The Power Structure of American Business

The Power Structure of American Business

Beth Mintz and
Michael Schwartz

The University of Chicago Press
Chicago and London

To the memory of our friend and colleague,

Eugene Weinstein

The University of Chicago Press, Chicago 60637
The University of Chicago Press, Ltd., London

96 95 94 93 92 91 90 89 88 87   6 5 4 3 2

Library of Congress Cataloging in Publication Data

Mintz, Beth.
        The power structure of American business.

        Bibliography: p.
        Includes index.
        1. Financial institutions—United States.
2. Corporations—United States. I. Schwartz, Michael,
1942-   . II. Title.
HG181.M556   1985   332.1′0973   84-8841
ISBN 0-226-53108-2 (cloth)
ISBN 0-226-53109-0 (paper)

Contents

Preface

In some sense this book began on a picket line in 1969 when the insurance adjusters at the John Hancock Insurance Company national office in Boston were striking for higher wages and job security. A small group of Students for a Democratic Society (SDS) members, including Michael Schwartz, were performing modest tasks of strike support including research into the relationship of John Hancock with other corporations, particularly those involved in the war in Vietnam. The SDS researchers discovered that John Hancock had so many directorate interlocks that the list was too unmanageable to compile for handouts to passersby. When a student commented to the strikers that Hancock was interlocked with all the other big companies, one striker replied, "You're wrong. John Hancock is connected to only half of the large corporations. Prudential is connected to the other half."

This casual (but surprisingly well informed) comment triggered a long chain of logic and research that has culminated in this book. It seemed to provide a sense of the divisions as well as the groupings within the business class, a subject of much speculation among those concerned with the role of corporations in American foreign and domestic political policy.

Although this was a provocative insight, it seemed impossible to test, considering the large number of interlocks maintained by both Hancock and Prudential and the lack of technical tools to test the insurance adjuster's theory. This methodological problem was solved in another casual conversation, one with Philip Bonacich at the University of California at Los Angeles who commented that he had developed a way of mathematically unscrambling the power structure of local high schools by analyzing the overlap among the various club memberships listed in yearbooks. This comment, which subsequently became formalized in Bonacich's (1972) pathbreaking article on centrality analysis, led Michael Schwartz to tuck away both the idea and the method of attacking the Prudential-Hancock issue.

Two years later at the University of New York at Stony Brook, Peter Mariolis happened along with the energy, interest, and mathematical creativity to put together the first large interlock data set in the current round of research into corporate interlocks. In a frenzy of work Mariolis developed a data set, adapted centrality analysis, and ran the first significant set of analyses. In some ways the results were wholly disappointing, since they revealed that Prudential and Hancock were not nearly as separate and competitive as the Hancock insurance adjuster had posited. Yet in another way they were dramatic and exciting, since they demonstrated the centrality of financial corporations—both commercial banks and insurance companies—in the corporate network. This pattern laid the foundation for the argument about the preeminence of financial institutions that became the major theme of this book.

Mariolis's preliminary work reinforced a conclusion that was emerging from our research on the structure of power in American society (Mintz, 1975; Mintz et al., 1976): the untangling of power relations in the modern industrial world rests on an understanding of intercorporate relations and intercorporate power wielding. These insights led to our formulating, with Peter Freitag, the grant proposal subsequently funded by the National Science Foundation (SOC 73-05601) that supported the data collection, program development, and data analysis upon which this book is based. Subsequent grants from the State University of New York at Stony Brook ("Social Background of Corporate Leadership") in 1978 and the Guggenheim Foundation ("The Power Structure of American Business") in 1980 provided further support for our research.

The MACNET (Mathematical Analysis of Corporate Networks) project, which was supported by the original National Science Foundation grant, provided the base for this book. We are indebted to our colleagues on that project for a range of creative inputs that we have incorporated here, including solutions to the wide variety of data collection problems, decisions about the nature and contours of the data set, innovative data analysis techniques, new and significant ideas that helped make sense of what became an increasingly complex and exciting intellectual puzzle, and ongoing constructive criticism of our efforts to report and reinterpret what was, and still remains, a collective analysis. Some of our colleagues' names appear as coauthors of the appendixes, which describe the basic techniques used in analyzing the pattern of interlocks among large American corporations. Others turned to their own specific questions about interlocking directorates or other related subjects that flowed partly from our common endeavors and partly from their independent intellectual interests. We wish to thank them here and to acknowledge that their work was absolutely essential to the completion of this project. In that sense we owe a lasting and impossible to repay intellectual debt to Peter Freitag, William Atwood, Jim Bearden, Carolyn Hendricks, Donald Palmer, Mark Mizruchi, Dan Clawson, Dana Powers, and Davita Glasberg.

As we struggled with understanding and reinterpreting a set of results that did not fit any existing theories (or our own intellectual predilections), we were constantly encouraged, criticized, and guided by Eugene Weinstein, who has become both a mentor and a guardian angel to us both. His apparently unlimited devotion and loyalty led him to criticize our worst errors and to encourage our best efforts. He forced us to keep after certain crucial points that we were ready to abandon, and he weaned us away from some unsubstantiable arguments that we entertained at various times in the creative process.

We must also give special thanks to Chick Perrow, who had the good taste to disagree with us when we were wrong and the equally good taste to encourage (and criticize) our best ideas, always urging us to make our work more accessible to the audience we hoped to reach. His encouragement and appreciation of the basic (and sometimes buried) ideas were particularly important in directing our efforts at revising and vitalizing the text in the course of many rewrites.

Four other scholars have played crucial roles in defining the final form of the manuscript. Edward Herman, Harrison White, Lewis Coser, and Stephen Fraser read the semifinal manuscript with great care and offered sharp criticisms that allowed us to reorganize the argument, emphasizing the main themes that contribute to our understanding of business politics and de-emphasizing the more speculative ideas that, in previous drafts, had confused and diverted readers' attention from the main thrust of the evidence. Our experience with these criticisms, coming from individuals who had varying degrees of commitment to competing theories and perspectives, has deepened our conviction that the debate among contending viewpoints is one of the great virtues of academic life.

To these names we would like to add the following list of individuals from whom we have borrowed or stolen ideas and extracted unpaid labor and the other personal resources essential to this sort of endeavor: Veronica Abjornson, Richard Alba, Howard Aldrich, David Bunting, Philip Burch, Jr., Tom Burns, Debbie Camaros, Robert B. Cohen, Donna DiDonato, G. William Domhoff, Peter Dooley, John Ehrenreich, Peter Evans, Dan Feshbach, Meindert Fennema, Robert Fitch, David Gersh, Robert Gogel, Mark Granovetter, Joseph Helfgot, Paul Hirsch, Floyd Hunter, Thomas Koenig, David Kotz, Joel Levine, Harry Mackler, Weeza Matthias, Dennis McCue, Robert Mokken, Harvey Molotch, Susie Orbach, Wanda Olivera, Mary Oppenheimer, Timothy Patterson, Richard Pelton, Jeffrey Pfeffer, Richard Ratcliff, Anna Rochester, Joel Rosenthal, Carole Roland, William Roy, Laura Anker Schwartz, Leon Schwartz, Joseph Schwartz, Rosemarie Sciales, John Scott, Peter Seybold, Theda Skocpol, Diane Smith, John Sonquist, Linda Brewster Stearns, Frans Stokman, Susan Strasser, Paul M. Sweezey, R. T. Tewarson, Michael Useem, J. Allen Whitt, Glenn Yago, Rolf Zeigler, Gerald Zeitz, and Maurice Zeitlin.

Introduction

This book began as the research report for a major study of corporate interlocks funded by the National Science Foundation (grant FOC 73-05606, 1974) and informally titled "Mathematical Analysis of Corporate Networks." Our original proposal argued that we could evaluate the validity of the contending theories of intercorporate relations by analyzing the shape and structure of the network produced by overlapping directorates in major corporations.

In a sense we succeeded all too well. Our analysis of the interlock network, reported in scholarly articles (e.g., Bearden et al., 1975; Mintz and Schwartz, 1981a,b, 1983) and summarized in Beth Mintz's doctoral dissertation (Mintz, 1978), indicated that banks and other financial companies play a coordinating role in the corporate world. No matter how we (or other researchers) manipulated the data, this result occurred and recurred in a convincing fashion. Nevertheless, the evidence also indicated that modern versions of bank control theory, which assert ongoing intervention by financial corporations into the daily workings of nonfinancial firms, were both misleading and inaccurate (see especially Fitch and Oppenheimer, 1970a-c; Menshikov, 1969; Pelton, 1970). By the time we finished the computer analysis in 1978, we were convinced that a new conceptualization of intercorporate power was necessary to explain the patterns found in the interlock network and that this reconceptualization would center on financial institutions and involve concepts of hierarchical domination and influence that were neither absolute nor deterministic.

The economic literature on banking systems was not helpful in developing such a reconceptualization. The traditional literature on money and banking, for example, pays little attention to the overall role of financial institutions in the corporate system. Instead their internal organization is studied and their function as intermediary stressed, as this quotation from a standard text in the field indicates: "The prime economic role and justification of financial institutions . . . is to serve as middlemen between savers and investors" (Hutchinson, 1971). Moreover:

> Commercial banks are the heart of our financial system. They hold the deposits of millions of persons, governments, and business units. They make funds available through their lending and investing activities to borrowers. (Reed et al., 1976)

Rather than considering their role as mediators, we wanted to analyze the behavior of financial institutions as active participants in the American economy—as coordinators of business activity.

In the scholarly articles reporting the interlock results, we tentatively sketched the outlines of an analysis that would allow us to explain this participation (see especially Mintz and Schwartz, 1981b). At the same time, we pursued a two-pronged search for a more substantive and concrete understanding of the processes that the interlock patterns appear to trace.

Part of this quest involved an exploration of Gramsci's notion of hegemony as a structural rather than an ideological phenomenon. Ideological hegemony has been discussed recently by a wide range of scholars and has become quite fashionable, especially in Marxist intellectual circles (see particularly Williams 1977). Another form of hegemony, which we call structural hegemony, has been left relatively unexplored and undeveloped even with the recent popularity of Gramscian analysis.[1] Structural hegemony operates when the actions of one social institution (or coordinated group of institutions) determine the viable options available to other institutions and individuals. If such constraint regularly occurs in a social system, the leadership of the dominant structure exercises a noninterventionist leadership that allows for coordination of the various contained social formations without either overt coercion or systematic ideological manipulation (see chapters 1–3).

It is this concept of hegemony that we have found most useful in analyzing the leverage capital flows create between financial and nonfinancial institutions in the upper reaches of the American corporate structure. It is particularly appealing to us because, while the hegemonic relationship is neither absolute nor inevitable, it explains the existence of episodic coordination among otherwise autonomous major American business enterprises. It also explains why, in the ordinary conduct of business affairs, the opinions and needs of financial institutions carry such great weight in the judgment and decision making of other corporations, even with the exercise of little overt leverage.

The second part of our investigation was an attempt to discover if the sort of interaction that the interlock networks trace could actually be identified and studied in the real world of ongoing business relations. There is a danger implicit in the abstraction of quantitative social science that we will "discover" relationships that simply do not exist in the real world.

The single most important theorem of network analysis, unstated in most work, is that we can discover the content of the relations among social actors by analyzing the shape of their structural relationships. In our case, when we discovered a structure we thought was the trace of hegemonic content, we suffered a significant failure of nerve. We felt it would be presumptuous for us to assert the existence of a whole set of intercorporate relationships based only upon the patterns of corporate interlocks, however elegant and convincing these patterns were to the small fraternity of interlock analysts.

This lack of confidence was deepened by the ongoing debate over the meaning of corporate interlocks themselves. We are hopeful that our work (both in this book and in our published articles) has contributed to the appreciation of the importance of corporate interlocks as a significant and multifaceted phenomenon in the world of big business. Different interlocks symbolize different types of connections among corporations and people, and the same interlocks can migrate from one kind of relationship into another. This shifting quality has led some to believe that interlock networks as a whole are either meaningless or uninterpretable. We think that this conclusion is both hasty and badly misplaced. Research in the last decade and a half has demonstrated over and over again that the patterns of interlocking directorates symbolize and trace real relationships that are very important in the business world and very useful to analysts of business structure. We will not dwell here on the evidence that substantiates this proposition, though we refer to it at some length in chapter 6. Nevertheless, it is important to acknowledge that the complex meaning of interlocks, and the transient nature of each particular tie, makes conclusions derived from the analysis of directorate networks problematic to many scholars.

For these reasons—our own need to validate the conclusions based on abstract quantitative analysis and the inevitable questions raised about interlock content—we sought more specific and concrete evidence for the relationships we had come to believe existed in the corporate community. We began a careful review of the business press, first as a matter of curiosity and then as a source of evidence to substantiate the conclusions we had drawn from data on interlocking directorates.

In a sense, then, the book is written in the reverse order of its own intellectual history. The interlock analysis, which appears in the last part of the book, is historically primary. We derived our ideas and our conclusions from the analysis of corporate interlocks reported there.[2] Examples from the business press are meant to substantiate, concretize, and embellish those insights. We present the evidence in reverse order because we find the examples drawn from the business world a more convenient vehicle for describing our argument and developing the details of our analysis. It is easier to explicate ideas with concrete, real life examples than with complex derivations from mathematical analyses.

Our use of the business press has raised a particular problem however. Some scholars who have read preliminary drafts of this book have challenged our apparent faith in the unerring accuracy of their reporting. It seems to them a substantial contradiction for scholars like ourselves, who are so critical of the behavior of business, to accept uncritically the word of *Business Week, Fortune,* and the *New York Times* on matters of such great importance. We have been gently accused of both cynical selectivity, choosing the evidence that supports our viewpoint and ignoring what contradicts it—and naive use of business gossip instead of developing hard evidence about real corporate relationships.

We plead not guilty to both of these charges, though we think them important enough to deserve a careful rebuttal. The business press is vast. It involves a great many newspapers and magazines as well as a large number of scholarly journals and books. At the same time there is a general fascination with the business world that expresses itself both in popular coverage of business subjects and in a great many best-selling books devoted to corporate activity, corporate malfeasance, and corporate hijinks. It is not clear that the modern fascination with the business world is greater or less than the fascination of earlier generations, but it is clear that there is a mass of contradictory and often unreliable information about every aspect of corporate America. One cannot uncritically accept everything that is presented to the public. For our research we have narrowed our sources to a handful of the most central media: *Business Week*, the *New York Times* financial section, and *Fortune*. On particular issues, we also consulted the *Wall Street Journal* and *Forbes*. We chose these particular sources for two reasons. First, they are the basic news sources about ongoing events within business. They attempt to summarize the main issues of the business world and to keep their readers abreast of what they consider to be the most important developments, especially among the major corporations. Second, they are generally considered the most influential magazines and newspapers within the business community. Because they are respected by business people themselves, we felt that they would be most likely to reflect the thinking of influential individuals in the business world.

This focus on the central business media did not, however, guarantee the accuracy of their reports. It would seem, especially to those unfamiliar with the business press, that such crucial journals might be particularly susceptible to the distortional loyalty that we frequently find in partisan literature. This is a problem that must be addressed by all researchers who use printed sources, and we have attempted to use the business press in the same way that any working historian uses journalistic evidence.

When an American historian studies the Civil War, using newspapers reporting the various events in that war, every fact or datum is looked upon with a jaundiced eye. Nothing is certainly true, but much of it is presumptively true. The knowledgeable researcher learns to recognize those kinds of reports and arguments that are likely to contain factual or analytic errors as well as those that are likely to be accurate. Patterns in the reports are used as flags for judging the accuracy of the information offered.

Much of this is subtle, at least to the beginning researcher. It becomes clearer and more easily managed as one becomes accustomed to checking and rechecking the efficacy of sources. This checking process involves a number of relatively standard techniques that most historians apply whether or not they explicitly reveal them to their readers. The most important of these is the simple test of time. A set of events reported contemporaneously in 1970 will be reviewed retrospectively when they become relevant in 1975 or 1980. If one compares the contemporaneous coverage of the events with retrospective analyses, the researcher gets a very good sense of what sorts of distortion occur in particular news media. In working with the business press, there is an ongoing retrospective quality, especially in *Fortune* magazine. *Fortune* specializes in analytic articles that review the history of a corporation, a sector, or a business issue. In doing so, the reporters for *Fortune* investigate, with interviews and with documentary work, the details of previous decisions and activities of the major firms involved in their report. Comparisons of the original coverage of *Business Week* and the *New York Times* with the retrospective analytic investigations of *Fortune* have allowed us to refine our own critical judgment as well as correct the errors inherent in contemporaneous reporting.

The efficacy of using these sources has also been confirmed by more formal means. Over the years, a number of important business events have been thoroughly researched and carefully analyzed by scholars, either inside or outside academia, and these case studies provide a useful assessment of the accuracy of careful analytic work based on the business press.

Consider four instructive examples. In 1969–70 the business press offered brief but sharply analytic reports of the attempt by Leasco Corporation to acquire Chemical Bank.[3] This acquisition effort was later studied by Davita Glasberg (1981, 1982) using documents uncovered by a detailed and elaborate congressional investigation of the incident. This investigation rendered public the internal documents of the contending factions and revealed the innermost details of the strategies and resources utilized by both contestants. These documents also demonstrate the accuracy of the reports of the business press. The story told by *Business Week*, the *Times*, and *Dun's* was by no means complete, but the part of the story they told was reassuringly accurate.

This same accuracy can be found in the case of the Chrysler rescue in 1980–81. Using standard historical methods, Yago and Schwartz (1981) put together a partial analysis of the government loan guarantees based on business sources. Glasberg (1982) once again consulted government investigations based upon subpoenaed internal documents to develop a definitive account. The information in the business press, when properly analyzed and carefully filtered, was accurate, though it was much narrower in scope than the information found in government sources.

The ouster of James Ling from Ling-Temco-Vought in the late 1960s was a spectacle that attracted widespread attention.[4] The research reported by Brown (1972), based on interviews and documentary analysis, was much more thorough and infinitely more detailed, but it basically confirmed the outline provided by the business press. And finally, the reports in the business press of the spectacular ouster of Howard Hughes from the leadership of TWA[5] are validated and deepened by the careful analysis offered by Tinnen (1973). This is perhaps the most interesting case, since Tinnen's work was based on five years of testimony from an elaborate antitrust suit and probably rests upon the most extensive evidence ever assembled for a single study.[6]

We conclude from these, and other, case studies that the business press is a valuable, perhaps indispensable, tool for business structure research. This does not mean that one can uncritically accept anything printed in the New York Times financial pages. There are many inaccuracies, and researchers must be sensitive to these. Nevertheless, this should not prevent the careful researcher from relying upon this as useful evidence of the ways corporations behave and relate to each other.

Speaking as researchers who have used magazines and newspapers as sources for other kinds of research (Schwartz, 1976, 1977; Mintz, 1975), we find that the business press is more reliable, by and large, than the general mass media. It is interesting to speculate upon the reasons for this greater accuracy, and it is our feeling, though we cannot prove it, that this is a result of the recursive relationship between these journals and their readers. The main audience of Business Week, Fortune, and the New York Times financial pages are the individuals whose activities are reported in these journals. This reflexive character—that the subject matter of the media is also its readership—places it in a particularly vulnerable position when inaccuracies appear. Such inaccuracies are likely to generate discontent among readers with substantial institutional power and therefore the wherewithal to publicize these errors. Since the business world depends on business news input in certain decision making, accurate reporting is seen as essential to corporate health. Any journal that was consistently in error would quickly lose readership.

An example will make this a little clearer. In 1979, Business Week published a long article comparing companies in the electrical manufacturing industry and concluding that General Electric was a fundamentally healthy firm while Westinghouse was faced with a major crisis. Such a report in Business Week could have driven away potential investors in Westinghouse and generally harmed the business atmosphere in which the company operated. Westinghouse's chief executive officer promptly wrote a long letter to Business Week protesting their characterization and offering a considerable body of evidence to counter the analysis. Whether or not this repaired the damage is not at all clear, but it is indicative both of the sensitivity of the business community to its image in the business press and of its capacity to articulate its contrary viewpoint. This allows the researcher to move with a little more confidence in accepting or rejecting the characterizations in the business press, because contrary opinions are likely to have been published and contrary evidence reported. At the same time, this capacity for rebuttal forces the reporters and the editors in the business press to be careful of their own statements and circumspect in their characterizations of corporate executives and the corporations they manage.

Despite these reassuring patterns, business press evidence is useful only in specific contexts and for specific purposes. In this book we rely on it heavily because we feel it is ideal for our type of investigation.

The patterns found in the interlock network indicate that financial institutions exercise a form of structural leadership over a wide range of nonfinancial corporations. This form of leadership is, in our opinion, episodic and problematic; but it is nevertheless ongoing and highly significant in terms of the overall shape of corporate decision making. What we needed from the business press were indications of the existence of such forms of influence and a sense of the ways this influence operated at the particular moments when it was exercised. We are confident that the evidence we present here is powerful support for our argument because it has two essential characteristics.

First, the evidence is against the grain of the bias of the sources we have consulted. If we were developing an argument that corporations were independent, rarely influenced by each other, and highly competitive, it would be difficult to rely on the reporting of the business press. Most business sources tend to glorify competition and independence among corporate actors. But since we are looking for cases of intercorporate dependence and influence, topics not often explicitly covered, we can have greater confidence in the reports of such occurrences. The ideology of the business world does not view banks and other financial institutions as wielding coordinated power that generates united action. This form of news is revealed begrudgingly, and only when an occurrence is incontrovertibly important. Most incidents of bank influence reported in this book involve teasing out information from a reluctant source, and we therefore feel confident in reporting this evidence as accurate.

Second, we are offering here what mathematicians call an "existence proof." If we believed that all events in the business world were the result of intercorporate power and that bank leverage represented an ongoing form of control in the everyday life of corporations, the examples we offer would hardly be proof of our position. We would then need to demonstrate that the independent actions of corporations were inevitably and always consequences of outside control. But our theory does not assert ongoing and total control. We are attempting to demonstrate the existence of important *moments* when intercorporate influence is exercised by financial institutions. Therefore, by looking at specific moments in the history of firms and demonstrating the importance of financial decision making in these instances, we are providing what we consider to be convincing evidence for the viability of our theory. The nature of our argument, therefore, fits with this sort of exemplary evidence.

In our view the combination of evidence from the business press and the quantitative analysis of interlock patterns produces a viable case for the existence of financial hegemony in the American business world. The anecdotal descriptions demonstrate the existence of financial leadership at crucial moments in corporate biographies, and the structural shape of the network demonstrates the general patterning that emerges from these particular interactions.

1 Constraint, Discretion, and Intercorporate Power

Banks are more dangerous than standing armies.

Thomas Jefferson

Leasco, a Long Island computer company, grew during the "go-go years" of the 1960s into a large conglomerate approaching *Fortune* 500 status.[1] In late 1968 Leasco's chairman, Saul P. Steinberg, embarked upon an ambitious campaign to acquire Chemical Bank of New York, one of the largest commercial banks in the world. His strategy was to exchange about eighty shares of Leasco stock for one hundred shares of the bank stock; since Leasco was selling at $140 and Chemical at $72, bank shareholders would be getting about $112 per share. This represented more than a 50% profit on their investment, and, as Chemical's chairman William S. Renchard commented, "it would be tough going persuading our stockholders not to accept" (Austin, 1973: 40).

Chemical's leadership decided to "resist this with all the means at our command" (Renchard, quoted in the *New York Times*, Feb. 6, 1969: 52). What followed was an impressive display of the coalescence of a variety of institutions with leverage over Leasco:

1. Leasco's lead lender, Continental Illinois, informed Steinberg of its opposition to the acquisition effort and indicated that it would not look favorably on future loan agreements.
2. Leasco's investment bankers, Lehman Brothers and White Weld, informed Steinberg that they would not participate in a Leasco tender offer for Chemical.
3. Major customers of Leasco threatened to cancel their contracts with the company if the merger attempt continued.

4. The management of Chemical threatened to resign if the merger succeeded and indicated that major depositors would withdraw their funds.
5. United States Senators introduced a federal bill that would make Leasco's plan illegal.
6. Nelson Rockefeller, governor of New York, called for a New York State law that would also make the acquisition illegal.

These actions, however, created no immediate bar to the acquisition. The coup de grace was delivered when institutional investors began dumping Leasco stock. This caused a price drop from $140 per share on February 3, 1969, to $106 per share two weeks later. As of February 20, Chemical shareholders would receive only $84 for the $72 Chemical stock they held. During the next year Leasco stock declined to $6 per share, an unprecedented drop for a company that was economically viable and continued to show substantial profit increases throughout this period. Chemical shareholders therefore had no incentive to tender their stock, and the bank was spared the fate of becoming "a mere division of an unseasoned upstart" (Austin, 1973: 39).

This episode is atypical of normal intercorporate relations in almost every respect: industrial firms, even the very largest multinationals, rarely attempt to acquire even the smaller regional banks; stock dumping is almost always a response to projected economic decline, not a device for resisting acquisition; and intercorporate conflict does not ordinarily involve the wide range of institutions mobilized in this instance. Nevertheless, this example is an ideal illustration of certain aspects of normal corporate decision making and behavior, because it brings into dramatic relief aspects of intercorporate processes that are often invisible to the naked eye.

All corporate action develops from a meshing of discretionary decision making and institutional constraint. Saul Steinberg was not compelled to acquire Chemical Bank. He, and his executive team, *decided* to seek the merger rather than undertake other activities Leasco might have pursued. This discretionary act was conditioned by a set of institutional constraints. The cost of acquiring Chemical by purchasing its stock would have been slightly more than one billion dollars; Leasco could not generate even 10% of this amount internally. A cash acquisition, therefore, would have necessitated borrowing over $900 million. While loans of this magnitude are frequently a part of major acquisitions—United States Steel, for example, borrowed over $4 billion to acquire Marathon

Oil—such an option was unavailable to Leasco in its Chemical acquisition.

The decision to offer Leasco stock in exchange for Chemical stock therefore represented a conjunction of discretion—the freely made decision to attempt the acquisition—and institutional constraint—the lack of access to sufficient capital to make a cash offer. We believe that the dialectic between constraint and discretion informs all social action and is the most fruitful vocabulary for understanding corporate behavior and intercorporate influence. It allows us, for example, to clarify and understand the process by which stock dumping frustrated Leasco's offer.

Once Chemical decided to resist the merger, it had two possible options. The unused alternative was to gain access to the discretionary aspect of Leasco's acquisition strategy: that is, to induce Steinberg to voluntarily withdraw the offer.[2] The chosen alternative involved structural constraint: stock dumping removed the only viable acquisition strategy by lowering Leasco's stock price and therefore making the offer unattractive to Chemical shareholders.

It is important to see the situational contingency in Chemical's strategy. If Leasco had had $1 billion in retained earnings (many companies do, in fact, accumulate such a capital pool) or could have borrowed the money, stock dumping would not have prevented the merger. It is only in this precise institutional circumstance that Chemical's strategy had the dramatic effect it did. (On the other hand, another set of circumstances might have produced another equally effective strategy.)

Intercorporate relations in general can be viewed using the calculus of discretion and constraint. Each time a company acts, its leadership attempts to determine all available options. It assesses the constraints on the firm's behavior and makes a judgment about the most profitable strategy—that is, it makes discretionary decisions. Once the firm pursues these strategies, it changes the structural environment for itself and other companies and therefore alters the profile of options in the next round of decision making. Thus, companies constantly influence each other's behavior in unanticipated ways by routinely altering the set of constraints facing executive decision makers.

Chemical's resistance to the Leasco takeover illustrates a small but very important subset of these processes of mutual influence: actions taken for the express purpose of altering another firm's behavior. Such actions are usually conceptualized as instances of intercorporate power or outside control, and the fields of interorganizational theory and business structure have been constructed around the exploration of these instances of deliberate influence and the assessment of their importance for corporate behavior.

The dialectic of constraint and discretion offers a framework with which to analyze this recent work on intercorporate relations and to build a coherent portrait of business structure. Intercorporate leverage can derive either from the alteration of the profile of constraint—as in the Leasco example—or from the access to corporate decision making, such as replacement of the top executives. The two forms of leverage are effective in different circumstances and produce different results. Moreover, in some circumstances constraint may provide access to discretion; in other circumstances discretion can alter the profile of constraint. The dual nature of corporate action underlies both the regularities and the complexities of intercorporate relations.

For almost five decades the debate over ownership and control in the modern corporation has continued without a clear conceptualization of what control of a large company involves. A considerable portion of the disagreement in this debate can be traced to the indiscriminate use of several meanings of the term; meanings that fail to confront the dialectic between constraint and discretion.

Intuitively, most people use the word control to imply the strongest sort of oversight and direction of the discretionary activities of people or institutions. In this sense, control refers to daily decision making within the options made available in a constrained circumstance. Consider a year in the life of a major American corporation such as General Motors, Ford, or AT&T. The chief executive officer is called upon to make a variety of decisions about the operation of the firm: he (occasionally she) will choose among candidates for high positions and pass on nominees for lower ones; will decide whether to continue or discontinue joint ventures with other firms; will reevaluate supplier and customer agreements; will make or approve major decisions regarding labor relations; will set guidelines for compensation of nonunionized personnel; will help set prices; will judge the activities of many subordinates; and will make choices about entry into new lines of business. Many times these decisions will be made in consultation with subordinates; sometimes they will be solely in the hands of the chief executive.

We do not expect this chief executive to have complete discretion. These decisions will be conditioned by the availability of qualified personnel inside or outside the firm, the strength of unions, the market for nonunion personnel, the company's creditworthiness, and myriad other constraints which he or she can at best partially influence.

Nevertheless, within the confines of structural constraint the summation of all these small and large decisions constitutes a policy, orientation, and business philosophy of the chief executive officer. The chief executive officer therefore controls the daily and yearly activities of the firm. Insofar as discretion is applied in overall decision making, he or she applies it. Insofar as other employees exercise discretion, it is delegated by the chief executive officer and can, in principle, be repossessed at any time.

A dominant stockholder can also control a company. In the post–World War II era, the epitome of owner control was Henry Ford II's domination of policy at the Ford Motor Company, in which his family held over 40% of the stock.[3] Appointed president (second in command) in 1945 at age twenty-seven (with no previous experience) Henry II served a fifteen-year apprenticeship while Ernest R. Breech ran the company. During this time, Ford was not a typical subordinate: he hired the famous Whiz Kids who rebuilt the firm in the late 1940s; he made the final decisions about financial and administrative decentralization; and he was even the key figure in the failure of the Edsel. As one Ford executive commented, "even when Mr. Breech was here, toward the end Henry had taken over and was in command" (Weymouth, 1978: 74).

Between 1960, when he officially became chairman and chief executive officer, and 1980, when he retired, Henry II ran the firm as a classic (even capricious) monarch; an owner-entrepreneur of the old school. In 1968 he fired the president, Arjay Miller, without warning and hired Semon Knudsen away from General Motors. This attempt to catch General Motors by hiring its top executive ended less than two years later with the sudden firing of Knudsen and the establishment of a three-person executive office. After seven years and much reshuffling, Lee Iacocca emerged as the main leader under Ford; but fifteen months later he too was fired.

During the entire period, Ford himself set the direction and redirection of the firm. He gave final approval to the successful introduction of the Mustang in 1963 and the Maverick in 1969. He resisted small-car production after the oil crisis of 1973; reversed a decision by Iacocca to produce a fuel-efficient "downsize" auto in 1978; and finally consented to small-car emphasis just before his retirement. In each case, he reinforced his policy decisions with oversight and direction in their implementation, just as he oversaw and often reversed his personnel decisions.

Henry Ford II qualified as a controlling owner by acting as chief executive officer making the major discretionary choices for his company. His regime was more chaotic than most, but his relationship to his company is replicated by a great many other corporate leaders.[4]

Most instances of corporate control involve domination of discretionary decision making. In some cases an owner can control a firm without formally leading the company. Howard Hughes did so when he held almost 78% of the stock of TWA. Although he was never an officer and only occasionally a member of the board of directors, from all accounts he controlled the company on a daily basis. All major decisions about personnel, business policy, joint ventures, labor relations, and the like were referred to him; and he personally discussed each issue with the chief executive officer (Tinnen, 1973). When Kirk Kerkonian held 25 percent of Columbia Pictures, the firm "had to consult with Kerkonian on any material financial transaction," thus creating a relationship similar (though much looser) to the one Hughes had established with TWA (*Business Week*, June 3, 1981: 119).

Control in this sense—either by owners or by nonowning chief executives—refers to access to the discretionary decision making roles in the company. Henry Ford II did not manipulate the constraints within which his firm operated; he was ultimately forced to build downsize cars in response to consumer demand in the face of increased fuel prices; he had to live with GM's domination of the domestic market; and he could not alter the cyclical character of auto sales. These constraints were givens in Ford's corporate environment. Control, as we intuitively use it, implies the ability to make the choices that remain after structural constraint has restricted available options.

A looser notion of control coexists with the concept we have just explored. We can posit an arrangement in which Henry Ford, or some other dominant stockholder, would be consulted only in the most important circumstances. Instead of being asked about all appointments, the owner would intervene only when the chief executive officer or another high-level official was under consideration. He or she might participate in a decision about a major expansion but would not be consulted about smaller projects. The owner would be involved when major borrowing was undertaken but not in the negotiation of smaller loans. He or she could be consulted during a major strike or confrontation with unionized workers but not about normal contract negotiations. Scott (1979) refers to this looser form of intervention as strategic control, as opposed to day-to-day administrative decision making, which he terms operational management.[5] Although the two phenomena sometimes fold into each other, the distinction is an important one.

Strategic control is illustrated by the case of Alexander and Baldwin, one of five corporations that dominates the economy of Hawaii. The two founding families, which together hold over 30% of the stock, maintain at least six representatives on the eleven-member board of directors. Nevertheless, all recent chief executives have been recruited from outside the controlling group. Stockholders, through their board positions, have remained active in policymaking. They have set and changed basic policy and have enforced their will by firing chief executive officers they felt were not honoring their wishes.

Long after the other major Hawaiian firms had diversified into food processing, hotels, building supplies, and the like, Alexander and Baldwin's board "stuck doggedly" to sugar, land, and transportation (*Business Week*, March 3, 1980). When diversification was undertaken, the board ousted a chief executive they decided "had gone too far" (ibid.). Another chief executive officer was ousted for failing to move vigorously into board-mandated land development; and a president was removed when his handling of sugar operations was not consistent with traditional board-endorsed procedures.

In sum, the owner-dominated board of directors set policy for the company and expected it to be enforced. *Business Week* commented when the firm appointed its fifth chief executive in ten years:

> The direction is likely to come more from the board than from Pfeiffer [the new chief executive officer], who, according to a local executive familiar with A&B's affairs, "will listen and do exactly what they say." Pfeiffer, who is highly regarded as an operational specialist, is not considered to be a forceful manager by those who know him. Says one man: "Really [A&B's board] does not want a very dynamic type right now." (March 3, 1980: 57)

Thus, the stockholding families "controlled" Alexander and Baldwin not with day-to-day operational oversight, but by enunciating policy and enforcing it through the ouster of executives who failed to honor it. Chief executives who are subjected to strategic control from outside, like Pfeiffer of Alexander and Baldwin, must make their policy decisions fit into the premises of board dicta. This does not necessarily mean a lack of creativity—in fact, it could require Pfeiffer to be very creative in generating programs consistent with the board's desires. But program development and implementation would have to be consistent with the broad guidelines of modest diversification, land development, and conservative sugar production methods that the controlling families had explicitly endorsed or implicitly established by their activities and decisions during the decade of the 1970s.

This control is not the sort of operational management we have just discussed; it is not the sort of control Howard Hughes or Henry Ford II exercised. It is a broad strategic control in which the owners dominate decision making while relieving themselves of the daily exercise of the power they ultimately wield.

This strategic control is frequently called outside control because it is exercised by people who are not part of the full-time executive team. It is important to search for, and understand, the incidence and consequences of outside control, to distinguish those managers who are subordinated to it from those who are not, and to evaluate its limitations or constraints. As Pahl and Winkler (1974) argue, control of this sort can be subverted by its subordinates. Outside policy establishment can be effective only in the context of creative compliance by the actual administrators. The uncertainty contained in this dependence of outside controller on inside executive was reflected at Alexander and Baldwin, both by the four firings and by the nervous intervention in numerous policy decisions.

And while Alexander and Baldwin was unusually chaotic, outside controllers are often quite nervous about chief executives' obedience to their mandates.[6] Their tension is well founded. The act of separating the establishment of broad guidelines from the implementation process creates a permanent contradiction; there is a constant tendency for one side to encroach upon the other's domain. At Alexander and Baldwin, a "coup d'etat" by professional management seemed to be a continual possibility, and the corporate world contains many similar examples.[7] In these circumstances it is not surprising that contolling stockholders often designate a family member (such as Henry Ford II) as chief executive, even if it involves a sacrifice in technical competence.

The acquisition of policymaking authority by the chief executive is seen by managerial theorists (see below) as more or less inevitable in the modern firm. Though their argument is appealing, it ignores the many documented instances of outside control, either by stockholders or lenders directly or, more frequently, by the board of directors acting as a representative of some defined outside interest (see chapter 2). The proper approach, in our view, is to accept this as a problematic relationship and to analyze the conditions under which outside controllers can successfully establish and change corporate direction.

Recent work on interorganizational relations has been weakened
by the failure to maintain this distinction between strategic control
and operational management and to focus attention on the conditions under which outside control dissolves in the face of the executive authority exercised by inside management.

The distinction between operational management and strategic
control is an important device for analyzing corporate interaction.
Nevertheless, it is important to identify their underlying similarity:
both refer to power derived from access to discretionary decision
making. A wholly different form of intercorporate power derives
from the manipulation of structural constraint, a phenomenon that
usually remains outside the scrutiny of theorists of corporate control. Consider an example. During the post–World War II period,
Robert Moses built a remarkable network of highways and bridges
around New York City (Caro, 1974). One of the consequences of
this development was the construction of bedroom suburbs on Long
Island. It is quite clear that without highways (or equivalent mass
transportation) the home builders on Long Island could not have
moved the new suburbanites from their homes to the jobs and other
activities that were essential to their lives. The executives of Levitt
and Sons, Incorporated, and other firms that chose to build houses
on Long Island may have strategically controlled their own firms,
they may have had their own financial resources, and they may
have had their own ideas about what a profitable investment looked
like. They may have consulted no one in their choices. Nevertheless, these choices were conditioned and made possible by the construction of this network of highways. In some sense, then, those
who made the decision to build highways created a circumstance
that determined—perhaps "controlled"—the subsequent decisions
of the home builders.

This form of influence is an example of the same process that
thwarted Leasco's attempt to acquire Chemical Bank. It has little
to do with an individual's ordering another individual or organization to do something, which is the essence of strategic control.
Instead, decisions and activities of one set of institutions created
and transformed the environment in which another set of institutions operated. When a major American corporation makes an
investment decision, that decision is influenced and conditioned
by numerous—perhaps innumerable—prior decisions by other corporations and other institutions. This interdependence characterizes all complicated social systems, from individual organizations
to whole societies.

Most times these interdependencies are not intentionally manipulated, but sometimes corporate action is intended to affect the operations of another firm in a predictable manner. In these circumstances, the affected firm may be forced to respond and adjust according to plan; the dumping of Leasco stock exemplifies this possibility. When, however, the second company is able to counter the first firm's action or is capable of frustrating the original goals of the first firm, "mutual deterrence" may arise. Baran and Sweezy (1966) argue that mutual deterrence, or corespective behavior, prevents the constant conflict and disruption that could result from the massive interdependencies among giant corporations.

The argument they construct derives from analyses of corporate interest during the era of large scale oligopolistic enterprise—the era of monopoly capital. The logic of competition is approximately this: when a great many firms make up an industry, a company can maximize profits either by reducing its costs and therefore increasing its profit margin, or by increasing its share of the market. These two processes are usually connected: a firm that successfully decreases costs through technological innovation, intensifying the work process, or finding cheaper labor or resources lowers its price. Some competitors may be able to match the price cut, but many cannot reduce costs and therefore cannot lower prices. In the short run, customers purchase from those with lowest prices, thereby increasing the market share and profitability of the innovator.

In the middle term, the least efficient firms are driven out of business, and customers become permanently wedded to the more efficient competitors. In the long term, the continuing application of these competitive practices results in the survival of a few large companies. Once this occurs, we arrive at the era of monopoly (or oligopoly), and a new set of pricing strategies develops.

Note that the company that reduces costs need not lower prices. Its leadership could choose to keep prices stable and increase its profit while maintaining market share. Competitive pricing, therefore, is at some level a discretionary decision, based on the hope that increased market share will compensate for lower per-item profit.

In a monopolistic setting, Baran and Sweezy (1966) argue, price competition is no longer a viable option available to corporate decision makers; it is structurally precluded by the capacity of other large firms to defend their market share. If one oligopolistic firm develops lower costs and therefore lowers prices, its competitors can lower their own prices and absorb the losses until they have copied the innovator's new production strategy. Price competition therefore makes no inroads into the others' market share. Consider the auto industry. Suppose Chrysler, which experienced repeated crises in the 1960s, 1970s, and 1980s, were to attempt to increase its market share by reducing its costs and prices. If it began to capture General Motors' market, GM would be forced to match this price decrease. Once the two prices were matched, Chrysler would not gain any further customers: instead it would find itself selling automobiles to its original market at a lower price. Even if Chrysler was making a profit on each car and General Motors was not, it could not hope to maintain the cost advantage long enough to drive GM into bankruptcy. Eventually GM would cut its costs also. Such a price-cutting strategy would serve no one except the consumer, who would be getting any car at a lower price. This type of strategy is known as "destructive competition" and is simply not in the direct, narrow economic interest of monopolized firms.

For Baran and Sweezy (1966), the key to a noncompetitive market is the understanding by monopoly capitalists that destructive competition cannot successfully maximize corporate profits—instead, it minimizes them. Moreover, the logic of corespective behavior extends beyond the relations among firms in the same industry:

> If one big corporation is not a competitor of another, it is quite likely to be either a customer or a supplier; and in this realm of corporate relations the sovereign principle is reciprocity, which enjoins corespective behavior as surely as competition does. (p. 50)

This point is nicely illustrated by the decision of Big Steel to forgo a price increase that would have exacerbated the problems of automobile manufacturers in 1973. This forbearance was not kindness; it was a recognition that such an increase could deepen the crisis and ultimately result in a large decline in orders from automobile manufacturers. Ultimately such a price increase would hurt, rather than help, the steel industry.

Mutual deterrence is a major form of intercorporate constraint. Companies, even the largest ones, find that otherwise attractive business decisions cannot be carried through because a predictable response by another firm will render the action unsuccessful. In these circumstances, influence is exercised without access to corporate discretion. The company is deterred by the possibility of a constraining action by another corporation. Baran and Sweezy's insight directs our attention to the other half of the discretion/constraint duality and introduces a form of outside influence that is fundamentally different from the types of control we have just discussed. We wish to expand on this idea by developing the possibility that a fundamental asymmetry may exist between two firms, or within a group of firms. If each of a group of institutions makes decisions and takes actions that directly and significantly affect the others, they are interdependent, and mutual deterrence should arise. However, if one set of institutions regularly makes decisions and sets policies that significantly affect the subsequent decisions of another group, but the second set does not often make decisions and/or take actions that affect the first, a hegemonic relationship may arise. This latter case is a form of domination that is rarely discussed or analyzed in the context of capitalist institutional relationships.[8] Baran and Sweezy (1966) avoid the issue by analyzing the government as a referee in such asymmetrical situations. While this may occur in some instances, it is by no means the inevitable consequence of asymmetrical interdependence. In innumerable circumstances, no government intervention takes place.

In our reckoning, hegemonic relationships exist between individual corporations and among subgroups of corporations; they are also the main organizing principle of the business world as a whole. The larger structure—particularly the hegemonic role played by financial institutions—will be addressed more fully in later chapters. For now, we wish to discuss the contrasts and similarities between hegemonic domination and the other sources of control and coordination in the corporate world.

We begin with yet another example. The American auto supply industry, which contains at least eight of the *Fortune* 500 corporations, has traditionally been dominated by the automobile manufacturers, although no formal control relationships appear to exist (*New York Times*, Sept. 13, 1979; *Business Week*, Sept. 24, 1979). A review of the recent history of the production and distribution of new parts for autos illustrates the nature and process of this hegemonic domination.

In the 1960s, General Motors, Ford, and Chrysler were experiencing a boom period and decided to manufacture their own new-car parts. While this decision excluded auto-parts manufacturers from their most lucrative business, they could not overturn it since they had no deterrent with which to threaten the Big Three. Even though nobody ordered them to abandon new-parts construction, they were nevertheless *forced* to do so, and they concentrated thereafter on replacement parts. The auto manufacturers therefore determined the corporate strategy of the parts industry to a degree usually reserved for chief executives, dominant stockholders, or other controlling forces. Yet they exercised this influence without issuing a single order; they did not gain access to the decision making authority of the auto parts executives. Their own decisions so profoundly affected the auto supply business that it did not matter whether they issued orders or not. The parts companies' executives were left to their own judgment in a changed institutional context, and they decided to remove themselves from the new-car-parts market.

In the late 1970s auto manufacturers fell on hard times, and all available capital was needed to develop smaller cars. Along with a great many other changes, the Big Three withdrew from substantial portions of their parts businesses and returned to outside contracting. This recreated a market for original equipment in auto parts, and the parts industry competed for the new contracts. Here again, the auto manufacturers exercised domination over the investment profile and business strategy of the auto-parts producers. Once again there was no direct control, either strategic or operational. No one ordered the chief executive officers of Bendix and TRW to begin new-parts construction. The policy change, however, was just as certain as —actually more certain than— it could have been had an owner-entrepreneur, like Henry Ford II, or active owning families, like the Alexanders and the Baldwins, intervened. The creation of a massive market for new-car parts was sufficient to produce the change.

It is important to note that the Big Three did not make "autonomous" decisions. Their own choices were heavily circumscribed by a multitude of decisions made by other firms, whose actions made up the economic reality the auto industry faced. But the Big Three were not, to any great degree, influenced by the decision making of the auto-part suppliers. The relationship was asymmetrical. The actions of the suppliers were a small—perhaps trivial—determinant of the reality within which General Motors, Ford, and Chrysler made their decisions; the actions of the Big Three were a fundamental determinant of the reality within which the suppliers operated.[9]

Hegemony implies both interdependence and differential power. A hegemonic relationship exists when:

1. One corporation (or corporate grouping acting in unison) makes decisions that directly and significantly affect the business conditions of another firm (or corporate grouping), thus forcing changes in company strategy.
2. The second corporation (or corporate grouping) cannot take actions that either nullify the effects on themselves or nullify

the benefits sought by the first group and therefore cannot achieve mutual deterrence.

3. The second corporation (or corporate grouping) is constrained to adopt strategies that complement those adopted by the dominant firm (or group of firms).

We should point out that a company frequently will find itself "at the mercy" of another firm for only a short period. In order to sell its large nuclear reactor plants, Westinghouse guaranteed its customers uranium fuel rods at fixed prices over a ten-year period. When the uranium cartel was formed in the mid-1970s, price rises of over 1000% forced Westinghouse to allocate a major part of its resources to uranium purchases.[10] In other words the uranium cartel, for that period, exercised a form of hegemony over Westinghouse, and Westinghouse had no counter action that could produce a situation of mutual deterrence.

A useful comparison can be made between the relationship of auto-parts suppliers to the auto companies and the relationship of Westinghouse to the uranium cartel. Westinghouse attempted to extricate itself from this relationship by refusing to honor its contracts, despite the anger of its customers. This was a reasonable effort, since the dependency was derived from a marketing strategy that, in the long run, could be ended or changed. Ultimately Westinghouse could cease to relate to its disgruntled former customers. For the parts industry, however, the dependence was at least quasi-permanent. Every decision of the Big Three profoundly affects the life of auto-parts manufacturers: a scaling down of car sizes implies major changes in the parts to be produced; a Big Three strategy of fewer cars and higher prices implies an overall decline in demand for parts; and so on and so forth. In this circumstance the relationship is virtually permanent, even if the specifics of the interaction change dramatically.

Moreover, the potential for strategic outside control is contained within these long-term hegemonic relationships—that is, structural constraint can sometimes be transformed into decision making power. In 1973, the Budd Company sold 82% of its product to the Big Three; 40% to Ford (New York Times, Nov. 11, 1974: F1). This made Budd exceptionally vulnerable to Ford's daily policies; a decision by Ford to find a new supplier would have destroyed Budd. Obviously, had Ford chosen to dictate policy to Budd's chief executives, they would have had an excellent chance of obtaining compliance.[11] And beyond this, imagine a situation in which Budd was considering an activity that would directly hurt Ford's interests. Budd leadership would be forced to think carefully before proceeding, since the leverage Ford exercised was so great. Thus, the hegemonic relationship contains the potential for both deterrence (although not "mutual") and outside control.

It is useful at this point to underscore the fundamental differences and similarities between the modes of control—operational management and strategic control on the one hand and structural constraint (mutual deterrence and hegemony) on the other.

Both operational management and strategic control operate through access to the discretionary decision making apparatus. Outside controllers force top management to obey their will through the threat of firing. Power is wielded in two steps: (1) the transmission of orders from the planning agency to the chief executive; (2) implementation of the new policies by the chief executive.

Hegemony and deterrence both operate through structural constraint, without the mediation of chief executive officers. In hegemony, the dominant firm takes an action, and the altered economic conditions force a complementary response on the part of the subordinate company. Management of the subordinate firm need not agree with, or creatively comply with, the overall plan; they are coerced by the new set of structural constraints to make appropriate changes. Under deterrence the same logic applies, but in this case the anticipated response invalidates the planned action and therefore deters it.

The different resource bases and capabilities of operational management, strategic control, mutual deterrence, and hegemony determine their different roles in the structure of interorganizational relations, but all four forms of influence provide the capability for intercorporate coordination and planning.

Operational management. A dominant stockholder may maintain administrative control over two or more companies and can therefore coordinate intercorporate activities simply by issuing the appropriate directives. Planning is straightforward: the controlling individual or family directly coordinates the actions of the target corporations. The limitations of this device lie in the inability of a single individual (or family) to run a large number of independent firms, since each unit requires at least one full-time administrator.

Strategic control. Intercorporate coordination is accomplished through directives from the outside controller to the top executives of the involved firms. Planning is done outside and imported to the company through directives or by the appointment of chief executives committed to the execution of the plan. Unlike administrative control, outside control does not suffer from limitations as to scope. However, there is always the necessity of creative compliance from the various chief executive officers. For this reason, planning or coordination through outside control can be problematic; one recalcitrant executive can disrupt the entire effort.

Mutual deterrence. Coordination occurs when each firm corespects the others' ability to affect corporate environments adversely. Certain actions are prohibited—notably destructive competition—and replaced by such devices as price leadership in the context of monopoly pricing. Planning is facilitated by the ability of each firm to predict the reaction of others to many proposed policies. This allows some degree of coordinated activity, since reactions can be predicted before a policy is actually implemented. Explicit cooperation, however, is usually transitory and temporary; it occurs only when all parties achieve more-or-less equal benefit from the alliance. Unlike control relationships, there is no possibility of planning and coordination when one of the firms is detrimentally affected, even if the overall benefits are large.

Hegemony. Coordination occurs in a dependency relationship: the dominant firm can force coordination because of asymmetrical dependency. It can undertake planning that involves all firms under its hegemonic domination, and coordination is not limited to conditions under which all firms derive some benefit. In this way hegemony is comparable to a control relationship. However, the absence of direct interaction implies an imprecision in the planning process and a limited realm in which its domination applies. A hegemonic institution cannot dictate the exact choices that subordinate chief executives will make, and therefore tight coordination—a possibility in control relationships—is especially problematic. On the other hand, since the leverage is exercised over the subordinate firm itself, hegemony is not as susceptible to disobedience by recalcitrant top managers as is outside control.

All four of these sources of unity exist in the modern business world, and they coexist with a great many of the autonomous relationships described by managerialists (see chapter 2). As we shall see, they often operate in tandem, in sequence, or in antagonism to each other. Each type can be transformed into all the others, given the appropriate circumstances. And each type can arise through myriad different processes. Nevertheless, there is a constancy to the patterns and an overall structure that reproduces itself at each moment in the history of business. The remainder of this book attempts to analyze the underlying processes at work and to identify the enduring patterns of coordination and domination that characterize the American economy.

2 Managerial Autonomy, Corporate Unity, and the Role of Financial Institutions

Finance capital is capital controlled by banks and employed by industrialists.

Rudolf Hilferding

Management Control Theory

The 1970s were marked by a debate within the academic world over the essential outlines of American business structure. The ascendant theory of the firm, managerialism, posited intercorporate autonomy and was challenged by three different perspectives, each assuming that widespread intercorporate unity shaped the overall structure and individual consequences of business activity. Each view, however, suggested a different source of unity: one perspective asserted that it was based on common economic and political interests; another found its basis in corporate interdependence; and the third posited its derivation from bank control of nonfinancial firms. Although the positions have become less distinct in recent years, this dispute is a convenient starting point for an analysis of the structure of American big business.

We begin with a brief expression of the managerial perspective as first stated by Berle and Means (1932) and developed further by a generation of economists and sociologists, most notably Robert Gordon (1945), Carl Kaysen (1957), Daniel Bell (1961, 1973), Robin Marris (1964), Herbert Simon (1966), and John Kenneth Galbraith (1967).

In some sense, American capitalism had never enunciated a fully developed theory of itself until 1932, when Berle and Means wrote *The Modern Corporation and Private Property*. Asserting that a trend toward stock dispersal and corporate self-finance had radically changed the structure of business, they argued that professional managers had replaced entrepreneurial owners at the helm of the modern corporation. "The surrender of control over their wealth by investors," Berle and Means argued, "has effectively broken the old property relations and has raised the problem of defining these relationships anew" (p. 4).

It was precisely this issue to which subsequent managerialists turned. The answer, incorporated into the thesis of managerial control, ran directly counter to the Marxian argument that there were irreconcilable antagonisms between those who directed major corporations—the owners and top executives—and the welfare of the general populace—the working class in particular. The "separation of ownership from control" meant that the modern corporation was no longer run by individuals whose main purpose was to maximize profits. This, in turn, resulted in a relaxation of the overwhelming drive to exploit both worker and consumer, since this drive was a consequence of the profit nexus (Berle, 1957; Galbraith, 1967).

The new manager, freed from the control of both stockholder and banker, sought to maintain and perpetuate his or her position. In order to accomplish this, managerialists argued, a moderate administrative strategy inevitably evolved. The technocratic executive sought to pacify and co-opt all those inside and outside the organization who might potentially upset the status quo. Instead of the reckless pursuit of high profits, a more responsive strategy developed, one that sought a smooth, undisrupted course of growth and transformed the modern firm into a "soulful corporation" (Kaysen, 1957).

It is important to emphasize the connection between stock dispersal and the argument for managerial control. Although the logic is straightforward, the details are crucial to an understanding of the contending theories of capitalist society. Managerialism sees owners as the source of the drive for high profits, a drive motivated by their desire to increase both stock value and dividend levels. A stockholder, therefore, will almost inevitably push for maximum returns; and the systemwide profit orientation is a reflection of the domination of most large firms by profit-seeking owners.

According to managerialists, stock dispersal in the twentieth century has severed this important bond. The traditional entrepreneur, who had owned the bulk of stock in the firm he created and managed, sold it off in dribs and drabs to a great many, mainly small, shareholders. The proof of this dispersion can be found in the annual report of any modern American corporation. In 1974 Exxon,

for example, reported 707,000 stockowners averaging fewer than
four hundred shares (worth $20,000) each; Consolidated Edison
reported 302,000 stockholders averaging fewer than one thousand
shares (worth $30,000) each; and Chemical Bank reported 43,000
shareholders, averaging fewer than five hundred shares (worth
$25,000) each. (Exxon Corporation 1975; Consolidated Edison, 1975;
Chemical New York Corporation, 1975)

For managerialists, this dispersion implies that a dissatisfied
stockowner must rally tens of thousands of other shareholders to
influence corporate policy. This is nearly impossible because of the
difficulty of making contact with so many individuals and by a
diversity of interests that makes agreement about policy problematic in many situations. Stockholder action therefore requires
enormous resources and unusual circumstances; it is not a day-to-
day threat to top management.

Moreover, chief executive officers tend to consolidate their positions. Through control of both the proxy mechanism and the flow
of information, they propagandize, mobilize, and organize the mass
of stockholders behind their regime; a dissident faces a well-
organized, entrenched elite with widespread stockowner support.
The process is summarized by Berle and Means (1932):

> As ownership of corporate wealth has become more widely
> dispersed, ownership of that wealth and control over it have
> come to be less and less in the same hands. Under the cor-
> porate system, control over industrial wealth can be and is
> exercised with a minimum of ownership interest. Ownership
> of wealth without appreciable control, and control of wealth
> without appreciable ownership, appear to be the logical out-
> come of corporate development. (p. 69)

Managerialists posit, therefore, that in normal times insiders
dominate corporate policy formation.[1]

> Experience shows that it is sufficient to own 40 percent of
> the shares of a company in order to direct its affairs, since a
> certain number of small scattered shareholders find it impos-
> sible, in practice, to attend general meetings, etc. The "de-
> mocratization" of the ownership of shares, . . . is , in fact, one
> of the ways of increasing the power of the financial oligarchy.
> (Lenin, 1917a; 54–55; see also Zeitlin, 1974, and Hilferding,
> 1910, part 1)

They use this power to seek a high return on investment, most
of which is kept as retained earnings they can control. They do not

pursue reckless profit maximizing in the style of their entrepreneurial forebears because this might lead to a crisis of sufficient proportions to trigger stockholder interest.

This strategy provides top management with maximum flexibility and insurance against disaster. It increases their control over capital resources by limiting dispersal to shareowners and relieves them of the necessity of seeking the outside funding that had traditionally been a mechanism of bank control. Thus, stock dispersion frees the firm from two important sources of outside influence: dominant stockholders and interventionist lenders.

Considerable disagreement has arisen among managerialists over the ultimate consequences of this type of inside control. There have been quarrels over whether managers pursue policies contributing to the general social welfare or whether they follow a parochial interest of their own. There have been quarrels over whether corporate positions are springboards for national leadership or whether the organization imposes a narrow scope on its incumbents, limiting their interests to the concerns of the firm. And there have been quarrels over whether the basic drive is toward maximum growth or stability.[2]

Managerialists have quarreled less, however, on two fundamental propositions. First, they agree that the drive to squeeze maximum profits from both worker and customer has been reduced substantially. And since the drive for maximum profit is the cause of many corporate problems—including bankruptcy, overextension, cutthroat competition, and a wide variety of other inefficient and often disastrous activities—control by managers implies a reduction in the amount of chaos and irrationality in the system as a whole.[3]

Thus, managerialism concludes that profit maximizing is not a satisfactory strategy for the survival of modern capitalism or for the long-term health of the individual large corporation. Management control rationalizes capitalist enterprise and makes it more effective in pursuing the interest of society as a whole.

In addition, implicit in the managerialist argument is the importance of inside control in preventing the development of intercorporate coordination. Once stock is dispersed, outside control declines, and the primary source of unity among companies dissolves. In the analyses of most early critics of capitalism (e.g., Lenin, 1917a; Hilferding, 1910), immense economic and political power derived from the capacity of empire builders like John D. Rockefeller, Sr., or J. P. Morgan to control several different enterprises simultaneously through stockholding, debt leverage, or both. By coordinating the activities of the many firms under their direction, they attained enormous power that they used to advance their interests at others' expense. By controlling whole industries, they could eliminate competition and raise prices without fear of losing business; they could suppress new products that undermined their interests (by refusing to produce them and by buying any companies that did); they could force highly profitable but undesirable products upon customers who had no alternative suppliers; and they could refuse to improve working conditions for those whose employment options were under their control.[4]

Traditional managerial control theory posits the termination of both the motive (profit maximizing) and the mechanism (outside, coordinated control) that permitted these abuses. It therefore implies the end of the possibility that a handful of great capitalist families can band together and impose their narrow political will on the country as a whole.

The managerial argument focuses exclusively on the locale of discretionary decision making. Reworded in our vocabulary, classic managerialism asserts that stock dispersion and financial independence have become so pervasive that stockholders and lenders rarely get involved in either operational management or strategic control. Discretionary decision making now resides with top management in most major corporations. Unfettered by outside control, executives select those options that guarantee their own security, thus transforming the fundamental thrust of corporate policy.

Managerialist conclusions rest, therefore, on two separate propositions—one explicit and one implicit. The explicit proposition is that management makes independent decisions about available options; that is, its discretion is not regularly subject to strategic control by outsiders. The implicit proposition is that available choices are extremely broad; that is, there are relatively few structural constraints that force executives to choose among a narrow range of options.

Mutual Deterrence and Class Cohesion Theory

Much criticism has accompanied the development of managerial theory: one set of researchers has shown that the concept of the "separation of ownership from control" is overstated and underdocumented;[5] another group has demonstrated the continued dependence on outside funds and the continued existence of strategic control by banks;[6] a third set has uncovered pervasive coordination and cooperation in the corporate world;[7] and a fourth set has documented the continued drive for maximum profits.[8] These arguments and evidence have laid a foundation for questioning the degree of decision making autonomy available to chief executives.

The managerial assumption that structural constraint plays only a minor role in determining the actions of the modern corporation was first challenged by Baran and Sweezy (1966), who questioned the conclusion that firms no longer try to maximize profits. They suggest that, since most high-level officials own substantial blocks of stock in their own and/or other corporations, they are personally tied to the profit nexus (Baran and Sweezy, 1966: 34–35). More fundamentally, the role of management in the operation of the firm involves it in the inevitable logic of capitalist enterprise. Personal ambitions and desire for high salary can be achieved only through the success of the corporation to which an executive is wedded. Insofar as the firm can purchase raw materials, exploit its workers, and sell these finished products at sufficiently high prices, there will be enough money to pay dividends, to maintain a high level of reinvestment, and to offer advancement and lucrative remuneration to leadership.

The chief executive must therefore strive to preserve his or her company, and this striving inevitably involves competition with other firms, including the constant growth and technological innovation that only high profits can fuel. Top management is simply carried along by this dynamic and does not have the option of pursuing low-profit strategies, since the ultimate outcome would be technological or marketing obsolescence, loss of market share, and corporate crisis. In this way the interests of top management—whether or not it holds stock in the firm—are tied intimately to the maintenance of high profit margins. Baran and Sweezy (1966) thus argue that profit maximizing remains the driving force of capitalist enterprise. And from this premise they dispute all managerialist claims about the amelioration of social problems emanating from the profit nexus.

In asserting the continued force of profit seeking in corporate life, Baran and Sweezy (1966) temporarily leave themselves without an explanation for the decline of cutthroat competition in the twentieth century. How can they explain, for example, the absence of price wars among the Big Three auto manufacturers, even during periods of major contraction and crisis?[9] As they note, the history of postwar American capitalism is replete with examples of cooperative activity among supposedly competing firms. We need only point to the great steel price rise controversy in 1962, when all major steel companies first raised, then lowered their prices, or the spectacular price-fixing indictments against the electrical industry, to illustrate this point (McConnell, 1962).

Baran and Sweezy resolve this contradiction by introducing the concept of corespective behavior, which is a theory of mutual deterrence. Since the vast resource bases of corporations allow them to resist fierce competition, price wars and the like become very expensive to all participants. Such strategies rest on driving competitors from business and capturing their markets. Since this is an unlikely outcome, it becomes self-defeating for large companies to compete in this manner.

The broader picture of corporate structure that Baran and Sweezy paint is an extension of this basic principle. Corporate managers, although autonomous, have many common interests that flow from the logic of mutual deterrence. These interests counter the huge pressure for profit maximizing, and they dampen the chaos of capitalism that would otherwise produce intense competition.

> The attitude of live-and-let-live which characterizes Big Business likewise derives from the magnitude of the corporation's investment and from the calculating rationality of its management. . . . The Big Business community is numerically small, comprising perhaps 10,000 or so people for the entire country, and its members are tied together by a whole network of social as well as economic ties. Conscious of their power and standing in the larger national community, they naturally tend to develop a group ethic which calls for solidarity and mutual help among themselves and for presenting a common front to the outside world. (Baran and Sweezy, 1966: 50)

Translated into our vocabulary, Baran and Sweezy assert that mutual deterrence removes price cuts from the competitive repertoire of large oligopolistic companies. A system of mutual constraint arises that imposes cooperative behavior on profit-seeking corporate executives.[10] This does not, of course, imply the abandonment of all competition; it implies the sublimation of price competition (and other deterrable forms) into cost-cutting marketing methods and other strategies that cannot be deterred.

Baran and Sweezy (1966) do not see mutual deterrence as the only mechanism for suppressing competition or as the sole source of intercorporate coordination: the government plays a key role in this realm. The detailed discussions of government processes in *Monopoly Capital* are not just exercises in political analysis. They represent an attempt to develop a thorough political economy, tied together by an overarching concept of the role of the state in late capitalism. This role, as Baran and Sweezy (1966) analyze it, is fundamentally prophylactic: the government tries to suppress or resolve the contradictions within the capitalist class and to execute policies that require more coordination than big business can muster on its own: "what appear to be conflicts between business and government are reflections of conflict within the ruling class" (p. 67).[11]

Three functions of the state are identified in this context. First, the profitability of crucial industries is regulated by the government to ensure that essential services are provided to the business class as a whole. Control of natural monopolies, for example, reflects the need either to suppress the potential hegemonic domination such monopolies could develop or to guarantee sufficient profits in the sector to prevent a collapse that would reverberate through the entire system:

> Now under monopoly capitalism it is as true, as it was in Marx's day, that the executive power of the . . . state is simply a committee for managing the common affairs of the entire bourgeois class. And the common affairs of the entire bourgeois class include a concern that no industries which play an important role in the economy, and in which large property interests are involved, should be either too profitable or too unprofitable. Extra large profits are gained, not only at the expense of consumers, but also of other capitalists (electric power and telephone service, for example, are basic costs of all industries). . . . Abnormally low profits in a major branch of the economy such as agriculture on the other hand, damage the interests of a large and politically powerful group of property owners who are able, through pressure and bargaining with the other capitalists, to enlist the necessary support for remedial action. It therefore becomes a state responsibility under monopoly capitalism to insure, as far as possible, that prices and profit margins in the deviant industries are brought within the range prevailing among the general run of giant corporations. (Baran and Sweezy, 1966: 64–65)

Second, certain sectors require support services that business cannot provide on its own, and these are pursued despite resistance from adversely affected fractions. The health of many major industries in the United States, for example, is directly dependent on auto production. In turn,

> the whole complex, of course, is completely dependent on the public provision of roads and highways. It is thus only natural

that there should be tremendous pressure for continuous expansion of government spending on highways. Counterpressures from private interests do exist—notably from the railroads, hard hit by the growth of highway transportation, but the railroads have been no match for the automobile complex. Government spending on highways has soared. (Baran and Sweezy, 1966: 173–74)

Finally, the government is the major instrument in the maintenance of full industrial production and overall economic health—the most fundamental requirement of monopoly capital:

> The structure of the monopoly capitalist economy is such that a continually mounting volume of surplus [production] simply could not be absorbed through private channels; if no other outlets were available, it would not be produced at all [and therefore production would decline, plants would close, recession or depression would occur, and profits would plummet]. . . . Since a larger volume of government spending pushes the economy nearer to capacity operation . . . both the government and the private segments of surplus can and indeed typically do grow simultaneously. (pp. 147–48).

Thus, in late capitalism, the government becomes a major agency of intercorporate coordination.[12]

Baran and Sweezy's perspective, known as class cohesion theory, posits a set of intermeshed constraints among major companies that limit the scope of options available to individual executives. Although these constraints provide the foundation upon which cooperative efforts are constructed, they are not sufficient to overcome all divisive tendencies. The government therefore implements any further action necessary for systemic survival. In this theory, little outside strategic control is established over managerial discretion. Corporate unity is achieved almost exclusively through intercorporate or state-imposed constraints.

Resource Dependency Theory

Baran and Sweezy's mutual deterrence argument is consistent with the basic assumptions of resource dependency theory, which in recent years has become a widely debated analysis of business structure. (See, for example, Aldrich, 1979; Pfeffer and Salancik, 1978; Pennings, 1980.) This perspective agrees with managerialism

that strategic corporate decision making is in the hands of chief
executive officers (see, for example, Aldrich, 1979: 317–21). It also
posits structural constraint, not invasion of managerial discretion,
as the source of interfirm unity.

Since large firms rely on each other for essential resources, the
paradigm suggests, the health of the corporation is dependent upon
predictable and profitable transactions with customers and suppliers. Top executives therefore must form structural bridges such
as mergers, joint ventures, and director interlocks that routinize
these relationships.[13] These structural ties reduce the degree of risk
while formalizing the constraints to which they respond. Thus
management discretion is preserved while structural constraint is
institutionalized. Although the outcome of this process can be either
outside strategic control or hegemonic domination, resource dependency theorists see little asymmetry and orderliness in the dependencies among major firms. They posit an assortment of symmetrical and asymmetrical relationships in which each company
or sector partially dominates some firms, is partially dominated by
others, and can mutually deter still others. Because of this complex
set of interactions, each major corporation continually searches for
stable, predictable connections with firms and sectors upon which
it must rely. Intercorporate coordination arises from this complex
interdependence and does not generally lead to control and coordination; the most frequent outcome is tenuous episodic cooperation.

Since stable hierarchies are not likely to arise from this loose
coordination, the main dysfunction in the system occurs when mutually interdependent corporations cannot arrange a structural
bridge to stabilize their relationships:

> When dependence is not capable of being managed by ne-
> gotiating stable structures of interorganizational action . . . or-
> ganizations seek to use the greater power of the larger social
> system and its government to eliminate the difficulties or pro-
> vide for their needs. (Pfeffer and Salancik, 1978: 189)

Resource dependency, therefore, arrives at a political theory similar to that of Baran and Sweezy: the government is the arbiter of
intercorporate conflict, because managerial autonomy cannot guarantee stable intercorporate relationships.

The debate among class cohesion theory, resource dependency
theory, and managerialism contains several areas of agreement and
disagreement. Managerialists contend that profit maximization is

no longer the driving force of capitalism and that many of the pathologies that characterized early twentieth-century business practice have consequently disappeared. At the same time, managerial autonomy has removed the main sources of intercorporate unity (stockholding and loan relationships). Large firms, therefore, are simultaneously less competitive and less unified than in the past.

The logic of both mutual deterrence and resource dependency rests upon the managerial assumption that top executives are free to make discretionary decisions without intervention from stockholders or lenders. However, these theories challenge the idea that managerial autonomy has reduced the profit motive, and instead they suggest that the forces of competition, conflict, and the drive for exploitation remain intact. Rather than greater competition, however, mutual deterrence and resource dependency have created structural constraints that encourage intercorporate cooperation. Thus, large firms are simultaneously highly competitive and highly constrained; the behavioral outcome is cooperation in a context of continued competition.

These contrasting portraits derive from different assessments of structural constraint in the system of intercorporate relations. For traditional managerialists the original profit drive reflected a discretionary choice made by owner-entrepreneurs. They did not pursue maximum profits because the system demanded it; they did so because they desired the enormous wealth such profits would produce. The reduction in the profit drive is also discretionary; it is an uncoerced choice made by autonomous executives who personally have little to gain from such activity.

In both class cohesion and resource dependency theories, the drive for profits is not an expression of individual greed by specific managers or stockholders, but a constraint of the system. Thus although price competition could, in principle, increase market share, guarantee growth, and ensure corporate health, it is suppressed by the threat of successful countermoves or by the withholding of needed resources. Cooperation or passive noncompetition is a result of system constraint, not executive discretion.

Bank Control Theory

The logic of structural constraint contained in mutual deterrence and resource dependency theory is the foundation upon which an accurate portrait of American business structure can be built. However, our understanding of this process has been limited by inattention to two critical issues: the interface between decision-making discretion and structural constraint, and the assumption of symmetrical interdependence among major corporate actors.

It is in this context that the recent revival of banker control theory is most important, since this posits an asymmetrical interdependence between banks and nonfinancial firms that is translated into strategic control of major industrials by financial institutions.[14] This view of intercorporate relations rests on a judgment that commercial banks are an overwhelming force in the business world. Their power is based on their ability to grant or refuse loans to major firms and to exert leverage through the vast stockholdings of their trust departments. It explicitly challenges the managerial assertion—endorsed by both mutual deterrence and resource dependency theories—that large corporations are no longer dependent on outside financing.[15] Instead, it argues that control of loan capital and stockownership enable banks to dictate policies to industrial firms and thus achieve coordination and planning that would otherwise be impossible.[16]

The classic example of strategic control by lenders, discussed by Fitch and Oppenheimer (1970a-c) and later carefully documented by Tinnen (1973), was the ouster of Howard Hughes from the leadership of Trans World Airlines. Beginning in 1939, Hughes built TWA into a major force in commercial aviation. In the late 1950s, when the first generation of commercial jets was entering the market, he used the airline's dominant position to bargain for favorable purchase agreements with financially strapped manufacturers. The most important privilege he gained was the right to purchase planes in the same way an ordinary citizen buys a car: the producer would construct the plane and TWA would pay for it in monthly payments (with interest) after delivery. This arrangement would have forced the manufacturers to borrow construction capital, thus adding to the already overwhelming debt they had accumulated in developing the planes.

The manufacturers and their creditors wanted a different payment schedule, one they had successfully negotiated with other airlines. Their policy involved prepayment, with the last installment paid at the time of delivery. In this way the weight of construction costs would be borne by the relatively debt-free airlines instead of the nearly bankrupt manufacturers. Hughes refused these terms; they would have reduced his profits. His market position allowed him to insist on delivery before payment as well as priority status; he received the first jets produced before other, more cooperative, airlines received their new aircraft.

During the 1959 recession, however, Howard Hughes's other major holding, Hughes Tool Company, was unable to repay a $25 million loan held by several New York banks. Under ordinary conditions a loan that small would have been renegotiated and repaid at a later date. In this instance, however, the lenders threatened foreclosure unless Hughes placed his TWA stock—which accounted for 78% of the outstanding common—into a voting trust under their control. Once this demand was met, the immensely successful Hughes was ousted and a new management installed. The purchase agreement was then renegotiated according to the specifications that lenders advocated, and after a long legal battle Hughes was forced to sell his shares in the company.

This episode illustrates two fundamental propositions of bank control theory: that loan leverage is capable of producing strategic control, and that banks can suppress competitive forces within the economy. Hughes, as an independent actor, was seeking to maximize his own profit even if it weakened the aircraft manufacturers. This was traditional capitalist cutthroat competition, and it was not suppressed by mutual deterrence, resource dependency, or state intervention.

It was the recession that placed Hughes in a constrained position vis-à-vis lenders. By refusing to roll over his $25 million debt, the banks offered him two unpalatable options. Bankruptcy implied that Hughes Tool would be run by a committee of creditors—that is, the banks; placing his stock in a voting trust implied that TWA would be run by the banks. Hughes was forced to relinquish his right to discretionary decision making over one company or the other. Loan leverage—a structural constraint—was thus translated into strategic control by lenders. Ultimately, this became long-term domination because the executive installed by the banks, Charles Tillinghast, remained at the helm of TWA for a dozen years.

Once in control, lender representatives used their newly acquired discretion to renegotiate the purchase agreements to conform to the banks' (not TWA's) interest. Loan leverage, mediated by strategic control, was thus capable of overcoming a competitive impulse.

Bank control theory is constructed upon the logic of this example. After initial intervention, banks use a variety of mechanisms to maintain control: they appoint their own leadership, strive to establish chronic capital dependency, and attempt to acquire controlling stock.[17] Increasing numbers of firms fall under the control of a specific bank, which coordinates activities for the entire group and transmits plans to the management of constituent firms for appropriate action. Interference in day-to-day operational management is unusual. Bank control theorists thus argue that financial institutions determine the broad policy orientations that managerialists, mutual deterrence theorists, and resource dependency analysts believe is now in the hands of inside management. In doing so, they also allocate to banks the integrative power these perspectives attribute to the state.

This difference in perspective is crucial to our analysis. Bank control theory asserts a dictatorship by financial institutions over both the business community and the state, since a united business sector is viewed as capable of dictating policy to government. Therefore it is consistent with a traditional Leninist portrait of the state as an instrument of (finance) capitalist will—a "dictatorship of the bourgeoisie."

In one respect bank control theory offers the most profound challenge to traditional managerialism, since it questions managerial autonomy itself. In another respect, however, it represents a return to managerial logic, which focuses on access to discretionary decision making as the principal vehicle of outside control. In this logic, the constraint of asymmetrical interdependence—industrial firms' crucial need for capital—allows banks to dominate decision making. This discretionary power is then used to suppress competition and coordination among a collection of firms—all in the interest of financial institutions.

In the resource dependency and mutual deterrence perspectives, competition is suppressed and coordination achieved without the enactment of such strategic control—it is, instead, a direct result of the application of (often reciprocal) constraint.

The Theory of Financial Hegemony

The publication of Fitch and Oppenheimer's three-part article "Who Rules the Corporations?" (1970a-c) offered a fully developed theory of bank control and triggered a complex debate over the nature of financial intervention that we will review in more detail in chapter 4. The crucial point of contention in this debate was bank control theory's assumption that lending relationships are in general asymmetrical; that, following the TWA example, they create more dependence among borrowers than among lenders; and therefore that bankers develop structural leverage over industrial firms.

In the case of TWA this asymmetry is clear, but this may not be true in general. Hence the recurring theme of critics has been that industrial dependence on lenders is balanced by the reciprocal dependence of lenders on their borrowers (Sweezy, 1972; Herman, 1973, 1981). This reciprocal dependence notion is an important one, and since it is central to the logic of our argument, it must be discussed in detail.

Clearly banks are dependent upon large nonfinancials, since without them they could not lend capital. Based on this Scott (1979), quoting Sweezy, argues that "banks and industry are involved in a relationship in which 'both sides hold strong cards, and their mutual lending and borrowing operations provide no basis for assuming that either controls the other' " (pp. 97–98). He concludes that "the notion of bank control has limited application to contemporary conditions" (p. 103).

Interdependence, however, does not eliminate the possibility of asymmetrical domination. In the case of bank-industrial relationships, two factors facilitate financial ascendancy: the ongoing systemwide shortage of capital and the crisis conditions that frequently accompany an industrial firm's search for loans. This argument was succinctly expressed by Ratcliff (1980b: 112):

> the leading segments of the capitalist class face an enduring shortage of capital to meet their investment needs and opportunities. Because of this shortage, banks become especially important types of private enterprises precisely because of their role in accumulating the surplus capital available in the broader community.

To illustrate the impact of these forces, consider the comparison between two sharply contrasting moments in recent business history: the 1976–78 period of capital surplus and the 1979–81 period of capital shortage. From 1976 to 1978, an unprecedented number of large corporations had large capital reserves.[18] *Business Week* summarized the situation:

> The 400 largest U.S. companies together have more than $60 billion in cash—almost triple the amount they had at the beginning of the 1970s. About 175 companies currently have caches of $100 million or more, and nearly a dozen boast $1 billion or more. (March 13, 1978: 62)

The business press was full of accounts of desperate searches by cash-rich industrial enterprises for profitable investments. The surpluses triggered a new wave of mergers and the development of an extensive commercial paper market, in which large firms lent their excess funds to each other without the mediation of bankers.[19] The surpluses caused enormous difficulties for major lenders, since their usual customers were simply not borrowing:

> Bankers are increasingly distressed by the lack of loan demand, and they are gradually abandoning caution as they tailor terms to make bank loans more appealing to big corporate borrowers. The major New York and Chicago banks are leading the drive for new business, pushing out all over the country to get it. (Business Week, Oct. 18, 1976: 91)

It also triggered competition among financial sectors: "Banks and life insurance companies, flush with lendable funds, are slugging it out for borrowers of intermediate-term (5 to 12 year) funds, and that means better terms for borrowers." (Business Week, March 23, 1977: 105)

One can imagine the development of industrial dominance over banks in these circumstances. Bankers might have curried favor with cash-rich industrials and been forced to alter bank policy and investment strategy to suit the needs of their former customers. This did not take place.

Instead, these constraints forced the banks to offer better financial terms or to place their investment capital in less attractive outlets. But there was no outside dictation of bank policy; at no time did nonfinancial firms intervene in the discretionary decision-making process of banks or insurance companies.

The banks escaped outside domination because, even in this period of great surplus, there was an underlying capital shortage. At the crest of this slack demand, with $80 billion in retained earnings held by industrial firms, top American corporations still needed to borrow 33% of their investment capital (Business Week, Sept. 18, 1978: 97). "If such giants as IBM are cash rich today, hundreds of smaller companies find their tills nearly empty" (Business Week, Jan. 30, 1978: 62).

Thus, though major banks were unable to reach their preferred borrowers, they still had many anxious, less-attractive customers to choose from. These options provided a satisfactory, if not ideal, alternative that prevented the development of industrial dominance over financial firms. The constraints imposed by the capital surpluses did not eliminate all options and thus did not produce sufficient leverage for intervention by potential borrowers.

Consider in contrast, the period 1979 to 1981, when an acute shortage of capital developed.[20]

The same message echoes from industry after industry—aircraft, appliances, steel, even textiles and shoes: Technology is not lacking; the know how that is needed exists; however, U.S. companies cannot raise the capital necessary to put the technology to work. (*Business Week*, June 30, 1980: 104)

In 1978 Ford held $3.4 billion in retained earnings; General Motors held $3.2 billion (*Forbes*, March 20, 1978: 80). By 1980, the two firms were searching desperately for over $10 billion in outside funding (Yago and Schwartz, 1981). Even the highly profitable semiconductor industry was strapped:

TI [Texas Instruments] President J. Fred Bucey has forecast that U.S. semiconductor companies will have to come up with $25 billion to $35 billion in new capital in the 1980s. . . . Intel's [chief executive officer Gordon E.] Moore puts the capital requirement at closer to $65 billion, only half of which could be financed out of earnings. (*Business Week*, June 1, 1981: 78)

The shortages were felt throughout the economy. Computer industry analysts saw "the capital crunch pinching profits over the next couple of years and precipitating a major shakeout" (*Business Week*, June 1, 1981: 78). In communications and aircraft construction, the message was the same (*Business Week*, June 1, 1981: 78; May 25, 1981: 149). Industrial firms and sectors competed for limited financial resources. As a consequence, industrials paid higher interest rates, maintained ample compensatory deposits, and sought out new funding sources. In many cases, however, such maneuvers were unsuccessful and firms were faced with abandoning capital-spending plans, even in the face of possible bankruptcy.

In certain circumstances capital shortages will spur a financial crisis that will force bank rescue. The resulting relationship can involve close coordination and external strategic control. Banks, unwilling to expose their money to undue risk, may insist upon careful scrutiny of the firm they rescue. Frequently, they will demand input into discretionary decision making and participation in the development of new programs.

Consider the case of Braniff Airlines.[21] Overcapacity in air travel grew slowly during the 1970s and crystallized into a crisis with federal deregulation in 1978. This produced rigorous price competition, forcing airlines to reduce costs dramatically. To a considerable degree, survival depended upon quick conversion to new fuel-efficient planes, and this required large amounts of capital. The capital shortage exacerbated an already difficult situation, and each airline was forced to develop strategies aimed at boosting profits despite lower air fares. They needed to generate capital internally for the conversion and to supplement this with borrowed funds.

Braniff's strategy relied on its recently purchased fuel-efficient Boeing 727-200s. It took advantage of deregulation to invade lucrative routes dominated by other carriers, hoping to gain a large market share, generate enormous profits, parlay this into fresh loans, and thus finance the rest of their conversion to new planes. However, the air-travel recession deepened, and the other carriers successfully resisted the invasion. Braniff could not meet payments on existing loans and could not borrow enough new money to finance the purchase of additional fuel-efficient aircraft.

Beginning in late 1979, lenders took an active role in corporate policy. At first they exchanged relaxed loan repayment plans (to "give Braniff more breathing room") for warrants convertible to a controlling 14% block of stock. They insisted upon the cancellation of a stock issue in July, 1980 (*Business Week*, July 28, 1980: 43); dictated the sale of fifteen of Braniff's Boeing 727-200s (to pay debt) in August (*Business Week*, Aug. 11, 1980: 26–7); participated in decisions to cancel trans-Pacific routes in September (*New York Times*, Oct. 7, 1980: D5); and finally ousted the chief executive officer in January, 1981 (*New York Times*, Jan. 8, 1981: D3). These actions were part of an extended rescue effort: "Wall Street analysts have long contended that the company's 39 senior lenders, owed nearly $700 million, would work closely with the airline rather than watch it go into bankruptcy" (*New York Times*, April 16, 1981: D5).[22] In this way, Braniff became a prototypical case of bank control.

The logic of bank intervention is clear: to protect an existing investment, the banks became involved in Braniff's decision-making process. This is hardly surprising if we note the $700 million exposure of the banks. With an investment of this size, bank officials would be irresponsible if they failed to take an active interest in the affairs of the company. As the crisis deepened, this interest matured into concern that Braniff would default; it was therefore transformed into active intervention.

This logic is openly expressed in the business community. During the 1981 International Harvester intervention, *Business Week* quoted a major bank executive:

"We don't take the attitude that time will heal the wounds." Rather than accommodate a troubled company, bankers try

to force the borrower to recognize its difficulty and mend its
ways. Accommodating a troubled company—as bankers did in
1975 with retailer W. T. Grant—may do both borrowers and
lenders a disservice. As a company's health deteriorates, so
too does the liquidation value of its assets. "The sooner you
say no, the better it will be for both you and the borrower,"
says one lender. "Sometimes a banker can provide a useful
discipline." (June 22, 1981: 70)

The key difference between the consequences of capital surplus
and capital shortage lies in the nature of the relationships established. Capital surplus had great impact on the specific features of
loan transactions: interest rates declined (for many firms), compensatory balances were reduced, and so forth. Real constraints
were placed on bank options. Capital shortage had the opposite
impact, and it therefore constrained many borrowers. But in some
instances it also produced lender inputs into corporate discretionary decision making. Braniff's banks dictated route contraction and
sales of new planes; no group of industrial firms dictated the investment decisions of banks.

This is the crux of the asymmetry: when large financials face
capital surpluses, "they tailor terms to make bank loans more appealing" (Business Week, Oct. 18, 1978: 91). When industrials face
capital shortages, they search for a "large investor who will provide
the cash without interfering with management" (Business Week,
Sept. 22, 1980). Capital surplus threatens lender profit margins and
forces changes in lending transactions; it does not facilitate borrower access to lender decision making. Capital shortages may result in the loss of corporate autonomy and the (temporary or permanent) transfer of strategic control to lenders. In some
circumstances, then, they allow for lender access to the discretionary decision making of borrowers.

This asymmetry derives from four sources. First, capital is a
fluid, almost universal commodity. It is useful in all realms of business and can act as a substitute for most resources required by large
companies. A firm faced with a shortage of a certain raw material
may either locate a new source or obtain capital and thus pay higher
prices to existing suppliers. The systemic shortage of capital reflects
this universality; insofar as corporations remain resource dependent, they are customers for capital. This universality also results
in lender involvement in all parts of the economy. Other industrial
groupings, even dominant ones like oil today or auto manufacturing
during the 1950s, maintain exchange relationships with a limited
number of sectors and therefore are not in a position to influence

or constrain a broad spectrum of other companies. Lenders are involved in every sector and therefore may constrain any part of the economy by withholding needed capital.

Second, the asymmetry arises from the unique role of capital as a commodity. While all other commodities are exchanged for a different commodity (usually money), finance capital is exchanged for itself. A lender gives its customers money in exchange for a larger sum at a later date. In between the two payments lies a period in which the lender has an interest in the financial viability of the borrowing enterprise. In some larger sense, it is "just" that the lender takes an interest in the management of the firm and in the uses to which its money is put, since repayment depends on the nature of these decisions. Although in many situations lenders allow (or are forced to accept) borrower autonomy, there are many other circumstances in which their interest dictates—and their power allows—a more active role. Hence the lender relationship suggests a partnership of sorts between the bank and the borrowing firm.

Third, industrial firms seeking large loans must approach a handful of major banks that regularly coordinate their activities (see chapter 5). Existing loan consortia consolidate the lending monopoly still further and force the firm to deal with a single source of finance capital. Banks and other lenders never face such a monopoly of borrowers; even the largest sums can be placed with literally hundreds of customers. If industrial firms could form a consortium and refuse to borrow unless the lenders compromised managerial autonomy, they could, under certain conditions, intervene in bank decision making. Without this comparable unity, intervention can occur only in one direction.[23]

Fourth, asymmetry derives from the urgency of the lending relationship. Industrial firms relinquish strategic control because without quick capital infusions they face bankruptcy. Capital surpluses do not threaten banks with bankruptcy because, as the surplus of 1976 illustrates, lenders were able to place their funds with less-attractive borrowers. Hence the degree of urgency is far from comparable.

That asymmetrical interdependency derives from the combined effects of these factors, rather than a single one, is illustrated by the example of certificates of deposit, a major source of commercial banking assets. These are funds banks borrow from nonfinancial firms, and this establishes a partnership in which the industrial company is the lender. The nonfinancial therefore has every motive to oversee the safety of its loan; that is, to participate in decision making. Such oversight does not occur, however, because no single depositor can generate sufficient power to enforce such a demand. Only if depositors were united and threatened simultaneous withdrawal could such a demand become viable.

In some circumstances, a de facto unity arises among borrowers: widely known problems at a bank may lead to a "silent run" in which major depositors protect themselves by switching their funds to other institutions. In these cases withdrawals create an urgency that threatens bank viability, but the lack of coordination among depositors makes intervention impractical. Collective action would require a decision-making apparatus among depositors that could hammer out a collective strategy. In a context of previously atomized, uncoordinated activity, the development of this unity among depositors is virtually impossible.

Ironically, banks faced by silent runs turn to other banks for rescue loans and therefore become susceptible to lender, not depositor, intervention. Lenders, unlike borrowers, can establish and maintain the necessary unity through well-established consortium arrangements and mutual deterrence processes that are reviewed in chapter 5.

The four aspects of control of capital flows that produce asymmetrical interdependency—the universality of capital as a commodity, the tendencies toward lender unity, the urgency among borrowers, and the partnership aspects of lending relationships—all contribute to the recurring pattern of financial intervention into the discretionary decision making of industrial companies. Such intervention occurs in the American economy. Each year a substantial number of major corporations are dictated to by outside financial interests as to broad policy and the recruitment of internal leadership (see chapter 4). However, long-term or permanent strategic control is a rare phenomenon; instances of financial intervention are almost always temporary. There may be a period when lenders dictate policy or the hiring of a chief executive officer, but they then withdraw from active participation. Very frequently they withdraw from the strict enforcement of loan agreements and stockholding privilege once the crisis is over.

This suggests a major paradox. On the one hand, without long-term control, finance capital apparently loses its capacity to plan and coordinate intercorporate activity, thus leaving the managerial vision of intercorporate autonomy intact. On the other hand, voluntary withdrawal is illogical: why would bankers give up control if they could, as Fitch and Oppenheimer (1970a–c) suggest, use it to increase their own power and profits?

In part this is explained by Gogel's (1977: 205–23) analysis of the
consonance between the interests of bankers and those of nonfinancial firms (see also Zeitlin, 1974: 1110–12). Except in rare instances, an independent, profit-seeking chief executive officer will
pursue policies that make the industrial firm a maximally attractive
investment for banks, either as lenders or as stock managers. Intervention and outside control are therefore necessary only in those
rare instances in which the firm is in trouble, or when grave mismanagement occurs. Regular intervention might, in fact, demor-
alize top executives and undermine performance.

Nevertheless, the capacity to coordinate several independent
companies offers the planner so many advantages that it is hard to
imagine bankers voluntarily abandoning this possibility unless such
unity could be achieved by other means.

It is our contention that structural constraint, rather than strategic intervention, is the main means by which such coordination
is achieved. Though the equation of forces that produce asymmetrical interdependence may express themselves on occasion as
intervention, they can also develop into hegemonic constraint that
accomplishes much the same result. Such constraint is illustrated
by the famous Leasco example discussed at the beginning of chapter
1.

A more instructive example of this process involved the 1976
proposal by aircraft manufacturers to develop and market a new
airbus that would:

> use up-to-the-minute technology, would mean lowest possible
> noise, enormous fuel savings, and a carefully calculated seat-
> ing capacity for the most profitable possible operations on in-
> tended routes. . . . Almost everyone concedes that large new
> plane programs will only be started with large orders that only
> United States airlines could be expected to provide. But these
> airlines' traditional lenders have repeatedly said they cannot
> provide financing unless the industry's financial health im-
> proves markedly, and not just in a one or two year spurt. . . .
> Conceivably, if the airline recovery continues, the lenders
> might relent and agree to provide financing. But they are wor-
> ried not just about short-run profit levels, but also about where
> the industry is headed in the long run. (*New York Times*, Sept.
> 3, 1976: D5)

Ultimately, despite vigorous lobbying by both airlines and manufacturers, the lenders withheld funding. The decision by the lenders was a determining, hegemonic one. Without formal interven-

tion, the financial institutions defeated the airbus plan, and the airbus was never built.

In this instance, the ingredients of asymmetrical interdependence produced a circumstance in which financial companies exercised their own discretion in a way that determined the policies of both the airlines and the aircraft manufacturers. The loans were not to forestall bankruptcy, but they were crucial for the airbus project. The partnership aspect of the lending relationship forced the banks to consider the long-term prospects for air travel and to discount the industry's prosperity in 1976. It was also reflected in the informed judgment of these prospects, which derived from the knowledge developed through previous investment in airplane development. The unity of lenders meant that a collective decision was made: the *New York Times* article quoted above expresses this coordination, which was a structural necessity born of the enormous investment required for such a project. The universality of capital is seen in the ability of lenders to refuse such a large project even during a period of capital surplus. The fluidity of capital allowed them to place these funds in other locales rather than to settle for a risky aircraft construction endeavor.

Ultimately, the decision to forgo a third generation of civilian jets was made by lenders and not by the aircraft industry. The decision was enforced by the refusal to supply needed funds and not by intervention into the decision making of the manufacturers. This instance of decisive external influence through structural constraint is prototypical of hegemonic domination: the leadership of the dominant institutions makes decisions that limit the options available to subordinate institutions and thus constrain their actions.

As we noted in chapter 1, constraints that determine corporate behavior can arise from many sources. The uranium cartel severely constrained the options of Westinghouse but did not maintain the ongoing leverage that characterized the hegemony exercised by the major auto companies over auto-parts suppliers. Consumers, by refusing to buy gas guzzlers, forced the auto industry to shift to small cars, but this was an episode of unity rather than an ongoing joint action capable of replication and therefore of systematic exploitation. Hegemony need not involve continuous domination or frequent intervention, but it does imply regular moments of dependence that impose a loose but consistent discipline on subordinate firms.

The remainder of this book will attempt to demonstrate that decision making over capital flows regularly confers upon financial institutions this hegemonic leverage. Large firms often retain strategic autonomy for short or long periods. Much corporate action is undertaken by individual companies without decisive financial influence or by groups of companies temporarily unified through mutual deterrence or resource dependence. Nevertheless, the major source of broad coordination and discipline in the system—when such coordination and discipline arise—derives from the leverage conferred by control of capital flows.

In some instances, like the one just reviewed, this leverage expresses itself as a veto power over proposed projects. In other instances, like the expansion of shipbuilding in the early 1970s reviewed in chapter 5 below, it expresses itself as lender-initiated projects that attract industrial firms because of the availability of capital. In still other instances, like the transformation of farm co-ops into capitalist enterprises, also reviewed in chapter 5, it expresses itself as lender insistence on certain policy changes before loans are approved. And in a few instances, usually associated with corporate crisis, it expresses itself as intervention into the discretionary decision making of nonfinancial firms.

The overall impact of this assortment of individual constraints is succinctly expressed by Gogel (1977: 50):

> the largest American corporations form an interconnected network which is dominated by financial institutions, especially commercial banks, [which] . . . maintain a greatly disproportionate amount of power to affect the normative orientations, determine the flow of information, and influence the policies and behavior of other members of the network.

We apply the concept of hegemony to this arrangement because it produces domination of policy without strategic control. The influence exercised by financials operates mainly through the elimination or creation of options for other institutions; that is, by altering the profile of constraint. A considerable degree of planning is facilitated by these hegemonic relationships that accrue to the lending, and more recently stockholding, functions of financial institutions. The flow of capital into or away from various sectors and firms is so crucial in modern capitalism that the capacity to plan derives from control of these decisions; intervention into discretionary decision making, though it occurs regularly, is frequently superfluous to systemwide planning and is often counterproductive.

Thus, hegemonic relationships are narrower than control relations. Because domination is exercised by eliminating or facilitating specific options, hegemony does not allow broad dictation of policy. It is rare (though not unknown) for capital-flow decisions to result in the ouster of top executives; major lenders do not ordinarily dictate design and production decisions as dominant stockholders do.

Bank hegemony theory, therefore, asserts and implies a loose but powerful hierarchy in intercorporate interaction patterns. This hierarchy is not just one of many dyadic relationships between banks (or other capital sources) and with all firms in the system. Quite the contrary: bank hegemony implies a set of hegemonic relationships that connect and unite one sector—financial firms— with subordinate sectors—large industrials like auto manufacturers—which connect with still other firms—like auto supply companies—and so on, until a large proportion of the economy is subject to coordination by corporate lenders in the center of the system. The theory does not argue that each and every corporation is under tight, or even loose, control at all times. It does suggest, however, that the behavior of major corporations are subject to and conditioned by their ongoing capital needs; and they therefore must fit their actions and strategies in the overall patterns determined by the major financial institutions.

This analysis does not suggest that banks are omnipotent in any way. Even direct intervention into the decision-making process at Braniff did not prevent eventual bankruptcy. And the investment of massive sums of capital in nuclear energy and in the Third World succinctly demonstrates the fallibility of banks. Nevertheless, the imperfect coordination and the sometimes faulty decision making of financial institutions condition, in broad strokes, the activities of the modern American corporation, and the effects of this reverberate through the system.

If we return to the auto industry example, we can interpret our description in chapter 1 in light of the conceptualization just developed. The domination the major manufacturers exercised over the auto-parts suppliers had to do with capital flows. The key moves, in both the 1960s and the 1970s, were Big Three decisions about the use of investment capital. In the first instance, they decided to use retained profits to manufacture parts in-house rather than invest in some other type of expansion. This drove the suppliers out of the new-car-parts business. In the second instance, the Big Three used all available capital (retained earnings and borrowings) on development of fuel-efficient small cars and forwent investment in the manufacture of parts. This brought the suppliers back into the business of new-car parts. Thus the structural domination exercised by the Big Three was tied directly to decisions about the flow of capital, even, in this instance, when financial institutions were not involved directly.

While the auto companies were exercising hegemony over the parts industry, large banks and insurance companies were exercising a similar form of hegemonic domination over the Big Three. When the manufacturers set out to spend $75 billion on the development of fuel-efficient cars, they faced a "need for tremendous outside capital," which lenders refused to grant in full (*Business Week*, March 24, 1980: 81–82). The high cost of construction of new-parts factories was a major consideration: "auto makers have a more pressing demand on their capital investment money—making their cars smaller" (*Business Week*, Sept. 24, 1979: 140). Thus the refusal of lenders to fund Big Three capital spending created, in good part, the circumstances in which the auto industry decided to abandon parts manufacture. This, in turn, led to the reentry of parts suppliers into the field. In some sense the lenders exercised a two-step hegemony; one set of decisions conditioned and delimited a second set, which conditioned and delimited a third.

Corporate lenders are often aware of many of the implications of their financial decisions. When a major expansion is proposed, they undertake impact studies that help predict the economic consequences of the enterprise. These studies, however imperfect, allow for planning inputs into the decision-making process: they aid the creditors in making an informed judgment about the viability of the project; they allow lenders to calculate what other industries and firms will necessarily be involved in the effort; and they thus allow an estimate of the overall costs and profits of the enterprise. Many times the decision to fund a large project turns on the subsidiary lending opportunities that might derive from it and the adverse effects of the proposed endeavor on other enterprises to which the banks are already committed. This planning therefore permits anticipation and prevention of "destructive competition" or duplication of economic development, a constant danger in the complex interplay of high-level corporate finance.

Thus, in order to evaluate an investment opportunity, the major lenders are forced, by their own size and by the diversity of their investment profiles, to assess and plan upon its consequences. This inevitably leads them to explore the entire profile of economic activity connected with a single major project. This planning, however imperfect it may be, is not just a "capacity" that flows from asymmetrical interdependence; it is a necessity imposed upon the hegemonic lenders by the logic of their position in the intercorporate network.

This logic also has important political consequences, since when a major economic enterprise is under consideration the political impact or prerequisites for all large projects must be assessed. Therefore the existence of economic planning, however imperfect, implies the collateral existence of political planning and suggests that business intervention in government is as inevitable as it is prevalent.

Consider again the postwar development of super highways and suburban housing projects discussed above. These enterprises involved such a wide range of interdependent construction that it is almost impossible to chronicle all the prerequisites and consequences of suburbanization. Suburban home building required huge infusions of investment capital. It also required the construction and maintenance of means of transportation from bedroom suburbs to places of employment. The decision to build highways instead of public transportation required huge infusions of capital to auto manufacturers (see, for example, Sloan, 1965) and suppression of competition from the mass transportation systems (Whitt, 1975, 1982; Yago; 1980, 1983). Automobile culture, in turn, necessitated a change in the shopping habits of the American population. Downtown areas create huge congestion in a car economy; the existence of decentralized shopping districts became an economic necessity and created yet another funding opportunity/obligation. The set of consequences can be spread out through the entire structure of suburban life and extends beyond decision making in the construction industry.

Governments were involved from the beginning in the construction of highways, public facilities, new schools, and even playgrounds, and therefore political action became an integral part of the planning process. Other major industrial capitalists who located their industries (or failed to locate their industries) at convenient locations were also involved. Commercial retailing firms, who developed a whole new system of supermarkets and department-store malls, were drawn in almost immediately. Even charitable institutions and hospitals had to revise their typical structure to suit the suburbanization process.

Only financial institutions were in a position to understand the implications of suburbanization, even partially, and to coordinate and plan, however imperfectly, the various sectors, including the government, needed for this enterprise. These sorts of relationships impose upon financial institutions the necessity of planning at every investment juncture.

Conclusion

Managerial theory posits the development of chief executives whose discretion was unhampered by outside control and whose options were not seriously limited by structural constraint. Both mutual deterrence theory and resource dependency theory have focused attention on the structural constraints that narrow the options available to corporate management. These constraints motivate the creation of intercorporate structures that suppress intercorporate conflict and create coordinated action.

These perspectives, however, neither question the assumption of managerial autonomy nor arrive at a portrait of hierarchical relations among sectors or firms. Unity is implied between independent actors who form coequal alliances.

Bank control theory asserts that managerial autonomy is undermined by hierarchical relationships between financial and nonfinancial companies. Asymmetrical interdependence leads to lender intervention into the discretionary decision making of industrial companies and ultimately produces a hierarchical unity coordinated by banks and other financial companies.

In this perspective, structural constraint is important only insofar as it produces strategic control; it is not a significant direct determinant of corporate behavior. The processes of mutual deterrence and resource dependency are seen as epiphenomenal in light of the enduring control relationships created by bank intervention.

The theory of financial hegemony embraces the structural logic of mutual deterrence and resource dependency theory and the hierarchical domination of bank control theory. Although asymmetrical interdependence sometimes produces intervention, it most frequently creates hegemonic structural ties between financial and nonfinancial firms. The constraints analyzed by earlier theorists thus result not in coequal collusive arrangements, but in unequal dominance relationships. The outcome is a loosely coordinated system broadly organized around the interests of financial institutions.

To demonstrate the viability of hegemony theory, we turn now to an exploration of the processes of capital flows and a demonstration of their pervasive influence over intercorporate affairs.

3 The Structure and Functions of Unity among Financial Institutions

You cannot put into operation any large project without the help of the New York banks.

Anonymous industrial leader (Katona, 1957)

The theory of financial hegemony outlined in chapter 2 rests on the assumption that financial institutions can achieve a unified posture toward investment possibilities; that nonfinancial corporations encounter periodic episodes of capital dependency; and that alternative pools of capital are unavailable. While we have already presented illustrations of this, in this chapter we present a more systematic exploration of these points. We will also investigate the differing roles played by national versus regional commercial banks and insurance companies versus investment banks in achieving financial unity and analyze the allocation of discretionary decision making within the banking world.

Financial unity would be unimportant if the modern corporation did not need external financing. Consider, therefore, a corporation seeking capital for a major expansion or retooling. The preferred source is retained earnings, but, as many authors have demonstrated (e.g., Lintner, 1966; Gogel, 1977), corporations cannot always depend on internally generated funds. In recent years well over 30% of all corporate capital has been borrowed (Lintner, 1966; Gogel, 1977), while the total long-term debt of American corporations jumped from $49 billion in 1940 to $363 billion in 1970 (Sweezy and Magdoff, 1975: 5). In 1977, a period of relative prosperity, only 2.5% of the 857 firms surveyed by *Business Week* (Dec. 27, 1977) had obtained over 90% of their capital from retained earnings; about 10% had obtained over 50% of their capital from outside sources.

The following year nonfinancial corporations invested a total of $236.5 billion, 43% ($102 billion) of which was borrowed. Of the borrowed funds, 70% ($71 billion) came from lending institutions (*Business Week*, Jan. 30, 1978: 62).

Even very healthy firms may require a constant flood of outside financing. AT&T, one of the most profitable corporations in the United States, owed $32.5 billion in 1978 (*Business Week*, Nov. 6, 1978: 119). Other companies may attempt to expand through retained profits only, but most borrow at some point in the corporate life cycle. Du Pont lasted twenty-five years (perhaps a record) between bond issues, but finally succumbed. And even IBM, the ultimate example of internally funded expansion, was forced to borrow $2.5 billion in the late 1970s. These loans do not necessarily indicate crises. For AT&T, Du Pont, and IBM, they were necessary measures taken by healthy firms ready to expand. The IBM analyst for Drexel Burnham Lambert (a top investment bank) commented on the IBM debentures, "We are pleased at the development. The debt offering tells me that the company will reveal exciting new computer products next year" (*New York Times*, Sept. 30, 1979: E1).

Almost all firms have periods of high capital dependency, either because of crisis or because major capital investment is mandated by the compulsion of the profit nexus. In 1977, the auto industry (except Chrysler) was basically debt free and in possession of large amounts of retained earnings. Ford had a cash surplus of $3.4 billion; GM retained $3.2 billion (*Business Week*, March 13, 1978: 63). By 1979 the collapse of the big-car market had gutted GM and Ford, dissipated the surpluses, and sent them in search of $10–25 billion in outside investment capital (*New York Times*, March 5, 1981: D1). This was not discretionary borrowing. A failure to retool for small-car production would certainly have resulted in bankruptcy (*Business Week*, March 24, 1980: 78–88).

Thus even healthy companies—like AT&T—and healthy industries—like the high-technology sector in the late 1970s—become dependent on outside funding when competitive pressures force major investment. The largest firms seek capital infusions at certain moments in their histories. However, capital dependence—either chronic or periodic—does not necessarily produce bank leverage. If borrowers can obtain access to other funding sources, or if the large banks compete among themselves, the conditions for structural hegemony do not develop.

Note that there are a variety of sources for loan capital: bank and life insurance assets, pension and other trust funds, profits of other nonfinancial corporations, the fortunes of capitalist families, and individual savings. A prospective corporate borrower might, in principle, deal directly with these alternatives and avoid the possibility of bank or insurance company dominance. Certificates of deposit from large corporations (in denominations over $100,000) are a case in point. Constituting a major part of bank funds (*Business Week*, March 30, 1980: 110–11), these moneys could, in principle, be lent directly from one nonfinancial firm to another, thus avoiding bank intermediaries.[1] The decade of the 1970s saw a dramatic increase in the use of commercial paper—so dramatic that it became a matter of competitive concern for money market banks. In 1970, large corporations borrowed nearly three times as much from banks as from the commercial paper market; by 1980, the amounts were nearly equal (*Business Week*, April 13, 1981: 82).

Despite this expansion, however, the commercial paper market does not offer an outlet for firms with pressing financial need and thus is not a viable alternative to financial intermediaries. Industrials that enter the commercial paper market know little about risks and opportunities in sectors outside their own and therefore cannot evaluate problematic borrowers. Moreover, since they do not routinely accumulate sufficient retained profits to become lenders, it is not efficient for them to develop this expertise. As *Fortune* (June 30, 1980: 86) noted:

> The average depositor or investor of liquid funds cannot evaluate the creditworthiness of the ultimate user of his money. So he lends instead to a bank, which substitutes its credit, founded on its ability to analyze a variety of loan risks, for that of the final borrower.

For the most part, therefore, commercial paper has encroached upon bank lending in areas that do not involve crisis, expansion, or other urgent corporate activities. Thus the commercial paper market has come to dominate nonproblematic lending—loans involving seasonal capital shortages, for example. This has been a matter of great strain for commercial banks since these sorts of bread-and-butter loans were major sources of profits. It has not undermined financial hegemony, however. While it has offered low-risk borrowers a viable alternative to commercial banks, these were the very firms that had little to fear in the first place; lenders rarely exercise constraint on borrowers whose ventures do not involve significant risk.

Pension accounts are a second potential source of investment capital. As of 1977, well over $200 billion had accumulated in these funds.[2] Since commercial loans amounted to about $100 billion that year, pension funds might have met a considerable portion of the demand, thus offering an alternative to bank leverage. In practice, however, most pension money is invested in secondary stock and bond markets; the funds purchase already issued stocks or already negotiated loans.[3] Federal law requires that pension funds be administered by a "responsible fiduciary" agency. This is usually either the management of the corporation whose workers receive the pensions or the leadership of a major bank or insurance company. In the middle 1970s, banks held 80% of pension assets; the top ten banks held 48% (Fortune, July 31, 1978: 75; Kotz, 1978: 69). This domination eliminated pension funds as an independent source of investment capital, since similar criteria are used by loan and trust departments to evaluate creditworthiness. Pension fund administration, then, was dominated by the same handful of major banks and was not an independent source of investment capital.[4]

By the late 1970s, the poor performance of bank fund managers had resulted in a substantial outflow of pension funds from bank trust departments. But by and large the new managers of these funds had honored the traditional segregation into the secondary market and pension fund investments have not changed significantly.

A similar logic applies to trust funds in general.[5] The one hundred largest bank trust departments control about 80% of all trust holdings; the top ten control about 30%. The remainder is either deposited in open-ended investment trusts (mutual funds) or independently administered. In 1974 the ten largest investment trusts (sponsored by major Wall Street institutions) controlled 58% of mutual fund assets. This places decision making in the hands of a small number of individuals drawn from the same circles as major bankers. Even independently administered trusts (Harvard's $1.8 billion endowment, for example) are usually managed by groups of prominent businessmen, once again drawn from the same circles as bank managers. Together, pension and trust funds account for over 70% of all stock traded on major exchanges and over 30% of the stock held in the largest industrial firms. The hegemony of money market banks over this enormous pool of capital confers on these few financial lenders considerable additional power and authority.

Money market funds, which in 1982 held over $200 billion (New York Times, Nov. 16, 1982: D1), are not managed by bank trust departments, and this posed a two-pronged problem for banks in the early 1980s. On the one hand, since they offered substantially higher rates of return to investors, they attracted away depositors. On the other hand, these funds often purchased bank certificates of deposit and withdrew large sums very quickly when banks showed declining profits. These withdrawals placed severe strain on bank liquidity and threatened to undermine the viability of some institutions (*New York Times*, Sept. 21, 1982). By late 1982, federal regulations were changed to aid banks in attracting deposits away from these competitors (*New York Times*, Nov. 16, 1982: D1).

These alternative pools of capital—commercial paper, pension and trust funds, and mutual funds—represent potential alternatives to traditional lending sources that could undermine bank leverage in the capital market. They have not become viable competitors, however, because banks have captured control of a substantial portion of these funds; because bank involvement in all aspects of the economy is the principal means of assessing the viability of the problematic loans that confer leverage on borrowing firms; and because these capital pools have found other locales for investment. There is a structural contradiction that remains unresolved, however, and therefore the possibility of such competition always exists.

At present, however, the 1957 statement of a chief executive of a large industrial firm is still apt: "You cannot put into operation any large project without the help of the New York banks" (Katona, 1957: 46–47). In the 1970s and 1980s, this remained a constraint of corporate life because these institutions, augmented by a handful of newcomers from Chicago and San Francisco, represented an accumulation "of money and economic power never before seen in modern times" (Egan, 1980: 30).

Corporate dependence on the financial community confers leverage only if the major banks establish a unified stance vis-à-vis potential borrowers. And unity among financials depends on high levels of concentration, since many small companies could not overcome the powerful competitive forces among them. As early as 1900, sources of investment capital were highly concentrated in the United States, and while the degree and form of concentration has fluctuated since that time, it has never fallen into a competitive condition. In the early 1970s, the fifty largest banks held over two-thirds of the lendable funds in commercial banks. The seven New York and Chicago money market banks alone controlled about 20% of all bank assets (*Business Week*, July 25, 1970). Life insurance companies, the other major source of commercial loan capital, were even more concentrated.

Competition among financials has not undermined a larger unity. Although present, it is not expressed in pricing because of the logic of mutual deterrence that Baran and Sweezy identified as a key factor in all oligopolized sectors. Katona's (1957) summary of his interviews with corporate executives underscores this point:

> Most . . . said that large New York banks differed from each other greatly. Yet, in discussing this point, they seldom mentioned differences in lending terms or quality of service. In their opinion the differences between these banks are mainly accounted for by differences in the personalities of the bankers. Sometimes, this feeling was expressed by speaking of differences in the ability and qualifications of the bank personnel. (pp. 48–49)

The banking industry has exhibited well-developed price leadership. The prime rate of major banks has for many years moved in lockstep, with certain institutions generally taking initiative for changes, followed shortly by all others. The introduction of "NOW" accounts (checking accounts that pay interest) illustrates this price leadership nicely: New York banks carefully managed the transition to NOW accounts in order to guarantee "price discipline"— that is, to limit the level of interest paid (*Business Week*, Nov. 13, 1978: 146).

The absence of price competition does not rule out other forms of competitive behavior. For our purposes, the most important instances are those in which one major bank funds a loan that others have refused. Consider the process of loan evaluation in this context. In judging a loan, a bank must make two separate assessments. First, it must decide whether the enterprise is economically viable. Although such a decision is sometimes problematic and discretionary, it always includes a technical component upon which all potential lenders are likely to agree. Competition will therefore derive from differing assessments of loan risk.

Second, lenders must evaluate the extent to which the loan complements other parts of its investment portfolio. Insofar as a borrower's plans will create hardship for other companies to which the lender is committed (destructive competition), the bank will be reluctant to become involved even if the enterprise has excellent chances of success. Insofar as major banks have different investment profiles, this will produce competitive cleavage; a prospective investment that endangers the portfolio of one institution may complement that of another. Such a loan institutionalizes bank competition by placing the fate of the two banks in contradiction with each other, since the success of one client suggests destructive competition for the second. On the other hand, similarity of investment profiles undermines this sort of cleavage. Mutual deterrence and similarity of investment profiles create constraints that inhibit bank competition without creating structural ties that more directly intrude on institutional autonomy. Initial unity, however, has produced a more tangible form of structural bond that follows from the dynamics of resource dependency. This bond is the result of the complicated system of interbank borrowing, which is designed to smooth the frequent mismatches between deposits and capital commitments. When banks experience a shortage of funds—their withdrawals exceed their deposits on a given day—they borrow from other banks. In this way they are not forced to call in loans or sell assets to raise necessary cash. By and large, this is a routine matter. If the same institution is forced to borrow large sums continually, however, the lending banks must question its viability and worry about its capacity to repay. Even so, needed funds are refused only when a crisis is thought to exist. When such refusals occur, they provide a glimpse of the stable patterns of ongoing interfirm discipline, as well as the breadth and limits of financial unity.

The events that led to the Chemical's acquisition of Security National Bank in 1975 provide a lucid example of bank crisis and the process of interbank discipline.[6] In the early 1970s Security National, like many other regional banks, attempted to enter the national and international capital markets. Security National's Long Island location allowed it to enter New York City with little difficulty, especially after it had recruited several prominent executives from major New York banks. By 1974, its financial situation had degenerated owing to persistent deficits in the international money market. The losses became widely publicized when Thomas W. MacMahon Jr., who had moved to Security from Chase Manhattan several years before, resigned in late 1974. Two other officers also resigned, and a report to shareholders revealed continuing financial difficulty (New York Times, Feb. 28, 1975: 51).

A week later a silent run began:

> The one thing a bank cannot do without is money. Banks never fail just because they have losses. They go under because depositors and money-market lenders lose confidence and stop putting money in them. In its severest form, this phenomenon is known as a "run on the bank," a phrase that conjures up images of lines of anxious depositors. But the

money that leaves first, without fanfare, is from big lenders, and this has been described as a "silent run." (Fortune, June 2, 1980: 49)

A silent run occurs when other banks refuse overnight loans and thus force the financially leveraged bank to call in loans or sell assets to pay withdrawals. If such transactions can be quickly accomplished and the deficits do not continue, the silent run may do no permanent harm. If, however, new deposits continually fail to match withdrawals, the bank must continually redeem loans or sell assets to cover the withdrawals. If this continues, the bank will at some point be unable to generate the necessary cash to pay withdrawals. For small depositors this may be a matter of concern, but there is no threat to their money since the Federal Deposit Insurance Corporation guarantees accounts up to $100,000. It is, however, of grave concern for corporations, since their certificates of deposit, generally in denominations greater than $100,000, are not insured.

The prudent corporate treasurer, therefore, moves his or her firm's deposits from a troubled bank to a healthy one as soon as the certificates mature; that is, within a few weeks of the bank boycott. These massive withdrawals can create enormous deficits for the troubled bank—deficits it is incapable of covering. The Federal Reserve is obliged to provide rescue moneys temporarily, but unless the silent run ends the Fed must finally refuse rescue money or find itself without funds.

The silent run is itself an excellent example of hegemony, since the refusal of bank loans triggers the withdrawal of nonfinancial deposits. Ultimately, the actions taken by bankers so constrain the decisions by industrial firms that their actions are determined without explicit interaction among the participating executives. Alternatively, a renewal of interbank lending to the troubled institution guarantees the security of industrial depositors and ends the silent run.

The executives of Security National responded to the silent run by seeking the advice of top New York bank executives—that is, by inviting bank intervention into their decision making process. The major banks instructed Security's executives to search for merger partners, and it was ultimately sold to Chemical at $8 a share.[7] Chemical immediately returned its new subsidiary to its Long Island base; it soon absorbed the company completely.

The Franklin National and First Pennsylvania crises had similar features.[8] In both cases attempts to enter the international money market led to financial difficulty. In both cases a silent run, initiated by the New York banks, created the crisis. In the Franklin National example, subsequent investigations revealed widespread malfeasance by top executives, and the outcome was bankruptcy, acquisition by a consortium of European banks, a name change to European-American, and contraction back to its Long Island base. In the case of First Pennsylvania, a lending consortium was established to rescue the company; a $1.5 billion line of credit was extended; a new chief executive was appointed; the major banks acquired 43% of the stock; and the bank withdrew from the New York money market.[9]

Beyond the many incentives for lender unity that emerge from concentration, mutual deterrence, and loan similarities, the interdependence among banks themselves (and the consequent threat of intervention during times of financial weakness) provides a major deterrent to rule breaking and disruptive activities by individual banks. The financial community sits above the individual institutions, and there is no firm—not even Citibank—that is immune to collective discipline. The Group of Thirty (1982) expressed the sense of this interdependence nicely:

> Interbank lines [of credit] are not always assured, and may indeed dry up for any individual bank when most needed. Many banks therefore take great care to maintain and test lines and cultivate overall relationships with other banks. Diversification of sources is clearly important. Banks employ various techniques to monitor their lines and try to gauge as well as possible how much they can tap from different sources and in different currencies and maturities. Additional business relationships may be developed to reciprocate for lines, and personal contacts may be deliberately cultivated as well.

This set of structural interdependencies mutes the competitive thrust among banks and also establishes substantial, although not inevitable, unity. This internal discipline is buttressed by the pervasive system of loan consortia, the basic mechanism of structural leverage between lenders and borrowers.

The business press contains daily announcements of lending arrangements between major industrial corporations and consortia of large financial institutions. For example:

> The Standard Oil Company (Ohio) of Cleveland announced . . . that it had entered into a $500 million revolving credit and term loan agreement with the Manufacturers Hanover Trust Company, as agent, and 18 other banks, to help pay for tankers

that would transport its Alaskan crude oil and to develop its
Alaskan north slope reserves at Prudhoe Bay. (*New York Times*,
Oct. 1, 1976: D12)

Loan consortia have become normal operating procedure, both
in the financing of new ventures and in the refinancing of troubled
corporations, because even the very largest banks cannot safely
provide the capital needed by huge modern industrial companies.
A large loan, the $500 million Standard of Ohio borrowed, for ex-
ample, would mean that the lender's economic well-being was cru-
cially dependent upon the health of a single firm. Such a risk is
always unwise, particularly when the borrower is in financial trouble or the venture is unavoidably risky, as is the case with many
large loans. Loan consortia allow banks and insurance companies
to divide both the risk and the benefit in major lending endeavors.

Lending consortia are joint ventures that impose cooperation on
their members and force a united financial interest vis-à-vis borrowers. Since it is very difficult for one lender to withdraw, the
needs of each bank are tied to the collective enterprise. The consortium members must therefore develop and maintain devices for
creating and enforcing common policy toward their joint venture.

The normal procedure is the establishment of a lead bank—
usually the member with the largest percentage of the loan and
the longest ongoing relationship with the corporate borrower. This
leader is responsible for broad supervision of the loan and for en-
suring that the borrower does not pursue policies that endanger
the investment of the group.

Nearly half of all United States consortia are headed by four
New York banks—Morgan Guaranty Trust, Chase Manhattan, Citibank, and Manufacturers Hanover; over 75% are led by fifteen
large banks centered in New York, Chicago, Philadelphia, and San
Francisco.[10] When a company seeks external financing, it must deal
with a handful of major financial institutions.

And this imposes upon the financial community a united policy
vis-à-vis any particular corporation. Thus, when a firm falls into
financial difficulty, it must make peace with its bankers rather than
seek out alternative funding sources.

This is illustrated by the bankruptcy of W. T. Grant, the sixteenth
largest retailer of 1974. [11] During the crisis preceding bankruptcy,
Grant borrowed from a consortium of 145 banks and insurance
companies. Almost every major and minor commercial lender was
involved. As the crisis deepened, the consortium attempted to protect its collective investment by controlling Grant's everyday ac-

tivities, but it ultimately decided that bankruptcy was the least costly alternative. Because the lenders recovered more of their investment than any other creditor group—suppliers, customers, stockholders, employees—this episode has become the subject of a major lawsuit, and it points to the potential power of a unified financial group.

By standardizing decisions about capital flow, consortium-produced unity reinforces the potential for bank hegemony. It also aids in the crystallization of power relations among lenders. Since the consortium must reach unity, differences of interest must be resolved. Most often, these divisions are minor and do not create problems. At times, however, the differences are major and the consortium becomes a forum within which differential power is exercised; inevitably some firms are forced to adopt and support financial policies they do not desire.

One example of such interbank power involved the near bankruptcy of a large number of real estate investment trusts (REITs) in the early 1970s. These companies, established and often owned by major banks to facilitate commercial construction (malls, office buildings, etc.), were large borrowers in the late 1960s. By the early 1970s, depressed real estate markets placed many REITs in grave financial difficulty. The major commercial banks were placed in an unusual bind: if the REITs went bankrupt, their stock would become worthless; if they remained in business, their loans would have to be renegotiated at very low interest rates, since the trusts were incapable of repaying the debt at the appointed rates and times. For the banks that owned REITs, the latter course was preferable; for the institutions with only loans outstanding, bankruptcy and sale of assets was a much better arrangement.

The resulting conflict was resolved in favor of the New York money market banks, which protected their equity investment. Using their position as lead banks in the consortia—as well as their dominance in the economy—the New York banks were able to engineer the renegotiation of loans at interest rates as low as 1%.[12]

Lending consortia, therefore, are a source of immense power in American corporate life. They are a crucial part of the unity of financial institutions that leads to their hegemonic leverage in the corporate world. We note three major consequences of consortium lending:

1. The negotiation of a loan between a corporation and a consortium of lenders creates a unified financial posture toward that company. The consortium, therefore, forces financial institutions into a united stance vis-à-vis corporate borrowers;

lender leverage is all the more feasible when other conditions are met.

2. The prevalence of loan consortia imposes upon financial institutions ongoing interaction and a collective decision making process. It also calls into play a wide range of power relations among the financial community.

3. The necessity of interbank consortia creates a framework within which broad decision making about the flow of capital can proceed. Since large-scale lending inevitably involves consortia led by fewer than fifteen banks, they facilitate a united decision making procedure within the financial community as a whole. They also encourage a consistent policy toward specific areas of investment as well as a unified posture toward particular industrial sectors or corporate entities.[13]

Lender leverage over nonfinancial companies is based on the concentration of loan capital, which forces large borrowers to seek loans from a small number of major institutions. Upon this foundation a superstructure has developed that activates this leverage, converting it into structural constraint or discretionary intervention. Mutual deterrence among financial institutions, similar investment profiles, and interbank lending all contribute to the lack of competition within the financial world; loan consortia provide the institutional device for collective action. The hegemony that is latent in the asymmetrical dependency of loan relations can be activated only if lenders are not *constrained* to offer certain loans to certain customers. Without discretionary decision making by bankers, unity cannot be translated into intercorporate leverage.

The logic of lender discretion contains two separate parts. The more explicit element is the existence of a problematic decision-making process. When a corporation applies for loans, a decision-making procedure must allow the lending consortium to evaluate the prospect. These decisions always involve predicting future events and conditions, and therefore they contain a degree (large or small) of indeterminacy. Ultimately the decision, however well informed, is still a judgment made by individuals trying to summarize and compare complicated factors, many of which are contingent on future events.

The second aspect of this discretion lies in the potential conflict between bank interest and the interest of the borrowing firm. A bank (or group of banks) could severely injure its own financial situation if it were to lend indiscriminately to floundering companies. Even were the borrowing firm to survive, the lenders might

have made a mistake. Consider, for example, the loans made to
real estate investment trusts, discussed above. When the trusts fell
into prolonged crisis and the loans were renegotiated, the banks
did not receive returns comparable to those available in other investments. Since banks lend money that they themselves have borrowed, they were lending at lower interest than they were forced
to pay. Despite ultimate repayment, several banks risked failure
during this period. It is interesting that, while the REIT repayment
schedules were being renegotiated, the banks were refusing to lend
money to New York City at a tax-free 10% level. This suggests that
banks follow their own financial interest even in the circumstance
of driving city government and city services into disarray.

It is equally true that banks cannot consistently refuse sound
loans. If a corporation applies for a loan and this represents the
best location for the lenders' money—in terms of profitability and
security—the decision to withhold the funds is damaging to the
banks' interest. While such decisions are often taken, in the long
run financial institutions that consistently withhold money from
profitable investments flounder. The crisis at First Chicago bank
was precipitated by a restrictive loan policy that produced refusals
for potentially lucrative loans to major Chicago industrials (see
below).

Bank leverage, therefore, does not apply when a potential borrower proposes a loan on a highly promising venture with little
risk. In this case, lenders are constrained by the profit nexus to
fund the venture. Failure to do so does not create leverage, because
these are precisely the circumstances in which commercial paper
is available and the mechanisms of unity (mutual deterrence, interbank dependency, the necessity of consortia) collapse.

Lender leverage thus arises under conditions of substantial risk
in which informed judgments are necessary and advantageous.
These circumstances occur regularly in the history of individual
companies, cyclically within industries, and occasionally at the level
of whole economies (Mintz and Schwartz, 1982). They are important because they are the moments when planning is possible and
discretionary decision making most influences corporate history.
The domination of these moments by financial institutions forces
upon financial executives the principal discretionary decision making in a highly constrained economic system.

The biography of American capitalism can, in a sense, be written
as a chronicle of the flow of capital into certain sectors and away
from others. The expansion of the post–World War II automobile
industry, for example, can be described as an enormous increase

in investment in auto manufacturing, highway construction, and collateral industries that are complementary to private cars. The history of public transportation during the same period can be seen as the absence of capital flows into rail transport and the support facilities that would have preserved and expanded this sector (Yago, 1980; Whitt, 1975; and Caro, 1974).[14]

Obviously, this characterization misses a great deal of the dynamics of this process, but it nevertheless illustrates the degree to which capital flows and economic development are correlated. An individual, or a collection of collaborating individuals, in a position to make unconstrained decisions over the flow of capital could significantly influence this history. This, of course, is never the case. No social actors, however powerful, are completely or even substantially unconstrained.

At the same time, large corporations, especially large lenders, are never completely constrained; they always exercise some discretion over the direction of capital flows. Only in the case of an uncentralized capital market where various active and potential lenders would make itemized, independent decisions under the imposition of market logic would discretion be absent. In this case, the ultimate flow of capital would be analyzable in terms of market logic, and decision making would not be a factor. If, however, an individual, or a group of collaborating individuals, can choose among several locales for investment, then a different process arises. The decision makers could (within limits) violate the law of narrow profit maximizing: they could favor their friends over strangers; they could introduce political decision making into the economic process, and they could choose maximum growth over maximum short-term profit.[15] They could also, at least on occasion, plan coordinated economic development. Investment in unprofitable projects or less profitable areas (e.g., roads) could be undertaken to facilitate highly profitable outlets in other areas (e.g., automobiles). Long-term strategic development could occur with the guiding hand of a broadly based plan rather than through the chaotic and atomized logic of market relationships.

It is our contention that the decision-making model has become a major feature of twentieth-century American capitalism, and that this decision making is largely devoted to choosing among various locales for capital investment. The logic was nicely expressed by Tom Burns (1974):

> Inevitably, the growth of the corporate system is matched by an increasing concentration and centralization of decision

making and communication control. However complicated the decision making processes and technically abstruse the information ... what issues from its various divisions ... are proposals for renewing, expanding, curtailing or initiating expenditure. And these proposals are considered by a superior body—the directorate, the cabinet, the board of control—in light of their respective merits, plus considerations of an external (political) kind.

The decision making or communication system involves, as one approaches the top, a perpetual translation of information bearing on choice and decision into an homologous language (money). All decisions emerge as decisions concerning monetary expenditure for current and future activities. This enables decisions to be allocative rather than lexicographic, but also allows for further integration and centralization of decision making in giant conglomerate enterprises, and over and above that, in consortia, international organizations and in government. (pp. 171–72)

At the very top, spending alternatives available in the economy are compared. Many of the options do not even appear as choices, and this tends to conceal their existence. Nevertheless, as a senior partner at Kuhn, Loeb remarked, their impact is felt:

I think bank loans are a case in point. Take one example: Ling-Temco-Vought borrowed a very substantial portion of $600 million to take over Jones and Laughlin. . . . There are lots of takeovers. I think this is what makes money scarce for constructive loans, loans to companies that want to expand and have every right to, or where there should be plant additions or new equipment purchased." (Ney, 1970: 106)

The availability of alternative investment opportunities provides a range of options for capital-flow decisions. The structure of financial unity funnels lending discretion into the executive offices of a small group of national commercial banks and insurance companies, and this provides the foundation for financial hegemony. This hegemony imposes a vast discretionary responsibility on financial leadership, couched in a system defined by structural constraint. While the result is far from the strategic control suggested by early finance capital theorists, the end product of hegemony produces the most significant power concentration in American society.

Berle and Means (1932) appreciated the existence and importance of this new era of corporate discretion, though they located

decision making in all large corporations, financial and nonfinancial:

> A society in which production is governed by blind eco-
> nomic forces is being replaced by one in which production is
> carried on under the ultimate control of a handful of individ-
> uals. The economic power in the hands of a few persons who
> control a giant corporation is a tremendous force which can
> harm or benefit a multitude of individuals, affect whole dis-
> tricts, shift the currents of trade, bring ruin to one community
> and prosperity to another. The organizations which they con-
> trol have passed far beyond the realm of private enterprise—
> they have become more nearly social institutions. (p. 46)

So far we have argued that, to a considerable degree, the discretionary decisions about broad economic policy are made by executives of the financial companies that dominate capital flows. We
have suggested, but not argued explicitly, that this discretion is
largely wielded by the leaders of money market banks. We have
not analyzed the reasons for this locale, and we have not analyzed
the complementary and conflicting roles of regional banks, large
life insurance companies, and investment banks. It is to this that
we now turn.

Regional Banks

Regional banks play three roles in commercial lending: they are
participants in large lending consortia; they act as lead banks for
smaller loans to locally based national firms; and they are principal
lenders to smaller companies whose annual sales range between
$5 million and $500 million.[16] They are tied to national banks
through their participation in consortium lending, and because their
large customers may borrow concurrently from small regional consortia and large national consortia. In both cases, national firms
headquartered in local regions help link regional and national banks.
The most important regional banks are therefore usually in those
areas that have produced many major national corporations: New
York, California, Chicago, Texas, Philadelphia, and Boston.

As local corporations increase in size, their increased capital
requirements force them to enter the national capital market and
thus establish ties to national banks. Since their ongoing activities
may remain concentrated in their regional area, they must also
continue their relationship with local banking institutions. In this

way, they become bridges between regional banks and the national money market. This bridging function becomes even more pronounced when a corporation embarks upon national or multinational enterprises, since local banks are usually incapable of providing investment information or financial support services for such ventures. Since regional banks have a financial stake in the continued profits and expansion of these firms, they become indirectly dependent upon the resources of the national banks.

At the same time, national banks are dependent upon regional lenders. The larger institutions cannot maintain accurate information on regionally based firms, despite the importance of these companies as future customers. By and large, the national banks must rely on local banks to seek out and provide initial financing for promising local enterprises.

A symbiosis has developed between the money market banks and their successful regional brethren. The financial history of Faneuil Hall in Boston illustrates the deference shown by the money market toward regional institutions. The Faneuil Hall project, organized by entrepreneur James Royce, transformed a decaying inner city marketplace into a successful innovative shopping area that has been copied in several other cities. The capital was supplied largely by New York money market banks, and $20 million in long-term loans and $10 million in short-term loans was promised before renovation and development began. However, these funds were made contingent upon Royce's recruitment of some $3 million from Boston financial sources. This clause effectively gave Boston financiers veto power over the entire enterprise; it reflected the unwillingness of the money market to fund a local effort without the endorsement of local bankers (*Fortune*, April 10, 1978: 85–91).

This symbiosis is fraught with tension. There is a constant push from successful regional banks toward national and international operations, and an equally constant structural resistance by the existing money market institutions against such efforts. The success or failure of such moves varies. In the past, First Chicago and Continental Illinois successfully ascended. More recently Bank America, historically a regional California bank despite its large size, successfully pushed into national and international markets. On the other hand Security, Franklin, and First Pennsylvania all failed, resulting in a return to their regional bases.

The push of regionals toward the money market is complemented by an equally insistent push by larger banks into local markets. Most of these attempts have floundered, however, because familiarity with the local economic situation has enabled the regionals to predict which firms would be successful, which industries should be nurtured, and which mix of investments was safest. In this way, they have outcompeted the larger national banks.

This tense interdependence is illustrated by a rapid economic growth period in Texas in the 1970s, which led to an enormous influx of national and international banks. Despite its competitive intent, this invasion did not win a significant share of the local market. The failure was partly institutional: out-of-state banks, although permitted to negotiate loans, were legally prohibited from providing full-service banking for local corporations. More important, however, was the expertise and understanding that allowed the Texas regional institutions to pick out the lucrative investments (*Forbes*, July 1, 1977: 71; *Business Week*, Dec. 5, 1977: 39). Richard G. Merrill, president of First City National Bank of Houston, told the *New York Times* (May 14, 1980: D1): "The out of state competition has not had any significant negative effect on the banks in Houston."

Here again we see the limits of hegemonic power; national financial leadership does not always achieve its ends. It dominates only at certain moments and in certain realms. In the early 1980s, acknowledging repeated competitive failure, national banks moved toward acquiring, rather than competing with, regional banks.[17] The relationship between national and regional banks, then, involves simultaneous unity and disunity.[18] Structural unity flows from the joint funding of national firms located in regional centers, from extensive interbank borrowing, and from an established division of labor in the evaluation of proposed ventures. Disunity derives from the impulse for maximum profit that pushes regional banks into the money market and propels national banks into regional markets. While the success or failure of these competitive efforts varies with the situation, the overall shape of this relationship creates a division of discretionary labor: the national banks direct capital flows at the national level, while the regional banks perform a similar function within their more limited domain.

Insurance Companies

Major insurance companies, which account for over 75% of the industry's assets, have much the same lending relationship to industrial firms as do major banks: they are highly centralized; they are constrained by mutual deterrence; they coordinate their decisions through consortium ties and other relationships; and they make collective judgments about which companies will receive the capital they control. It is tempting, therefore, to simply fold insurance companies into banks and analyze them together, as we have done so far. There have been some attempts to untangle the differing roles of banks and insurance companies (Mariolis, 1975), but these efforts have not focused on the relationships between these two sets of institutions. We address this issue here in order to clarify the division of discretionary labor between banks and insurance companies.

Banks and insurance companies borrow the money they lend to their customers. Banks borrow from corporations and other purchasers of certificates of deposit; from consumers with savings or checking accounts; from institutions or capitalist families whose funds are administered by trust departments; and from other banks which provide short-term overnight loans. Insurance companies borrow from their policyholders, who pay premiums monthly, quarterly, and so on, and withdraw their investment (with interest) upon death.

Banks tend to borrow short-term money: certificates of deposit have maturities from one day to a few months; individual savers tend to leave their money on deposit only for short periods; trust department holdings are removable at any time; and interbank loans are specifically designed to be short term. Bank assets therefore are fundamentally transient, and they can flood out of the bank in relatively short periods. Life insurance borrowing, on the other hand, is long term. Individuals pay for insurance over their lifetimes, and the companies pay them back, with interest, when they die. Thus, insurance companies keep premium money for as long as several decades.

The first dictum of lending is, "Never borrow short to lend long; never borrow long to lend short." To understand this, consider the fate of First Pennsylvania Bank, which was rescued from bankruptcy in 1980.[19] In the late 1960s, attracted by high interest rates, First Pennsylvania purchased $1 billion in long-term government bonds. To do this, the bank was borrowing short-term money at very low interest rates and therefore borrowing "short" (for short periods of time) from depositors and lending "long" (for long periods of time) to government at high interest for enormous profits. However, by the mid-1970s, short-term interest rates had increased from 7% to more than 15%. The bank's commitment to long-term government bonds forced it to borrow additional funds at a rate of interest higher than it was receiving. By mid-1978 First Pennsylvania had recorded losses of $315 million, greater by $8 million than its total equity. After a silent run, money market banks intervened, ousted the chief executive officer, and brought in new leadership and new policies, including contraction back into its regional market.

The same sort of process can occur in reverse, though it is much rarer. An insurance company sets premium notes according to actuarial tables and the rate of interest it can obtain from reinvestment. If it invests in the long-term market, it guarantees that its ultimate return will cover the cost of death payments. But if it invests in the short-term market, it risks a decline of interest rates that would make its return less than the ultimate insurance payout.

For this reason, a division of labor has developed between insurance companies and banks; insurance companies dominate long-term lending, and banks dominate short-term lending. This division of labor has had three important consequences for the structure of capital flow in American business. First, the complementary roles played by the two types of institutions have produced a structure of cooperation between them. The most visible symptom of this structure is the high density of director interlocks between major banks and major insurance companies (see below, chapter 8).

It is important to note that most major life insurance firms are mutual companies, whose policyholders are the legal owners. This implies management control, since ownership is completely dispersed. The board of directors is therefore very important, since it is the only source of structural power over management. Multiple interlocks between banks and insurance companies thus suggest genuine collective leadership capable of developing coherent lending policy.

These complementary functions are cemented further by coparticipation in lending consortia, either through short- and long-term lending to the same institutions or through joint participation in a single middle-term loan. Thus, the same forces that coordinate and consolidate the interests of different banks tend to coordinate and consolidate the interests of banks and insurance companies. This consonance of interest creates a further incentive for coordinated investment policy.

The second major consequence of this division of labor is that banks are often forced to make the crucial judgment about the viability of loans. In chapter 2 we explored the importance of urgency on the part of the borrowing firm in producing lender leverage and therefore structural hegemony for financial institutions. Moments of corporate crisis, especially, involve mainly short-term loans, and therefore the banks must make these crucial—sometimes life-or-death—lending decisions.

Bank dominance of short-term lending, therefore, forces banks to establish the capacity for loan evaluation. Once this facility is established, it becomes useful in other contexts and thus creates a further structural preeminence for banks. For these reasons, commercial banks have become the visible representatives of lenders in intercorporate affairs.

It would be a mistake to press this distinction too far. Many corporations fall into crisis when already deeply in debt, and quite frequently the debt is long term. This forces insurance company scrutiny and intervention. Therefore insurance companies must also maintain the capacity to make judgments about the viability of firms to which they are already committed. In most instances, large ventures involve both long- short-term capital commitments, so that both types of firms are involved. The preeminence of banks, therefore, is only a question of emphasis. Shifting arrangements and specific circumstances often produce insurance company initiatives. The broader patterns that emerge from this unsettled symbiosis require careful study.

The third consequence of the division of labor between banks and insurance companies is the creation of another axis around which conflict can arise. As in the case of regional and national banks, the conflict is both endemic and irretrievable; in the area of middle-term loans, each side has the incentive to invade the other's domain. Consider this account of conflict during the 1977 period of capital surplus:

> Banks and life insurance companies, flush with lendable funds, are slugging it out for borrowers for intermediate term, five to twelve year funds, and that means better terms for borrowers. . . . "We've pushed out and insurance companies have pushed in," says Raymond J. Dempsey, executive vice president of Bankers Trust Co. "We are clashing in the intermediate term area. . . ." This is not a comfortable spot for banks, which prefer to lend short because the maturity on the money they borrow runs an average of only four months. By tying up their money for longer terms, banks run the risk of getting squeezed if interest rates take off. But, says Horgan [vice-president of Citibank], "we're doing it because we have a pile of money in and haven't been able to put it out." Insurance companies are in similar straits, with millions of dollars worth of investable funds yet to lend out. (Business Week, March 28, 1977: 105)

The existence of separate bank and insurance company consortia also provides an institutional contradiction capable of generating sharp conflict. When the expensive and ambitious Colony Square Development in Atlanta, Georgia, fell into bankruptcy, a fifteen-month conflict over proportional sacrifice erupted among the lenders, with the main antagonism between two consortia—one led by Prudential and one led by Chase Manhattan (Business Week, Jan. 31, 1977: 39).

Banks and insurance companies exist in a contradictory relationship. Their joint interest, consolidated through lending consortia and other institutional ties (and facilitated by the dangers of mismatched maturities), creates deterrents against full-scale invasion by either party. During times of prosperity, high profitability, and ample lending opportunities, cooperation predominates. During periods of capital surplus, lines of conflict tend to develop.

The Role of Investment Banks

One of the most important transformations in American financial structure in the twentieth century has been the displacement of investment banks by commercial banks at the center of the United States economy (Kotz, 1978; Mizruchi, 1982a). In the early 1900s, major industrial firms depended upon investment banks with connections to the diverse sources of capital to construct large blocks of lendable funds. Since the number of major investment bankers was quite limited, they could command the respect and obedience of major industrial firms.

During the first few years of the Great Depression, the drastic decrease in security offerings by nonfinancial corporations temporarily undermined the influence of investment banks. The Glass-Steagull Act of 1933 institutionalized this decline. By separating deposit banking from security underwriting, it made investment houses dependent on commercial banks for loan capital (Kotz, 1978: 52–54). While investment banks still possessed the information and understanding of the economy necessary to make broad decisions, commercial banks (and insurance companies) now possessed the concentrations of capital necessary to fund the actual enterprises, having consolidated the previously dispersed sources under their institutional roof. A division arose in which investment banks acted as intermediaries between the now concentrated lenders and their industrial borrowers. This circumstance created the incentive for commercial banks to develop and apply the capability of discretionary decision making. Leverage deriving from control of lendable funds was thus transferred to commercial banks and insurance companies.

By the end of World War II this transformation was more or less complete. Investment banks had been relegated to a lesser role in the system of capital-flow decision making. They became long-term advisers to various industrial clients, making informed recommendations about areas for expansion, helping to design stock or bond offerings, and locating appropriate customers for the offering. Insofar as the issue involved little risk, it could be sold to the investing public with little concern for the opinions or policy objectives of commercial banks. If the offering involved considerable risk, however, the investing public was usually not accessible. In these instances, the main source of funds was private placement with banks or insurance companies, a procedure that exposed the borrower to the constraints of bank/insurance company decision making about the direction of capital flows.

We see that investment bankers have little leverage over borrowers. In nonproblematic loans, they advise about market conditions and help set interest rates; in problematic circumstances, they orient their customers to the policies and standards of the major lenders. According to the *New York Times*, investment banking has become "somewhat of a misnomer. Investment banking is more closely related to the brokerage business, with most stock brokerage firms also acting as investment bankers" (May 25, 1975: F1).

The preservation and transformation of investment banks reflects the complicated role of information in intercorporate relationships. We will argue below (chapter 6) that the mass of knowledge accumulated in the boardrooms of major financial institutions (a direct consequence of their investment decision making) becomes a resource in and of itself. This importance is a consequence of the uncertainty of business life. All investment decisions require reliable, broadly based information. When industrial firms consider major expansion, they must understand the economic and technical climate of the sector into which they are venturing. When they seek out funding, they must understand the orientations and prerequisites of the lenders with whom they negotiate. This sort of information is sporadically necessary and requires general knowledge that industrial leadership does not ordinarily develop. The investment banker, who must understand the broad spectrum of investment opportunities and lending sources, is a useful resource when this information is needed. This functional, efficient depen-

dence has preserved investment banks in the changing context of
the corporate world.

This informational function does not, however, carry with it the
sort of structural leverage that lending creates. Information is rarely
the crucial ingredient in rescuing a troubled firm; it is rarely an
irreplaceable necessity for a firm contemplating major expansion;
and it is rarely a monopolized commodity unavailable from other
sources. While banks and insurance companies are usually forced
into a united front vis-à-vis potential lenders, investment banks
tend to compete because they lack any particular incentive for
cooperation. The investment bank cannot withhold information in
order to develop leverage.

Investment banking is subject to the evolving circumstances of
corporate life, and this has produced a constantly changing profile
of activities. As direct communication between capital sources
(banks especially) and industrial borrowers has expanded consid-
erably in the past decade, the role of investment banks in lending
has further declined. In response, they have sought out new roles
for themselves—most significantly arranging, managing, and de-
fending against acquisitions. For the top houses:

> The merger and acquisition departments have provided re-
> cord profits over the last several years, offsetting the erosion
> of income that has come with the end of fixed stock market
> commission rates. At the same time these departments have
> irrevocably altered the way investment bankers do business
> as well as the public's perception of them. (Business Week,
> June 25, 1979: 72)

The fundamental function of investment banks in the world of
big business has remained unchanged: they possess and provide
information that nonfinancial firms must have occasionally. At the
same time, they have declined in importance because they no longer
exercise institutional leverage over capital flows. This decline reflects both the impermanence of any particular structural arrangement and the continuing importance of control of capital flows in
determining the central institutions in American capitalism.

Conclusion

The world of big business contains a maze of crosscutting constraints that inhibit the discretionary decision making of corporate
executives. A substantial proportion of these constraints are un-

touchable by the subject firm and therefore appear as environmental givens within which corporate leadership must operate, although of course the profile of constraint is different for each company at each decision-making juncture. Another substantial proportion of these constraints derive from processes of mutual deterrence and resource dependency. They are therefore susceptible to negotiated alteration, either through direct collusion or through less overt forms of cooperation among interdependent companies. A final group of constraints derives from asymmetrical dependency and can be seen as a form of interorganizational coercion accomplished with or without direct intervention into the subject company's decision-making procedure.

This last group of constraints is the least analyzed and most important source of intercorporate coordination. It can be seen as the preemption by one company of another's discretion. Consider the example, reviewed in chapter 1, of the auto companies' domination of the auto-parts suppliers. Viewed from a distance, we see the suppliers choosing to leave the new-car-parts business in the late 1960s and choosing to return to this niche in the late 1970s. A closer analysis reveals, however, that these choices, apparently made by the suppliers, were actually made by the auto manufacturers, who first decided to produce their own parts and later decided to return to outside contracting. These metadecisions by the Big Three systematically altered the profile of constraints for the suppliers and left no viable options except to first withdraw and then return.

This particular form of intercorporate constraint—the preemption of one company's discretion by another firm—is the foundation of financial hegemony. A meaningful proportion of apparently nonfinancial decisions are actually made by financial leadership in the course of determining the direction of capital flows. In the example just mentioned, the auto companies' decision to return to outside contracting was a choice dictated by the refusal of lenders to fund fully the development of fuel-efficient small cars. Bank executives preempted the auto companies' decision, though they may have had good reason to do so.

Financial hegemony depends ultimately on the unique nature of capital as a resource that creates a temporary partnership between the supplier and the consumer. During this period of partnership, the supplier of capital is constrained to protect its investment by monitoring and evaluating its partner's activities. As long as capital is dispersed, the consumer of capital is not unusually constrained by this relationship. If new funds are needed and the enterprise is viable, competition among the various sources prevents a systematic boycott that could produce significant leverage. If the enterprise is unreasonably risky, no single supplier could credibly negotiate changes in the prospectus, because it could not, by itself, guarantee that the capital would be forthcoming. In this circumstance, the borrower is constrained by the market and not by the discretionary choices of financial institutions.

Once control of capital flows is centralized, however, the unique nature of capital matures into a unique set of constraints in the world of business. The development of a unifying superstructure—mutual deterrence among lenders, lending consortia, and interbank borrowing—allows for collective action by capital sources vis-à-vis their customers. Large projects become subject to a double set of decisions—industrial leadership must choose to pursue it, and lenders must choose to fund it. The fate of a great many projects rests with the lenders; discretionary decisions made in corporate headquarters are conditioned by decisions made by executives of lending institutions.

Within the financial community, decision making over the largest and most problematic projects migrates to the boardrooms of a few dominant firms, those capable of handling and managing immense loans. Within this they migrate further toward the banks, which typically make the initial commitment.

Ultimately, decision making over capital flows is highly concentrated. The major choices are made by fewer than fifteen companies, who are constrained to communicate and coordinate with each other. Thus a substantial portion of the discretionary decision making of the most significant enterprises in our economy is conditioned by decisions made by the leadership of financial companies. This is the process that confers upon financial executives the necessity and the opportunity to undertake coordinated action that melds the activities of one company or sector into those of other companies and other sectors.

The resonance within the system toward financial decision making varies as the degree of dependence on outside capital increases or declines. When individual firms or sectors seek capital infusions, they are particularly responsive to the structural leverage created by capital flows; when they are rich with retained earnings or uncompelled by expansionary forces, their responsiveness wanes. When the system as a whole is capital short, the overall resonance is high; when capital is widely available, it declines.

Although the leverage deriving from the control of capital flows is episodic and chronically problematic, it is the main source of systemic coordination. When large-scale unity of action occurs, it is a very broad coordination and is usually managed by the dominant financial institutions. When these institutions are incapable of producing coordinated action, such action rarely occurs.

4 Bank Intervention, Institutional Stockholding, and Bank Control

> Talk about centralization! The credit system which has its focus in the so-called national banks and the big money-lenders and usurers surrounding them, constitutes enormous centralization, and gives to this class of parasites the fabulous power, not only to despoil periodically industrial capitalists, but also to interfere in actual production in a most dangerous manner— and this gang knows nothing about production and has nothing to do with it.
>
> Karl Marx

The Controversy over Bank Control

In earlier chapters, we outlined the theory of financial hegemony and compared it with four other paradigms of corporate organization: managerialism, class cohesion theory, resource dependency, and bank control. In this chapter we extend our discussion of bank control and compare it with financial hegemony. To do this, we examine (1) bank intervention into the discretionary decision making of nonfinancial corporations and (2) institutional investors as potential sources of corporate constraint. At issue is the question how bank intervention and institutional stockholding contribute to the broader pattern of financial hegemony.

Bank control theory concentrates on the ongoing corporate need for capital. Extensive cash infusions are necessary at moments of crisis (when firms cannot pay debts) or during periods of major expansion when companies cannot internally finance the research, development, retooling, or capital construction required to remain technologically competitive. The dependence that flows from the need for outside funds provides the foundation for bank control. At these moments bankers are able:

> to *ascertain exactly* the financial position of the various capitalists, then to *control* them, to influence them by restricting or enlarging, facilitating or hindering credits, and finally to

entirely determine their fate, determine their income, deprive
them of capital, or permit them to increase their capital rapidly
and to enormous dimensions. (Lenin, 1917a:34–35; italics in
original)

The theory of bank control further asserts that this power is used
(a) to develop strategic control over the borrowing firm (Lenin,
1917a:64; Hilferding, 1910: 172) and (b) to dictate policies that, in
the long term, are consistent with the needs of the financial institutions. This occurs even when the policies are harmful to the
interest of the dependent industrial firm.[1] As Fitch and Oppenheimer (1970c) argue:

> under finance capital the rate and mode of corporate growth
> are no longer determined independently within the corpo-
> ration. Rates of accumulation, dividend payout ratios, debt
> policy, relations with other corporations, and purchasing and
> sales relations differ, depending on who controls the corpo-
> ration. (p. 34)

Important systemwide consequences occur when bank control
dominates the economy:

> a *system* of corporations dominated by finance capital . . . op-
> erates differently from a system in which independent, self-
> financing corporations are the supreme economic decision-
> making units. These differences show up primarily in a de-
> clining rate of capital accumulation . . . and in the erosion of
> purely market relations between giant corporations. . . . Fi-
> nance capital is far more centralized, far more socialized: it
> is able partially to transcend market forces in order to shape
> economic activity to a conscious social purpose. (Fitch and
> Oppenheimer, 1970c: 34–35; italics in original)

Since the advantages of maintaining strategic control are so great,
bank control theorists assume that banks regularly intervene in the
affairs of client corporations in an attempt to maintain constant
capital dependency. This produces long-term control. Following
this logic, bank control theorists posit the segregation of the economy into financial groups, each composed of companies that remain
under the control of a financial institution. Though there may be
collapse and evolution in these collectives, the trend is toward an
economy of grouped corporations.[2]

In a very cohesive financial group, each constituent non-financial corporation would act, not to maximize its own profits, but to maximize the long-run profits of the group. . . . It would imply that the individual corporation should not be treated as the basic, independent decision-making unit for economic analysis but rather the financial group should be treated as the basic unit. (Kotz, 1978: 146)

Recent theorists have also stressed the role of bank stockholding in creating control relationships.[3] Kotz (1978) writes:

When a financial institution is the holder of record of a large block of a corporation's stock—even if the financial institution is not the beneficial owner of the stock—this may be a source of power for two reasons. First . . . it can vote against management proposals, and it can initiate or join a proxy fight to replace the existing board. Second . . . an institution can sell its holding suddenly, which would depress the price of the stock and hence harm the interests of management and other stockholders; or it could sell its holdings to a group attempting a takeover. (p. 19)

Bank control theory has been subjected to three imposing criticisms. First, there is a denial that bankers regularly intervene in the decision making of borrowing firms. Second, there is disagreement over the extent to which bank trust departments can be used as mechanisms of bank influence. Finally, there is doubt about the existence of financial groups. Based on our own evidence as well as the findings of other researchers, we believe that the third criticism is true for the current era of American capitalism. We present our argument in chapter 10 below.

It is with the first criticism, however, that we take issue. In this chapter, therefore, we present an analysis suggesting that bank intervention into the discretionary decision-making process of non-financial corporations is a recurring event in corporate life; that institutional stockholding is a potential source of power for financial institutions; and that bank intervention and institutional stockholding may be fit into a broader context of financial hegemony. At the same time, we maintain our distinction between bank control and bank hegemony and argue that intervention and institutional stockholding rarely produce relationships of long-term strategic control but contribute to an overall pattern of a looser financial hegemony. We begin with an investigation of bank intervention into the discretionary decision making of industrial firms.

The notion of bank intervention as a typical and significant event in business life has been criticized by every opponent of bank control theory. Baran and Sweezy (1966), for example, have asserted that:

> Each corporation aims at and normally achieves financial independence through the internal generation of funds which remain at the disposal of management. The corporation may still, as a matter of policy, borrow from or through financial institutions, but it is not normally forced to do so and hence is able to avoid the kind of subjection to financial control that was so common in the world of Big Business fifty years ago. (p. 16)

Similarly, Edward Herman (1973:25), another critic of bank control theory, agrees that banks may exercise coercive power through "their ability to grant, withhold, or impose special terms on loans to borrowing customers." He argues, however, that "such provisions and interventions are usually . . . invoked only as a last resort." In his review of Kotz's book *Bank Control of Large Corporations in the United States*, he states his case more sharply, declaring that, although financial institutions can exert significant influence over the affairs of major corporations, "almost without exception" this intervention falls "far short of control" (Herman, 1979: 55).

Herman's argument captures the crucial issues of bank control theory—the frequency of bank intervention and its impact on the behavior of industrial firms. The dispute is one of degree: bank control theorists argue that intervention is an ongoing reality with far-reaching consequences for major nonfinancial corporations; their critics argue that intervention is infrequent and usually insignificant in terms of systemwide impact. This theme is echoed repeatedly, as Herman's (1981:125) latest work on the topic illustrates: "when large corporations get into serious financial difficulty, banker power tends to increase markedly and may eventually include veto power . . . and influence . . . that qualifies as full or shared control." He concludes, however, that "direct bank intervention and virtually unilateral displacement of management . . . are rare among very large corporations."

Systematic investigations of bank intervention into the internal affairs of industrial firms have yet to be undertaken. Instead, research has concentrated on the existence of lending, stockholding, or interlock relationships that could facilitate, motivate, or impel intervention. In this consideration, we wish to establish four points.

First, bank intervention in the internal affairs of major industrial corporations is a relatively infrequent, but consistent event in business life, so consistent that chief executive officers often take bank needs into account in planning the activities of their enterprises. Second, such intervention is effective in altering corporate policy; it is therefore an important component in the strategic decision making of major firms. Both of these points support traditional bank control theory.

Third, the typical instance of bank intervention is short term, although it may have long-term implications or consequences. This contradicts Fitch and Oppenheimer's (1970a-c) argument that long-term intercorporate exploitation is a major feature of bank intervention. Fourth, incidents of intervention are part of a broad set of financial relationships that fit together to produce the financial hegemony that permits and necessitates a loose bank coordination of overall investment policy in American business. These other relationships, and the consequent coordination, will be discussed and analyzed in subsequent chapters.

In sum, we concur with Kotz (1978), Fitch and Oppenheimer (1970a-c), and other bank control theorists that bank intervention is an important factor in determining corporate behavior, but we emphasize that intervention intrudes only on discretionary decision making. While we disagree with Sweezy (1972) and Herman (1973, 1981) in their contention that financial institutions do not play a unique, dominant role in intercorporate affairs, we concur that long-term control relationships are not a major feature of the corporate landscape.

Instances of Bank Intervention

Table 4.1 lists forty-two instances of lender intervention into the internal affairs of nonfinancial firms during the five-year period between 1977 and 1981. This listing was compiled from a thorough reading of *Business Week* and less complete surveys of the *New York Times, Fortune,* the *Wall Street Journal,* and *Forbes.* Since our sources cover only the most important and newsworthy business events, since our survey did not involve a complete scrutiny of available sources, and since we did not consult more specialized publications that would cover less spectacular events, our listing is far from complete. While the information obtained is accurate, we are certain that the number of interventions is larger than table 4.1 suggests.[4]

Table 4.1
Bank Intervention in Major American Corporations, 1977–81

Company	Dates	Trigger	Mechanisms	Major Changes Dictated by Interveners
Arlen	1977	$24 million loss in 1976	Stock dumping Loan refusal	Divestiture of real estate holdings
Barwick Industries	1976–79	Failure to repay loan	Voting trust for stock Debt renegotiation	Ouster of founder/chief executive with 83% of stock Divestiture of major subsidiaries
Braniff Airlines	1980	Failure to repay loan	Debt renegotiation	Ongoing bank decision making, including sale of new planes (for debt repayment) Abandonment of new routes Ouster of chief executive
Eastern Airlines	1980–81	Proposal to acquire Braniff	Debt renegotiation	No acquisition
Chrysler	1980	Heavy losses	Debt renegotiation	Ongoing bank decision making, including decision to retreat from full line production
City Stores	1977	Many years of losses	Debt renegotiation	Stock cannot be traded Divestitures of subsidiaries
	1979	Many years of losses	Bankruptcy	Policy changes unreported Lenders write off debt for controlling block of stock
Colgate	1979	Decline in profits	Board of directors' action under bank leadership	Ouster of chief executive Dediversification
Commonwealth Oil	1977–80	Reported failures to repay loans	Debt renegotiation Loan covenants Bankruptcy	Bank balances seized to pay debt to Gulf Daily lender review of decisions Ouster of top executives

Table 4.1 (cont.)

Company	Dates	Trigger	Mechanisms	Major Changes Dictated by Interveners
Cook Industries	1976–77	Heavy losses	Stock dumping Debt renegotiation Loan covenants	Sale of profitable subsidiaries to pay debt Covenant preventing company's executives from buying all stock and making it private Covenant preventing further investment in futures trading
Daylin	1974–78	Heavy losses	Bankruptcy	Ouster of founder/chief executive Sale of 40% of stores, layoff of 60% of employees
Farah	1977	Heavy losses	Debt renegotiation	Ouster of dominant stockholder as chief executive Prohibition of ouster of new chief from any part of management (later reversed)
Genesco	1977	Heavy losses	Board of directors' action	Ouster of top executives from founder's family Changes in personnel policy Divestiture of subsidiaries
Grolier	1977	Heavy losses	Refusal of rescue	Dediversification Internal reorganization Management layoffs
Gulf	1976	Watergate revelations	Controlling block of stock Board of directors' action	Ouster of chief executive
International Harvester	1980–81	Heavy losses	Debt renegotiation	Executive salaries cut by 20% Sales of subsidiaries Altered business relations with retail dealers
Kennecott	1980	Attempted takeover by Curtiss-Wright	Loan covenant	All loans would default if Carborundum subsidiary sold (thus preventing Curtiss-Wright takeover)

Company	Dates	Trigger	Mechanisms	Major Changes Dictated by Interveners
Korvette	1978	Declining profits / Acquisition by Arlen	Loan covenants	Covenant preventing transfer of Korvette funds to Arlen
	1980	Bank seizure of accounts to pay off debt	Bankruptcy	Sale of assets / Liquidation
Lockheed	1974–77	Exposure of overseas bribery	Debt renegotiation	Ouster of chief executive / 13% equity for lenders
Mattel	1975	Decline in profits	Debt renegotiation	Ouster of chief executive/owner/founder / Dediversification
Microdot	1976	Decline in profits	Loan covenant	Daily oversight by banks / Attempts to find takeover partner
Okonite	1976	Losses	Debt renegotiation	Ouster of chief executive/founder
Pan American	1974–80	Ongoing crisis / Heavy debt	Loan covenants	Oversight of daily operations
Penn Central	1970–78	Bankruptcy	Bankruptcy committee	Comprehensive reorganization / Financial executive becomes chief executive
Placid Oil (Privately held by Hunt family)	1980	Hunt brothers owe $1.1 billion in silver futures, borrow from banks	Loan covenants	Hunt brothers withdraw from silver market
Pullman	1970–80	None—ongoing control by Mellon	Domination of board of directors / Stock dumping (by banks other than Mellon)	Install several chief executives / Ongoing control of policy
	1979–80	Decline in profits		Ouster of chief executive / Takeover attempts lead to White Knight merger
Rapid American	1970–78	Heavy losses	Loan covenants	Sale of profitable subsidiary / Prohibition of acquisitions

Table 4.1 (cont.)

Company	Dates	Trigger	Mechanisms	Major Changes Dictated by Interveners
Rock Island Railroad	1975–80	Heavy losses	Loan refusal leads to bankruptcy	Liquidation
Rohr	1975–80	Failure to repay loan	Debt renegotiations	Ouster of two chief executives Dediversification 50% layoffs
Seatrain	1975–81	Six years of losses (bankruptcy 1981)	Debt renegotiation	Ongoing consultation and policymaking by lenders
Tesoro	1976–77	Debt renegotiation	Loan covenants	Sale of specific subsidiaries Prohibition of acquisitions Prohibition of loans to Commonwealth Oil
Textron	1976	Attempted acquisition of Lockheed	Stock dumping	Acquisition attempt discontinued
UM&M	1976–77	Two years of losses	Debt renegotiation	Ouster of chief executive Sale of financial subsidiary
	1977	Dispute over proceeds of sale of financial subsidiary	Seizure of bank balances leading to bankruptcy	Debts repaid Complete shutdown
Uniroyal	1980	Debt renegotiation	Loan covenants	Sale of accounts receivable to repay loan
United Brands	1976	Suicide of chief executive	Loan convenants	Prohibition of dividends
Wheeling-Pittsburg	1979–80	Bond offering	Refusal to purchase bonds/covenants	"Stiff restrictions" on use of bonds Guarantees from government
White Consolidated Industries	1977	Request for loan extension	Debt renegotiation	Prohibition of acquisition of White Motor
White Motor	1976 1980	Delinquent loans Bankruptcy	Loan covenant Nomination of bankruptcy committees	Sale of major subsidiaries Ongoing control

More important, since the press tends to report spectacular cases of corporate crisis or corporate conflict, our listing systematically excludes lender-borrower consultations that influence corporate policy (perhaps dramatically) without the trappings of crisis or conflict. In late 1980, for example, Archie McCardell, the chief executive officer of International Harvester, "invited Harvester's eight lead banks in for an informal 'informational' chat when it appeared that company coffers were running low" (Business Week, June 22, 1981: 67). Had these consultations succeeded in correcting the problems, this meeting would not have been reported. However, three months later Harvester fell into a major cash crisis requiring massive infusions of capital, and the story burst into the business press.[5]

Despite the incomplete nature of our survey, it is useful in two ways. First, the forty-two instances reported here demonstrate the ongoing existence of outside intervention by lenders. We recorded only instances that involved Fortune 500 firms (fewer than a thousand companies in all). This indicates that at least one in twenty experienced such intervention; the actual figure may be much higher. Since these cases include only important, well-established companies, we assume that nonaffected chief executives are aware of these instances and that this can influence corporate policy and condition the responsiveness of individual firms to the interests and opinions of the financial community.

Second, this listing allows us to describe the process of bank intervention and begin an analysis of the precipitating conditions and strategic consequences of this phenomenon. Our purpose is twofold: we address the controversy over bank control by documenting the existence of direct intervention as a mechanism of bank influence. However, since we argue that hegemonic relationships are the major form of dominance, our analysis emphasizes the conditions under which intervention occurs and the ways intervention intermeshes with broader decision making by financial institutions. Thus, we go beyond traditional bank control theory by analyzing intervention as one component of a larger process of bank influence, and we emphasize that intervention is possible only in specific circumstances.

We begin by reconsidering Howard Hughes's ouster from TWA, an episode described in chapter 2. Hughes, the major owner of TWA, was forced to retire from a company that was pursuing its interests in a very profitable way. What must be asked, however, is how frequently creditors are in a position to exercise this sort of control. Moreover, do banks intervene every time they disagree with corporate policy? The answer to both questions is that banks have neither the opportunity nor the desire to intervene at every juncture. Intervention occurs when opportunity and inclination intersect. In the Hughes case, it took creditors two years to unseat him. With Colgate's chief executive officer, in time the opportunity arose as well:

> David Foster's fall was largely caused by a series of long running differences of opinion with key members [three bankers] of the Colgate board over his managerial style and acquisition policies. So long as all went well, Foster was safe, but once some trouble began to surface, he was vulnerable. (*Fortune*, Sept. 24, 1979: 92)

Financial intervention, then, is sporadic. Under certain conditions banks are unable to pursue their interests when they conflict with the policies of an individual corporation. At other times and in other circumstances, they act with both speed and force. Among these uncertainties, however, we can identify situations in which financial leverage is institutionalized and bank intervention is a typical response.

Bankruptcy: Court-Ordered Bank Intervention

Although bankruptcy is the most serious crisis a corporation can face, it is generally quite different from the immediate shutdown, massive layoffs, and mountains of unpaid debts of public perception. Every so often, as in the case of W. T. Grant, bankruptcy conforms to this pattern (Bearden, 1982; Glasberg, 1982). These, however, are the exceptions and not the rule. Of the eight instances of bankruptcy in our study, only two (UMM—Robert Hall stores— and Korvette) involved the demise of the entire enterprise. In these cases, despite the shutdown, lenders retrieved most of their money through liquidation of assets.[6]

Among large corporations, chapter 11 bankruptcy predominates.[7] When the court grants chapter 11 status, the firm is temporarily freed from its debt obligations while continuing to operate just as before: it may order new supplies and pay for them; it may meet its regular payroll; it continues to sell its products at normal prices; and it generally conducts business as usual. It may even borrow new money. The only change in status is that it does not pay existing debts—mainly loans—when they fall due. The company then attempts to reorganize its operations on a profitable footing.

The reorganization is not, however, controlled by the chief executive officer. Bankruptcy law requires that a committee of creditors be convened and that these creditors agree to the proposed reorganization before it is approved by the court. In principle, this committee should represent everyone with a claim against the corporation, including banks, insurance companies, individual lenders, customers who have paid money for future deliveries, suppliers who have not yet received payment for previous deliveries, employees whose pension fund or wages are in arrears, and landlords seeking past-due rent. Despite this potential for pluralism, however, chapter 11 creditors' committees are virtually always dominated by financial institutions, both because the troubled company generally owes far more to lenders than to any other creditor and because bank debt is generally senior (it has the first claim on corporate resources). In our search of the business press, we found only one case of a creditors' committee that was not controlled by banks or insurance companies or both.[8]

In some sense, therefore, chapter 11 bankruptcy is a legally mandated form of bank control involving the subordination of corporate policy to bank dictation.[9] Scott (1979) argues that the predominant mode of corporate control in mid-twentieth-century capitalism has been "control by a constellation of interests": a group of influential institutions that must find some unity in order to direct a company. The creditors' committee is a formalized institutional effort to achieve this unity among lenders; it is based on the notion that the dominant creditors can negotiate a compromise of their interests that will serve the group better than closing the firm and liquidating its assets. "Creditors, of course, usually want to see a bankrupt company pull through because they stand a much better chance of getting more of their money back" (Business Week, Nov. 15, 1976: 44).

Chapter 11 usually succeeds among giant firms: it produces new directions, financial rescue, and renewed corporate health. Consider the example of Daylin, which filed bankruptcy in 1975, "when it could no longer meet its current financial obligations" (New York Times, Feb. 28, 1975: 51).[10] In the late 1960s, Daylin had grown into a Fortune 500 corporation by acquiring a huge number of small retail firms and putting together a loosely connected merchandising empire with fifteen thousand employees, six hundred retail outlets, and over $500 million in revenues. In 1974, however, the company reported a $28 million loss coupled with a negative cash flow. Lenders reacted by bringing in Sanford C. Sigoloff to revive the firm. Six months later, Sigoloff filed for chapter 11, citing $160 million in unpayable debts. The resulting creditors' committee was chaired by Peter Finch of First Chicago Bank—one of Daylin's three major lenders—and debt restructuring and company reorientation negotiations began. In less than a year the firm emerged from chapter 11; two years later it was healthy enough, with bank backing, to bid $62 million in an attempt to take over Dymo Industries.

Sigoloff described his relationship with the creditors' representatives: "We had an excellent disciplined creditors' committee and superb well trained counsel. People could talk and disagree and still trust in each other. The financial investors, including the creditors, wanted the company to survive" (*New York Times*, June 11, 1978: F11). Note that the fundamental decision about the future of the firm lay with the lenders. The restructuring, however, was a carefully negotiated agreement among all parties.

The financial plan demonstrates the intersection of interests represented in a bankruptcy proceeding. First, the debt was restructured. The lenders immediately collected $31 million, and the remaining debt was reissued as long-term debentures carrying little or no payment of interest. In exchange for interest losses, creditors were given stock that would appreciate enormously if the company survived. The lenders therefore gambled (successfully, it turned out) their interest payments against equity investment.

Second, the company dediversified. The acquisition of innumerable small firms with little in the way of a unifying theme was considered to be a major cause of Daylin's problems. The company sold off nearly half its retail outlets and narrowed its business focus to two areas: hospital supply and electronic marketing. Its sales dropped about 30% as a consequence. Subsequent to its emergence from bankruptcy, the company continued to pursue this new, limited focus; the policy trajectory developed under bank control continued after the control ended.

Third, the company was allowed to keep a substantial cash reserve. During bankruptcy proceedings, it is tempting for creditors to insist upon using every available resource for debt repayment, but this did not occur in Daylin's case:

> The plan ... envisaged providing the surviving company with an adequate amount of working capital and with enough eventually to develop a new product line to add to its retailing and health service. ... It was largely Mr. Sigoloff's persuasion of creditors that Daylin should not be cash poor following its bankruptcy that allowed it to become a suitor of Dymo [and thus attempt to acquire the planned new product line]. (*New York Times*, June 11, 1978: F11)

This illustrates the crucial role of creditor discretion in bank control situations. In the Braniff example discussed in chapter 2, the refusal of lenders to refinance debt forced the airline to try to "sell 15 of its best, most modern planes" (*Business Week*, Aug. 11, 1980: 28). A rival executive was proved correct when he said that the decision "is undermining its medium and long term future in an effort to buy time now" (*Business Week*, Aug. 11, 1980: 28). At International Harvester, insistence upon maximum repayment "hampered" Harvester in "bringing out new products to keep up with rivals" and "imposed" restrictions on sales financing that could "seriously weaken Harvester's far-flung dealer network."

During chapter 11 bankruptcy the fate of the company is determined by lenders, based on the complex of interests they represent. The decisions taken influence future ownership (through such devices as acquisition of stock), long-term corporate strategy (as in the channeling of Daylin into certain business sectors), and even the future existence of the company itself (through determination of capital resources or the total refusal to refinance). The right to decide the policies, size, direction, and health of the emergent entity is given to the creditors, and they make their decisions based on the protection of their collective interests. The constraint imposed by corporate crisis is thus transformed into strategic control by lenders; discretionary decision making passes into the hands of banks or their representatives.

Since the consequences of a particular option cannot be foreseen these decisions are not based exclusively on technical grounds. Creditors must apply a combination of judgment and expertise, always protecting their own stake. If foreclosing maximizes return on bank investment, this choice may be their best option, even if it is the worst alternative for stockholders, employees, and customers of the firm. In some sense the immense gravity of lender decision making is captured by *Business Week*'s (March 4, 1977) assessment of Grolier's chances of surviving its 1977 crisis: "Whether Grolier goes under or not depends on how far the banks are willing to go" (p. 32).

Consider another example, the bankruptcy of the Penn Central Railroad. This incident, the largest bankruptcy in American business history, has been a focal point in the debate over bank control. Fitch and Oppenheimer argue that bank domination contributed to the Penn Central crisis by imposing policies that benefited lenders while undermining the company's viability (1970a–c). Sweezy (1972: 182–84) argues convincingly against this view, citing evidence that lenders suffered enormous losses from the incident and that the major banks were "hoodwinked by a crooked management into approving and pouring money into what . . . was in fact a series of investment fiascos" (p. 184). Daughen and Binzen's (1971) authoritative account of the bankruptcy supports Sweezy's argument in this case, although it also demonstrates that the bankruptcy was primarily a consequence of broader economic forces and not a direct result of the extensive management malfeasance.

However, Daughen and Binzen (1971: 259–336) suggest—and subsequent events demonstrate—that the crucial bank control issue arose after the Penn Central crisis matured into a major business catastrophe. Penn Central was not under the direct control of banks or other financial actors when the crisis developed. It was only after grave trouble was identified that creditors intervened in the operational management of the company. This illustrates that financial institutions are not all-powerful, that financial hegemony cannot keep close track of managerial decisions, and that financials cannot control or prevent corporate crisis. Once the crisis matured, however, strategies for responding to it were developed by creditors, and discretionary decision making went to them. This began in May 1970, a month before the official bankruptcy declaration when lenders took control. They dictated leadership changes, made financial decisions, and ultimately formed long-term corporate policy (Daughen and Binzen, 1971: 280). Even after the government provided loan guarantees, the lenders—and only the lenders—took an active role (p. 280).

The Penn Central bankruptcy lasted until 1978.[11] The creditors' committee, led by John Ingraham of Citibank and dominated by major commercial banks and life insurance companies, worked throughout this period to arrive at a viable restructuring. They explored various options, made leadership decisions, and determined the direction of the reorganized company. In doing so, they kept careful track of their own interests. They installed an Equitable Life Assurance executive as head of the new company and obtained a 55% stock interest in the new firm. They also sacrificed between 30% and 60% of their loans in an attempt to preserve the company.

Penn Central was the largest transportation firm in the United States when it entered bankruptcy proceedings. The organization that emerged was "a viable real estate and energy company" (*Business Week*, Jan. 24, 1977: 46). The decision to withdraw from the railroad industry was made by the creditors—mainly banks and insurance companies—in their own interest; the consequences continue to reverberate through the entire economy. Rail employees, commuters and long-distance rail travelers, manufacturers and purchasers of products shipped by rail—in short everyone in the United States—were affected by these decisions. Thus bankruptcy, which institutionalizes bank control, also institutionalizes lender discretion over decisions that condition and constrain the lives and prospects of workers, customers, and other citizens affected by the fate of corporations in crisis. Capital-flow decisions can have similar effects. Intervention, however, is a more direct, immediate, and surefire method of implementing decisions.

Bank Intervention without Formal Bankruptcy

That corporate bankruptcy is infrequent should not minimize the importance of the power wielded by bank-dominated creditors' committees. As one banker told the *New York Times*, the same financial problems can occur without the legal formalities: "It is easy to disguise a default in today's world. You merely have a rescheduling" (Aug. 31, 1980: F1).

A corporate crisis rarely reaches the bankruptcy stage. Penn Central was unusual, since internal management actively concealed major financial difficulties. In most cases, there are ample warnings. Typically, the company's quarterly or yearly financial report reveals a decline or loss of profits. This alerts the interested public, including lenders, customers, suppliers, stockbrokers, and stockholders. If the case is sufficiently dramatic or important, the business press investigates. The careful scrutiny resulting from any danger signal—a missed loan payment, delayed payment for supplies, ouster of top officials—generally identifies impending crisis long before chapter 11 becomes wise or necessary.

This scrutiny often guarantees that officials will make changes before the problem becomes unmanageable. Since this often requires new borrowing, restructuring of old loans, or both, the lenders are usually party to these changes. And since large financial institutions have no desire to risk additional capital, loans arranged under these conditions are carefully investigated to ensure that the investment will not be lost. This can produce substantial bank leverage, since the consortium arrangements discussed in chapter 3 make it difficult for the troubled firm to exploit competition among potential lenders. The leadership of the consortium, therefore, plays approximately the same role as the creditors' committee under bankruptcy. And while the negotiations do not take place under the color of law or the official sanction of the government, the similarities far outweigh the differences.

Negotiations between troubled corporations and current or potential lenders thus involve an evaluation of corporate policy and leadership that could lead to a vindication of current practice, a major overhaul of the firm, or any of a large number of intermediate results. The same sort of strategic control exercised under conditions of bankruptcy may occur, in a more routine and less flamboyant way, under conditions of financial distress.

Less dramatic lender interventions, then, are also part of corporate life. In many circumstances this is the best method banks have of conserving their capital investment in a troubled organization. At other times this is the only alternative to a wave of bankruptcies. As one banker explained it in relation to Great Southwest Corporation (GSC):

> If GSC was a unique situation we'd push them under. But if we did that to all companies in the same boat, we'd throw the economy for a loop. In any case, some interest is better than none. It gives the company a real opportunity to come out of its troubles, and it stretches out future losses for us. (*Business Week*, April 25, 1977)

Sometimes the ensuing intervention is almost routine, as this anecdote reported by Myles Mace (1971) indicates:

> In one case, poor management by the president resulted in the steady decline of sales and profits in a once-profitable and distinguished midwestern company. ... although there was mounting evidence that the president was incapable of leading the enterprise no action was initiated by the board members. Finally, after a succession of three loss years, a vice president of the principal lending bank, and not a director of the company, asked to meet with the board, and stated that unless a change was made the bank loans would not be renewed. With this leverage from the bank, the outside directors made the decision to ask the president to resign—but, it should be noted, with considerable reluctance. (pp. 37–38)

Such incidents are unobtrusive and difficult to uncover unless a specific study of the firm in question is undertaken. James and Soref (1981) have demonstrated that chief executive firings are largely a consequence of declining profits or losses; this anecdote suggests that such ousters are sometimes a consequence of bank intervention.

The instances of bank intervention that reach the major business publications tend to be more spectacular and involve a more comprehensive restructuring of the company. Consider the case of Rohr Industries, another of the high-flying firms of the late 1960s that ran into difficulty in the 1970s.[12] Cofounder Burt F. Raynes developed the company from a narrow aircraft-parts supplier into a *Fortune* 500 manufacturer of trains, subway cars, and buses. A series of financial setbacks in the mid-1970s left it with heavy, unpayable debt, and in late 1975 Raynes was ousted and replaced by Fred W. Garry, an aerospace engineer. Garry immediately sold off viable subsidiaries to repay some of the debt and "persuaded the lenders to stretch out the repayment schedule" (*Business Week*, Feb. 28, 1977: 87). Over the next three years, he dediversified back into aircraft by selling off other sectors of the company, instituted large-scale layoffs and general contraction in the remaining sectors, undertook decentralization of leadership, and ousted most of top management.

During this process, one of Rohr's bankers told *Business Week* (Feb. 28, 1977) that, while there was a clear "downside risk . . . we feel very comfortable about its ability to repay" (p. 87). However, the lender was wrong: after the contraction (motivated by the need to repay loans), "Rohr found that its production capacity, which had been overlooked, could not be brought up to the level necessary to meet demand" (*New York Times*, July 30, 1980: D5). This ultimately led to a failure to meet delivery schedules, thus triggering another financial crisis and the replacement of Garry by another chief executive officer.

In this example, we see all the elements of the Daylin bankruptcy without the legal accoutrements. The financial crisis triggered the ouster of the dominant executive, new corporate policies, and a new organizational structure. The debt was renegotiated, though not as favorably as in Daylin's case. The extraction of capital led to an overcontraction, a new crisis, and a new intervention. This is a more typical pattern than formal bankruptcy. In table 4.1 twenty-six instances of bank intervention involved loan negotiations or restructuring; several others appear to have involved the threat of such a restructuring.

The accounts of bank intervention we have reviewed so far imply that the lenders hold incontrovertible leverage that they translate into access to the discretionary decision making of the troubled company. Although this is sometimes the case, the initiative and expertise of top executives, as well as their day-to-day control of

the corporation's fate (see chapter 1), make them formidable ad-
versaries in some circumstances. Consider the following example.

Cook Industries is another firm that grew very rapidly in the late
1960s and then fell into difficulty in the mid-1970s.[13] During its
expansion, Cook borrowed heavily to finance entry into grain trading and reaped enormous profits on these operations. By late 1976,
however, spectacular losses left it in grave financial distress. This
led to meetings between Cook executives and bank lenders "to go
over the financial condition of the company" (Business Week, June
13, 1977: 42). These meetings produced sales of assets (to pay debt),
a major reorganization of the company's grain merchandising operations, and a new loan agreement containing covenants that "imposed some strict limitations on what Cook could do in merchandising and in futures trading" (Business Week, Jan. 30, 1978: 22).
When new losses were reported in December 1977, chairman Edward W. Cook went to the lenders with "plans to bring its grain
merchandising divisions back to profitability"; but these were rejected by the consortium. Rather than follow lenders' dictates, Cook
sold off the bulk of the company to Pillsbury, repaid the debt, and
remained in control of the resultant entity: "The 55-year-old chief
executive will be left with an extermination company, an insurance
brokerage firm, and a cotton warehousing operation, or about what
he started with in the late 1960s" (Business Week, Jan. 30, 1978:
23).

This conflict turned on the grain-trading and merchandising subsidiaries of Cook Industries. Edward Cook and his allies among the
firm's executives (who collectively controlled 57% of the stock)
desired continued expansion and flexibility in a sector that, in the
early 1970s, had produced enormous profits. The lenders, after wit-
nessing the volatility of the sector, insisted on limiting and re-
straining the company's activities in the area until the company
was safely on a profitable course: " 'Cook's banks were aghast' re-
calls one source close to the events. 'They realized that the company could lose money even faster than it was capable of making
it' " (Business Week, Jan. 30, 1978: 22).

Neither side won. Edward Cook escaped the dictates of the banks
by selling off the grain-trading operations and using the proceeds
to repay the debt that had produced lender leverage. In doing so,
he also satisfied the lenders' interest. It is not always possible, of
course, for a chief executive officer to achieve even as self-crippling
an escape as the one Cook engineered. The combination of his
control of the stock (which prevented his expulsion by the board
of directors) and the marketability of the grain operations (which

allowed him to raise sufficient cash to escape debt) makes this an unusual situation. In other circumstances, Cook's choices would have been more limited; he might have been forced to accept bank dictates or have been expelled from his position.[14] This is an instructive example because the lenders' constraints left Cook with two options: following their directives as to corporate policy (that is, giving up discretionary decision-making power) or reducing the company to a shadow of its former self in order to repay the loans. Hegemony, in its most efficient form, operates in this way. It restricts the choices of the dominant firms to those that are consistent with lender interest. Whichever choice Cook made, the banks' interest was served.

Moreover, loan renegotiations exemplify the asymmetry between lender and borrower. By and large the lenders dominate the interaction. They establish policies for distressed firms, and they protect their own interest, even when it conflicts with those of other actors. This domination, spread across many troubled firms and sectors, influences the profile of American industrial decision making, and this reverberates through all aspects of American life. Corporate viability, regional employment opportunities, even individual life-style possibilities become subject to capital-flow decisions made by financial institutions.

Loan Covenants

Although the Penn Central crisis produced eight years of bank intervention, most bankruptcies take less than two years to resolve. The end of formal proceedings generally signals the end of bank input and a return to the normal quasi-autonomy of modern corporate life. Bank intervention during loan negotiations may produce ongoing oversight (as in the case of Chrysler), but usually the period of intervention ends when the new lending agreements are signed. The cases of Rohr and Cook, reviewed above, are typical: instead of constant oversight, the lenders intervened, negotiated a new policy, and withdrew. In both cases they intervened again (after three years at Rohr, after three months at Cook), and this sort of reintervention is more typical than ongoing direction of corporate policy. In our compilation, only Chrysler offered visible evidence of ongoing oversight by loan consortia. In two other cases, Gulf and Pullman, Mellon Bank controlled the firms for several decades through a variety of means; and in four cases—Daylin, City Stores, Lockheed, and Penn Central—after the intervention the lenders acquired commanding blocks of stock that could have been used to perpetuate strategic control.

The typical intervention, then, does not result in the consolidation of the industrial firm into a bank empire or sphere of influence. Instead, the lenders intervene decisively to reset corporate direction, then they withdraw. Loan covenants serve to modulate the renewed independence of crisis companies and enforce a certain degree of lender involvement in subsequent discretionary decision making; the involvement, however, is narrow and episodic instead of long term and encompassing.

The covenant negotiated in the initial phase of the crisis at Cook Industries set limits on grain trading and hence is a good example of this process. It served as an extension of bank intervention beyond the first round of loan renegotiations. This was a definite constraint on Edward Cook, as subsequent events demonstrated. Thus, a permanent bank presence was inserted into the policy process of an otherwise autonomous industrial firm.

Most loan agreements contain covenants, but many of them are pro forma: they contain standard clauses that do not interfere with management discretion. In some circumstances, however, covenants actually inhibit policies that might have been undertaken—in these cases they embody a long-term bank influence on the affairs of industrial corporations.

Bankers see loan covenants as instruments of intervention rather than ironclad policy dictates: R. J. Wynn, vice-president of Morgan, wrote in *Business Week* (Jan. 17, 1977) that covenants are " 'triggers' intended to give lenders a chance to appraise unforeseen developments and decide whether or not to take protective action" (p. 5). Loan provisions, then, force consultation with lenders before discretionary actions are taken. If the lenders agree to the action, the loan covenant is waived and the policy is pursued. If not, the loan covenant is enforced and the action is inhibited, despite the desires or judgment of the company's leadership.

This process is illustrated in the case of Omega-Alpha, which was owned and operated by conglomerator James Ling. *Fortune* (June, 1973) reported:

> Omega-Alpha's bankers have insisted on unusually restrictive loan agreements that prohibit the company and most of its subsidiaries from merging, selling off assets, or paying dividends without express permission. The main reason for the restrictions, says Drennan [commercial loan officer of First Pennsylvania Bank] is not concerned about the security of the

loans, but the desire to slow down Ling's wheeling and dealing a bit. "Ling is probably a financial genius in his own right," Drennan says. "He moves very quickly and I want to be able to keep up with him." (p. 234)

The Omega-Alpha covenants were particularly encompassing. They reflected Ling's notoriety, and they were part of a long series of efforts by lenders to control his wheeling and dealing (Brown, 1972). Covenants have been underestimated as instruments of control; with the exception of Herman's (1981) work they have been left unanalyzed in the bank control debate.[15] Nevertheless, quite frequently they are a part of loan agreements, and a surprising number of corporate crises involve the activation or establishment of covenants that constrain corporate behavior. Sixteen of our instances of bank control—over 33%—visibly involved covenants, and since covenants frequently remain unpublicized, the actual proportion may have been larger still. The constraints created by this mechanism are therefore largely unmeasurable by the methods of our study; they require and deserve a systematic research effort.

Despite the limitations of our method, our evidence demonstrates that covenants are enforced. There are many instances of encompassing or dramatic restrictions imposed by them. In 1974, for example, a Grumman loan agreement prohibited all acquisitions and restricted policymaking contact with Bank Melli Iran, which was a substantial stockholder in the firm (New York Times, Jan. 14, 1975: F1). In 1978, Rapid-American, a conglomerate that concentrated on buying and selling subsidiary corporations, was forced to restrict its merger activities (Fortune, July 17, 1978: 80). A Farah Industries rescue loan carried a covenant that forced William Farah—the founder, dominant stockholder, and chief executive officer of the firm—to withdraw completely from the company.[16] Kennecott Copper, an attractive candidate for acquisition during the 1970s, signed a loan agreement by which it would automatically be in default if its Carborundum subsidiary was sold or if a high dividend was declared. This was designed to prevent an unfriendly takeover of Kennecott by Curtiss-Wright, since Curtiss-Wright's leadership could have financed the acquisition by subsequently selling Carborundum. Korvette, 57% of which was owned by Arlen Realty, negotiated a loan containing a covenant preventing the transfer of any of Korvette's assets to the parent firm (Business Week, Nov. 13, 1978: 30). A loan to Placid Oil, the main corporate instrument of the Hunt brothers, prohibited them from further speculation in silver or in any other commodity, even if the speculation took place outside Placid Oil's organizational shell. This put an end to the celebrated Hunt brothers silver crisis (*New York Times*, May 1, 1980).[17]

Loan covenants illustrate the conflict of interest between lenders and borrowers. We see this in the provision that prevented the transfer of Korvette funds to Arlen; the banks had no desire to ameliorate the financial insecurity of Arlen if it in any way damaged the financial integrity of Korvette. Because their loans were to Korvettes (and they refused to help Arlen), this made perfect sense to them; it also made perfect sense for Arlen to seek to transfer funds as it chose, in order to attend to the health of the overall enterprise.

In the case of the Hunts, loan covenants were used to impose the broader interest of the business community upon the brothers. The provisions were designed to remove the Hunts from the futures market, since their speculation had repeatedly resulted in severe market disruptions. The lenders, representing the broadest alliance of the corporate world, utilized a moment of financial dependence by the Hunts to impose these divestitures upon them:

> A spokesman for the Morgan Guaranty Trust Company said that a condition imposed on a third party who was not directly involved in a loan [the Hunt brothers as individual citizens] would not be that unusual. He said that some paper indicating the Hunts' agreement to those conditions [no commodity speculation] would probably be put together. "It could be policed by the banks because they could throw the loan into default if the conditions were not met," he said. (*New York Times*, May 1, 1981: D1)

Insofar as a corporation's interest is expressed through the policies undertaken by its leadership, then all forms of bank intervention represent an imposition on the corporation's interest by the financial world. An even narrower sense of corporate interest, which would acknowledge the possibility that outside bankers might represent the interest of the firm better than the internal leadership, simply reverses the analysis: a considerable proportion of firms are then being run by managers whose policies contradict the interests of their companies. In either case, the success of banks in imposing their version of corporate interest over that of chief executive officers is a highly significant and important phenomenon in the corporate world.

Bank Intervention and Financial Hegemony

Let us return to the issues raised at the beginning of this chapter. We argued that our evidence would demonstrate that banks intervene in the internal affairs of major corporations; that this intervention results in the direction and redirection of corporate policy; that intervention is typically short term but nevertheless profound; and that this intervention is part of a broader pattern of financial hegemony.

How prevalent is bank intervention? Our evidence indicates that, over a five-year period, nearly one intervention per month was mentioned in the most important business publications. This can be viewed as many or few, depending upon one's perspective. Independent of one's interpretation of frequency, however, we argue that the importance of these interventions is found in the role they play in the corporate world. The leaders of major American companies read about them almost once a month. In all likelihood, they hear about other instances through informal channels. It is our contention that most prudent corporate leaders are aware of, and concerned with, the possibility of a major loan renegotiation in which their own performance would be scrutinized by their bankers. In this context, the prudent executive would be concerned with bank relationships and with the possibility that bankers could profoundly affect his or her personal career as well as the direction of the firm. We believe that this logic enters the policymaking considerations of major corporate executives.

For us, the importance of awareness of potential bank intervention is that corporate leaders will be attentive to and concerned with the opinion of bankers and that they will consider bankers' judgments in deciding corporate policy. It is crucial to recall that a major consequence of corporate crisis has been the ouster of chief executive officers. Of course, there is no substitute for corporate success, which not only maintains lender trust but also prevents lender leverage. But in the world of modern American capitalism, no chief executive officer can guarantee success. Hence the continuing incentive is to establish cordial, friendly relationships with current or potential lenders. A prudent executive will therefore think carefully before undertaking policies he or she knows bankers would oppose. Thus, the potential for bank intervention creates the reality of bank influence even in times of prosperity and corporate health.

Does bank intervention result in the redirection of corporate policy? In this instance little argument can be made. The purpose of intervention is to assess corporate policy in order to determine what directions would avoid a crisis. There can be little doubt that the renegotiation and bankruptcy processes are designed to influence policy. The capacity of bank decision making at the exact moment when corporate policy must be assessed makes the injection of financial interest inevitable. Moreover, corporate crisis and bank intervention are two faces of the same coin in a situation in which crisis breeds financial need. Thus the injection of bank interests into the crisis process represents a crucial influence over corporate history and future.

Finally, our evidence suggests that long-term bank intervention and control of captive firms is not a frequent phenomenon. This is important because it undermines the possibility of interest-groups and interest-group conflict, for which many bank control theorists have argued. We shall turn to this in chapter 10, where we address it more directly. Here it is important to note only that the consequence of a process of intervention followed by return to autonomy is not the creation of independent firms. Instead the intervention becomes a part of the broader system of hegemonic relationships outlined in chapters 2 and 3. However, bank intervention is best viewed as an adjunct to hegemonic domination rather than as a core component. It is a mechanism needed when control of capital flows does not sufficiently constrain the options available to corporate decision makers. Although the potential for intervention creates a longer-term bank influence, the conditions for successful intervention are available only under special conditions. Thus, although the threat of intervention carries weight in the corporate world, intervention is not the primary base of hegemonic domination.

Moreover, intervention intrudes upon the discretionary component of corporate decision making, while the major method of intercorporate coordination is the alteration of structural constraint. Financial hegemony, then, relies on intervention as a tuning mechanism; as a vehicle for formalizing financial input into corporate decision making. Capital-flow decisions, on the other hand, are part of the routine functioning of the financial world. They set— or sometimes follow—a rhythm of corporate investment that can ripple through the economic sector. Intervention is neither routine, far-reaching, nor guaranteed. It is a one-to-one control that does not routinely characterize intercorporate relations, and it is only in very special circumstances that banks attain sufficient leverage to accomplish intervention. Nevertheless, banks do intervene in the affairs of nonfinancial corporations, and, we argue, this is best understood as the most direct portion of a loose coordination system.

Institutional Investors

As a force in intercorporate relations, institutional stockholding is gaining more and more attention as an ever-increasing proportion of investment capital is given over to professional management. Although institutional investing first developed in the early part of the twentieth century, rapid growth followed the successes of the CIO campaign for pension funding just after World War II. Today, pension moneys, mutual funds, trust funds, and the endowments of foundations and universities, as well as the assets of individual capitalist families administered by financial experts, have made institutional investors significant actors in the world of big business.[18]

With the rise of pension fund expansion, in particular, commercial banks have become major institutional investors. As early as 1955, thirteen New York banks managed 60% of all pension fund dollars (Baum and Stiles, 1965: 30). By 1972, seventy-one trust departments controlled 72.3% of all trust department assets (Herman, 1975: 20). Although institutional investments are not confined to common stock purchases, they have become a dominant force in equity markets. In 1949, approximately 12% of the common stock listed on the New York Stock Exchange was held by various institutions; in 1962, pension funds alone purchased 80% of the new common stock issues of that year (Baum and Stiles, 1965: 44). By 1977, institutional investors accounted for 60% of all stock traded and 40% of all stock held (Newsday, Aug. 1, 1977: 56).

This concentration has enormous potential for corporate control, a potential that was recognized even before the post-World War II spurt of institutional investment activity. An early SEC study (United States Securities and Exchange Commission, 1938–42), for example, investigating the possibility of control of portfolio firms by investment companies, found ownership of voting stock to be an effective mechanism of control.[19] In 1955, the Stock Market Study of the United States Senate Committee on Banking and Currency addressed the effect of institutional investor activity on stock market rate fluctuations and concluded that it was indeed a factor. That corporate control was an issue in this period is further illustrated by the congressional testimony of John McCloy of Chase National Bank: "I must say I am impressed at the moment, at least, by the efforts which are made by the pure investor not to control. . . . He is diffident about getting too much control in a particular company" (quoted in Baum and Stiles, 1965: 64).

McCloy's opinion on the matter aside, the possibility of control of the corporation through institutional investor holdings has remained a serious issue. Formalized in 1965 by Baum and Stiles, the question was given important publicity with the 1968 release of the Patman Report. The findings that forty-nine bank trust departments individually held 5% or more of at least one class of stock of 5,270 corporations startled most observers (United States House of Representatives, 1968: 3). What had been a consistent but weak admonition about trust department concentration took force at that time. Other government investigations followed (United States Senate, 1973, 1976); the Twentieth Century Fund addressed the question as part of its series on conflict of interest within the securities industry (Herman, 1975); academic curiosity was piqued (Soldofsky, 1971; Schotland, 1977), and institutional investment activity was incorporated into the debate over banker control (Fitch and Oppenheimer, 1970a-c; Kotz, 1978).[20] Though all participants agree that institutional investors are important sources of capital, the major disagreement is over the implications for corporate control.

Fitch and Oppenheimer (1970a-c) took a strong position in the controversy. Using the institutional stockownership data supplied by the Patman Report, they argued that the concentrated holding of bank trust departments may be used to secure control of many nonfinancial corporations. Their argument, deepened and enriched by Kotz (1978), suggests that the large blocks of stock held by a limited number of trust departments could be voted to determine corporate policy. The main opponents of this view were Herman (1973, 1975, 1979, 1981) and Herman and Safanda (1973), who argued that institutional investors rarely vote against management and that trust department stockholding is "mutually supportive" (Herman, 1973: 25) of banks and portfolio companies. Moreover, "the reciprocal and protective element is . . . more characteristic of the bank-client relationship than any thrust toward control by either party" (Herman, 1973: 26).

Much evidence has been generated to support the contention that institutional investors typically vote with management, although significant exceptions do exist (Herman, 1975: 67; Kotz, 1978: 126). Instead, the Wall Street rule advises the sale of a corporation's stock rather than an attempt to influence internal policy. And, indeed, the sale of large blocks of stock has become commonplace among institutional investors. As Robert Metz, *New York Times* stock market columnist, put it: "These days, institutions commonly dump shares of any corporation that issues a disappointing earnings report" (*New York Times*, Dec. 17, 1976: D2). And this type of large-scale sale has an effect on the corporation at issue. Research-Cottrell, for example, a manufacturer of pollution control devices, saw its stock drop from $60 to $4 because design errors had led to a decline in profits and triggered institutional dumping (*Forbes*, April 1, 1977: 78). Even IBM, seemingly invulnerable to outside influence, was subjected to mass selling by institutional investors and was forced to purchase its own stock to keep equity prices up (*Business Week*, April 4, 1977: 110).

The Wall Street rule, then, is not necessarily a neutral mechanism for divesting of a problematic holding. As blocks become larger, the sale of concentrated holdings has greater and greater impact on the price of the stock, and this translates into potential influence over corporate policy. As Lewis H. Young, editor-in-chief of *Business Week* (1978: 45), wrote:

> In Wall Street, people argue that that is the best way for institutions to influence management. Selling the stock in large blocks pushes the price of the stock down, increasing the company's costs of raising capital, and punishes the management for poor performance.

Thus, the Wall Street rule may become an instrument of policy rather than a method of withdrawing from corporate affairs. The threat of stock dumping, however, makes its use less necessary. As the Conference Board reported: "some proposals or programs never see the light of day simply because management discerns that these institutions [trust departments] have looked askance at these proposals" (Bacon and Brown, 1977: 90).

Similarly, the respect shown for potential stock dumping is illustrated by the experience of Becton, Dickinson, a New Jersey pharmaceutical firm, controlled and operated by owner-founder Fairleigh Dickinson. "In 1974, Dickinson voluntarily surrendered the chief executive's post to his handpicked successor, Wesley J. Howe, in a move calculated to assure Wall Street of continued professional management in the company" (*Business Week*, Oct. 3, 1977). The "Wall Street" referred to here was the institutional investment community, which held 8.3 million of the 19 million Becton shares outstanding (*New York Times*, Jan. 19, 1978: D2). Dickinson feared that his continued leadership would result in wholesale

selling of these shares, which would lower stock prices (making
the firm vulnerable to takeover), undermine credit ratings (making
the firm less able to finance expansion), and alienate prospective
economic allies.

Under certain conditions, then, the policy preferences of large
institutional investors can be a major influence in determining individual corporate policy. Nevertheless, it is crucial to stress that
the constraints on corporate autonomy created by institutional
stockholding are rarely the active, long-term process of control en-
visioned by Fitch and Oppenheimer (1970a-c) and critiqued by Herman (1973, 1975, 1979, 1981). Institutional investors do not purchase
stock with an eye to influencing corporate policy; purchases are
typically made on the basis of market position. Assuming the practice of the "prudent man," trust department holdings are not determined by the needs of the larger financial institution.[21] However,
the same corporations are ultimately at issue. Trust departments
invest in a broad range of firms; commercial banks lend to a broad
range of firms, and overlap is present. When the needs of the larger
institution correspond to a trust department holding, a coincidence
of interest between the two units occurs.

This suggests, then, that institutional investing cannot be viewed
as a systematic mechanism for establishing bank control or for gaining a position of influence over a set of corporations. Instead institutional stockholding, like bank intervention, is available only
in certain circumstances or under special conditions. And, like bank
intervention, it is a useful support for bank hegemony rather than
a mechanism of bank control. Although the larger argument that
we are developing stresses a loose but long-term influence over the
nonfinancial world, with control over capital flows the major mechanism underlying this influence, institutional stockholding can be
quite effective in influencing corporate policy. And it does so on
several levels.

First and most important, it establishes a set of constraints under
which portfolio companies operate. In the most successful cases,
"Corporate managements ... pander to institutional preferences
and ... adopt whatever policies are favored by ... large investment
institutions" (Business Week July 25, 1970: 54). Under other conditions investor preferences are considered, but with less force. In
still other instances, institutions are ignored, corporate policy pro-
gresses, and banks may attempt to influence policy by stock dumping. Sometimes this strategy is successful, at other times it is not.
While the Leasco example described in chapter 1 illustrates the
potential power of stock dumping, complete failure occurred in the

case of Skaggs Drug Centers, when it and Albertson's markets announced the end of a highly successful partnership in jointly operated combined drug and food supermarkets. Institutional stockholders began dumping Skaggs's stock because they believed the leadership could not profitably manage food operations. The stock price dropped nearly 22% in the three months after the announcement, with top bank trust departments accounting for 17% of all shares sold. This did not disrupt the proposed separation. And when Skaggs announced a hefty profit in the first quarter of independent operation, the institutions returned and the stock jumped 6% in one month (Schotland, 1977: 131, 228, 231; *Business Week*, June 6, 1977: 56). In this case, stock dumping produced no effect on Skaggs's economic performance or on its strategic decision making.

In other instances, dumping constrains corporate activity without completely determining it. Institutional dumping of stock in General Public Utilities and other electrical plants after the Three Mile Island disaster contributed to the cancellation of other nuclear facilities, but it has not led to an enduring resolution of the industry's financial problems (*Business Week*, May 28, 1979: 108–24). Dumping of International Harvester stock after a $397 million loss in 1980 did not force basic policy changes, but it contributed to the necessity for debt renegotiation, which allowed the banks to intervene massively (*New York Times*, Feb. 23, 1981: D4; March 10, 1981: D3; March 31, 1981: D1). Hence we stress the variability in outcomes when institutional investors attempt to use stock dumping as a lever in corporate affairs.

Stock dumping is most effective, of course, when many institutions sell simultaneously. *Business Week* (July 25, 1970: 53, 55) explains:

> As institutions buy and sell ever larger blocks of stock, they develop greater power in corporate affairs—power they occasionally exercise with the impact of a sledgehammer. . . . When institutions sell as a group they have a devastating effect on a company—squelching financing and expansion plans and sometimes destroying morale.

Thus, the coordinated trading of large institutional investors has been noticed, and its consequences can be devastating. When, for example, LTV moved to break up newly acquired Jones and Laughlin Steel despite opposition from bondholders, LTV stock declined so precipitously that it triggered a corporate crisis culminating in the removal of James Ling, who was the principal individual stockholder and architect of the giant conglomerate (Brown, 1972: 166, 240).

Moreover, coordinated stock dumping, even when it does not produce immediate consequences for the company, represents a warning that financial leadership has lost confidence in the firm. The loss in stock price not only implies a lower net worth and therefore lower lending limits, but also reflects a pessimistic judgment by lending institutions. This could lead to lowered bond ratings, higher interest rates, loan refusals, and vulnerability to acquisition. It could also suggest lender intervention to reorient corporate strategy, if loan renegotiation became necessary.

But what about the argument that stock dumping results in monetary losses for the dumping institutions? As the price of the stock drops, the sellers receive less and less for each sale and therefore do not emerge with reasonable return on investment.[22] Though this danger creates a financial deterrent, it is only one factor in institutional decision making. The 1970s were marked by an ongoing controversy over the failure of institutional stockholders to perform as well as the average investor. Despite their technical skills and enormous financial clout, bank trust departments have consistently paid their customers a lower rate of return than could be achieved through a random selection of stocks.

Fortune (July 31, 1978: 72–78) contains a fascinating discussion of this underperformance. During 1973–74, the Standard and Poor's market index declined 40%, while pension funds dominated by bank trust departments declined by 52.5%. While the S&P index lost 0.3% from 1973 to 1977, the average customer of Morgan, the largest trust department, lost 4.1%.[23] In 1976, Business Week (Dec. 20, 1976: 54) reported that 84% of money managers had underperformed the market in the preceding decade. In 1980, it reported that institutional investors returned an average of 7.3% per year to their customers during the 1970s (less than the 8% average inflation), while the S&P average returned 9.1% (Aug. 11, 1980: 57).[24] These findings suggest that trust departments are following investment strategies that consistently fail to maximize return on the moneys entrusted to them.[26]

In sum, then, institutional stockholding can be an effective mechanism in influencing corporate affairs. It should be stressed, however, that our own analysis of institutional stockholding deviates from traditional bank control theory in two ways. First, we accept Herman's (1973, 1975) argument that bank trust departments do not often vote against nonfinancial management, and we suggest instead that stock dumping is the more typical method of influencing corporate policy. Second, we argue that institutional stock-holding—and bank intervention—are not part of the everyday repertoire of major banks. Instead, we suggest that, although the possibility of bank intervention or institutional stock dumping establishes a degree of long-term discipline within the nonfinancial world, the specific circumstances that allow the use of these mechanisms are not everyday events; they develop sporadically.

Hence, neither institutional stockholding nor bank intervention is a systematic method for establishing bank control. Instead we view both as reinforcements, rather than core components, of intercorporate influence. As important, the influence itself is far short of bank control. Instead of intercorporate domination as described by control theorists ranging from Lenin (1917a) to, more recently, Fitch and Oppenheimer (1970a-c), we outline a process of looser coordination and influence; a process that favors financial institutions in the long run rather than one-to-one interactions; a process in which financial power is limited in both the short run and the long run but is nevertheless profound; and a process that depends on the alteration of structural constraint rather than on strategic control. We argue, therefore, that financial hegemony is quite different from bank control, both in scope and in process; that financial hegemony conditions the economic sector but does so in broad strokes; and that financial hegemony is the most important feature of intercorporate relationships.

Institutional stockholding and bank intervention play different roles in this process. While bank intervention invades the discretionary decision making of the target firm, stock dumping as a vehicle for financial influence alters the environment in which the corporation operates. It thus alters structural constraint. Stock dumping cannot ensure a particular outcome, and it is thus consistent with the hegemonic process. To the extent that dumping can trigger a crisis, it can create circumstances in which banks can intervene in the discretionary decision making of the target firm. Intervention is direct influence—influence consistent with the process of bank control. This distinction suggests that, when possible and necessary, financial institutions utilize mechanisms of bank control to maintain hegemonic domination. Although the larger structure of intercorporate relations is mediated by financial hegemony, components of bank control reside in the system and contribute to the hegemonic process. Thus, components of bank control and financial hegemony combine to produce an overall, long-term hegemonic domination.

5 The Texture of Financial Hegemony

Does he [Herbert P. Patterson, former Chase Manhattan Bank president] miss the pomp and power..."if you are interested in prestige and...power and you want to play God with people's lives, you obviously are going to miss it. I wasn't interested in prestige or power or playing God. I don't miss it at all."

Forbes, May 15, 1978: 96

Constraint and Discretion

The relationships that produce financial hegemony have been analyzed in chapters 1–4. This catalog, although necessary for understanding the structural outcomes of intercorporate relations, is misleading because it creates the impression of well-defined episodes of intercorporate constraint separated by equally well-defined periods of relative autonomy. More realistically, loan negotiation and renegotiation, lender intervention into the internal decision-making process of borrowers, and the symmetrical dependencies imposed by resource dependency and mutual deterrence are intermeshed and are part of the larger process of corporate life. Decisions made during periods of relative autonomy are altered by changes in structural constraint; choices made under severe constraint may ultimately produce expansion in discretion. Thus, while we can identify specific instances of financial influence on a particular corporation, the interplay of forces is part of the everyday environment of business life. Corporate decision making, in its most routine or most constrained form, is carried out in the context of a system of interrelated parts, with past and future relationships influencing current options. Financial hegemony, then, is not static or episodic. It is a process with long-term development and long-term consequences.

Financial hegemony, however, does not suggest unlimited discretionary decision making by commercial banks and insurance companies. Occasionally, decisions made by financiers are wholly constrained—no viable alternatives exist. In these cases banks become the agencies of systemic constraint, the enforcers of structural determinism. Other decisions have a huge discretionary component—financial executives must choose among several viable locales for capital. In these cases, financiers make choices that may determine the future of the economy, and, by inevitable implication, the entire country.

Since the direction of capital flows is so important to the general welfare, it is crucial to understand the process and assess the consequences of financial decision making. In this chapter we offer a general portrait of these consequences, focusing upon the influence of financial hegemony on corporate, sectoral, and economic behavior. In chapters 6–10 we analyze the network of interlocking directorates, which is the main structural apparatus for managing this process of decision making.

Bank Decision Making and the Corporate Life-Style

Within the business sector, structural constraints result from the complex rhythms of economic life. At the most general level, despite a permanent overriding need for investment capital there are periods of relative surplus and relative shortage to which both lender and borrower behavior must adjust. Industrial sectors experience periods of growth, stability, and recession that influence their need for outside capital. Individual companies undergo expansion, consolidation, and contraction. These cycles influence the availability of and need for capital and therefore the fabric of intercorporate relations.

The overall rhythm of financial decision making is, in the first instance, responsive to the ebb and flow of capital supply. As illustrated in chapter 2, when a capital shortage exists banks must compete for deposits and choose among worthy borrowers. When they are cash rich, they must seek out new lending locales, either through creation of new customers or through re-establishment of traditional markets. Both surplus and shortage constrain financial behavior and produce discretionary decision making, which in turn constrains industrial firms, creating still new constraints for financial institutions.

A second rhythm that conditions bank hegemony follows recessionary and expansionary cycles of particular industrial sectors. This pattern is illustrated by the growth of large farm co-ops in the 1960s and 1970s.[1] Developed during the period of farmer revolt in the 1920s and consolidated in the Great Depression, these cooperatives emerged from World War II as an important force in agriculture. During the 1960s, they became a dominant force in many sectors of agribusiness. By the mid-1970s, cooperatives accounted for over 50% of all farmer purchases and nearly 33% of all farm sales. The five largest had sales of over $1 billion each; the ten largest accounted for nearly 10% of all farm revenues.

In addition, the co-ops integrated vertically and horizontally. In the late 1940s, they began building oil refineries to supply fuel for farm machinery. They developed the capacity to produce, distribute, and sell farm chemicals; they encroached upon the previously uncontested terrain of food processors (and by 1977 accounted for some 15% of grain processing); they became a major force in grain exports; and they even developed a presence in the manufacture of farm machinery. Cooperative banks, acting as an internal finance system, guaranteed the co-ops' access to capital sources.

This enormous growth led, however, to major changes in co-op structure. By the late 1970s, co-op financing needs outstripped the supply of capital available from traditional funding sources. The invasion of new sectors necessitated costly product development. Monopoly control over certain products drove a substantial number of suppliers out of business and forced the co-ops to expand into these vacated sectors. The great successes also led to pressure from members for increased rebates. Though extremely profitable and dominant in their competitive niches, the co-ops became dependent on outside finance. This dependency made them responsive to the rules of corporate behavior. Co-ops began to hire outside executives (who were more experienced with the business methods of stockholding corporations); they were forced to disclose their financial figures; and they began to adopt standard business methods. The chief executive officer of Grain Terminal Association, a billion-dollar grain co-op, commented, "co-ops are being run damned near like companies now because if we are going to be as good as our competition, we better act like it" (Business Week, Feb. 7, 1977: 63).

Farm cooperatives demonstrate the frequent connection between profitable growth and increasing dependence on capital markets. Grand expansion may force entry into lending markets. Once this occurs, even the healthiest firm or sector becomes subject to the process of capital-flow decision making. In times of capital shortage, it must compete with other attractive locales by proposing appealing projects that do not injure existing commitments and that offer profitable secondary investment. At the same time, continually expanding giant corporations are crucial to the health of the financial industry, since they generate the capital banks lend. Moreover, it is these very firms that are profitable investment outlets for the capital other firms provide. Hence, on the general level, the relationship between corporate expansion and financial hegemony is dialectical. Capital dependence generates structural constraints for industrial firms, which in turn alters the environment in which financial institutions operate. In the long run, however, financial decision making is determining, at least in broad strokes, and the intersection of financial and nonfinancial constraint is financial hegemony.

The experience of the shipping industry in the last decade illustrates another component of capital-flow decisions which ultimately produce financial hegemony.[2] As part of a larger plan of expansion into overseas finance, the leading American banks made available a huge pool of capital to expand the international tanker fleet. Unusually generous terms were offered: whereas construction loans rarely cover more than 50% of the total cost, shipbuilders could borrow up to 75% of the cost of construction at relatively low interest rates.

Citibank, which led the stampede, announced its intention to become "the principal bank of the world's major ship owners" (New York Times, July 14, 1980: 3.11), and by 1978 shipping loans represented 4.6% of its portfolio. The top ten American banks held over $7 billion in shipping loans by 1978.

The decisions of banks drastically altered the profile of constraint for the shipbuilding industry. This led to an enormous boom in construction and a dramatic increase in the world's capacity to move goods, especially oil, by sea. However, the 1973 oil crisis struck with 100 million tons of shipping capacity under construction and triggered a long recession in the shipping industry. To make matters worse, the Soviet Union invaded the shipping market, using low prices as a way of capturing market share. Overcapacity, Soviet competition, and the absence of long-term leases created havoc in the industry; many shipbuilders could not repay their loans.

During 1977 and 1978, the banks were forced to reassess their commitment. They scrutinized each loan and each corporation, deciding upon rescue or abandonment. While rescue terms were often generous, abandonment could be brutal: a French firm was forced to sell a four-year-old, $30 million supertanker for $10 million; two others sold off three supertankers for scrap; two American corporations were themselves sold at distress prices after they failed to negotiate debt moratoriums; and another, Pacific Far East Line, declared bankruptcy, leaving the United States government with $98 million in loan guarantees.

This chronology demonstrates the importance of sectoral cycles. The expansion of shipbuilding was triggered and conditioned by the incentives created by bank decisions to direct capital into the industry, decisions conditioned by the availability of capital. The contraction was caused by systemic constraints—constraints beyond the reach of any corporate executive. Bankers, however reluctantly, were forced to choose among distressed firms. The largest proportion of discretion, in this case, rested with the lenders. And the determining decisions were enforced through constraint, not intervention.

The social waste involved in reducing several hundred million dollars worth of shipping to scrap is a symptom of the dysfunctions of a system dominated by financial hegemony. The calculus of maximum profit—in this case, minimum loss—combined with the leverage that allows lenders to impose their needs upon dependent sectors, frequently ends in the sacrifices of public welfare and economic efficiency to the interests of financial institutions.

This is the general outline of the relationship between finance capital and industrial sectors. Aircraft manufacturers were lavishly funded in the middle 1950s in order to produce the first generation of passenger jets. A period of financial independence was then followed by a period of excess capacity, financial stringency, and careful lender scrutiny and even intervention (Tinnen, 1973). The steel industry had easy access to capital during its period of strength in the 1960s, but it could not find conversion capital in the late 1970s when a worldwide recession and foreign competition threatened its viability (Business Week, Sept. 22, 1980: 103). The auto industry was nurtured for thirty years after World War II. In the late 1970s, during its gravest crisis, sufficient loan funds were not available for a quick conversion to small, fuel-efficient, vehicles.

The ebb and flow of capital supply in the economy as a whole and the rhythm of expansion and contraction in various industries are major environmental forces influencing the fate of the particular firms in American big business. Most important, however, decisions over capital flows are fit into the uncontrollable complexities of the interaction of systemic, sectoral, and corporate economic cycles. Financial institutions do not have absolute power; they too are continually subject to a wide assortment of structural constraints.

The Patterns of Corporate Conduct

The consequences of financial dominance are elastic and inconsistent. Bank leadership is confronted with a changing, uncontrollable external reality that imposes a shifting profile of institutional constraint. Nevertheless, those who lead financial institutions make decisions with far-reaching consequences and institutional reverberations. The institutional patterns that emerge from bank influence can therefore be roughly identified and analyzed. While they often complement and reinforce other tendencies in the economy, they sometimes contradict and overwhelm them. Among the most important of these broad trends are the continuing pressure for profit maximizing; the redirection of this profit nexus away from destructive competition; and the resistance to industrial development that threatens financial hegemony—conglomeration for example. In this section we consider these patterns. We begin with profit maximizing.

Despite managerial assertions concerning the rise of soulful, profit-satisficing companies, recent evidence suggests that the profit nexus remains the fundamental force in corporate life. Since Zeitlin (1974) outlined the weakness of managerial evidence, recent research has supported the proposition that large modern corporations profit maximize.[3]

It is important, however, to understand the somewhat different dynamics that impel the modern profit nexus:

> The glamor has not gone out of the pursuit of profit, even for management-controlled banks. Certainly, there would be far-reaching reverberations for a bank's survival if the principal owners of capital . . . found that the bank was giving them, on the average, a lower rate of return than other banks and, therefore, shifted their trusts elsewhere. . . . Such a general "loss of confidence" would drain the bank's funds, render it incapable of honoring its contractual obligations, and drive it into collapse. Thus the "discipline of the market" . . . requires the banks not to deviate significantly from profit-maximizing policies. To the extent, therefore, that the management-controlled banks are both the creditors and principal shareholders of the largest management-controlled corporations, and interlock tightly with them, these banks will, in

turn, impose their own profit-maximizing requirements on them." (Zeitlin, 1976: 900)[4]

This argument suggests a two-step structural imperative: capital markets impose profit maximizing on banks, and the banks (as lenders) impose it on nonfinancial firms. Hence, despite the decline of profit-maximizing owner-entrepreneurs, chief executives cannot pursue profit-satisficing behavior. This is illustrated by the farm co-op example presented above. Though they are the ultimate managerial-controlled firms—each farmer is restricted to a handful of shares and top management remains in power year after year in a self-perpetuating oligarchy—the co-ops' increasing dependence on outside financing forced them to profit maximize. Without returns as high as other firms, farm co-ops could not compete for necessary outside funding, because loans are given to those firms that can afford to pay the highest rate of interest.

This process occurs over and over again. In mid-1981, for example, Consolidated Edison requested and received a 15.5% rate increase from the Public Service Commission because:

> Unless utilities can provide investors a good return on their money, state P.S.C. commissioners said, companies such as Con Edison will be unable to issue new stock of a high enough price to let them raise the capital necessary to meet future demands on service. (New York Times, April 20, 1981: D1)

That is, since investors (largely institutional) could find returns of over 15% for their money, Con Ed could not obtain funds for less. Hence they requested and received a rate hike that would generate a profit high enough to pay these dividends rates and thus allow them to sell new stock. They did this despite their highly profitable condition and user rates, which were already the highest for any United States metropolitan area. Insofar as major corporations are hooked into the flow of capital, they are also part of the profit nexus.

This pressure for profits is, however, limited to certain situations. Financial institutions must resist profit maximizing among their clients if such behavior endangers investments in other firms or sectors. They do not want to encourage a company to profit maximize if high profits come "at the expense of other firms" to which the banks are financially tied. This was illustrated in the example of Howard Hughes's separation from TWA (see chapter 2), an ouster motivated by attempts to profit maximize even though it threatened the financial viability of commercial jet manufacturers.

This is also illustrated by the experience of A&P, once the dominant force in retail foods. In the early 1970s, after decades of decline in market share and profitability, A&P found itself in chronic financial difficulty, despite its 28% share of supermarket sales. To reverse the trend it initiated a price war, publicized as the WEO campaign ("where economy originates"), involving price cuts on approximately 3% of its products. While 3% does not appear to be large, the margin in retail food is so small that these reductions immediately threatened the profitability of several major competing firms. The Chicago area, where A&P dominated, was particularly hard hit. *Fortune* reported the consequences of this pressure:

> In the course of the war A&P picked up some new enemies it could ill afford. In a most extraordinary statement last month, the First National Bank of Chicago declared that A&P had aimed at a "cutting of corporate throats." J. L. Dody, a vice president of First National's loan division, told the meeting of 1,500 of its correspondent bankers that it was up to them to come to the rescue of well managed firms that suffered from the WEO offensive by offering them loans at unusually generous terms. He added "this is your opportunity to assist those good chains which can outlast and survive WEO." (*Fortune*, Jan., 1973: 108).

These rescue efforts were successful; A&P suffered massive losses from its price-cutting campaign without achieving compensatory increases in market share. Lenders eventually intervened, removed the leadership, and replaced it with new, less competively oriented executives.

In the cases of TWA and A&P, banks intruded directly into the relations among contending companies to prevent "destructive competition" (see chapter 2). These were not generous acts: competitive practices that threaten the financial viability of major firms threaten financial backers as well. Insofar as they are capable of countering these moves, banks are more or less required to do so by the logic of their own drive for profits. Mutual deterrence is therefore much deeper and more thorough than Baran and Sweezy suggest (chapters 2 and 3), because price competition by one company may produce financial support for the companies under attack. The competitive firm must be prepared, therefore, to defeat both its sectoral competition and the financial community.

The deterrent against price competition channels the profit-maximizing impulse into cost reduction. By lowering production costs while maintaining prices, large companies can increase their profit margins without threatening the health of their competitors, suppliers, or customers. This channeling effect, a consequence of both mutual deterrence and financial influence, has generally negative consequences for society as a whole. Customers pay higher prices when price competition is deterred, and cost reduction may spur worker/owner conflict, since it often involves declining or less-than-maximum wages. Either of these effects may involve a net loss for ordinary citizens and a net gain for corporations, as well as their stockholders and lenders.

The incentive for high profits is so overwhelming that the daring or desperate chief executive officer is sometimes forced or enticed to pursue destructive competition. This is especially prevalent during times of industry overcapacity. Since the fixed costs of maintaining idle plants are often extremely high, executives in depressed industries have enormous incentive to increase sales, even if it involves price competition aimed at luring customers away from other large companies. The airline industry, for example, experienced extreme competition in the late 1970s as a result of the shrinkage in the consumer market for air travel, which threatened many airlines with bankruptcy unless they filled their planes. The resulting "shake out" drove some companies into bankruptcy and others into rescuing mergers because they lost so many customers. Others survived and were even strengthened, because they attracted business from the less-successful firms.[5] Episodes of price competition, however, are usually short-lived. American capitalism is marked by such brief episodes, minimized by the mediation of financial actors.

In addition to imposing the profit nexus, financial hegemony must attempt to protect itself from structural changes that might undermine the logic of asymmetrical dependency, since this is so central to the preservation of its institutional role. This tendency is illustrated by bank resistance to conglomeration in the 1960s and 1970s.

Conglomerate acquisitions, unlike their predecessors, involve the merger of two firms with no intrinsic economic connection. Conglomerates are generally made up of relatively discrete profit centers under common leadership. They are therefore very similar to the empires of early capitalists who controlled and led several firms through external stockholding.

Conglomerates present difficulties for banks. They are, for example, less dependent on outside capital than other companies.[6] Since much borrowing takes place because of sectoral cycles, conglomerates can often finance one subsidiary with earnings from another in a different cyclical stage. Conglomerate mergers are often undertaken for precisely this reason.

Carrier, an air conditioner manufacturer, acquired Inmont, an ink producer, "to buffer the effects of off-years in its air conditioner sales" (Business Week, Aug. 29, 1977: 26). The acquisition of St. Joe Minerals by Fluor, an engineering firm, was partly motivated by the expectation of "Fluor's businesses acting as cash generators and St. Joe's businesses as cash users" (Business Week, April 27, 1981: 104). Fuqua sought a "consumer products company that would off-set the cyclical fluctuations of the other divisions" (New York Times, Aug. 15, 1980: D1). Koehring agreed to acquisition by Freuhof because it "needed the financial muscle of a well heeled parent" (Business Week, Jan. 24, 1977: 27); and in the mid-1960s Bendix "began acquiring a variety of operations for the same reason that many other corporations have done so—to ease the impact of cyclical downturns" (New York Times, Dec. 15, 1976: D1).

Smoothing of recessionary cycles within conglomerates represents a loss of business for lenders. If the constituent firms were independent, they would necessarily use financial intermediaries—those with surpluses would deposit their money in financial institutions; those with cash needs would borrow from these same firms. Conglomeration therefore short-circuits the lending process and harms the interest of financiers.

When conglomerates do seek financing, the lenders are faced with complicated decisions. For example, during a recession in the steel industry, financial institutions must choose which firms to nurture. One of the major steel producers is Jones and Laughlin, a subsidiary of the conglomerate LTV. In order to support Jones and Laughlin, lenders must lend to the conglomerate and risk the possibility that the loans will be directed to different subsidiaries. Conglomerate entities therefore make lending decisions more difficult and imprecise and reduce lender control over the ultimate fate of capital flows.

Since 1970, there has been consistent financial antagonism to conglomerate mergers, and while this antagonism has not eliminated such mergers, bank intervention into the affairs of conglomerates frequently involves dediversification.[7] Loan covenants often prohibit the use of funds except for specific earmarked subsidiaries or purposes. More generally, financial institutions have attempted to erect barriers to the establishment of institutional forms that undermine their dominance.

The existence of financial hegemony, therefore, creates a set of rules of conduct that impose themselves on corporations, sometimes more successfully than other times. Nevertheless, the structures that evolve from these rules emphasize profit maximizing in the absence of destructive competition and discourage institutional developments that threaten this hegemony.

Corporate Leadership and Bank Confidence

Outside domination of the discretionary decision making of a corporation is temporary (chapter 4); rules of conduct are inconsistently obeyed; financial institutions cannot inevitably work their will on the economy; and broad strategic planning is therefore the exception rather than the rule. The rarity of wholesale coordination, however, does not imply that market relationships are the principal arbiter of intercorporate behavior. Corporate "good citizenship" provides a middle ground between strategic control and the chaos of total competition. It is within this intermediate area that financial hegemony operates most successfully.

Although there appears to be a set of broad rules prohibiting competitive practices that advance one firm at the expense of many others, these guidelines seem easily evaded. The rhythm of corporate life includes periods of relative autonomy alternating with short spans of high capital dependency. Corporate leadership is usually under loose constraint and is rarely susceptible to overt intervention. When nonfinancial firms must seek capital, lenders are often constrained to respond favorably: existing loans may remove the option of abandonment; expansion may be mandated by broader economic imperatives; and the plan may be so appealing that refusal is financially improper. In many of these cases, industrial borrowers could ignore the rules of good citizenship with virtual impunity. They could proceed with their own strategies and gamble that future moments of dependency would occur in propitious circumstances.

Such corporate lawlessness certainly occurs. The ongoing oil crisis, for example, raised the share of United States industrial profits claimed by oil companies from 12% in 1970 to 40% in 1980. In engineering this massive increase, oil executives broke the cardinal rule of civilized competition: "Rather than increasing total corporate earnings, the high oil profits are coming at the expense of other industries" (quoted in *Business Week*, Aug. 18, 1980: 84). *Business Week*, calling for higher dividend payouts by oil companies, argued that "since much of these dividends will probably be reinvested, this would allow the private capital markets ... to determine where the oil profits could be most efficiently employed" (Aug. 18, 1980: 88). This suggestion was not honored by the oil firms, who chose instead to indulge in "misdirected" mergers, largely in extractive industries (*New York Times*, March 30, 1981: 46). In this case, then, there was little financial leverage capable of inducing compliance: highly profitable cash-rich oil companies could not be threatened with loan refusals or with outside takeovers through declining stock prices. They therefore proceeded with their own actions, impervious to financial discipline.

In contrast to successful oil company disobedience to the rules of corporate good conduct, many executives have been disciplined for rule breaking. James Ling, acknowledged as a "genius" even by his enemies, has no standing in the corporate world because, in due course, he arrived at moments of great vulnerability and was expelled not once, but twice from the leadership of large firms.[8] The Hunt brothers, who violated normal business ethics repeatedly in the 1970s and escaped discipline because of their enormous family fortune, were finally forced to borrow $1 billion to cover losses after they failed to corner the silver market. The banks imposed unprecedented covenants, including sale of all silver holdings, prohibitions on all futures trading in any commodity, and other constraints on the Hunt brothers' investment.[9]

Yet, as the oil industry example illustrates, punishment for nonresponsiveness to financial opinion is by no means inevitable. Hence lenders develop an interest in the personalities and loyalty of executive leadership. And because corporate autonomy is an essential part of the structure of modern capitalist enterprise, a responsible executive with experience in leadership and knowledge of the industrial atmosphere is essential. The executive must be given discretionary decision-making power, since bankers could not expect to decide the best course of a nonfinancial company. For this reason, lenders must become expert at judging the reliability and quality of corporate leadership. Thomas Labrecque, president of Chase Manhattan, summarized this concern: "Part of lending is knowing the management of the company you're lending to. Not everything is numbers" (*New York Times*, April 5, 1981: 22).

The importance of responsive officers reveals both the validity and the error in managerial theory. The contradiction between outside domination and managerial autonomy focuses on the choice of chief executives and magnifies the importance of leadership. A maverick who obtains profits at the expense of other industries, who squanders precious investment capital, or who undertakes (even profitable) expansion into already saturated markets can produce economic havoc before any effective counter can be generated. Early removal or refusal to fund incompetent or unreliable executives can prevent disruption and economic difficulty later on; careful recruitment to top positions can forestall later ousters, crises, or bankruptcies. And because lenders are careful about evaluating corporate leadership, corporate leadership has become extremely protective of its standing with the financial community.

The evaluation of leadership is, of course, intertwined with the evaluation of corporate performance. Even if lenders are forced to rescue a company or finance a new enterprise, however, they can insist on the removal of executives who lack their confidence. Thus, even when bankers are constrained to renegotiate loans, corporate leadership may not be protected. As a consequence, an important concern of chief executives is the opinion lenders hold of them: "the only thing that really counts is how well the company is doing, and what the investment community thinks of its management" (chief executive officer of large firm, quoted in Mace, 1971: 91).

We argued in chapter 2 that outside control of corporations depends upon a chief executive who creatively complies with the controllers' policies, using the discretion of his or her office to implement and not sabotage the overarching plan. The ongoing evaluation of industrial leadership by financial firms provides a massive incentive for creative compliance, given the protection banks offer their trusted clients. This principle was expressed by a top executive at Crocker National, who referred to "obligations to long standing customers" even if the loans to them were "unproductive" (Business Week, Nov. 5, 1979: 91).

"It's naive to look at (interest) rates in the abstract," says John W. Ingraham, senior vice-president and member of the credit policy committee at Citibank. Bankers stress the borrower's overall relationship with the bank in pricing decisions. (Business Week, Sept. 1, 1980: 66)

The personal network that emerges from the structural relations among large firms is an important decision-making resource. When companies, especially financial firms, exercise discretion that will create systemic constraints, they must assess the most accurate information and best judgments. The many imponderables in such decision making are reduced greatly by personal knowledge of those who will implement or respond to these actions, and they are further reduced by the informal and formal access to these individuals before options are chosen. Ultimately, the shape and content of executive loyalty is the major determinant of discretionary decision making. Thus, the focus upon leadership evaluation produces the most subtle and effective form of hegemonic leadership: responsiveness to bank opinion without overt disciplinary constraint or intervention. This in turn reinforces information sources from which emerge a developed information-gathering apparatus (see chapter 6 for a discussion of the crucial role interlocks play in this process). This mass of information further develops lender hegemony, since financiers can then offer nonfinancial firms expert advice on investment opportunities. This informational function complements the leverage over corporate behavior that derives from primary control of capital flows and provides a nonantagonistic occasion for financial consultation in corporate planning.

The structure of constraint and the application of discretion combine to give shape to the policies of the corporate world. The hegemony banks exercise, however, remains problematic. Violation of corporate good citizenship occurs with some regularity, but it is mediated by the risks involved in such actions. The rules of corporate conduct, then, serve as a middle ground between bank intervention and corporate autonomy. And adherence to these rules makes financial hegemony part of the everyday process of corporate life rather than an episodic influence on economy.

Financial Hegemony and Social Process

The rules of corporate conduct produce regular patterns of corporate behavior. Broad economic developments that appear as reflections of market logic are frequently shaped by ongoing hegemonic decision making. This dissociation between appearance and dynamics is nicely illustrated by the role of the United States in the upheavals in Poland in 1980 and 1981.

The Polish crisis began as an apparently classic confrontation between the East and West, with the United States supporting rebellious workers against the Polish and Soviet governments. This perception was, in fact, inaccurate. The business ties that had arisen in the 1970s between Poland and Western banks had created profound economic contradictions between Western business and the demands of the Polish workers. These contradictions help to explain many paradoxes in the United States during the crisis.

Despite the anti-Soviet posture of United States foreign policy, Secretary of State Muskie told the press when Solidarity began its major protests that the United States would "refrain from any words or actions" (*New York Times*, Aug. 30, 1980: 1) that might be seen as provocative. American business was even more restrained. Some financial leaders suggested that:

> Soviet intervention could aid Poland's credit position. Both the Communist authorities and the capitalist bankers recognize a convergence of interest in stability—so much so that one Western banker . . . said that if the Russians actually did intervene in Poland, the nation's creditworthiness might actually increase. (*New York Times*, Aug. 31, 1980: 3.1)

This ironic harmony between United States banks and Soviet interventionism was the outcome of a series of decisions made over a ten-year period by large American and European banking institutions, decisions that determined the shape and context of American involvement overseas in the 1970s and early 1980s. The story begins in 1967, with a First National City Bank business prospectus that was so successful it propelled Citibank past Chase Manhattan into the role as the world's premier financial firm.[10]

This report has become a landmark document in the history of banking because it predicted a great many of the developments of the 1970s, most particularly financial expansion into the Third World.

Citibank had opened offices in many foreign countries during the early 1960s, but after the 1967 report it attempted to make itself into an "international bank, rather than a bank with international presence" (*Business Week*, Nov. 7, 1977: 64). During the 1970s, overseas activities accounted for 70% of the company's profits; in 1977 they reached a peak of 82%. The results made Walter Wriston, chair of Citicorp, the most respected businessman in the world: he "turned Citibank into a global financial department store—an accomplishment likely to win him a place in the annals of banking along with such titans as J. P. Morgan and A. P. Gianini, the creator of Bank of America" (Egan, 1980: 33).

Among the most active areas of foreign lending were loans to less developed countries (Poland is considered an LDC). By the late 1970s, 30% of Citicorp's profits came from such investments. This commitment was particularly significant because it illustrates the process of bank decision making and demonstrates how this decision making conditioned, delimited, and imposed itself upon other institutions. During the period 1967–1974 loan consortia, organized by Citicorp and other New York money market banks, sponsored a variety of loans that determined the profile of the economic development of LDCs and the nature of American business involvement in these countries.

Two basic principles were enunciated in the 1967 prospectus. First, careful consideration of the overall economic and political situation (called "risk assessment") in each country would allow a judgment as to the borrowing capacity of that country's economy. This policy evolved into a set of informally enforced lending limitations for each American international bank (Group of Thirty, 1982). It thus provided the guidelines for foreign investments by multinationals and constrained industrial investment within boundaries that suited bank interest. Second, to protect itself from social instability and possible expropriation, Citibank attempted to maximize the number of loans made to local subsidiaries of multinational corporations and to minimize the number of loans made directly to governments or to locally owned industrial firms. In this way, if problems developed within a particular country the multinational parent firm could still be held accountable for repayment of loans (Business Week, Nov. 7, 1977: 66). (This doctrine had little utility in Eastern European countries, where there was little opportunity for private investment.)

In 1969 there was $4.6 billion in outstanding loans to less developed countries. By 1974 the figure had risen to $14.7 billion, an increase of 220%. Most of this increase took the form of private loans, just as Citicorp had advocated. These had begun at $1.7 billion (30% of the total) and risen to $8.4 billion (51% of the total), an increase of 400% (Hancock, 1980: 287).

The oil shortages of 1973–74 produced economic and political crises in many LDCs. The industries that had begun to develop in these countries, the transportation systems that serviced them, and the cities that had become increasingly dependent on various forms of mechanized activity all required a constant flow of oil. As oil prices doubled and redoubled, enormous pressure was placed upon the economies of these countries. They needed to renegotiate existing loans and to borrow more money to finance their survival. The multinational banks, led by the New York money market, came to the rescue of these countries despite considerable risk and substantial criticism from various observers. Walter Wriston justified the rescues on the basis of the profitability of the loans and on broader political grounds: "If the commercial banks had not financed the LDCs," he told Business Week, "the world would have exploded" (Nov. 7, 1977: 68). Bank decision making, therefore, was based on the most general political-economic principles: "No corporation can be healthy in a sick society" (Egan, 1980: 35), Wriston declared.

Because these rescues led to an even deeper commitment, the banks became deeply involved in the financing and the survival of the economies of the Third World, including an increasing number of Eastern European countries. Here we see the hegemonic force of financial decision making. The loan limits set by the banks represented available capital for various countries. The favoritism offered to multinational firms provided incentives for American investment. Each country's need to repay existing debts led to the development of export industries that attracted still other international firms. A multitude of American and European companies were therefore drawn into the process. Phillips Brothers and other grain traders, for example, began handling and organizing large agricultural ventures. Investment banks, enticed by large fees, became consultants to Third World governments seeking loans and refinancing.

The developing interdependence between Western capitalism and the Third World entrapped both sides. By the late 1970s, Citicorp was netting 30% of its overall profits from LDC loans, a proportion large enough to create structural dependence. Chase reached 30% by 1979, and even Chemical, the least involved, by 1980 derived about 15% of its profits from Third World loans (Egan, 1980). On the other hand, the LDCs developed a growing dependence on imported goods, imported capital, and imported oil. Together with the constantly escalating price of fuel, this dependence produced a continuing crisis in the late 1970s. By this time there was no longer a real choice for the European and American financiers; their actions were highly constrained. As loans came due they had to be renegotiated, since default might actually threaten the lenders' solvency. The banks agreed to these rollovers because refusal could produce borrower default and the loss of the entire investment. "Banks are in so deep in LDC debt that there may be no way out except to lend more money to repay existing debt" (Business Week, Nov. 7, 1977: 67). The impossibility of sudden withdrawal from LDC loans produced a new policy: banks began treating these countries in much the same way that they treat crisis corporations (see chapter 4).

The banks therefore intervened into the internal affairs of countries and attempted to set policies that would generate sufficient cash flow to repay the debt. The "first public showdown with the international banking community" (New York Times, May 31, 1978: D11) occurred in Peru. This involved debt rollover as well as a $54 million loan to Southern Peru Copper Corporation, 53% owned by Asarco, a major American mining company. The banks refused to lend the additional money to complete a $750 million project, designed to increase copper production for export, until the Peruvian government drastically revised its taxing policy. The government was taxing the exports of Southern Peru and using the proceeds to subsidize the purchase of food imports for poor people. The lenders, led by Chase, insisted that the tax be eliminated so that the entirety of foreign credits gained through the sale of this copper could be used for debt financing. The food subsidies were eliminated, wage controls were instituted, and three left-wing cabinet members were expelled from the government.

Many observers commented that the banks' "passing judgment on Peru's economic performance raises troublesome questions about foreign business interference in the affairs of a sovereign state" (Business Week, March 27, 1977: 117). The lenders insisted, however, that "they did not interfere in Peru's affairs," that "the Peruvian authorities independently decided how they would make themselves creditworthy" (ibid). This defense is supported by scholarly evidence (Stallings, 1982), but it hardly lessens the significance of the events. It only demonstrates that in some circumstances structural constraint (the withdrawal of credit) can determine government actions as effectively as decision-making intervention (that is, overt dictation of policy). In certain circumstances, therefore, governments are as susceptible to financial hegemony as are corporations.

By 1980 banks became much more comfortable in their role as policymakers in the Third World and often resorted to overt intervention. Though they were constrained to renegotiate LDC loans, they became adept at extracting desired concessions. During Brazilian negotiations in 1980, a local banker commented:

> We are witnessing a big poker game. Deep in his heart, Delfin Netto (the Brazilian Planning Minister) knows that the United States banks cannot do anything but roll over the debt due next year. On the other hand, the banks know that Delfin Netto, for all his confidence, is churning inside over whether he is going to raise the billions of dollars needed. (New York Times, Dec. 8, 1980: D3)

Eventually Brazil agreed to reduce growth and to honor bank-defined fiscal discipline.

In South Korea, all new funds were refused for two years owing to political instability while banks reviewed conditions and developed a set of financial guidelines for the country. The Nicaraguan revolution produced a long period of negotiation over a wide range of government policies before new loans were considered. When the Manley government in Jamaica refused to accept certain loan conditions, the banks cut the flow of capital, deepened the ongoing economic and political crisis, and openly declared their support for the opposition political party. When the incumbent was defeated, they promptly renegotiated the loans at much better terms for themselves, though this meant increased austerity for the already desperate general population.

Bank intervention during this period generally pressed for two policies: fiscal discipline and increased exports (New York Times, April 21, 1980: D7). Fiscal discipline implied harnessing the maximum amount of resources to debt repayment, even at the expense of food imports or subsidies to living standards. Increased exports meant the further development of extractive and plantation industries in an attempt to increase the amount of foreign trade and hence increase cash for debt repayment. Such policies typically led to increased dependency on erratic world markets and to unbalanced economic development (Frank, 1966; Evans, 1979; Magdoff, 1978). In short, the banks' policies for these countries have become a force for increasing poverty and aggravating an already desperate economic dependency.

Poland, despite its advanced industrial base and its important economic ties to the Soviet Union, developed a similar profile of financial dependency between 1970 and 1980. It borrowed $20 billion from Western banks, all of which was due to be repaid by 1984. Even before the workers' revolt, the general consensus in American banking was that such repayment was virtually impossible, thus demonstrating the fallibility of financial decision making. In the spring of 1980 a delegation of Western bankers, following the pattern established in other LDCs, went to Poland to renegotiate the debt. Fortune (Sept. 20, 1980) reported the stance of the banks:

> They wanted Poland to stop investing hard currency in industries such as farm machinery that couldn't earn their own keep in foreign exchange, and . . . they hammered hard at the Polish pricing system, particularly for food, under which the prices for goods like sugar and meat were kept far below market levels, at an annual cost to the Polish government of more than $6 billion. (p. 125)

The food subsidy system the bankers wanted abolished was a particularly important feature of the Polish welfare state. The removal of subsidies meant that many workers could no longer afford to feed their families.

Soon after this meeting, the Polish government announced the removal of many subsidies for staple foods in order to repay debt more quickly. This announcement triggered the first large workers' strike and initiated the period of protracted struggle in Poland. Though bank intervention was certainly not the only cause of this wave of rebellion, the lenders' role—"a combination alter ego and financial policeman of Poland's government" (Fortune, Sept. 22, 1980: 128)—was considerable.

The role of major banks in Poland was parallel to their previous interventions in other countries. In Poland—as in Peru, Brazil, Jamaica, and elsewhere[11]—the lenders pressed for increased exports and decreased food subsidies so that debts could be repaid more quickly. Such policies undermine living standards (at least in the short term) and are therefore opposed by common citizens. In Poland this opposition developed into a major rebellion. The ambivalent actions of the United States government are explained by a contradiction: tangible support for the workers could have led to a default on loans and economic catastrophe for American and European banks. The United States government therefore could not offer such support. Ultimately, the policy of the United States government in the early 1980s was determined by the actions of lenders, which brought about a $20 billion dependence on the successful defeat of Solidarity.[12]

American involvement in Poland took a significant turn in early 1982—after the initial strikes had produced Solidarity, the national trade union; after a series of successful protests by Polish workers had led to many economic concessions; after these concessions had led to concessions by Western leaders; after repeated threats of Soviet military intervention (quietly applauded by Western banks) had failed to control the insurgency; after a year of martial law had finally quelled the movement; and after it became patently clear that Poland's disrupted economy could not possibly repay its massive debt (or even the interest) in the early 1980s. At that time the American government, in a particularly anti-Soviet period, nevertheless refused to declare Poland in default, despite the prospect that such an action could potentially undermine the economic and political viability of the Polish government. Instead, the United States government chose to pay American banks millions of dollars owed to them by Poland, thus protecting both the banks and the Polish government from fiscal crisis. This act, defended as economically necessary in light of the huge investment in Poland and

America's economic interdependence with Europe, brought the United States government full circle. Though its ideological stance remained anti-Soviet and it continued, rhetorically at least, to support the insurgency in Poland, its policies had become fully consonant with the interests of the Polish government.

Investments in LDCs, in general, came full circle when a combination of overproduction, conservation efforts, and worldwide recession threatened crude oil prices. Despite the fact that the high cost of oil had been a major ingredient in the inflationary spiral that had gutted the American economy, American business and political leadership sought to maintain price levels. This apparent paradox reflected the massive debt of Mexico ($80 billion) and several other oil-producing countries. Lower prices would have meant massive defaults and consequent financial crises among major American lenders. The importance of these institutions to the American economy made it necessary to maintain inflated and economically catastrophic price schedules (*Business Week*, Sept. 6, 1982: 80f.; *New York Times*, Dec. 17–25, 1982: D1).

The lenders' decisions throughout the 1970s thus conditioned and constrained the actions of a broad spectrum of other actors. Financial institutions, by directing capital into LDCs, produced and directed the involvement of nonfinancial companies in these countries. This matured into an overarching pattern of American economic involvement in the Third World and led to a whole host of new involvements when defaults threatened Third World governments enmeshed in the nexus of bank domination. Ultimately the United States government experienced the constraint of financial hegemony.

The 1967 Citicorp prospectus did not include a vision of what would occur. Initial involvement was intensified by an oil crisis that was not foreseen. The threat of insurrectionary explosions forced another critical choice in 1973–74. The impending bankruptcy of LDC governments imposed yet another problem in the late 1970s. This was not a "grand scheme" fully executed; it was the summation of many smaller decisions into a major policy profile.

The resulting policy, however episodically it developed, nevertheless carried the sort of legislative force we normally associate with sovereigns. This is the hallmark of hegemonic leadership. The decisions made by the executives at Citicorp and other financial firms constrained the choices of a wide range of institutions.

As the economies of LDCs became dependent upon the newly developing industries, the decisions over capital flows—especially the threat of decreased investment—became crucial to their ongoing economic viability. Since economic and political viability are so intimately connected, the political life of the Third World became intertwined with decisions over capital flows. Ultimately, political policies such as the continuation of food subsidies and the alleviation of dependence on exports became subject to the constraints imposed by capital-flow decision making. The interests of the citizens of client countries were, at least part of the time, subordinated to the interests of international lenders.

The economic viability of the banks themselves became wedded to successful imposition of bank interest on client countries. This carried vast political implications for the United States government, since it is constrained to maintain a healthy national economy. This led to a defense of bank interest, even when this defense involved acceptance of Polish martial law, support for South African apartheid, or a host of other antidemocratic foreign policies. It also implied support to Chrysler's management against the interests of Chrysler's workers and customers (Yago and Schwartz, 1981), and a host of internal policies that nurtured lending institutions to the detriment of the public interest.

Lenders rarely achieve this level of coordination, but when it does occur it is almost always achieved by capital-flow decision making. The interests of bankers do not always contradict the interest of the corporate community, but when such contradictions occur they remain unresolved or else find resolution in financial hegemony. Coordinated actions produced by financial hegemony do not always produce dire results for American and foreign publics, but a substantial proportion of the social problems we face are produced or aggravated by such actions. Financial hegemony is a major force in American business, and it is a major source of economic and political pathology.

Conclusion

Relationships among financial institutions place the money market commercial banks at the focal point of the financial structure. They are therefore the locus of decision making over the direction of capital flows in the American economic system. As chapter 3 suggested, the decisions made in these institutions are modulated by decision making of regional banks and the largest life insurance companies. They are further modified by the constrained decisions of nonfinancial companies.

The asymmetry in relationships between financial and nonfinancial firms is not always in evidence. Industrials typically enunciate their own policies and pursue them with considerable autonomy. Hegemonic relationships create limited coordination and provide an assortment of signals about financial opinion and perferred financial policy. In many situations, industrial leadership can ignore these signals with relative impunity and pursue an independent course. However, if such action creates difficulty for lenders (as in the A&P case), the firm's leadership runs the risk of financial intervention or nonsupport in capital raising. In many instances (e.g., the oil industry), nevertheless, corporate leaders successfully avoid any consequences for violating corporate norms.

This institutional independence does not, however, create reciprocal, mutually co-respective relationships between financial and nonfinancial firms. Only financial institutions can plan policies that embody, organize, and compel the cooperation of other sectors. Only financial institutions could have directed and channeled long-term expansion into the Third World. Only finance institutions could orchestrate the expansion of the oil tanker industry. This sort of leadership that can coordinate the activities of diverse sectors of the economy—however broadly—resides only with financial institutions, because only they control the flow of investment capital.

Those who lead these institutions are therefore politicians in the broadest sense:

> The active politician is a creator, an awakener, but he neither creates from nothing nor moves in the turbid void of his own desires and dreams. He bases himself on effective reality. (Gramsci, 1957: 163)

6 Interlocking Directorates

> We find in this practice banking institutions, through membership on the board of directors, controlling the fiscal policies and, indeed, we may say, the business policy of railroads, manufacturing companies, and commercial enterprises.
>
> Max Pam, *Harvard Law Review,* 1913

The practice of interlocking directorates, the sharing of a director by two or more corporations, has provided an important data source for the study of business behavior during the past decade.[1] Although studies of corporate interlocks originated in the early part of the twentieth century, the recent development of sophisticated methods for analyzing interlock networks has stimulated interest in the field and has generated evidence that questions traditional interpretations of the meaning of director exchanges.[2]

Until the early 1970s most social critics assumed that the presence of an officer or other representative of one company on the board of directors of another reflected a control or a coordination relationship between the two firms.[3] The outside board member was viewed as a reflection of his or her firm's influence on the host company. Most often the interlocks were assumed to symptomize either controlling stock or lending relationships or collusion between the two corporations. Interlocks themselves were not the primary instrument of control or coordination, but a reflection of such activity.

Recent research has replaced this assumption with a variety of viewpoints about the content of director interlocks. They are now seen as indicative of one of several types of relationships: control, nonhierarchical coordination, communication networks, personal networks among corporate leaders, and inner-circle groupings. It is now clear that these many different types of relationships exist, side by side, in the interlock network.

In earlier chapters, we developed the concept of financial hegemony and examined the types of structural constraints posed by capital-flow decisions. In the remainder of this book, we support our theory with data on interlocking directorates. We argue that, as earlier research assumed, interlocks sometimes trace control relationships and that, as recent studies have demonstrated, some interlocks reflect dyadic relationships between companies. An overwhelming proportion, however, do not trace specific ties among corporations. The common attribute of all director exchanges is that they are part of the discretionary decision-making apparatus of the corporate world and hence are best understood as instruments of discretion within a system defined by structural constraint. In chapters 1 and 2, we suggested that the debate over the structure of control of the corporate sector could be clarified by distinguishing between access to discretionary decision making and the alteration of structural constraint. In this chapter we argue that this same distinction provides a framework for understanding the admittedly diverse phenomena represented by interlocking directorates. To do this, we turn to a consideration of the meaning of director exchanges.

Interlocks That Trace Control

When interlocking directorates are analyzed as reflections of control relationships, either strategic control or operational management is at issue, and three power bases are typically identified: stockholding, lending, or customer/supplier leverage. Even given this limited conceptualization, however, not all of these conditions inevitably yield control; not all control relationships involve interlocks, and not all interlocks suggest or reflect control. Thus, although interlocks are sometimes indicative of dyadic control, they are neither necessary to nor sufficient for its existence. That interlocking directorates occasionally, but not consistently, reflect structural relations of this sort has undoubtedly contributed to the confusion surrounding interlock content; the changing methods of control have confounded issues further.

Historically, individuals or families with ownership interests in multiple companies could obtain board positions in those firms and use those directorships to coordinate the activities of the companies involved. In 1936, for example, Vincent Astor sat on the boards of the Illinois Central Railroad, Western Union, International Merchant Marine, and at least seven other firms in which his family held interests (Myers, 1936: 175). The interlocks he created traced common ownership; they also traced the strategic control of the Astor family.

This form has declined in importance over time. A more common phenomenon today is intercorporate stockholding (in which one firm holds a common interest in another), either as an expression of mediated family interest or as strictly interorganizational control.[4] Many small industrial empires have been constructed in this way and sustained over considerable numbers of years. Victor Posner of Sharon Steel,[5] Elmer Singleton of Teledyne,[6] Saul Steinberg of Leasco and Reliance Industries,[7] and Charles Mellon Evans of H. K. Porter and the Crane Company[8] illustrate this pattern.

Stockholdings of over 10% are often "covered" by a director exchange, typically through the election of a top executive of the stockholding company onto the board of the target firm. At times these interlocks produce links among the controlled corporations, thus creating a small network of interrelated companies. In the 1960s, for example, the Kaiser family owned over 60% of the stock of Kaiser Industries, which in turn controlled at least 30% of Kaiser Aluminum, 35% of Kaiser Cement, and 50% of Kaiser Steel. In 1962, these relationships were traced by seventeen interlocks among Kaiser Industries and the three partially owned companies and sixteen interlocks among Kaiser Aluminum, Kaiser Cement, and Kaiser Steel.[9]

These empires may or may not engage in coordinated action. Teledyne has shown very little interest in the internal affairs of the companies in which it holds controlling blocks. Sharon Steel, on the other hand, has systematically attempted to reorganize or redirect corporate policy. These reorganizations have involved both director interlocks and the expulsion of top executives.

While family or interorganizational stockholding is a potential source of intercorporate power and coordination, the existence of such links and the interlocks that trace them is not a guarantee that coordination will in fact take place. Moreover, even if stockholder control were consistently traced by director interlocks, concentrated stockholding by nonfinancial firms or wealthy families in multiple corporations is not commonplace, while interlocks among the largest corporations are pervasive. Hence, only a very small proportion of total director exchanges would be indicative of these types of control relationships.

Institutional stockholding, another potential form of stock control, is sometimes traced by interlocks between the managing bank and the held company. In his survey of bank trust departments, Kotz (1978: 122) found that 14% of blocks of between 5% and 10% (six of forty-two) and 60% of 10% or larger holdings (six of ten) were reflected by interlocks. This has been the only systematic effort to assess the role of interlocks in trust department stockholding, and further analysis is certainly necessary. We note, however, that there is much controversy over the role of institutional stockholding as a mechanism for the strategic control of a corporation (see chapter 4), and the use of these interlocks for intervention or control has never been investigated in a systematic way.

Lending relationships are the second major source of control interlocks. When a nonfinancial firm becomes highly leveraged, when it has a large amount of debt, or when its financial condition deteriorates, lending institutions may place representatives on the borrowing firm's board. The representatives attempt to ensure that problems that endanger repayment or violate covenants are addressed quickly and efficiently. The lending institutions may be uneasy about the leadership of the borrowing firm, or they may feel that the degree of their investment necessitates ongoing input into the operational management of the corporation. The interlock thus may be a symptom of important alterations of policy for the host corporation, or it may be a sign of banks' latent power to impose their will. Both Penn Central and Southern Pacific, during their crisis periods in the 1960s, had many creditor representatives on their boards.

Although financial representation on industrial boards may reflect lender interest, bankers are attractive candidates for outside directorships for many neutral reasons, including their expertise, prestige, and access to capital. Hence, while some interlocks reflect lender control, many bankers accept directorships in noninterventionist contexts, and only a small number of these ties are valid indicators of control relationships.

A third form of intercorporate control that may be traced by interlocks is vendor intervention. In certain instances a firm may have a single dominant customer, or it may purchase from a single dominant supplier. This implies enormous potential for strategic control, and interlocks may become an instrument for coordination or surveillance. Globe-Union, the largest manufacturer of automotive batteries, for example, sold about 50% of its product to Sears in the 1970s and elected a Sears representative to its board. When a possible acquisition by U.V. Industries was considered, Sears threatened to take its battery purchases elsewhere, thus preventing the merger (Business Week, Jan. 23, 1978: 27–28). Such dependencies, like other control relationships, are traced by interlocks, only some of the time. Though Sears was the dominant customer of Whirlpool in the 1960s, it did not maintain interlocks with that firm. Similarly, though Budd Company sold 40% of its output to Ford Motor Company, Ford representation was absent from Budd's board. Hence in this case, too, dyadic power relations are imperfectly traced by interlocks, and many interlocks have little to do with control either in terms of operational management or in its strategic form.

That interlocks do not regularly trace control is consistent with the theory of financial hegemony.[10] Whereas the traditional models of bank control assume strategic control of nonfinancial corporations by banks and insurance companies—control thought to be reflected and institutionalized by director exchanges—financial hegemony asserts influence over corporate decision making by altering the environment in which the firm operates. This alteration does not require direct contact with corporate management as strategic control would; instead it assumes a process in which executives are forced to respond to a change in the operating climate of the corporation. Rather than adjustment based on instructions from a controlling body, managerial decisions are guided by the availability of options given the structural conditions under which the company must operate. Direct intervention by an outside director attempting to determine policy, or pressure from a majority stockholder, rarely can alter structural constraint. Instead, the strategic control of this sort only affects the strategies for managing an environment. Structural constraint defines available options; strategic control invades the discretionary decision-making process and hence is effective in forcing management to select a particular response to existing conditions.

When interlocking directorates are used to study business behavior, then, they are measures of one component of that behavior: discretionary decision making. The many examples of interlocks that reflect control relationships show this aspect of corporate behavior. Although in certain circumstances interorganizational or family stockholding may be an effective mechanism for altering the constraint within which a company operates, this does not happen often, and the availability of resources with which to accomplish this is situationally specific. If the Kaiser group transferred resources among included firms, for example, this could potentially alter the structural constraint of a particular company within the group. The effectiveness of this is limited, however. For example, no amount of intervention could increase the demand for steel, the most relevant variable in the environment of Kaiser Steel. Input from Kaiser Industries could determine strategies for managing a depressed market, but it could not alter the market itself.

To make sense out of interlocks, then, we must interpret them in the following way. Director exchanges, at best, trace attempts to control or intervene in the management of corporate discretion. They never reflect hegemonic relations, although occasionally they reflect attempts by one firm to control another company's response to the structural constraints imposed by hegemonic relationships. This pertains to the various types of control that interlocks reflect. When institutional stockholding is formalized by a director interlock, the link may represent the potential for institutional invasion into the discretionary decision-making process of the held firm. Stock dumping by bank trust departments can, but does not always, alter the structural constraint of the target firm. When constraint fails or does not adequately limit the options of the corporation at issue, strategic control may be attempted, and the presence of a director on the board of that company facilitates the attempt.

A similar description applies to lender relationships. The availability of capital conditions the options of corporations and industries and, in broad strokes, tunes the environment in which companies operate. Although constraints of this sort are typical, at certain points in the corporate life cycle, and often in times of crisis, lenders reinforce constraint by intervening in the discretionary decision-making process of a debt-ridden firm. This intervention does not alter the constraint created by capital-flow decisions: it is an attempt to control reactions to constraint.

Similar constraints operate in certain customer/supplier relationships. The effectiveness of this process was demonstrated by the auto industry example explored in chapter 1. In times of need, the hegemonic position of dominant customers or dominant suppliers can be augmented by direct intervention into the discretionary decision-making process of the dependent corporation. This may be done via a representative on the weaker firm's board or by an alternative form of direct pressure. The point to be underscored, however, is that, in the absence of input into the discretionary component of corporate policy setting, the effect of the hegemonic position of the dominant firm continues; decision making is still confined to available options, and the process is limited by the constraints created by the behavior of the dominant company. Even pervasive interlocking between customers and suppliers would not alter this condition; it might reflect, however, a mechanism for intervention into the discretionary component of corporate decision making.

Structural Ties without Dominance

Co-optational interlocks occur when a corporation invites onto its board the leader of a company on which it is dependent. In doing so, the host corporation attempts to co-opt the invited firm into pursuing a more favorable policy. A New York Times article (Nov. 4, 1980: D2) provided a clear expression of this motive: "The election of Sullivan S. Olayan, a prominent Saudi businessman, to the board of Mobil Corporation . . . may further Mobil's interests in Saudi Arabia."

Persuasive interlocks are a close cousin of co-optational interlocks. A company may (if it can) place a representative on another firm's board in an attempt to persuade that company to adopt favorable policies (Pennings, 1980). The same interlock can be both co-optational and persuasive: the host firm attempts to co-opt the sending company into a positive stance toward itself, while the sending firm hopes its representative will influence the host in the other direction. In a nonantagonistic situation, both could succeed. In a situation of conflict of interest, one, both, or neither might succeed.

Resource dependency theorists have amassed an impressive body of evidence demonstrating the existence of potentially persuasive and co-optive interlocks.[11] There can be no remaining doubt that corporate interdependencies are sometimes traced by interlocks, although the effectiveness of these links has not been demonstrated. Moreover, it is clear that this is only one of several possible motives for interlocking. This point is reinforced by Burt, Christman, and Kilburn (1980), who found that sectors with substantial interdependencies interlocked about 85% of the time, while those sectors with low interdependencies interlocked 60% of the time. This suggests that at most 25% of all interlocks are motivated by interdependence. Findings of Palmer (1983a,b) and Ornstein, (1982), to be discussed below, suggest that the figure is probably much lower.

Hence, as in the case of interlocks that trace control, ties that reflect resource dependencies are present in the interlock system, although many instances of interdependence are not formalized by a director exchange, and many interlocks are not indicative of resource relationships. Moreover, co-optational and persuasive interlocks, like control ties, are attempts to influence the discretion of the target corporation rather than altering its profile of constraint. Input into discretionary decision making in this case, however, is aimed at affecting the constraints within which the co-opting firm operates. Co-optational and persuasive interlocks, then, influence the discretionary decision-making process of the other company, which in turn affects the environment of (and therefore the constraints upon) the co-opting firm.

Communication Networks and Inner-Circle Groupings

Interlocking directorates provide enormous potential for information exchange. The logic of this is apparent: when a top executive of an outside firm sits on the board of a particular company, he or she obtains information about that company. At the same time the director gives advice and information useful to the host corporation. In some cases the information is used to benefit one of the firms, even at the expense of another. In his role as director of McGraw-Hill, for example, Richard Smith, president of American Express, was privy to the most confidential details of the publisher's financial situation. When American Express began searching for an acquisition, it decided to tender a bid for McGraw-Hill. As the target firm pointed out in its documents opposing the takeover, it was impossible for Smith to ignore his intimate knowledge of McGraw-Hill's financial condition in forming his decision to acquire the company (*Fortune*, Nov. 6, 1978: 95–106).[12] Although examples of dyadic communication of this sort exist, many argue that information about the specifics of a corporation's profile is not of interest, but that broad business and economic information is the valued prize of multiple board memberships. Useem (1982) quotes a British executive in this regard: "I would be totally worried if I found I was ever getting specific information of value to [my company]. I would wash my young man's ears if I ever found anything of special interest to us from any company I am involved in" (p. 210).

Interlocks as component parts of a communication system, then, are gaining much attention and seem to be among the most interesting aspects of interlock content. Implicit in this approach is the recognition that dyadic relationships represent a variety of interfirm arrangements—control in its varying forms, resource dependencies, friendship networks, convenience, and the like—but that the conglomeration of motives produces a system of information as a source of power. Mokken and Stokman (1974) argue that firms at the center "of the communication network possess power by virtue of their position" (p. 30). Scott (1979: 100), incorporating findings of recent studies that found financial prominence in the interlock system, suggests that the large banks at the center of the network are focuses of information flows and that the ability to control these flows is a way of influencing corporate strategy. We argue below that control of information is not the primary source of financial hegemony. Rather, bank centrality in the network of interlocking directorates, which many researchers have identified and which we document in the chapters that follow, is the result of bank attempts to collect sufficient information to make decisions—discretionary decisions—about the direction of capital flows. The informational centrality that results from this process creates further structural constraints to which corporations are forced to respond. We view information, then, as the most important product of director exchanges, but this information is not a source of power in a traditional sense; it is a mechanism for identifying options in that part of bank decision making that is discretionary.

The second approach to interlocking directorates as a communication system concentrates on the question of elite cohesion and emphasizes the importance of multiple directors in reconciling differences of interest within the capitalist class (Useem, 1979, 1983; see also Domhoff, 1967, 1970, 1975, 1978). These directors, referred to as members of the inner group, are drawn from the wealthiest segment of society and from the ranks of the financial world. When unity is measured by social club membership, they are found to be more cohesive than the larger class of business leaders (Domhoff, 1967, 1970, 1975; Soref, 1976; Koenig and Gogel, 1981; Useem, 1978, 1983). Their interests—both directorate and investment—in several companies place them in a position to identify with the problems of diverse corporations and hence to generate policies reflecting a broad class interest.[13] Although from an organizational point of view multiple directors function primarily as a mechanism for maximizing a corporation's business scan or information collection, "the unplanned consequence of such interlocking directorates," Useem (1982: 211) suggests, "is the formation of a communication network that inevitably helps a segment of the corporate elite identify its members' shared political interests."

We agree with this analysis. We suggest, however, that the institutional function of interlocking directorates is more specific than a broad business scan. Instead, it is an information-collection system that forms the basis for managing corporate discretion. We further suggest that by viewing interlocks within the context of discretionary decision making, both on the dyadic level as mechanisms for managing discretion and on the network level as a system of information collection for managing discretion, we can make sense of the meaning of interlocking directorates and of the bank centrality found within the interlock network.

Interlocks as Personal Relationships

The interlocks thus far considered are assumed to reflect intercorporate relationships, either in a dyadic or a network form. Mace (1971) has maintained that this underlying structural assumption is largely incorrect, that interlocks do not typically reflect relationships among companies but are emanations of the social and business networks of the chief executive officer of the home firm. Though Mace accepted the existence of business connections traced by interlocks, he concluded that managerial domination implies that the board would reflect the power and discretion of the chief executive. Ultimately, in Mace's (1971) view, outside directors are drawn from among businessmen whose stature matches that of the host firm and who are personally compatible with the host chief executive. He notes that "criteria used in the selection of outside directors stressed descriptive words and phrases such as 'friendly,' 'sympathetic to management,' 'non-controversial,' and 'our kind of people'" (p. 108).[14] In extreme cases, choices appear to be almost frivolous:

> In a large midwestern company ... meetings were held quarterly and never lasted more than one hour. The outside board members were chairmen or presidents of well-known companies, and most of the outsiders shared the president's interest in golf. Board meetings consisted of a review of the financial results of the period, and the presentation of management's requests for approval of capital appropriations, which were automatically voted without any questions from the board. (Mace, 1971: 82)

In other cases, they seem to have little to do with narrow business concerns:

> Former Vice-President Walter F. Mondale and Robert S. Strauss, a factotum in the Carter White House, have joined

the board of Columbia Pictures Industries Inc. "It's the government in exile," cracks one Wall Street wit. They are friends of Herbert A. Allen and a Columbia shareholder. Their appointments reflect the influence of Allen, who becomes Columbia's chairman on July 1. (*Business Week*, May 11, 1981: 123)

Nevertheless, even Mace (1971) agrees that interlocks have some implications for corporate fortune. He accepts the possibility, for example, that outsiders may provide useful, perhaps crucial, business information (pp. 13–27). More important, he implies that the personal prestige of outsiders may have beneficial consequences for the company. An impressive board may facilitate loans, joint ventures, and other corporate activities. What he fails to see, and what Koenig and Gogel (1981) suggest, is the reverse possibility: that prestigious outsiders may infringe upon executive autonomy if they are dissatisfied with corporate policy:

The prestigious, socially well-connected outside director may have little or no financial power of his own within the company but still be able to harm or destroy a management team simply by quitting his "window dressing" position on the board, since to leave is to publicly accuse the firm of misbehaving. (Mace, 1971: 22–23)

Moreover:

If a couple of outside people with some prominence depart from the board of a company, it is not going to do the company any great commercial good in the eyes of the investment community, the commercial banking community, and all those guys. This starts putting a question mark around the company itself. There again, I think most management with much brains doesn't have directors leave for no good reason. You start getting write-ups in the financial magazines, a *Wall Street Journal* reporter calls, and it's just no good. The first thing you know a New York bank asks, "What's the problem here:" And maybe you owe them 10 million bucks. You've got lines of credit. This is bad. (Mace quoted in Koenig and Gogel, 1981: 45–46)

Although we do not have precise information on the frequency of such resignations, they certainly occur, and they helped trigger crises at Great Western United (*Business Week*, July 25, 1970: 24), Security National Bank (*New York Times*, Feb. 28, 1975: D4), and Becton-Dickinson (*Business Week*, Oct. 3, 1977: 40–41).[15] Thus, even when director selections are based on friendship networks, the placement of an outside director on a corporate board has a potential impact on the fortunes of the receiving company.

More important, however, is the contribution of these appointments to inner-circle groupings. Independent of the motivating factors behind director selections, the result of individual decisions is a larger network of interlocks that function as a communication system as described by Useem (1978, 1979, 1982) and others (see above), with multiple directors playing an important role in maintaining cohesion. Thus, even if individual appointments reflect friendship networks and personal ties among corporate executives, the result is the creation of numerous multiple directors and the formation of a larger system with important implications for corporate behavior.

The Role of Interlocks in the Corporate World

Although there has been much controversy over the meaning of interlocking directorates, it is becoming quite clear that some, but far from all, director exchanges reflect dyadic relationships between corporations. This was suggested in earlier sections of this chapter and is underscored by the findings of Palmer (1980, 1983a,b) and Ornstein (1982).

Despite the ambiguity in evaluating interlocks, it is possible to obtain rough estimates of the proportion of links that actually reflect dyadic ties of significant structural content. Palmer's work (1980, 1983b) systematically assesses these ratios for the United States. Ornstein's (1982) does so for the Canadian example. We concentrate on the United States studies. Palmer (1980, 1983a,b), applying logic developed by Koenig, Gogel, and Sonquist (1979), studied corporate response to the departure of individuals who created interlocks. Such "broken ties" occur if an individual who sits on multiple boards dies, retires, moves to another company, or takes a job outside business (most often in government). His or her departure from the board of one or both companies breaks the institutional link connecting them. Palmer argued that if the tie was structural—if it traced a control relationship, a co-optative or persuasive relationship, an ongoing coordinative relationship, or an important informational flow—the firms would act quickly to renew the link and therefore the relationship the link represented. If, on the other hand, the interlock reflected personal ties or executive convenience, it would not be renewed, since the recruitment pool for replacement would be quite different.

Palmer's results undermine a strict dyadic interpretation of interlocks. His three main findings were:

1. Interlocks created by executives of one firm who sat on the board of a second firm were renewed only 14% of the time. That is, about six of every seven executive interlocks did not appear to reflect ongoing dyadic relationships.
2. Interlocks created by individuals who were outside board members of both firms were renewed in very rare cases. These ties do not seem to trace dyadic ties of substance.
3. Multiple interlocks—two companies sharing more than one director—were renewed more regularly than single ties. Between 25% and 85% of such interlocks trace structural relations.

These results suggest that relatively few interlocks represent dyadic relationships between firms.[16] Although it is tempting to view this as support for Mace's position that interlocks are extensions of friendship networks and have little to do with intercorporate relationships, such an interpretation would ignore the overwhelming body of evidence accumulated recently in support of structural assumptions.[17] To make sense out of these diverse findings, then, we note that some interlocks represent strategic control, resource dependencies, dyadic communication relationships, and the like. Often interlocks reflect both structural and personal relationships simultaneously. In the late 1970s, for example, Laurence Rockefeller sat on Eastern Airlines' board, representing the Rockefeller family stock interest and expressing the personal ties between himself and chief executive Frank Borman (New York Times, Nov. 18, 1979: F3; Jan. 4, 1977: 37).

At times, the combination of the structural and the personal generates still other relationships. This is illustrated by the case of Harper Sibley of Stirling Homex, who joined Western Union's board because business relations had led to a friendship with Russell McFall, Western Union's chairman. There he met several other outside directors and formed business associations that led to joint ventures and additional interlocks (Fortune, Jan. 1975: 118–26, 130). In this instance, the personal and the business aspects were completely tangled.

Still other interlocks change in form over time. In the 1970s, for example, Genesco, controlled for five decades by the Jarman family, had representatives of First National Bank of Chicago and Equitable Life on its board. These interlocks were apparently examples of successful co-optation, since both financial firms were also major lenders. In early 1977, however, after four troubled years, the financial directors led in the ouster of Franklin Jarman and in the reorganization of the firm. Co-optational interlocks became instruments of bank intervention.[18]

Finally, some interlocks are established to cement dyadic relationships but eventually deteriorate. When this occurs the interlock can be broken, as in the case of the Grumman Corporation, which, in the early 1970s, maintained a combination of ties to Bankers Trust: Bankers Trust held 12% of Grumman stock; it participated in its lending consortium; it invited Grumman's chairman onto its board. When Grumman experienced business difficulty in 1972, the bank cut off its credit, and Chairman Towl resigned from the Bankers Trust board to avoid an "awkward" situation (Newsday, Jan. 19, 1975: 4, 24; New York Times, Jan. 14, 1975: F1). This, of course, is a tie we would not expect to be renewed even though it reflected a structural relationship between the two companies. In other instances, the symptomized relationship could change without a corresponding resignation. When the tie did eventually break, we would still not expect renewal.

These variations suggest that the same interlock may reflect a diverse set of personal and structural relationships and that not all structural ties would necessarily be renewed if broken. Moreover, when we consider interlocks in the context of discretionary decision making we would not expect stable dyadic pairings. The theory of bank hegemony argues that the behavior of large corporations is conditioned by the movement of capital into and out of companies, industries, and sectors. While the environment is defined by this movement of capital, individual companies retain options and alternatives for operational management within the constraints defined by capital-flow decisions. Day-to-day policies are carried out by internal management in attempts to maximize control, given available options. Interlocks that reflect control, resource dependency, dyadic communication, and so forth, are attempts to control or co-opt the discretionary strategies of another corporation. Since this process is dialectical, a change in the structure of constraint alters the options management may select, and a change in strategy of one firm may alter the structural constraints within which a second company operates. This suggests that the system is dynamic—that it changes—and that intervention into or co-optation of another corporation's decision-making process could have valuable results.

However, since structural constraint rather than strategic intervention is the major mechanism for coordination within the corporate world, the success of dyadic relationships is sporadic and subject to changes beyond the control of either firm. Thus, since the system is fluid and since changes in capital-flow decisions reverberate throughout the economic sector, the possibility that paired firms will maintain stable relationships is minimized. What was established for a particular purpose can become ineffective over time, and the likelihood of stable dyadic ties characterizing the interlock network is minimal. Hence, we are not surprised that a majority of interlocking directorates are not renewed when broken or do not represent substantive relationships between paired corporations.

At the same time, as we noted earlier, there are other motives for sending and receiving board members. The most compelling interpretation of the overall network created by the collection of individual reasons for and responses to director recruitment is a general communication system. Within this system, three different functions can be identified. First, on the level of the organization, Useem (1982) suggests that interlocking directorates maximize a corporation's business scan and hence offer a very useful device for general information collection. Second, in terms of upper-class cohesion, the same business scan is used by inner-group members to collect general information on economic and business conditions in order to evaluate alternatives and generate an overall class interest. Third, on the level of the network, corporations in the center of the system use this business scan to make decisions—discretionary decisions—about investment options, capital commitments, and the like. At the same time, information collection is carried out on three different levels in response to three different but overlapping sets of needs.

When we merge the relationships forming the interlock network, then, we find a system in which individual firms attempt to manage their discretion, either by influencing other corporations' postures toward them through co-optation or strategic control or through maximizing information collection. This set of interactions is overlaid by a larger system of communication exchange. At the center of this system is a set of organizations—financial institutions, as chapters 7–9 will demonstrate—and a set of multiple interlockers—inner group members, as Bonacich and Domhoff (1977), Useem (1978, 1979), Ratcliff (1979–80,1980a,b), Koenig, Gogel, and Sonquist (1979), and others have demonstrated. Financial institutions need the broadest scan, since they are involved in capital formation in all sectors of the business community. Although many lending outlets are determined by the structural constraints under which banks and insurance companies operate—sectoral growth and contraction, loan portfolio composition, and so on—the details of loan activity are part of the discretionary decision-making process of the institution. To make these decisions, current, sweeping information is necessary. Hence, the institutional function of interlocks is information collection. However, control of information is not the foundation upon which financial hegemony is built. Bank centrality in the interlock network is the result of the need to collect sufficient information to manage the financial discretion upon which their power is founded.

Inner-group members also need a broad business scan. Like banks and insurance companies, they are either personally or institutionally linked to corporations in all sectors of the economy. And as with the banks and insurance companies, their actions are limited by the structural constraints defining viable options. Nevertheless, within the system bounded by structural constraints, inner-group members make decisions—discretionary decisions—about investment profiles of firms with which they are affiliated, about personal investments, about broad strategies for maximizing capital as a whole. And for these decisions, broad business information is necessary. For inner-group members as well as financial institutions, therefore, interlocking directorates are crucial sources of information; information necessary to manage the discretionary decision-making process in which inner circle members are engaged. And as in financial institutions, information is not the source of inner-group power but a crucial resource in managing that power.

Finally, inner-group members and financial institutions use the same networks and overlapping affiliations for information collection. As Bearden (1982) has demonstrated, bank boards are dominated by multiple interlockers, and bank boards are rich arenas for information exchange. On the boards of major financial institutions, then, inner circle members collect and evaluate information that serves as important input into the discretionary decision-making process of both the inner circle as a group and the financial institutions themselves. Both are subject to structural constraints that define available options; decisions by one group may alter the constraints under which the other operates. At times the financial institutions and their board members need the same type of information. At other times the decisions to be made are on quite different topics. In general the inner group as a whole, and financial institutions as representatives of finance capital, work together with overlapping interests. Occasionally, individual members of the inner group may deviate from the collective pursuit, but in general there is consonance between the most active fraction of the capitalist class and the most effective allocator of resources in advanced capitalism.

7 The Structure of the Interlock System: The Meaning of Bank Centrality

> James Stillman made National City Bank ... a leader in financing of industry by attracting to his Board of Directors the heads of the greatest enterprises in the country. These men brought to his bank not only money for deposit, but they brought what the subtle Stillman prized even more, and that was their knowledge and their brains. At his board meetings Stillman learned, at first hand, the inside facts about every business in the country, and this priceless information gave him the key to all the mysteries of financing that lay at the bottom of his success, and at these meetings Stillman had for the asking the advice and counsel of the shrewdest businessmen in the land.
>
> Hans Morganthau, *All in a Lifetime*, p. 77

Since interlocking directorates are formed by a combination of institutional and individual actions, interpretations of interlock networks must encompass both the structural compulsions and the personal decisions that underlie them. Such interpretations, however, must avoid the temptation of reducing conclusions about overall patterns into a determinist assertion about the genesis of particular interlocks among a small set of specific corporations.

This caution, of course, does not undermine carefully developed analyses of the significance of interlocks as major corporate phenomena. In this chapter we offer a fresh interpretation of the role of interlocks in intercorporate affairs. We begin by outlining the shape of the network produced by directorate exchanges and interpreting its significance. In succeeding chapters, we will analyze particular aspects of the network, focusing upon the ways interlocks reflect and produce unity and cleavage in the corporate world.

We concentrate on four main results. First, major money market banks and insurance companies are the most heavily interlocked firms in American business. Second, these major financials are tied to the most important nonfinancial firms in the country; that is, large industrials are not structurally isolated from the financial community. Third, unlike banks, major industrial companies are not necessarily the most heavily interlocked nonfinancial firms; network centrality reflects an intense relationship with banks and not necessarily economic domination in an industrial sector. Finally, based upon these findings, we conclude that the interlock network is in large part a reflection of patterns of capital flow, and that interlocks facilitate decisions relating to the allocation of loan capital by supplying investment information to the financial world.

Our study of interlocking directorates encompasses every firm included in *Fortune* magazine's list of major companies in any year from 1962 to 1973. This includes not only those corporations that were important in the years of our study (1962 and 1966), but also those that rose to prominence in succeeding years. Using standard techniques, we identified all members of the board of directors for each firm in 1962 and 1966 and then determined every instance in which the same individual sat on the boards of two or more companies.[1]

Our results are consistent with other studies that found interlocks to be a major phenomenon in American corporate life.[2] Four patterns are by now familiar to specialists in this area. First, the average corporation interlocked ten times, about the same as in smaller samples collected since 1960.[3] This means that the leadership of the average firm participated in the affairs of ten other companies and interacted with the leaders of some one hundred additional firms in the process.

For all categories of corporations, larger companies interlocked more frequently than smaller firms (see also Pennings, 1980; Mintz and Schwartz, 1981a; Meussen and Cuyvers, 1984). This undermines the notion that as companies become large or dominant, they adopt a stance of splendid isolation (see, for example, Wright, 1979). Third, commercial banks and insurance companies interlocked much more frequently than nonfinancial firms. Banks, for example, averaged 25.1 interlocks, while industrials maintained an average of 8.8 ties.[4] This implies that the leadership of major financial institutions participates in the decision making of a vast number of firms and interacts with a substantial proportion of the American corporate elite.

Fourth, in 1962, 998 of 1,131 firms in our population were connected into a single continuous map; each of these 998 companies could reach every other company through a chain of shared directors. Moreover, the overwhelming majority of these chains had fewer than three links. None exceeded six links. Figure 7.1 illustrates the meaning of this finding. It shows Daniel Construction and First National Bank in Saint Louis, two economically unconnected companies. Charles E. Daniel, the chief executive office of Daniel Construction, sat on the board of Chemical Bank, whose chairman, Harold Helm, was an outside member of the Ralston Purina Board.

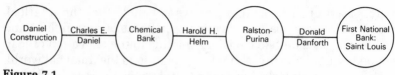

Figure 7.1

Donald Danforth, a Ralston Purina executive, was a member of the First National Bank board, thus completing a chain of three links connecting the two companies. Some heavily interlocked firms, such as Chemical Bank, had two-link chains to the vast majority of companies. This means that Chemical's leadership had personal contact (on the board of directors of a third company) with at least one member of the board of a vast majority of major corporations in America.

Although it is tempting to assume collusion and domination in this vast network, this would be quite exaggerated. As we indicated in chapter 6, both collusion and control certainly exist, but most interlocks cannot be interpreted in this way. The major significance of this intertwined business and personal network is its function as a crucial informational adjunct to capital-flow decision making.

To see this, we turn to a number of less well established results. Table 7.1 indicates that commercial banks send and receive interlocks more frequently than other types of corporations.[5] This is a subtle, yet critical finding. Until recently interlock research had not recorded the direction of interlocks, despite the fact that all structural theories of corporate interaction attach great importance to this. Bank control theorists, for example, expect officers of financial institutions to sit on the boards of client firms to oversee their investment. That directional interlocks imply control is reinforced by the limited evidence of direct control that has been adduced (see Kotz, 1978; Bearden, 1982; Fitch and Oppenheimer, 1970a-c). Most instances of overt outside intervention involve exactly this arrangement: an officer of the controlling company sits on the board of the client firm. This has encouraged some analysts (Sweezy, 1939; Menshikov, 1969; Perlo, 1957; Pelton, 1970; and Knowles, 1973) to assume that directional interlocks imply external intercorporate influence.

Bank control theory, which argues for direct domination of industrial companies by financial institutions, therefore predicts that many bank and insurance company officers will sit on nonfinancial boards providing a tangible enforcement apparatus for financial domination. The data reveal this to be a kind of half-truth. On the

Table 7.1
Mean Number of Interlocks for Each Corporation Type, 1962

Corporation Type	Mean Number of Interlocks			Correlation of Rank to Number of Ties[a]	Mean Number of Interlocks per Director
	All	Sending	Receiving		
Financial firms					
Commercial banks	25.9 (66)[b]	3.7	5.6	.579	1.1
Insurance companies	13.9 (55)	1.3	1.1	.536	0.7
Investment banks	5.6 (47)	0.8	0.1	—[c]	0.3
Diversified financial firms	9.2 (40)	1.4	0.8	—[c]	0.6
Nonfinancial firms					
Industrials	8.8 (689)	1.4	1.4	.457	0.7
Transportation	11.3 (73)	1.0	1.2	.670	0.8
Public utilities	10.9 (59)	1.8	1.5	.481	0.9
Retailers	8.4 (65)	1.3	2.2	.346	0.6
Miscellaneous	5.5 (37)	0.8	0.3	c	0.5
Total	10.1 (1,131)	1.5	1.5		0.7

[a]Positive correlations indicate that larger firms have more interlocks. Technically, correlations between rank and number of interlocks would produce negative correlations if larger firms had more interlocks, since the lower rank numbers 1, 2, 3, etc., would be associated with more interlocks. We report these as positive size correlations instead of negative rank correlations because it avoids the confusion of reversed intuition.

[b]Number of corporations in each category in parentheses.

[c]Rank unavailable for 1962.

one hand, financial executives sit on a remarkable number of non-financial boards: over 80% of the companies in our study have financial directors, and many have representatives from several different lenders. On the other hand, bank boards themselves are dominated by the chief executives of industrial firms.[6] This reciprocity undermines a straightforward control argument, since it implies that banks and industrial firms simultaneously control each other.

On the other hand, this pattern is quite congenial with resource dependency theory. Pfeffer and Salancik (1978), for example, argue that directional interlocks reflect attempts by the host firm to co-opt the needed resources of the sending company and of the sending company's desire to influence the policies of the host. This logic implies, however, that industrial firms devote a disproportionate amount of their co-optational energy to stabilizing relations with banks. Thus, Pennings (1980: 74) interpreted his finding that 43% of all directional interlocks involved financials as an indication that:

> the transactions between financial and nonfinancial organizations are among the most important for American corporations. The high propensity of corporations to place their own officers and directors onto the boards of banks and insurance firms also signals the importance to nonfinancial firms of maintaining close connections in the financial community. (p. 75)

On the other side of the equation, the main uncertainties for banks lie in locating corporate depositors and good-risk borrowers. By inviting executives of large industrials onto their boards and accepting reciprocal invitations onto industrial directorates, lenders stabilize both sources and outlets for funds.

This is an appealing argument, and we believe it points to important aspects of lender-borrower relationships. However, it is incomplete. Consider a board invitation from a bank to an industrial chief executive. Resource dependency theory would interpret this invitation as an effort to "have an edge on its rivals in getting company deposits and other valuable business" (Herman, 1979: 55). If the invitation were accepted, this might imply a desire by the industrial firm "to protect [itself] against the problems of short term financing" (Pennings, 1980: 119).

If bank-industrial interlocks reflected this dynamic, the overall network would be dispersed into loosely connected groupings around financial institutions. If one firm was co-opted by a particular bank, other banks would seek out other companies in that industrial sector. This is not the case. The major banks tend to interlock with the same, rather than different, industrial firms. Sears executives sat on the boards of several regional and national banks; National Distillers (a large chemical company) maintained no such links. From a resource dependency perspective, these patterns imply either fierce competition among banks for the business of a few firms or a simple neglect of basic interinstitutional logic. If Sears had long-standing relationships with Continental Illinois, then First Chicago would be advised to approach Montgomery Ward if it desired deposits and loan placements in the retail sector. If Chemical Bank had established a relationship with National Distillers, Morgan should search elsewhere—perhaps seek out Du Pont—for a promising, profitable chemical company. Instead of pairwise relationships between industrials and banks, which resource dependency logic predicts, we find industrials that connect competing financial institutions.

Moreover, resource-dependency logic cannot explain the basic finding of all interlock research: financial institutions have more interlocks—both outgoing and incoming—than industrial companies do. This suggests that there is something unique about finance capital: companies that possess it are the most important sources of uncertainty for industrial firms (since so many financial executives are invited onto nonfinancial boards), and they are also among the most vulnerable to the actions of other companies (since they invite so many industrial executives to sit on their boards).

This becomes even more perplexing when we remember that, within each sector, larger firms are more interlocked than smaller companies. When directionality is considered, larger companies have more incoming as well as outgoing interlocks, thus suggesting that they are more susceptible to environmental uncertainty than smaller firms. This contradicts every extant theory of corporate structure.

It seems likely that these patterns are not a result of strict resource dependency, and this doubt is reinforced by the evidence presented in table 7.2. Though they make up 11% of the corporations studied, 85% (seventeen) of the twenty most interlocked firms are commercial banks or insurance companies. All of the major money market firms are included in this list: Morgan, Chemical, First National City Bank, Chase Manhattan, Manufacturers Hanover Trust and Bankers Trust, among the banks; Equitable New York and Metropolitan among the life insurance companies. The seventeen financials on the list are involved in 986 of the 5,699

Table 7.2
Twenty Most Interlocked Corporations, 1962

Rank	Corporation	Type[a]	Total Number of Interlocks	Interlocks Sent	Interlocks Received
1	Equitable Life Assurance	Ins	75	6	13
2	Morgan Guaranty Trust	Bank	72	20	13
3	Chemical Bank of New York	Bank	70	20	13
4	First National City Bank	Bank	69	19	14
5	Chase Manhattan Bank	Bank	66	17	13
6	New York Life	Ins	61	9	10
7	Mellon National Bank and Trust	Bank	59	20	14
8	Manufacturers Hanover Trust	Bank	59	13	11
9	Bankers Trust	Bank	55	21	11
10	Harris Trust	Bank	54	10	11
11	First National Bank of Chicago	Bank	52	17	14
12	Insurance Company of North America	Ins	52	6	10
13	Metropolitan Life	Ins	51	7	8
14	Southern Pacific Railroad	Trans	50	0	8
15	First National Bank of Boston	Bank	49	9	14
16	Pennsylvania Railroad	Trans	49	15	6
17	International Harvester	Ind	48	6	8
18	Irving Trust (charter of New York Corporation)	Bank	48	8	12
19	Penn Mutual	Ins	48	6	10
20	Continental Illinois Bank	Bank	46	13	13

[a]Type abbreviations in this and following tables are as follows: Bank = commercial bank; Div = diversified financial; Ind = industrial; Ins = life insurance company; Inv = investment bank; Mer = merchandiser, retailer, or wholesaler; Misc = miscellaneous; Trans = transportation company; Util = utility.

interlocks in the system, 17% of the total. This suggests that, fundamentally, the network traces the connections between a relative handful of highly central companies—mainly banks and insurance companies—and the rest of the corporate world.

It is our contention that these results reflect a single phenomenon: that the network of interlocks is largely a structural trace of capital flows, and that it reflects and consolidates financial hegemony. To understand how the pattern is constructed, we must emphasize that interlocks are not simple expressions of interfirm relationships. The structural ties created between two companies by an interlock are mediated by the individuals who actually sit on the two boards. We must consider a whole host of issues if we wish to understand these interlocks: the personal interests of the executive who is sent from one company to the other; the relationship between the outsider and the chief executive of the host firm; the relationship of the host executive to his or her own company; and the changes the new board membership may produce in the dealings of the outsider with his or her own firm. This complicated set of roles introduces a personal aspect into the institutional arrangement. It also suggests that the content of the interlock can shift from one focus to another.

In our view, bank boards have a great many incoming ties because the individuals who lead important firms are eager to participate in decisions about capital flows. There is no other institutional locale that is consistently involved in decisions of economy wide importance. When a vacancy occurs at a major bank, there is no difficulty in locating a corporate leader who wants to become a part of the major decision-making apparatus of American capitalism.

Banks are eager to recruit these leaders because they possess information and expertise both about sources of deposits and about investment opportunities in their industries. This expertise is crucial for lenders, whose institutional survival depends upon attracting large amounts of corporate deposits and, in turn, lending this money in promising investment locales. They are therefore interested in recruiting important, informed, respected executives of major companies that either have large sums of surplus capital or are major borrowers. Pennings (1980) found this pattern when he demonstrated that ties to banks correlated with current assets and with amount borrowed (see also Koenig and Gogel, 1981).

On the other side of the equation, industrial firms invite bank executives onto their boards to obtain important information about lending opportunities. Bank executives, however, are often less interested in this connection, since it may not represent the same type of opportunity for personal advancement that entices industrial leaders onto bank boards. It may, however, involve a necessary reciprocity for industrial representation on the bank's board or an opportunity to broaden the banker's (and the bank's) understanding of an important industrial sector. Since the personal attractions here are less compelling and the consequences less encompassing, we believe that bank presence on industrial boards is less significant for the operation of bank hegemony than is the presence of industrial executives on bank boards.

There is a strong element of resource dependency in bank-industrial interlocks. When an industrial executive sits on a financial board, the bank may hope or expect to develop policies that will appeal to the outsider's home firm and thus attract deposits or potential borrowers. The home firm may hope for or expect advantageous lending policies. Though we acknowledge the structural motivation in the establishment of interlocks, resource dependency is not the principal aspect of outside board memberships. If the outsider provides useful advice and information that helps to guide bank policy in a profitable direction, loans or deposits from his or her home company become secondary. Sometimes the advice of an outsider suggests that investment in the director's home firm, region, or sector is unwise. In this situation, the relationship between the outsider and the bank is primary; his or her relationship with the home firm temporarily becomes secondary.

Would an executive act against the interests of his or her home company? This is a major issue in the business press. Important corporate leaders are rarely wedded to their home companies. Besides outside board memberships, they often have large personal fortunes to invest, friendship and kinship ties to other firms and individuals, and personal ambitions beyond their current institutional affiliation. Membership on a money market bank board, where fundamental and far-reaching decisions are debated and concluded, is very often an important step in an executive career. Home-firm loyalty, therefore, cannot be assumed, although we of course cannot assume disloyalty either.[7]

The opportunity to participate in capital-flow decisions is a central attraction for outside directors on bank boards. The power of financial institutions is therefore created not by interlocking directorates, but by control of these decisions about capital. Nevertheless, the interlock network is a working part of a larger system of bank hegemony. It functions in this capacity because it allows banks to appropriate the firsthand knowledge, information, and expertise of the chief executive officers of major corporations. Scott (1978) has made this point forcefully:

> Within a system of corporations a "substructure" of capital exchanges constrains the actions of any particular company and is the basis upon which patterns of strategic control can arise. Where such relations involve the establishment of shared directorships, which is generally the case, they generate a "superstructure" of information flows through a network of interlocking directorships. The resulting communication network is an important condition for the stability of the very exchange network which produced it. (p. 2)

Summarized in our vocabulary, outside directors on bank boards are essential to the management of discretionary decision making about capital flows and are therefore crucial actors in the system of financial hegemony.

Moreover, financial interlocks reflect the sectors of the economy in which the particular bank is most involved. Thus, interlock networks nicely reflect the resource dependencies of major banks and, by implication, the relative financial importance of industrial sectors. At the same time, they only vaguely trace the nonfinancial interdependencies of major industrials; these are expressed more directly through mergers, joint ventures, and other nonmediated institutional ties.[8]

This modified resource dependency analysis helps explain many of the results of previous interlock studies. Mizruchi (1982a), for example, found that railroads, highly central in early twentieth century interlock networks, declined in centrality as their economic importance waned. Oil companies, on the other hand, did not achieve centrality levels in the 1970s consistent with their rising economic import. Our interpretation suggests that the economic decline of the railroads was matched by their decline in importance to major banks, while the oil industry did not generate either investment capital or borrowing commensurate with its rising economic position. Pennings (1980: chapter 5), for example, found that firms that either generated or utilized large amounts of investment capital were highly interlocked, both in general and with financial firms.

In our view, then, the presence of large numbers of industrial chief executives on bank boards is not a reflection of bank dependence on large industrial customers, although such dependence does exist. In a sense, it is just the reverse: industrial executives are eager to become members of bank boards because financial decisions about capital flows determine the fate of a great many industrial corporations. Interlocks facilitate that hegemony and perfect it by providing banks with the information necessary to refine their investment judgments. On the other hand, a bank executive's presence on an industrial board does not imply industrial hegemony. It may be another symptom of bank importance. It may, for example, reflect the desirability of having a banker on one's board as a method of attracting loan capital.

Interlocks, therefore, are both traces of financial hegemony and instruments of financial decision making. This dual role complicates the interpretation of interlock patterns but helps unscramble some puzzling patterns that interlock research has uncovered.

The Logic of Centrality Analysis

To use interlocking directorates to their fullest, we introduce more refined and serviceable techniques for analyzing the network of connections created by board overlaps. So far, we have noted that the boards of major money market financial companies contain many industrial executives and that the officers of these banks sit on a great many industrial boards. We interpret this pattern to suggest that outsiders on bank boards are important business leaders who are knowledgeable about corporate affairs. Moreover, these individuals come from firms or industries that are important capital users, and many possess broad knowledge of business conditions beyond the narrow confines of their own companies. They typically have personal and business ties to a considerable number of important corporations. It is these business diplomats who are chosen for outside membership on a wide variety of boards and who can invite prestigious outsiders onto the directorates of their own companies (Koenig and Gogel, 1981; Useem, 1982, 1983).

Bank directors, therefore, should typify the network patterns illustrated in figure 7.2. Hegemonic financial firms should attract outsiders from (and place their own officers on the boards of) companies that are heavily interlocked (figure 7.2a). Nonhegemonic firms are less able to attract corporate diplomats and therefore should interlock with more isolated companies (Figure 7.2b). Using this logic, we note that in figure 7.2, corporation B interlocks with five companies, while corporation A interlocks with only four. Nevertheless, corporation A is the more important of the two, and this is due to its indirect ties (through companies 1–4) to sixteen other firms. This suggests that the individuals who connect corporation

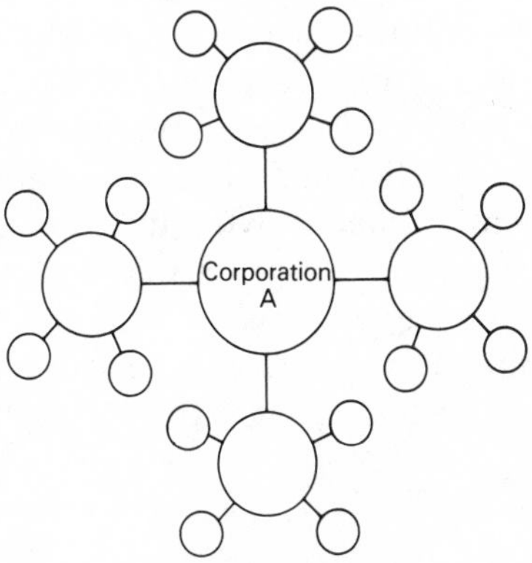

Figure 7.2a 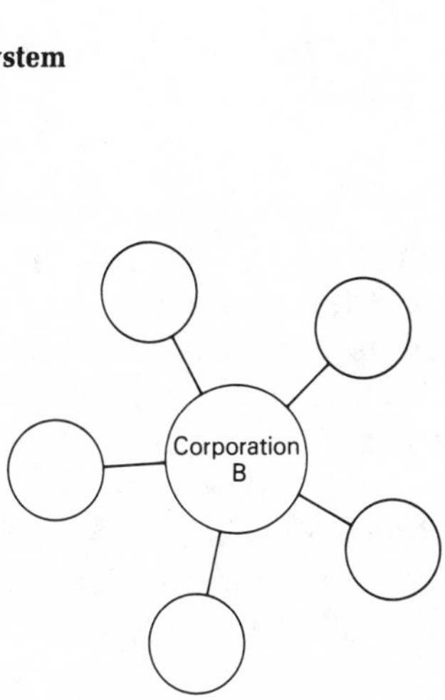   Figure 7.2b

A to its partners are far more cosmopolitan than their counterparts in corporation B.

To test our hegemony argument, we must scrutinize the interlock patterns of major banks: if they tie mainly to firms with a great many interlocks of their own, this is consistent with our argument. If their partners are poorly connected, however, the argument is disconfirmed.

To test this, we simultaneously assess the connectedness of the banks as well as their interlock partners. Centrality analysis, originally developed by Bonacich (1972), modified by Mariolis (1975), and remodified by Bearden, et al. (1975), allows such an assessment by evaluating:

1. The number of companies with which each corporation interlocks.
2. The number of companies with which each partner is tied.
3. The intensity of the interlocks among each pair of corporations.[9]

The effect of combining these criteria is illustrated by comparing Eastman Dillon, an investment bank with eleven interlocks in 1962, and Kodak, an industrial firm maintaining ten ties in that year. The eleven companies connected to Eastman Dillon were, in turn, linked to ninety corporations. Kodak, on the other hand, indirectly interlocked with 258 firms.[10] If we look only at the number of interlocks, we would conclude that Eastman Dillon was more favorably situated than Kodak. Centrality analysis, by weighing indirect interlocks as well as multiple ties, rated Kodak among the top 25% (rank 242) in network importance, while Eastman Dillon was in the bottom half (rank 594).[11]

In our view, centrality analysis provides a more accurate assessment of a company's importance in intercorporate affairs because it takes into account the importance of the individuals who sit on its board, the importance (by implication) of the companies to which it ties, and the degree of exchange with its partners. Mizruchi and Bunting (1981) demonstrated this superiority for the early twentieth century by comparing qualitative data about the importance of particular companies in intercorporate affairs with network measures of importance. For this era, centrality was by far the better indicator.

The 1962 Corporate Network

When we apply centrality analysis to the 1962 network of 5,699 interlocks among 1,131 corporations we confirm the impression, formed from number of interlocks, that financial firms are the key nodes in the network. Table 7.3 illustrates this point. It lists the twenty most central corporations, their *Fortune* ranks, and the number of interlocks each maintains, as well as their interlock ranks.

There is considerable discrepancy between this list and the corporations included in Table 7.2. Five of the most central companies do not appear in the list of most interlocked firms, and ranks within each list are quite different. Nevertheless, we note that the money market banks and insurance companies, which dominated the list of the most interlocked companies, top this list as well. The seven most central companies (Morgan, Chase Manhattan, Equitable Life, Chemical, New York Life, First National City, and Metropolitan Life) are all from the New York money market.

This eliminates the possibility that financial interlocks represent connections to small or isolated companies. Table 7.4, which lists Morgan Guaranty's interlocks, illustrates the centrality of the money market. Of the eleven nonfinancials among the twenty most central companies, Morgan interlocked with seven. It tied to each of the Big Three auto companies (General Motors, Ford, and Chrysler), with the biggest steel company (United States Steel), with the largest chemical company (Du Pont) and with a long list of other major firms including Coca-Cola, General Dynamics, ARCO, Consolidated Edison, Scott Paper, and B. F. Goodrich. This pattern is replicated for each money market company and, to a lesser extent, for important regional financials.

Table 7.3
Twenty Most Central Corporations, 1962

Rank	Corporation	Type[a]	Fortune Rank	Interlock Rank	Number of Interlocks
1	Morgan Guaranty Trust	Bank	5	2	72
2	Chase Manhattan Bank	Bank	2	5	66
3	Equitable Life Assurance	Ins	3	1	75
4	Chemical Bank of New York	Bank	6	3	70
5	New York Life	Ins	4	6	61
6	First National City Bank	Bank	3	4	69
7	Metropolitan Life	Ins	1	13	51
8	Southern Pacific Railroad	Trans	2	14	50
9	Mellon National Bank and Trust	Bank	14	7	59
10	Manufacturers Hanover Trust	Bank	4	7	59
11	American Telephone and Telegraph	Util	1	30	43
12	Pennsylvania Railroad	Trans	1	15	49
13	Insurance Company of North America	Ins	—[b]	11	52
14	Bankers Trust	Bank	9	9	55
15	General Electric	Ind	4	33	40
16	United States Steel	Ind	6	42	37
17	Westinghouse Electric	Ind	17	28	44
18	Irving Trust	Bank	12	17	48
19	Harris Trust	Bank	23	10	54
20	Phelps Dodge	Ind	164	55	33

[a]For type abbreviations, see table 7.2.
[b]Not ranked by Fortune in 1962, owing to its diversified nature.

This finding is consistent with results of other studies. Allen (1974) and Mariolis (1975), for example, found a positive correlation between the number of financial interlocks and corporate assets. Similarly, Gogel and Koenig (1981) found a correlation of .62 between assets and the number of financial interlocks in the primary metals industry. This means that larger firms interlock more frequently with financial institutions than smaller ones do. Pennings (1980: 90) found a substantial correlation between total number of interlocks and number of financial interlocks maintained, thus demonstrating that well-connected industrials are also heavily tied to banks and insurance companies.

Table 7.4
Morgan Guaranty Trust's Interlocks, 1962

Corporation	Asset Rank	Number of Ties to Morgan	Total Number of Interlocks
Industrial companies			
Standard Oil of New Jersey	1	1	8
General Motors	2	1	33
Ford Motor Company	3	2	38
United States Steel	4	1	37
General Electric	11	2	39
Chrysler	20	1	31
Cities Service	21	1	15
Continental Oil	26	1	25
Eastman Kodak	31	1	11
Proctor and Gamble	32	1	25
Atlantic Refining	43	1	16
Kennecott Copper	50	1	23
Continental Can	53	2	31
National Dairy Products	55	1	22
American Cyanamid	59	1	7
B. F. Goodrich	66	2	29
American Smelting and Refining	89	2	46
Phelps Dodge	98	1	33
Campbell Soup	107	2	23
J. P. Stevens	110	1	13
American Radiator and Standard	113	1	7
Scott Paper	117	1	23
Johns-Manville	120	1	26
American Viscose	124	1	23
Air Reduction	128	1	16
Standard Brands	150	1	17
Raytheon	154	1	13
Merck	159	1	13
Eastern Gas and Fuel	172	1	12
Corning Glass	194	1	19
Owens-Corning Fiberglas	196	1	23
Gillette	211	2	31
American Brake Shoe	250	1	30
Wilson	256	1	9
Grumman	271	1	5
Smith Kline and French	278	2	15
SCM	376	1	27
Pepperell Manufacturing	463	1	12
Clorox	—ᵃ	1	5
Texas Gulf Sulphur	—ᵃ	1	14

Table 7.4 (*cont.*)

Corporation	Asset Rank	Number of Ties to Morgan	Total Number of Interlocks
Transportation companies			
Pennsylvania Railroad	1	2	49
Southern Pacific Railroad	2	1	50
Atchison, Topeka and Santa Fe	5	1	31
Norfolk and Western Railway	9	1	26
American Airlines	17	1	23
Wabash	31	1	23
United States Lines	35	1	17
Utilities			
AT&T	1	2	43
Consolidated Edison	2	2	37
Columbia Gas System	11	1	10
Duke Power	34	1	6
Panhandle Eastern Pipe	38	1	18
Insurance companies			
Prudential	2	1	22
New York Life	4	2	61
Mutual of New York	9	1	47
Diversified financials			
Discount Corporation of New York	—ᵃ	1	23
Insurance Company of North America	—ᵃ	2	52
Commercial banks			
First Pennsylvania Banking and Trust	19	1	35

ᵃNot ranked by *Fortune* in 1962.

It seems clear that money market financial institutions attract business diplomats onto their boards and place their own executives as directors of major nonfinancial companies. That they are more successful in this endeavor than even the largest and most important industrial companies indicates the attractiveness of financial board memberships; and this attractiveness reflects the importance of these institutions in the economy as a whole.

The enormous overrepresentation of financial companies, especially banks, among the most central firms is indicative of the preeminence of capital in determining and shaping intercorporate affairs. These interlocks give lenders access to the expertise of corporate diplomats who are knowledgeable about the viability of investment in their home sectors. These leaders, in turn, obtain vital information about capital flows, influence lending decisions, and obtain a variety of personal rewards. Although other director interchanges contain elements of the same symbiosis, they lack the salience that derives from capital-flow decision making.

This interpretation is strengthened by a closer examination of table 7.3. Most of the financials in the top twenty, even those not in the money market, are in some sense obvious choices for inclusion. The presence of this particular set of nonfinancials, however, is not immediately understandable.

Consider the financial firms. Table 7.5 demonstrates that they are the dominant forces in commercial lending and institutional stockholding. The money market banks—Morgan, Chase Manhattan, Chemical, First National City, Manufacturers Hanover, and Bankers Trust—which were second, third, fourth, fifth, sixth, and ninth in assets in 1962, were ranked first, second, third, fourth, tenth, and fourteenth in centrality. The three remaining banks on the list, Mellon, Charter, and Harris, were major regional lenders whose position among the most central firms is hardly surprising, though several other regional institutions might have been substituted.[12] The absence of the largest bank, Bank of America, validates the interlock analysis, since Bank of America achieved its high ranking from its retail—noncorporate—trade and was a second-tier regional bank in 1962.[13] Three of the most central insurance companies, Equitable, New York Life, and Metropolitan Life, were very large and intimately connected to the New York financial markets. The absence of Prudential (second in assets, fifty-seventh in centrality) and John Hancock (fifth in assets, 138th in centrality) reflects the relative isolation of Prudential and Hancock from major commercial banks.

Beyond their large size, these institutions are the key actors in capital-flow decisions. By 1967, five years after our data year, six of the nine commercial banks among the most central companies in the network were among the largest institutional stockholders in the country; together the nine held approximately 31% of all bank trust department assests (United States Congress, 1968: 584, 755, 760). The six New York money market banks included among the most central companies together held 25.6% of all such holdings (ibid., 1968: 680). These concentrations can be best appreciated if we remember that in 1963 institutional investors held over 20% of all stock listed on the New York Stock Exchange (Baum and Stiles, 1965: 6). In 1962 pension funds alone purchased 80% of all net new equity issues (Baum and Stiles, 1965: 43). Moreover, in 1967 the six New York banks held at least 5% of the outstanding stock in

Table 7.5
Commercial Lending and Institutional Stockholding of Major Financial Institutions

	Centrality Rank	Assets Rank, 1962[a]	Trust Department Holdings, 1967[b] Rank	Trust Department Holdings, 1967[b] Percentage of All Bank Trust Assets	Loan Consortia Leadership, 1976[c] (N = 128) Rank	Loan Consortia Leadership, 1976[c] (N = 128) Percentage of All Consortia	Percentage of Major Stockholdings (≥5%) in Controlled Nonfinancials, 1967–69[d] (N = 69)
Money market banks				25.6		49.9	44.8
Morgan Guaranty Trust	1	5	1	6.7	3*	7.8	10.1
Chase Manhattan Bank	2	2	2	5.4	2	13.2	23.2
Chemical Bank of New York	4	6	11	1.8	7*	4.7	0.0
First National City Bank	6	3	4	4.4	1	15.6	4.3
Manufacturers Hanover Trust	10	4	7	2.9	4	7.0	0.0
Bankers Trust	14	9	3	4.4	16*	1.6	7.2
Major regional banks				5.3		7.8	4.3
Mellon (Pittsburgh)	9	14	6	3.0	8	3.9	4.3
Irving Trust (New York)	18	12	30	0.7	10*	3.1	0.0
Harris (Chicago)	20	23	14	1.6	NA	0.8	0.0
Insurance companies				—		6.3	0.0
Equitable Life Assurance	3	3	—	—	16*	1.6	0.0
New York Life	5	4	—	—	16*	3.6	0.0
Metropolitan Life	7	1	—	—	10*	3.1	0.0
Insurance Company of North America[e]	13	—	—	—	—	0.0	0.0

Table 7.5 (cont.)

| | Assets Rank, 1962[a] | Trust Department Holdings, 1967[b] | | Loan Consortia Leadership, 1976[c] (N = 128) | | Percentage of Major Stockholdings (≥5%) in Controlled Nonfinancials, 1967–69[d] (N = 69) |
	Centrality Rank		Rank	Percentage of All Bank Trust Assets	Rank	Percentage of All Consortia	
Other financials not among twenty							
most central				6.6			10.1
Bank of America	271	1	15	1.5	7*	4.7	0.0
Security First National	164	7	22	0.9	NA	NA	0.0
Continental Illinois Bank	34	8	10	2.0	NA	NA	1.4
First National Bank of Chicago	26	10	9	2.2	3*	7.8	8.7
Prudential	57	2	—	—	6	6.2	0.0
John Hancock	138	5	—	—	NA	NA	0.0

[a]From *Fortune* (August 1963: 144-45).

[b]From United States Congress (1968: 35-36).

[c]Compiled from an unpublished study by Robert Cohen (Columbia University). We are grateful to Cohen for permission to use this very important evidence.

[d]Compiled from Kotz (1978: 159-75). Control, in Kotz's study, involves a combination of stockholding (over 5%), loan leadership, and interlocks (see pp. 75-96). This table includes bank holdings in companies Kotz classifies as under full or partial financial control.

[e]Not ranked by *Fortune*, since it was too diversified to be considered an insurance company.

*Tie ranking.

NA = not available.

965 companies or an average of 160 firms per bank (United States Congress, 1968: 680). Mellon and Harris, the two important regional banks among the most central corporations, held over 5% of the stock in 274 companies (United States Congress, 1968: 602, 760). Many researchers consider a 5% holding sufficient for control; almost all analysts (including the federal government) view 5% as a potentially influential holding. This implies that the eight most central banks are now in a position to collectively influence the affairs of most major United States corporations (Kotz, 1978).

The only extant study of loan consortium leadership (Cohen, 1980) reinforces the importance of these centrally located firms. Despite a fourteen-year time lag between our data and the Cohen study, the twelve most central financial institutions accounted for seven of the top ten and eleven of the top twenty consortium leaders. Our twelve central banking institutions led 64% of all national consortia. Four money market banks—Morgan, Chase Manhattan, First National City, and Manufacturers Hanover—led 43.6%.

The Kotz study (1978) underscores these conclusions still further. Kotz identified instances in which a single financial institution had accumulated large amounts of stock, loans, and/or interlocks with nonfinancial firms. Of sixty-nine instances of such major holdings, thirty-three (48%) were accounted for by five (Chase, Morgan, Bankers Trust, Citibank, and Mellon) of our most central financials. Chase Manhattan alone accounted for 23% of that total.

These results reveal that a handful of centrally placed financial institutions have dominated capital-investment decision making for decades. They directly control a significant proportion of all stock that changes hands; they lead a majority of lending consortia; and they are involved in almost half of all large financial holdings in major nonfinancial firms.

These results underscore the value of interlock research and the method of centrality analysis. With the exception of First National Bank of Chicago, no financial absent from the top twenty can claim consistent major influence on these dimensions. Thus, for financial institutions, interlock centrality is an indicator of substantive preeminence in the process of decision making about capital flows.[14] The nonfinancial corporations on the list of most central firms present a more complex analytic problem. On the one hand, they are among the largest firms in their sectors: AT&T among utilities, Penn Central and Southern Pacific among railroads, United States Steel among steel producers, and General Electric and Westinghouse among electrical equipment manufacturers. Only Phelps Dodge, a relatively small mining company, was an exception.

Whereas previous interlock research has demonstrated that corporate size is highly correlated with network importance, table 7.6 illustrates that there is an ambivalent relation between size and centrality for nonfinancial firms. We see that General Motors and Ford are quite central (though not among the top twenty), and this reflects the importance of auto manufacturing to the economy. The high rankings of Consolidated Edison and PGE, the largest public power companies, Sears, the largest retailer, and General Telephone and Electronics, the second-largest telephone company, are similarly reassuring. In fact, of the seven nonfinancials on our list of the twenty most central corporations, five are among the twenty largest companies in our time period.

Table 7.6
Twenty Largest Nonfinancial Corporations by Assets, 1962

Rank	Corporation	Assets[a]	Centrality Score	Centrality Rank
1	American Telephone and Telegraph	$26,716,536,000	.61	11
2	Exxon	11,487,697,000	.12	273
3	General Motors	10,239,463,000	.44	32
4	Ford Motor Company	5,416,474,000	.49	27
5	United States Steel	5,059,749,000	.54	16
6	Gulf Oil	4,243,609,000	.25	108
7	Texaco	4,165,829,000	.34	52
8	Mobil Oil	4,136,463,000	.15	223
9	Standard Oil of California	3,353,105,000	.10	314
10	Standard Oil (Indiana)	3,108,876,000	.10	318
11	Du Pont (E.I.) de Nemours	3,095,670,000	.04	539
12	General Electric	2,846,988,000	.55	15
13	Pennsylvania Railroad	2,846,322,000	.59	12
14	Consolidated Edison	2,830,615,000	.50	25
15	Pacific Gas and Electric	2,809,136,000	.38	35
16	Sears	2,792,139,000	.35	45
17	General Telephone and Electric	2,563,593,000	.32	61
18	Southern Pacific Railroad	2,518,897,000	.68	8
19	New York Central Railroad	2,382,112,000	.04	520
20	Bethlehem Steel	2,212,204,000	.00	Isolate[b]

[a]From *Fortune* (July 1963: 177-94; August 1963: 139-49).
[b]Isolates had no interlocks with included corporations in 1962. The 128 isolates are therefore all tied for the bottom rank in centrality.

There are also a number of unclear results in this table. Exxon, the largest oil company and the second-largest firm in the country, was 273d in centrality and was far below other, smaller oil companies. E. I. Du Pont, the largest chemical firm by far and eleventh in total assets, was 539th in centrality. It was less central than most firms in the sample and far less central than many smaller chemical companies. New York Central Railroad, the third largest transportation firm, with assets almost equal to Southern Pacific (the most central nonfinancial), was 520th. Bethlehem Steel, the second-largest steel company and twentieth-largest company in 1962, did not maintain any interlocks within our sample.

Table 7.7 lists the twenty most central nonfinancial firms of the interlock network. This list underscores the results of table 7.6. Many of the companies included are large and dominant; they match

Table 7.7
Twenty Most Central Nonfinancial Firms, 1962

Rank	Corporation	Type[a]	Fortune Rank	Centrality Rank	Centrality Score
1	Southern Pacific Railroad	Trans	2	8	.68
2	American Telephone and Telegraph	Util	1	11	.61
3	Pennsylvania Railroad	Trans	1	12	.59
4	General Electric	Ind	4	15	.55
5	United States Steel	Ind	6	16	.54
6	Westinghouse Electric		17	17	.53
7	Phelps Dodge	Ind	164	20	.52
8	Otis Elevator	Ind	238	21	.52
9	American Smelting and Refining	Ind	109	22	.51
10	International Harvester	Ind	24	24	.51
11	Consolidated Edison	Util	2	25	.50
12	Ford Motor Company	Ind	3	27	.49
13	Chrysler	Ind	12	28	.47
14	Corn Products	Ind	59	29	.47
15	Continental Can	Ind	36	30	.47
16	General Motors	Ind	1	32	.44
17	National Distillers	Ind	110	33	.43
18	General Foods	Ind	34	35	.43
19	American Brake Shoe	Ind	258	37	.42
20	Consolidation Coal	Ind	197	38	.41

[a]For type abbreviations, see table 7.2.

our intuitive sense of their importance. But others are not easily explained. Phelps Dodge, the seventh entry, was a medium sized mining firm and the 164th largest industrial. Otis Elevator, the eighth entry, was the largest elevator manufacturer in the world, but it was hardly a dominant force in American industry (238th in size). American Smelting and Refining (ninth), National Distillers (seventeenth) and Consolidation Coal (twentieth) are all similarly out of place. American Brake Shoe, which was a relatively small auto-parts supplier, appeared as the nineteenth most central nonfinancial (thirty-seventh overall), despite its position as the 258th largest industrial. Exxon was seventy-five times the size of American Brake Shoe, yet it was far lower in centrality.

For banks (especially) and insurance companies (less dramatically), we found an orderly relation between control of capital and network centrality. For nonfinancials, however, the situation is less clear:

1. Size and rank within a sector appear to account for high centrality ranks in many cases.
2. Certain large industries, however (e.g., oil and chemicals), appear to be much less important in the network than their size would suggest: firms from these sectors do not appear among the most central companies.
3. Certain firms (e.g., Exxon , Du Pont, Bethlehem Steel), when compared with other companies in their sectors, are not as central as their size would suggest.
4. Some smaller corporations (e.g., Phelps Dodge and American Brake Shoe), despite their relative lack of size and sectoral prominence, are highly central in the network.

We believe that these discrepancies reflect the preeminence of financial institutions in interlock networks. Since a substantial proportion of board exchanges function as transmitters of information regarding capital flows, nonfinancial firms become highly central if they are in some way crucial to capital flow decision making. Since large corporations are typically in a position to play this role, central industrial companies are usually large or dominant in their sector. But since capital flows are not evenly distributed among sectors and firms, the patterns are not neat replications of asset size.

To illustrate, consider two anomalous results in the 1962 list of central organizations. First, Du Pont, the major chemical company and eleventh largest firm in America in 1962, ranked 539th in centrality. It maintained only eight interlocks and did not tie to a major bank. Its top leaders, W. S. Carpenter and Crawford H. Greenewalt, did not sit on any outside boards. This isolation is explained, in part, by Du Pont's policy of avoiding substantial outside finance. Until 1965 it had no long-term debt, and it did not borrow large sums until the 1970s (*Moody's Industrial Manual*, 1975).

During this period, though, the chemical industry borrowed quite substantially. This made Du Pont's leadership attractive to bankers, who could gain access to their expertise in evaluating the direction of the industry. This attractiveness found expression in 1964, when Du Pont leadership joined the boards of both Morgan Bank and Chemical Bank. Even so, the lack of participation in capital markets limited both their usefulness to lenders and their interest in gaining access to bank boardrooms.

National Distillers, a much smaller chemical company, was ranked as the 110th-largest industrial in 1962. In that year, its long-term debt amounted to $192 million, up from $144 million in 1958 and climbing toward $236 million in 1967. (*Standards and Poors Stock Market Encyclopedia*, 1969). It was ranked 33d in 1962 centrality, a standing that reflected thirty-nine interlocks, including ties to five major banks. Its chief executive, John S. Bierworth, was an outside member of eight major boards, including the board of First National City Bank. The second-in-command, Austin R. Zender, was a member of Chemical Bank's board, and Hulbert S. Aldrich, a top leader at Chemical, had accepted an invitation to sit on National Distillers' board.[15]

The popularity of National Distillers reflects the importance of the chemical industry as a locale for investment, Distillers' involvement in major borrowings, and also the respect for its leadership in the business world. It was more central than Du Pont because of its experience in capital markets and because its dependence on outside finance motivated its officers to acquire informational and institutional leverage over the lending process.

Consider another anomaly in the 1962 list of most central firms. Both General Electric and Westinghouse were highly connected, achieving centrality ranks of fifteen and seventeen. Double representation among the most central firms was certainly out of proportion to the importance of the electrical manufacturing industry in the economy as a whole. Their inclusion is less puzzling, however, if we note that these two firms formed what was then called the "duopoly" of nuclear power. Several billion dollars had been invested in nuclear generating plants that had yet to be proved viable, profit-making ventures (Grossman, 1980). General Electric was carrying $228 million in long-term debt, with the figure rising toward its 1968 peak of $749 million. It also maintained substantial credit lines for short-term borrowing. Westinghouse's situation was similar: its $290 million in bonds, which reached $583 million by 1970, was accompanied by very significant short-term borrowing (*Standard and Poor's Stock Market Encyclopedia*, 1963, 1969, 1971).

With a substantial proportion of loan capital flowing into the development of nuclear power, financiers needed ongoing information about the industry.[16] This is reflected in the overall ranking of the two companies as well as in their specific connections to major financial institutions. General Electric maintained interlocks with seven different financials, including two money market banks (J. P. Morgan and Bankers Trust) and three money market insurance companies (MONY, New York Life, and Metropolitan). Top officers of Morgan (Charles D. Dickey) and Bankers Trust (S. Sloan Colt) were members of the General Electric board.

In the Westinghouse case, geographical proximity and historical ties to Mellon Bank made it unsurprising that two top officers accepted invitations onto Mellon Bank's board, while Frank R. Denton, a Mellon executive, joined Westinghouse's board. Westinghouse's importance to the financial community as a whole was reflected in the presence on its board of John J. McCloy, a top official of Chase Manhattan, as well as interlocks with First National City Bank, Metropolitan Life, Insurance Company of North America, and Harris Bank in Chicago.

The Interlock Network in 1966

These analyses suggest that the anomalies in centrality among industrial companies are reflections of the status of capital flows at particular moments in corporate history. To demonstrate this with more precision, we consider the interlock network in 1966. In this investigation we are testing two propositions derived from the argument we have presented thus far:

1. Major financial firms should remain at the center of the network, since their centrality is the result of the long-term dependency of industrial firms on capital sources.
2. There should be shifts among the most central nonfinancials that reflect their changing role in the flow of capital.

It is, in principle, possible that the overrepresentation of financial concerns among the twenty most central corporations in 1962 was a temporary perturbation in business history. Although this is unlikely considering the unanimity of findings of previous research,[17] there has been no systematic examination of the short-term stability of director interlocks.[18] If the patterns changed drastically between 1962 and 1966, this would refute our contention that interlocks reflect financial hegemony and undermine the prevalent use of interlocks as indicators of stable intercorporate relationships.[19]

The four-year period between 1962 and 1966 was a brief moment in the history of American business, but it encompassed major alterations in the circumstances of particular companies. If our argument is correct, the interlock network should reflect these individual changes. Consider, for example, Xerox Corporation, which rose on the *Fortune* list from rank 423 in 1962 to rank 145 in 1966. In 1962, it interlocked with only two firms: Gannett Company, a medium-sized chain of newspapers centered in Rochester, New York (and thus a neighbor of Xerox, which was headquartered in Rochester), and First National Bank of Boston, a regional bank.

By 1966, Xerox had added ties to Sybron (then called Ritter Pfaudler), another rapidly growing Rochester company (five interlocks and 458th in centrality); Massachusetts Mutual Life, the tenth-largest insurance company (twenty-one interlocks and 141st in centrality); and, most notably, First National City Bank, a major money market firm ranked fifth in centrality in 1966. The interlocks with Massachusetts Mutual and First National City were created by Joseph C. Wilson, a top Xerox executive who had been invited to join the boards of the financials in 1964 and 1966 respectively. In our view, these invitations were the result of two connected developments: the sentiment in the financial community that Xerox was an important firm in a growing economic sector, and respect for Wilson's competence and knowledgeability as an executive. As potential lenders to this promising sector, Massachusetts Mutual and First National City had much to gain by access to Wilson's expertise. At the same time, both Wilson and Xerox had much to gain from membership on these financial boards, including information about available capital sources, the possibility of greater access to finance, and important personal ties to major corporate lenders.

Xerox was 911th in network centrality in 1962—over 90% of the companies under investigation were more connected. In 1966, it had risen to rank 491; it was more central than 50% of the other corporations. This change reflected its growth in size and in significance as a site for capital investment.

Ethyl Corporation, on the other hand, experienced a dramatic decline in network status. In 1962, it was jointly owned by General Motors and Exxon, and it maintained multiple interlocks with these companies as well as with six others. In 1964, the company was spun off as an independent unit, and its entire board composition changed. The eight ties with major national corporations were broken, largely because of the departure of Exxon and General Motors executives from its board. They were replaced by five new interlocks with smaller southeastern firms. In 1962, Ethyl had achieved a centrality rank of 307th. This reflected its importance to General Motors (thirty-second) and Exxon (238th), since a firm's centrality is based in good measure on the centrality of its interlock partners. In 1966, despite five interlocks (the same number as Xerox), it had dropped to 828th, largely because its new partners were unimportant in the network.

This decline is particularly instructive. Ethyl's economic importance was undisturbed by this change in ownership. It remained a major supplier of tetraethyl lead and therefore was involved in the same network of resource dependencies. Its trading partners remained as dependent upon it as they had been in the past, but it nevertheless declined drastically in network importance. This decline in centrality reflected the change in its importance in the system of capital flows: it was no longer a significant investment of two major companies, and it was no longer a significant bridge creating a joint interest between these firms.

Corporations may experience considerable shuffling among board personnel while their position in the network remains relatively stable. Consider, for example, Union Carbide, which ranked forty-first in centrality in 1962. In the next four years, four of the original twelve board members left; one of the four replacements also left. Seven of its twenty-four interlocks (including ties to highly ranked Mutual Life and Goodyear) were broken by these departures and by the resignations of Union Carbide directors from outside boards. Three of these seven broken interlocks were renewed, while four others remained permanently severed. New ties were established with seven firms, including Chrysler, Bankers Trust, and Metropolitan Life. In 1966, after all this change, Union Carbide maintained twenty-eight interlocks (four more than in 1962) and ranked thirty-fifth in centrality, compared with forty-first in 1962. This is not an unusual example. United States Steel had thirty-seven interlocks and a centrality rank of tenth in 1962; by 1966 it had lost eighteen interlocks, gained twenty-five, and ranked ninth in centrality.

A systematic analysis of corporate board turnover and the corresponding short-term changes in interlock patterns has not yet been undertaken. The examples just reviewed suggest that much could be learned from such a study. For our purposes, however, it is sufficient to note that the numerous changes in interlock profiles indicate that stability in network position is a meaningful independent result, not a simple extension of board stability.

Table 7.8 provides evidence that financial domination of corporate networks is a consequence of ongoing structural relationships. Although conditions for many of the top firms had changed substantially during four years, the list of most central corporations is quite similar. Of the seven most central firms of 1962, only New York Life failed to reappear in 1966. The others—Morgan, Chase Manhattan, Equitable Life, Chemical, First National City, and Metropolitan Life—dominate the 1966 network with only a reshuffling

Table 7.8
Twenty Most Central Corporations, 1966

Rank	Corporation	Type[a]	Fortune Rank	Centrality Rank in 1962
1	Equitable Life Assurance	Ins	3	3
2	Morgan Guaranty Trust	Bank	4	1
3	Chase Manhattan Bank	Bank	2	2
4	Chemical Bank of New York	Bank	6	4
5	First National City Bank	Bank	3	6
6	Metropolitan Life	Ins	2	7
7	American Telephone and Telegraph	Util	1	11
8	Lehman Brothers[b]	Inv	2[c]	152
9	United States Steel	Ind	8	16
10	Westinghouse Electric	Ind	19	17
11	Mellon	Bank	15	9
12	New York Life	Ins	4	5
13	United California Bank[b]	Bank	14	248
14	General Motors[b]	Ind	1	32
15	International Harvester[b]	Ind	18	24
16	Pacific Mutual[b]	Ins	33	91
17	Bankers Trust	Bank	7	14
18	First National Bank of Chicago	Bank	10	26
19	Southern Pacific Railroad	Trans	2	8
20	Western Bancorp[b]	Bank	—[d]	58

[a]For type abbreviations, see table 7.2.
[b]Not among the most central corporations of 1962.
[c]Ranking based on total dollar amount of underwriting for 1961–70.
[d]Not ranked by Fortune in 1966.

in order. Nine of the top ten and twelve of the top twenty reappeared in 1966.

Financial and nonfinancial companies did not reappear with the same frequency, however. Of the thirteen financials listed in 1962, nine reappeared in 1966; only four of the seven nonfinancial firms retained top twenty status. This pattern is more dramatically demonstrated in table 7.9, which traces the fate of the most central companies of 1962 in the 1966 and 1969 corporate networks. Of the thirteen financials in the 1962 list, seven reappear in both 1966 and 1969; of the seven nonfinancials, only two reappear in both of the later lists. More significantly, the seven financial repeaters are all from the New York money market (Morgan, Chase, Equitable Life, Chemical Bank, New York Life, First National City, and Metropolitan Life), a further indication of the persistent importance of

Table 7.9
Most Central Corporations, 1962, 1966, and 1969

Corporation	Type[a]	1962	1966	1969[b]
Morgan Guaranty Trust	Bank	1	2	8
Chase Manhattan Bank	Bank	2	3	5
Equitable Life Assurance	Ins	3	1	2
Chemical Bank of New York	Bank	4	4	1
New York Life	Ins	5	12	11
First National City Bank	Bank	6	5	4
Metropolitan Life	Ins	7	6	6
Southern Pacific Railroad	Trans	8	19	—
Mellon	Bank	9	11	—
Manufacturers Hanover	Bank	10	—	—
American Telephone and Telegraph	Util	11	7	3
Pennsylvania Railroad	Trans	12	—	20
Insurance Company of North America	Ins	13	—	—[c]
Bankers Trust	Bank	14	7	—
General Electric	Ind	15	—	—
United States Steel	Ind	16	9	7
Westinghouse Electric	Ind	17	10	—
Irving Trust	Bank	18	—	—
Harris Trust	Bank	19	—	—
Phelps Dodge	Ind	20	—	—

[a]For type abbreviations, see table 7.2.
[b]From Mariolis (1975).
[c]Not included in the Mariolis data set.

these firms in intercorporate relations.[20] The 1966 results confirm the pattern found in the 1962 analysis. The newly included financial firms are Lehman Brothers, the second-largest investment bank; First National Bank of Chicago, the largest of the Chicago banks; and three important Western financial institutions. These are no more out of place than the financials they replaced (Manufacturers Hanover, Insurance Company of North America, Irving Trust, and Harris). The new nonfinancials include General Motors, the largest auto maker, and International Harvester, the preeminent farm machinery company. These are not particularly surprising, though once again the industrial firms seem to be arbitrarily selected from among a much broader population.

When we compare the two years more closely, the results are less intuitive. Table 7.10 indicates that many of the changes in

Table 7.10
Corporations Entering or Leaving the Top Twenty, 1962 and 1966

Corporation	Centrality Rank		Centrality Score[a]	
	1962	1966	1962	1966
Financials that left top twenty				
Manufacturers Hanover	10	27	.63	.47
Insurance Company of North America	13	41	.55	.39
Irving Trust	18	61	.53	.33
Harris Trust	19	29	.52	.46
Nonfinancials that left top twenty				
Pennsylvania Railroad	12	23	.59	.50
General Electric	15	24	.55	.49
Phelps Dodge	20	192	.52	.17
Financials that joined the top twenty				
Lehman Brothers	152	8	.20	.71
United California Bank	248	13	.14	.62
Pacific Mutual	91	16	.28	.56
First National Bank of Chicago	26	18	.50	.55
Western Bancorp	58	20	.33	.54
Nonfinancials that joined the top twenty				
General Motors	32	14	.44	.62
International Harvester	24	15	.51	.59

[a]For a technical discussion of the meaning of centrality scores, see Appendix 2. For technical interpretation of changes in centrality scores, see Appendix 3.

ranking were relatively small, suggesting that high board turnovers may create perturbations in the rankings. Pennsylvania Railroad dropped from twelfth to twenty-third; Insurance Company of North America from thirteenth to forty-first, and Harris Bank from nineteenth to twenty-ninth. General Motors rose from thirty-second to fourteenth; International Harvester from twenty-fourth to fifteenth, and First National Bank of Chicago from twenty-sixth to eighteenth. These are small shifts that do not seem to indicate fundamental changes in the status of these companies in the corporate world.

On the other hand, the comparison produces three major shifts:

1. Phelps Dodge dropped from twentieth to 192d.
2. Three western financial firms (United California Bank, Pacific Mutual, and Western Bancorp) suddenly appear among the most central firms. United California Bank, in the most dramatic shift, rose in centrality from 248th to thirteenth, Pacific Mutual Life rose from ninety-first to sixteenth, and Western Bancorp rose from fifty-eight to twentieth.
3. Lehman Brothers, a major investment bank, suddenly rose from 152d in 1962 to eighth in 1966.

These changes are important because they bring into focus the process of interlock formation. They allow us to test our contention that network centrality, by and large, reflects the importance (temporary or permanent) of a company, sector, or geographic region in the system of capital flows.

Consider the decline of Phelps Dodge. It was the result of the withdrawal of four outside directors: William S. Gray of Manufacturers Hanover; Thomas S. Lamont of Morgan Guaranty; Richard S. Perkins of First National City; and Percy L. Douglas, the retired chairman of Otis Elevator. Since each of these individuals also held several other directorships, they accounted for seventeen of Phelps Dodge's thirty-two interlocks, including seven to major financials. The seven financial interlocks they created produced 32% of Phelps Dodge's 1962 centrality and 52% of its lost centrality.[21] Their replacements produced only four inconsequential new ties.

Phelps Dodge typifies highly central nonfinancials. Their centrality is, in large part, a consequence of interlocks with major banks and insurance companies. Not only were its most important ties to such companies, but many of its other interlocks were created by bank officers who also sat on other boards.

Above we noted that the 1962 centrality of General Electric and Westinghouse reflected their role in the development of nuclear power, a capital-intensive effort which required massive investment. The reason for the importance of Phelps Dodge is not as easily discerned. To understand its temporary centrality, we would need to investigate its particular role (and the role of the copper mining industry) in the system of capital flows in that period. Such an analysis is beyond the scope of this study, but it underscores the need to consider its specific role in corporate interaction and the history of its relationships with other actors.[22] However, this example illustrates that financial interlocks are crucial in determining the network centrality of nonfinancial companies. Consider the five nonfinancials among the most central firms of 1962 that were also included in either the 1966 or 1969 list (table 7.9).

AT&T, which appeared among the top twenty in all three years, maintained a constantly changing profile of multiple interlocks with major money market institutions. Only in 1962 did it fail to connect to six of the seven dominant New York financials (Morgan, Chase, Chemical, First National City, Equitable Life, Metropolitan Life). Each year it maintained over a dozen interlocks with the twenty most central financial institutions and these accounted for a minimum of 50% of its overall score.

AT&T's importance appears to reflect its ongoing role as the largest single corporate borrower, sometimes accounting for 20% of all long-term bonds. In 1966 it carried $10 billion in debt, an enormous amount by standards applied to normal corporations (General Motors, the largest company in terms of sales that year, owed only $287 million in total debt). For AT&T this debt load was not considered dangerous; Standard and Poor's assessed the firm's prospects as "highly promising" (Standard and Poors Stock Market Encyclopedia, 1969). The attention paid by financial institutions, was not, therefore, a consequence of crisis; it reflected financial interest in the company and the industry as an investment locale. This is suggested by the reciprocity of the firm's relations to lenders. Three financial executives sat on AT&T's board, while five top telephone company executives had accepted seats on seven financial boards, including Chase, Morgan, Manufacturers Hanover, Chemical, and Metropolitan Life.

United States Steel, the only other nonfinancial to appear among the most central firms in all three years, was ranked sixteenth in 1962. This position was due in large part to twelve financial interlocks, including ties to Equitable Life, First National City, Chemical, Morgan, New York Life, and Insurance Company of North America. It rose to 9th in 1966, almost entirely because of the addition of five new financial interlocks, including two to Chase, one to Mellon, and additional links to Equitable and Chemical.

Although it remained profitable throughout the 1960s, the steel industry suffered from a variety of economic maladies, among which excess capacity, threatened strikes, and outmoded equipment were the most salient. These led to high capital expenditures and, in some cases, high debt levels. United States Steel, for example tripled its debt (from $422 million to $1.25 billion) between 1960 and 1966 and increased it still further to $1.4 billion by 1969 (*Standard and Poor's Stock Market Encyclopedia*, 1971). As a major locale for capital investment, therefore, the steel industry was a focus of financial attention throughout the 1960s. This was reflected in the presence of financial executives on United States Steel's board, as well as in the invitations extended to top United States Steel executives to sit on the boards of Chase, Chemical, Mellon, and Metropolitan Life, where their working knowledge of steel could inform lender decision making.

Pennsylvania Railroad maintained eighteen financial interlocks when it was twelfth in centrality rank in 1962, including multiple ties to Morgan (two), Insurance Company of North America (three), and Mellon (two). In 1966, when it was twenty-third, it had lost three important links while acquiring five new ties, including interlocks with Equitable and Chase. By 1969, after merging with the New York Central Railroad the former year to become Penn Central, it ranked twentieth. It had lost its connection with five financials while establishing new ties to eight others.

Penn Central's importance in the network was rooted in its ongoing crisis, which culminated in bankruptcy by the end of the decade. It entered the 1960s with a considerable debt load (over $600 million), which it was unable to reduce. During the period, there was an ongoing crisis in the railroad industry, with frequent bankruptcies, reorganizations, and receiverships. Lenders were in desperate need of creative leadership and informed advice about the industry as a whole. This, together with Penn Central's own problems, explains the popularity of the company as a locale for financial directors as well as a recruiting ground for outside directors for several major financial boards (Daughen and Binzen, 1971).

Southern Pacific's role in the network is similar, although its ties were primarily to western, rather than eastern, banks and it did not fall into bankruptcy.

Westinghouse, which appeared in the top twenty in 1962 and 1966, maintained fifteen financial interlocks each year, including ties to First National City Bank, Metropolitan Life, Chase, Harris, and Mellon. In 1969, when it dropped far down the list, it had lost two-thirds of its financial interlocks, including links to Chase and

Metropolitan. Its slip from network prominence seems to reflect that lenders had begun to recover their massive investment in nuclear energy.

These profiles of centrally situated nonfinancial corporations illustrate the pattern of multiple ties to major financial institutions that underlies their prominence in the interlock network. Retention or loss of centrality was largely a consequence of retaining or replacing bank and insurance company interlocks, and financial ties were a reflection of corporate or sectoral prominence in capital flows.

Consider the vast difference between the profiles just discussed and that of United California Bank (UCB), which increased its centrality rank from 248th in 1962 to thirteenth in 1966. Two different processes produced this rise (and the comparable rises of Pacific Mutual Life and Western Bancorp): the ascent of Pacific Coast business into national prominence and the merger of UCB into Western Bancorp, one of the earliest bank holding companies.[23]

Western Bancorp acquired control of UCB in 1959, and three interlocks were immediately established between the holding company and its subsidiary. In 1964 a process of absorption began, and by 1966 the number of shared directors increased to nine. This allowed for more detailed coordination among the banks controlled by Western Bancorp. It also created multiple interlocks between the banks and a great many related industrial firms. For example, Edward Carter, the chairman of Broadway-Hale Stores, had long been an outside member of Western Bancorp's board, as well as a director of several other industrial firms. The consolidation process led him to join UCB's board; he consequently created interlocks between UCB and Southern California Edison, Pacific Mutual Life, Northrop, and Broadway-Hale. Since UCB had already established ties to Southern California Edison and Pacific Mutual, Hale's interlocks created redundant multiple links with these companies. This consolidation thus produced unintended multiple ties among UCB, Western Bancorp, and Pacific Mutual, on one hand, and eight West Coast industrial firms on the other.[24] Moreover, these multiple ties substantially increased the centrality of UCB, Western Bancorp, and Pacific Mutual.[25] By 1969, the consolidation had been completed, UCB was no longer listed as a separate company, and Western Bancorp was ranked sixth in assets among commercial banks.

At the same time, West Coast business was growing more rapidly than the traditional industrial centers. The enhanced centrality of UCB reflected this trend in three ways:

1. UCB itself began to establish economic and interlock ties with major firms outside California, including new links with General Mills, Marcor, ITT, and Lehman Brothers.
2. UCB established new economic and interlock connections with growing nonfinancial firms in the West, including new links with Cyprus Mines, Pacific Gas and Electric (PG&E), and Rockwell International.
3. Industrial companies with which UCB had long maintained relationships began establishing ties to major eastern corporations, therefore increasing their own centrality in the interlock network. The maintenance of UCB's connections to these firms resulted in enhanced importance for UCB, both economically and within the interlock network. Litton, whose centrality rose from .09 to .29, Lockheed (.06 to .21), Southern California Edison (.23 to .39), Times-Mirror (.21 to .48), TWA (.23 to .47), and Union Oil (.18 to .51) were the main firms in this group.

As a result of these factors, UCB increased its centrality from .14 in 1962 (based on nineteen interlocks with sixteen firms) to .62 in 1966 (based on fifty-eight interlocks with thirty corporations). Using the calculus of centrality presented in Appendix 3, we can partition this increase into its various sources (table 7.11). We see that nearly half (45%) of UCB's increased centrality derived from the merger process, and this explains why Western Bancorp dropped from the top list in 1969 once the merger had been completed.

On the other hand, 41% of the increased centrality can be attributed to the changing position of West Coast business. It is important to note that the increase deriving from Western ascent (which would have placed UCB about fifty-fifth) was mainly (63%) a result of UCB's relations to West Coast businesses; only a small proportion derived from new interlocks to the East. This is consistent with the patterns discussed in chapter 5: regional banks become more important when industrial firms in their areas become more important. They remain profoundly regional. Money market banks deal directly with nationally important industrials, no matter where they are located. Regional banks remain tied to their local corporations, and their prominence increases when locally based industrials become more economically dominant and tie into the money market.

This is underscored when we investigate the sources of UCB's new nonwestern interlocks, those with Lehman Brothers, General Mills, Continental Corp., Marcor, and ITT. The first two were created when Charles Thornton, the chief executive officer of rapidly

Table 7.11
Sources of Increased Centrality for United California Bank (UCB)

Source	Degree	Percentage	
Increases due to growing importance of West Coast firms	.199		41
New UCB ties to western industrial firms	.067	14	
Increased centrality of western industrial firms already tied to UCB	.059	12	
New UCB ties to eastern firms	.073	15	
Increases due to process of merging UCB into Western Bancorp	.215		45
Redundant interlocks with western industrial firms	.155	32	
Multiple ties to Western Bancorp and Pacific Mutual	.060	13	
All other sources[a]	.060		14
Total increase			
Centrality in 1962	.480		
Increase in 1966	.140		
Centrality in 1966	.620		

[a]See Appendix 3. These include changes in density of the network, interlocks with minor firms, and interaction effects.

expanding Litton Industries (and a long time member of UCB's board) was invited onto the boards of Lehman and General Mills. The tie to ITT was the result of the election to that board of Dwight Cochran, the head of Kern County Land. These new ties to eastern industrials were therefore really an incidental result of the elections of Litton and Kern County executives to those boards, and not a consequence of direct UCB relationships. Only the ties to Continental Corporation and Marcor can be attributed to unmediated connections to the East.

Thus, of the increased UCB centrality attributed to the rise of western business, 89% derived from connections established by industrial firms. This emphasizes the regional character of California banking, which remained local through the 1970s (Business Week, April 17, 1978: 66–72).

In analyzing UCB's interlock profile, we note one further pattern: unlike major industrials, UCB (despite six interlocks with Western Bancorp and Pacific Mutual) derived less than 20% of its 1966 centrality from ties to other financials. This is typical of all large banks—regional or national.

Consider Morgan, Chase, Chemical, and First National City, the most consistently central banks. The Clayton Antitrust Act prohibits interlocks among competitive banks, but not between money market and regional institutions. Nevertheless, only Chase maintained ties with more than one important regional commercial bank: First National Bank of Chicago (1962 and 1966), Harris (1962), and First Pennsylvania (1966). Morgan had only one bank interlock during the period under study (with First Pennsylvania in 1962); First National City had a total of six with very minor institutions, and Chemical had three, including a 1962 tie to Continental Illinois.

Interlocks with insurance companies, on the other hand, were more extensive: each of these major commercial banks maintained at least five ties to insurance companies in each year. Metropolitan Life, Equitable, and New York Life (the main money market institutions) were tied to all four at least once in 1962 or 1966. Nevertheless, these links accounted for only a small proportion of the centrality of the major banks. Only for Chase, in 1962, do they contribute more than 20% of the banks' centrality. For Morgan in 1966, its six financial links contributed less than 10%.

The detailed examination of the interlock profile of United California Bank has produced three important general patterns. First, the specifics of a firm's history (in this case a complex merger) greatly influence its centrality. Second, regional banks rise (or fall) through their connections to regional industrial firms, and not because of substantial numbers of interlocks outside the region. Third, banks, unlike nonfinancials, do not derive their centrality from financial interlocks.

Now consider Lehman Brothers, which rose from 152d in 1962 to eighth in 1966. Until the early 1960s, almost all investment banks operated as partnerships rather than corporations. Interlocks between investment banks and other companies, therefore, involved the election of a partner of the investment bank to the board of the host company. Since investment companies do not have formal boards of directors, corporate representation on investment house boards could not exist. Between 1962 and 1966, Lehman Brothers became a pioneer in investment banking by reorganizing into a corporation, thus laying the foundation for its subsequent transformation into a diversified financial institution. One by-product (or motive) of the change was the creation of a board of directors and the recruitment of outsiders with interests or connections that would facilitate both traditional investment banking and expansion into new enterprises.

During this period, Lehman Brothers had considerable turnover in personnel and interlocks: of the forty ties existing in 1962, thirty-three were broken, largely because of the departure of eleven partners. Three new inside directors were added, creating eleven new interlocks, including important ties to General Motors, American Express, and Southern Pacific. The addition of nine new outside board members created twenty-eight more interlocks to important industrial firms such as Ford, TWA, Westinghouse, and Litton, and ten interlocks with financial firms, including Morgan, Metropolitan Life, and Bankers Trust. These ties could not have existed under the partnership arrangement.[26] From 1962 to 1966, Lehman's centrality rose from .20 to .71; 97% of this rise is due to the addition of these outsiders to the board; 32% derived from the ten new financial ties.

The rise of Lehman Brothers was a consequence of the restructuring of the firm and did not reflect an abrupt change in status. In its new corporate form, it could attract the outside directors appropriate to a leader in its sector. Of particular importance is the significance of financial interlocks in establishing Lehman's centrality. In this respect it resembles highly central industrial companies rather than banks, which are not heavily tied to other financials.

We interpret this as suggesting that investment banking, like other sectors, is important enough to merit representation among the most central firms but is not dominant in a manner akin to commercial banks and insurance companies. As Kotz (1978) has convincingly argued, the predepression ascendancy of investment banking was undermined by the growing centralization of capital into money market institutions and permanently eclipsed by the financial legislation of the 1930s.

Conclusion

In chapter 6 we outlined the multiple functions of interlocking directorates in late twentieth century American business and suggested that an understanding of the role that interlocks play can derive only from an analysis of the underlying capital-flow patterns among major corporate actors. In this chapter we have attempted to document this proposition by demonstrating and analyzing the correlation between network centrality and the role of different firms in the system of corporate finance. We need not review the evidence in detail, but a summary of our findings will introduce our analysis of these patterns as well as lay a foundation for the more detailed calculations offered in chapters 8–10.

First, the stable core of the network is the money market banks and insurance companies, whose centrality persists throughout the 1960s despite considerable turnover in specific interlocks. Morgan, Chase, First National City, Chemical, Bankers Trust, and to a lesser extent Manufacturers Hanover, Mellon, and First National Bank of Chicago, maintain themselves as central banks. Equitable, New York Life, and Metropolitan Life are the central insurance companies. These firms, although not necessarily the largest or most prominent in retail financial markets, are the acknowledged leaders in commercial lending; their dominance in the interlock networks substantiates the intimate connection between board relationships and capital flows.

Second, the most central nonfinancials, although usually among the one hundred largest companies, are not necessarily the most important industrial companies either from the viewpoint of size or from the perspective of their resource interdependence with other firms or sectors. The extremes of this pattern are expressed by Exxon and Du Pont on the one hand, which maintained relatively few interlocks, and Phelps Dodge and American Distillers and Chemical on the other, which were centrally located in the network. These anomalies, as well as the less dramatic inconsistencies between economic and network importance, are explained by the dominance of financial interlocks. Industrial companies become network stars if they attract outsiders from major boards. This popularity is itself a reflection of corporate and/or sectoral prominence in the network of capital flows.

This association of interlock prominence with capital flows is reflected in temporal changes of network status. Industrial companies rise and fall in status in relatively short cycles, as they (or their sectors) become major sources or recipients of investment capital. The leaders of corporations that are large borrowers are especially useful as outsiders on bank boards, since they provide both information and insight into the prospects for successful investment. But when these sectors are no longer important locations of new capital, these companies slip in prominence.

Financial institutions rise insofar as they supply major nonfinancial companies. The money market firms remain central because they consistently lead major lending consortia and institutional investment in nationally prominent nonfinancials. The rise of regional institutions in California, Chicago, and Dallas generally reflects the increasing importance of their customers. As regional industrials become prominent, the regional banks to which they are tied also gain in stature.

The relationship between capital flows and interlocks is a result of the complementary character of the two. In chapter 2 we explored the unique quality of capital as a resource; unlike other economic relationships, lending and stockholding create a temporary partnership. This partnership is an "arm's length" arrangement, because it is not meant to create control—that is, intervention into discretionary decision making. On the other hand, large investments create a common fate; both lender and borrower depend heavily upon successful use of capital.

This implies the need for reliable information about this joint venture. Interlocks are an ideal vehicle for this because they provide information about the ongoing conditions of the institutions involved. In cases of specific questions about specific loans or stock purchases, however, interlocks are relatively inefficient and unnecessary. Instead, documents and other hard evidence are typically the preferred method of evaluation. Necessary information often involves speculation about an unpredictable future, however, and interlocks are ideal for this because they rely on personal trust and individual integrity to a much greater degree than a business transaction.

For this reason, interlocks have evolved into the major form of strategic information exchange in the corporate world. They provide the mechanism for the circulation of general information about investment policy and opportunity, for informed speculation about trends in capital flows, and for promulgating the variety of values and norms that constitute a corporate culture based on financial hegemony.

8 Directional Interlocks and the Integration of Regional Groupings into the National Corporate Network

A personal union, so to speak, is established between the banks and the biggest industrial and commercial enterprises. The merging of one with another through the acquisition of shares, through the appointment of bank directors to the Supervisory Boards (or Boards of Directors) of industrial and commercial enterprises, and vice versa.

V. I. Lenin, *Imperialism*

It is tempting to interpret our findings thus far as support for bank and insurance company control of the most important industrial firms in the American economy. The dominance that financials exhibit in the interlock network evokes images of bank representatives sitting on industrial boards and suggesting, encouraging, or dictating action that reflects bank policies and interests.

As we indicated in chapter 7, however, such a conclusion would not be consistent with the evidence. The interlocks that create financial centrality are not usually created by bank officers. Most often they are created by chief executives of major nonfinancial firms who have accepted invitations to sit on bank and industrial boards. Bearden (1982), in a detailed analysis of the board composition of the twenty largest banks, found that 79% of bank board members were outsiders, that almost all of these were chief executive officers of major industrials, and that these individuals created well over 50% of the banks' interlocks.

Consider, for example, First National City Bank. In 1962, its board included Amory Houghton of Corning Glass, John Kimberly of Kimberly-Clark, Roger Milliken of Deering-Milliken, and Reginald Taylor of the Taylor-Pyne interests. All were industrial executives and leading members of propertied families. The First National City directorate also included executives of General Foods, Metropolitan Life, NCR, United Aircraft, and Exxon.

These patterns undermine traditional bank control theory, since in every documented example of interlocks that trace outside control (see especially Kotz, 1978; Mizruchi, 1982a; Fitch and Oppenheimer, 1970a-c) the dominant firm sent its officers to sit on the board of the subordinate firm. If we were to interpret major bank interlocks as traces of control, we would have to conclude that major industrials collectively controlled the banks, not vice versa. This would reinforce Herman's (1979) conclusion (based on other evidence) that "bankers are powerful servants of the largest nonfinancial corporations, rather than their masters" (p. 56; see also Herman, 1973, 1981; Sweezy, 1972; O'Connor, 1968, 1972).

All recent work, however, has pointed to the interpretation offered in chapters 6 and 7: that while the selection of a corporate officer as an outsider on another board may signify an important tie between the companies, it does not usually reflect intercorporate control. Instead, it represents one or more of a variety of relationships between the companies or the corporate leadership.

In this chapter we explore the patterns of primary interlocks, those ties created when an officer of one company in our population is elected to the board of another. Such interlocks differ from secondary interlocks, which are by-products of primary ties. In the case of primary interlocks we can assume that the outside officer is a representative of her or his home company. This can therefore be analyzed as a directional tie.

To illustrate, consider Stanley Powell, president of Alexander and Baldwin, one of five diversified companies that dominate the Hawaiian economy (see chapter 2). In 1966, Powell sat on the boards of two other companies, Matson Navigation and Bancal Tristate Corporation. In doing this, he established primary interlocks between his home company and the other two (see figure 8.1). We

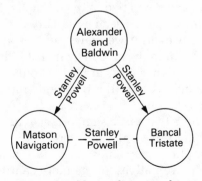

Figure 8.1. Alexander and Baldwin, directional interlocks.

can safely assume that in some sense he represented the interests of Alexander and Baldwin in the board deliberations of both Matson and Bancal Tristate. With this assumption, the interlock becomes directional, implying that Alexander and Baldwin sent its representative to the receiving corporations.[1] Although Powell also created an interlock between Matson and Bancal Tristate, this tie is neither directional nor primary.[2] One can argue that this was the accidental by-product of the election of an Alexander and Baldwin representative onto the two other boards.

In 1962, Alexander and Baldwin owned 93.7% of Matson (Burch, 1972: 87), and this fact clarifies the motive of these interlocks. First, Powell's position on Matson's board represented a control relationship. The interlock therefore was not symptomatic of the importance of Matson in the larger network. Quite the contrary, it indicated the differential importance of the two firms. Second, Powell's election to the Bancal Tristate board must have been a consequence of his role at Alexander and Baldwin (A&B), the parent firm of which he was a leader. The interlock he created between Matson and Bancal Tristate was therefore redundant and not a symptom of Matson's importance in the network.

Hence, the calculation of centrality developed in chapter 7 exaggerated Matson's position in two ways: by interpreting the Matson–Alexander and Baldwin link as signifying equal importance for both parties and by interpreting the Matson–Bancal Tristate link as significant at all. A more accurate portrait would necessarily take this into account.[3] The full impact of these conclusions is illustrated by examining the role played by Henry T. Mudd, chairman of Cyprus Mines, in the 1962 network. Figure 8.2 is a presentation of the interlocks he created in that year. His presence on six other boards created a total of twenty-one intercorporate links: each of the seven companies was tied to the other six. In most interlock analyses each firm would be seen as equally central in this region of the network. However, if we view Mudd as a representative of Cyprus Mines, we obtain the map in figure 8.3. While Cyprus maintains its ties, the six other firms are linked only through their Cyprus connection and thus are the recipients rather than the initiators of network relations.

This logic suggests that a firm's importance can be best measured by considering only those interlocks created when its officers sit on the boards of other companies. The more companies an organization sends representatives to, the more central it is in the network. Any corporation that does not send many officers to other

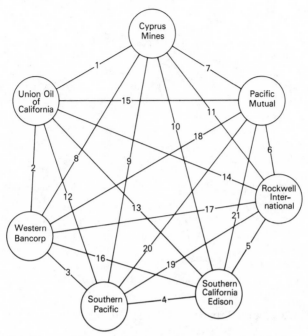

Figure 8.2. Cyprus Mines, primary and secondary interlocks.

boards would be very low in centrality, no matter how many outsiders it received.

Consider, however, the Chicago, Burlington and Quincy Railroad
(CB&Q), which sent one representative, Harry C. Murphy, to First
Chicago Bank while receiving six directors from the following firms:
Inland Steel, Great Northern Railroad, Quaker Oats, Northern Pacific Railroad, and John Morrell. Compare this with Chromalloy
American, which also sent one director to another company, Fron-
tier Airlines, but did not receive any outsiders. The two firms are
not equivalent. Had the CB&Q been inconsequential, Clarence Ran-
dall of Inland Steel and five other important Chicago area executives would not have joined the board. Thus, the fact that CB&Q
received interlocks from major midwestern corporations is an indication of its importance in the network. That Chromalloy American had no such ties may indicate independence, but it may also
reflect the fact that important outsiders refused board membership
because of its relatively insignificant position.

To take this into account we evaluate incoming interlocks as less
significant, but not inconsequential, in determining the centrality
of a company. The most central firms in the directional analysis

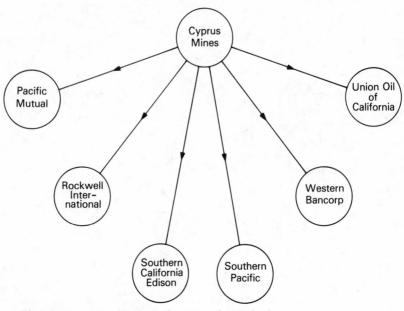

Figure 8.3. Cyprus Mines, directional interlocks.

are therefore those that send many officers to other firms whose officers, in turn, sit on the boards of still other firms, which in turn receive officers from companies that receive still other companies' executives.[4]

In 1962, 28% of all interlocks in our system were directional; that is, the individual who created the link was an active executive of one of the companies. We performed a centrality analysis on the network created by these ties, eliminating nondirectional links and giving only minor credit to incoming ties. To illustrate this method, we return to our Cyprus Mines example. Asa Call, executive officer of Pacific Mutual Life Insurance Company, sat on seven boards in 1962, including that of Cyprus. He therefore created an incoming directional link from Pacific Mutual to Cyprus and also connected Cyprus to five other companies. In the directional analysis, the five extra links were not considered, and Cyprus Mines lost a third of its fifteen interlocks. The tie to Pacific Mutual was considered to be one-ninth the strength of the links created by Cyprus's president (figure 8.3).

Table 8.1 lists the most central companies in the directional networks of 1962 and 1966. In 1962, ten of the top twenty companies were financials; in 1966 nine of the top twenty were financials. The

Table 8.1
Twenty Most Central Corporations, 1962 and 1966: Directional Analysis

Corporation	Type[a]	1962	1966
Mellon	Bank	1	1
Sears[b]	Mer	2	2
First National Bank of Chicago	Bank	3	4
Continental Illinois Bank[b]	Bank	4	8
Chase Manhattan Bank	Bank	5	38
First National City Bank	Bank	6	3
Commonwealth Edison[b]	Util	7	24
International Harvester	Ind	8	10
Inland Steel[b]	Ind	9	27
Quaker Oats[b]	Ind	10	20
Bankers Trust	Bank	11	37
Equitable Life Assurance	Ins	12	19
Chemical Bank of New York	Bank	13	5
Morgan (J. P.)	Bank	14	7
American Telephone and Telegraph	Util	15	11
Corning Glass Works[b]	Ind	16	30
National Distillers and Chemical[b]	Ind	17	13
Marshall Field[b]	Mer	18	83
Pacolet Industries[b]	Ind	19	18
New York Life	Ins	20	71
Broadway-Hale[b]	Ind	—	6
United California Bank	Bank	—	9
Litton Industries[b]	Ind	—	12
Gillette[b]	Ind	—	14
Southern California Edison[b]	Ind	—	15
Pacific Mutual	Ins	—	16
Cyprus Mines[b]	Ind	—	17

[a]For type abbreviations, see table 7.2.
[b]Not among the most central corporations of the full interlock network.

money market banks, which dominated the full network, also appeared among the most central in the directional system. Eight New York financials—including Morgan Guaranty, Chase Manhattan, Equitable Life, Chemical Bank, New York Life, and First National City Bank—appeared in the 1962 list, and four of them—Morgan, Equitable, First National City Bank, and Chemical—were also found in the 1966 directional listing. Important regional financials—Mellon, First National Bank of Chicago, Continental Illinois, United

California Bank, and Pacific Mutual—prominent in the full network were among the most central in this network as well. In fact, they were more central than major money market financials. Mellon National, a Pittsburgh commercial bank with quasi-money market status, was the most central firm in 1962 and 1966. In 1962 both First National Bank of Chicago and Continental Illinois, the largest Chicago banks, outranked the New York financials. Morgan Guaranty, a key money market institution, ranked fourteenth in 1962 and rose to seventh by 1966; Chase Manhattan ranked fifth in 1962 but dropped to thirty-eighth in 1966. These institutions were the key units in the full network.

These patterns indicate that the dominance of the money market in the full network rested to a considerable degree on the presence of major industrial executives on their boards. The introduction of directionality downgraded the importance of these ties in assessing centrality, and this resulted in a decline in network importance for the New York financials. At the same time, most regional banks maintained or enhanced their centrality, indicating that their executives were more active than money market officers as outside directors of important nonfinancials. We shall return to this pattern below, since it reveals the texture of the relationship between national and regional capital flows.

In 1962, only two of the seven nonfinancial firms that appeared among the top twenty in the full network were recorded among the most central in the directional analysis. These were AT&T, whose chairman (Frederick Kappel) and president (Eugene McNeeley) sat on six major boards, and International Harvester, whose three top executives sat on five major boards. Southern Pacific ranked eighth in the full network in 1962, maintaining fifty interlocks with forty-one other firms. Since only eight of these ties were directional and all were incoming, Southern Pacific plunged to 385th most central in the directional analysis.

The nonfinancials that appear among the most central in the directional network are by and large regional companies with national connections. Sears, Commonwealth Edison, International Harvester, Inland Steel, Quaker Oats, and Marshall Field—which ranked second, seventh, eighth, ninth, tenth, and eighteenth respectively in 1962—were all Chicago-area companies; Corning Glass Works, National Distillers, and Pacolet Industries—which ranked sixteenth, seventeenth, and nineteenth—were regional New York area concerns. Broadway-Hale, Litton Industries, Southern California Edison, and Cyprus Mines—ranked sixth, twelfth, fifteenth, and seventeenth in 1966—were western companies; Gillette, the fourteenth most central in 1966, was located in New England. AT&T, the only national company among the fourteen nonfinancials in table 8.1, was ranked fifteenth in 1962 and eleventh in 1966.

These results indicate that the leaders of regional industrials are far more popular as outside directors than the leaders of national industrials, a result that parallels the relationship between regional and money market financials. These two results are highly significant: in our view they provide an insight into the sources of unity and coordination of the American corporate system.

To understand these results and to utilize them in constructing a comprehensive interpretation of both interlocks and intercorporate structure, we offer table 8.2 and figure 8.4. These provide information about the main sources of centrality for the top firms in the directional network of 1966.[5] From table 8.2 we conclude that the sources of centrality are very different for industrial and financial corporations, a result that parallels the analysis in chapter 7. The top industrials received most of their directional centrality from interlocks with a small number of centrally located financials. Pacolet Industries, for example, sent an officer to the boards of First National City Bank and of Irving Trust, a New York regional institution. These two interlocks alone produced 34% of Pacolet's centrality in the directional system. Southern California Edison derived 65% of its directional centrality from the placement of its chief executive officer on the boards of United California Bank, Pacific Mutual Life, and Western Bancorp. Among eleven nonfinancials in the top twenty, ten took their largest single quantum of directional centrality from a bank interlock. Of the thirty-three most important links that these firms maintained, twenty-one were to banks and insurance companies. On average, these industrials derived 48% of their directional centrality from links to two or three large financial institutions.

Banks, especially regional banks, exhibited the opposite pattern: their centrality derived almost exclusively from ties to a few industrials. Over 50% of United California's centrality came from its placement of directors on the boards of Cyprus Mines, Litton Industries, and Times-Mirror Company. Mellon derived 37% of its centrality from links to Consolidation Coal, Gulf Oil, and Alcoa. Even the national banks (though the percentages are lower) derived substantial proportions of centrality from links to two or three industrials.[6]

This pattern is graphically displayed in figure 8.4, which presents a mapping of the major links among the twenty most central corporations of the 1966 directional network, as well as the ties of less

Table 8.2
Sources of Centrality, Twenty Most Central Corporations, 1966:
Directional Network

Industrials	Centrality Score	Percentage Derived from Top Three Banks	Largest Contributors
Sears	.88	53	Chemical, Continental Illinois, First National Bank of Chicago
Broadway-Hale	.76	43	Bank of America, UCB, Pacific Mutual
International Harvester	.67	43	Harris, First National Bank of Chicago
American Telephone and Telegraph	.61	41	Metropolitan, Chemical, Chase Manhattan
Litton Industries	.59	56	Western, UCB, Lehman
National Distillers and Chemical	.54	52	First National City, Chemical
Gillette	.52	46	Morgan, First National Bank of Boston
Southern California Edison	.51	65	UCB, Pacific Mutual, Western
Cyprus Mines	.50	50	UCB, Pacific Mutual, Western
Pacolet Industries	.50	34	First National City, Irving Trust
Quaker Oats	.48	40	First National Bank of Chicago, Northern Trust, Continental Assurance

central companies that maintained interlocks with two or more of the top firms. The companies are grouped according to their regional locations. An arrow between two companies indicates that an executive of the sending firm is a member of the receiving firm's directorate *and* that this link is an important (over 10%) contributor to the sending firm's centrality. As the chart demonstrates, regional banks exchange directors with major regional industrials, while these same industrial firms send unreciprocated representatives to national bank boards. National banks receive directors from regional and national industrials and send a bewildering set of representatives to important and unimportant corporations.

This diagram illustrates the existence of dense regional networks, each tied to the New York money market. The most central

Table 8.2 (*cont.*)

Banks	Centrality Score	Percentage Derived from Top Three Nonfinancials	Largest Contributors
Regional			
Mellon	1.00	37	Consolidation Coal, Gulf, Alcoa
First National Bank of Chicago	.78	44	Sears, Inland, Marshall Field
Continental Illinois Bank	.72	53	International Harvester, Commonwealth Edison, Consolidation Coal
United California Bank	.68	55	Cyprus Mines, Litton, Times-Mirror
National			
First National City Bank	.85	32	NCR, United States Steel
Morgan	.73	42	Gillette, Campbell, United States Steel
Chemical Bank of New York	.78	38	Associated Dry Goods, National Distillers

Insurance Companies	Centrality Score	Percentage Derived from Top Three Nonfinancials	Largest Contributors
Pacific Mutual	.51	41	UCB, Western Bancorp
Equitable Life Assurance	.49	73	Chemical, Chase Manhattan, First National Bank of Chicago

firms in each region are financials, but important industrials account for a large proportion of total interlocks and therefore of overall centrality. Continental Illinois, First National Bank of Chicago, International Harvester, and Quaker Oats, all located in Chicago, appear among the twenty most central corporations of the directional analysis. This high centrality is the result of each firm's sending officers to the boards of several other companies in the area.[7] Moreover, these regional groups are tied into the national network, largely through a series of connecting industrials. Sears is a perfect example: it exchanged officers with one Chicago-area

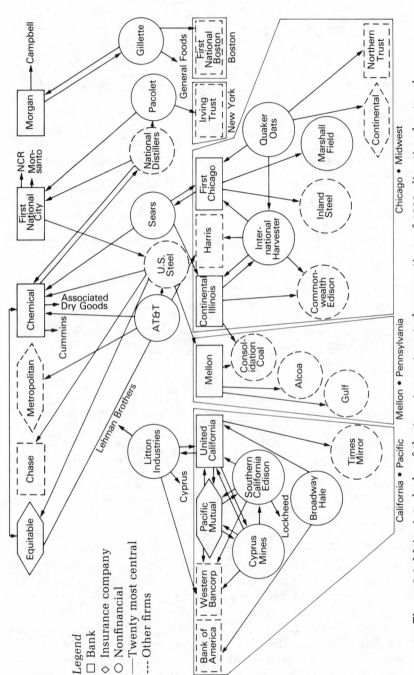

Figure 8.4. Major interlocks of the twenty most central corporations of 1966: directional network.

bank and sent representatives to Continental Illinois, another regional financial, as well as to Chemical Bank, a money market firm. Pacolet Industries, a regional New York industrial, sent a representative to Irving Trust, a New York regional bank, and to First National City Bank, a major money market institution. Gillette, a New England regional firm, sent representatives to a regional bank, First National Bank of Boston, and exchanged directors with a national bank, Morgan Guaranty. Litton Industries, in 1966 a rapidly rising West Coast company, maintained representatives on the boards of regional financials United California Bank and Western Bancorp as well as Lehman Brothers, a major national investment firm. Were we to consider the full array of directional interlocks, we would find this pattern replicated over and over again. Alcoa, which exchanged officers with Mellon National Bank in its region, sent a representative to the board of Metropolitan Life, a money market insurance company. Commonwealth Edison, which exchanged directors with Continental Illinois, sent representatives to First National Bank of Chicago and Nortrust—both midwestern banks—as well as New York Life.

We conclude that regional industrials achieve high centrality in the interlock network for two reasons: they exchange directors with regional banks, and they send representatives to the New York money market. The regional banks derive their centrality from their interlocks with regional industrials. Money market firms derive their directional centrality from placing representatives with a broad array of national firms and receiving a large number of outsiders from prominent regional industrials. These patterns suggest a system of regional groupings, each tied into the national network. Their significance for the integration of the system as a whole is immense, and it is to these implications that we now turn.

We begin by exploring the meaning of the dense interchanges among regional companies. These reflect long-term business relationships among local elites, one expression of which is board interlocks. In Houston, for example,

> as in many regional cities, social and business life are closely intertwined. And this puts Mr. [James A.] Elkins [chairman of First City Bancorporation of Houston] in a privileged position. On the golf course and in the private clubs it is particularly easy for him to build relationships with his peers, at the area's top companies. (New York Times, May 25, 1980: F1)

As regional chief executive officers pursue their own careers as well as the economic interest of their firms, they gain reputations as shrewd or naive, innovative or traditional, dynamic or organizational. Executives who are invited onto regional bank boards are selected because of the size and importance of their companies and because of their own achievements as executives. Regional bank boards thus recruit the local corporate all-stars to help obtain opportunities for investment in the region and thus to decide the direction of capital flows in the area.

At the same time, the chief executive of each regional industrial attempts to assemble a useful board of directors to provide information relevant to allocative decision making, institutional connections, and personal support for his or her leadership. Since industrials require a narrower range of expertise, their boards do not usually reflect the entire regional spectrum. However, most will seek out bankers and find local regional banking executives receptive to their invitation, since these positions often advance their own careers as well as the institutional interests of their banks.

Thus, regions tend to develop a tightly knit set of interlocks that represent economic, institutional, and personal interdependencies. These connections become a working reality in the daily business of the locality. The prevalence of these formations has been documented by earlier interlock research (Allen, 1974; Dooley, 1969; Sonquist and Koenig, 1975), and tight regional groupings are now assumed to be part of the world of business.[8] Chicago, for example, is "known for its close corporate ties, with friends sitting on each other's boards" (Business Week, June 25, 1979: 74); Houston was dominated, until the early 1960s, by "about a half dozen influential businessmen" (Houston Chronicle, June 27, 1977: 2–6); and Cleveland's "chief executives spend as much time—often more—doing charity work and serving on each other's boards as they do running their own companies" (Business Week, Dec. 13, 1976). Every serious study of a major metropolitan area has discovered tight interlock networks with banks as the central nodes.

As the individual company or the region as a whole grows larger, local financial institutions are no longer able to supply the capital needs of the major firms (see chapter 5 above; Katona, 1957: 43, 46–47, 82). This sends the leading regional industrials into the New York money market. If growth continues and more local companies seek out national lenders, the money market banks must acquire expertise and detailed knowledge of the conditions and possibilities for investment in the area. Their best sources for such information are the same executives who play a leading role in the regional economy—both because of the importance of their firms and because of their individual standing and knowledge within the local elite. A regional chief executive officer who commands respect as an innovative, dynamic leader—and is an outsider on important regional boards—is therefore the ideal candidate for a national bank board membership. He (only rarely she) is eager to join a national bank board because it represents an important structural connection for the firm and a major career move for him personally.

This is the process by which the unifying connections in figure 8.4 are created, and it underlies the national network of personal ties documented by Bonacich and Domhoff (1977) and Useem (1979, 1983). This also explains the prominence of local industrials in the directional network: the outsiders from these companies are actually representatives of the entire region. They provide information about, and insight into, the economic functioning of their home communities.

These types of ties may, however, be impermanent. By the mid-1970s, Litton Industries, a California regional in the 1960s, had grown into a national corporation. It was hardly representative of California industry, and its executives were no longer experts on western investment opportunities. Sears had become so large and locationally diverse that it was no longer a midwestern firm. Such companies become less involved in regional business affairs, and their leaders become less useful as informational links with the money market. Their knowledge is limited to the specific industrial sector in which they operate. Wright (1979), for example, describes the extreme isolation of General Motors leadership in the early 1970s. They were not deeply involved in the local Detroit business community, nor were they well integrated into the national network (see also Ewen, 1978).

National industrial companies, though they do not represent regional economies, find places on national financial boards because of their knowledge of crucial business sectors. AT&T, for example, sent representatives to Chemical, Chase, and Metropolitan (see figure 8.4). United States Steel, the second most central nonfinancial of 1966 (rank nine), sent representatives to Chase, Equitable, Chemical, and even Mellon, a regional firm with historical ties to the steel industry. But since these national companies are not integrated into local networks, they do not acquire the centrality that derives from the dense interchanges among regional firms. In these instances there may be a single corporation in each sector whose leadership is trusted and therefore asked to serve on money market boards. This helps to explain why Bethlehem, the second largest steel producer and twentieth largest nonfinancial, did not maintain any interlocks in 1962; United States Steel had monopolized the "steel" position on money market boards, and Bethlehem was no longer integrated into a regional economy. (By 1966, Bethlehem had established a number of important *incoming* ties but had only one outgoing interlock—to Continental Illinois Bank.)

National nonfinancial corporations are less central in the directional analysis because they do not tie regions together. Although in a strictly economic sense these companies are more important than regional firms, they are less crucial in the intercorporate network because they can represent only themselves and their sectors. Major regional companies, on the other hand, provide information about, and potential relationships with, an entire geographic area as well as an industrial sector. Thus, the network is not a one-to-one mapping of the economic or financial importance of the particular firm, but a trace of broader patterns involving groups of firms.

Consider now the role of national and regional bank executives as outsiders on industrial boards. Outgoing financial interlocks function differently than the incoming ties discussed above. Leaders of industrial firms tend to seek out bankers for their boards, both because of the importance of banks in their environment and because they can "provide a panoramic view" of an industry or a region (Pennings, 1980: 105). This explains, at least in part, Bearden's (1982) findings that 64% of the one hundred largest nonfinancials had at least one banker on their board, and that 26% of all outsiders on these boards were from financial firms.

Friendship networks are an important part of this process. Especially in regional contexts, industrial executives have personal relationships with bank leadership. Individual trust and mutual loyalty enhance the attractiveness of the banker as an outside director and ensure his or her acceptance of the invitation to serve. As one inside officer put it:

> Our relations with our bank are very close. We see each other on the street, we have lunch, we meet at parties, and a banker from the _____ Trust is on our board. Our president is on the board of a bank. (Katona, 1957: 54)

Similarly, there are various incentives for a bank executive to join the board of a nonfinancial firm. Friendship networks account for much of the personal incentive, and this explains many of the reciprocal interlocks we have noted in this chapter. It might be more than impolite for a banker to ask an industrial chief executive officer to join his or her board and refuse the reciprocal offer. Local bankers, especially, may derive personal and institutional prestige from membership on a board with national visibility.[9]

On an institutional level, we can identify still other reasons for bank representation on industrial boards. In certain circumstances, banker participation is a useful vehicle for obtaining information about the host company, though it is usually quicker, easier, and more reliable to consult an active executive in the company or industry. In times of corporate crisis bank creditors especially may feel that direct representation will offer more reliable information than depending on the chief executive officer. In the case of the Penn Central bankruptcy in 1969, for example, Stuart Saunders, one of the key leaders of the railroad, sat on the boards of Chase, Equitable, and First Pennsylvania. Nevertheless, the lenders knew little about the seriousness of the crisis and were "furious" that they had gotten "so deeply involved without knowing what a hole the Penn Central was in" (Daughen and Binzen, 1971: 260). To prevent this sort of problem, bank officials can be sent to borrowers' boards.

In situations of potential or actual conflict, however, industrial leaders are most reluctant to offer directorships to bankers who might disrupt the peaceful deliberations of the board. Such relationships are therefore generally developed from interlocks undertaken before the need for surveillance arises. In specific circumstances, the bank can insist on board representation. One executive expressed his ambivalence nicely:

> I don't think a bank should be in a position where they are actually setting policy for a company, but I think it is nice to have someone check your thinking and your approach to the problem. (Katona, 1957: 38)

Bankers, therefore, serve as outsiders on the boards of industrials for a combination of personal and institutional reasons. Unlike the case of outsiders sitting on the boards of commercial banks, though, bank representation may reflect stockholding or other overt control, heavy lending exposure, or interference because of corporate crisis. These situations provide both the incentive and the leverage for bank representation, although in most instances coercion—or even threat—is not necessary to convince the industrial leader to invite bank membership.

The outcome of these linkages to the money market is a community of executives from financial companies, national industrial firms, and representative regional corporations. This community, though it is more loosely knit than its regional counterparts, combines structural connections with personal relationships and produces broad understanding among its members of the common interests facing them. This information becomes the raw material for the collective decision making concerning national capital flows as well as producing the classwide rationality that characterizes the top leadership of American business.[10]

The network of directional interlocks traces and facilitates the flow of investment capital from financial to industrial firms, from the national money market to regional and industrial sectors. Within each region, certain local banks attain network prominence because their decision making about the allocation of capital to various firms and sectors requires the informed collective judgment of local business leadership. This judgment is managed by bringing the most respected and successful industrial leaders onto their boards and by placing bank officers on the boards of leading nonfinancial firms. These interchanges create the personal trust, as well as the institutional structure, for an informed collective judgment, whether the decisions are made at official board meetings, through individual consultation, or as part of informal gatherings at social clubs, parties, or golfing dates.

The prominence of regional banks in the directional network reflects their crucial role in the American economy. They exercise discretion over local investment, and they determine (within the considerable constraints placed upon them) which local sectors merit infusions of capital and which should not be encouraged to expand beyond their potential.

This local coherence provides the raw material for national capital-flow decision making. The money market, in assessing investment opportunities in various regions, must tap reliable expertise about new sectors and companies with which they have had little experience. The information/expertise available from major regional executives is particularly useful if these leaders are integrated into the local business community. They are sources of reliable information, both about their own and other sectors and about the leadership capabilities of local businessmen who seek capital from national money markets. Insofar as regional economies become attractive for national investment, local leaders become attractive as outside members of money market boards.

This unifying function, in a way, cancels itself out. Successful integration into national corporate life allows both executives and companies to expand nationally and internationally and therefore to project themselves away from their regional origins. In doing so, these executives transform themselves from regional to sectoral representatives and therefore create a void. Financial institutions must find new representatives from regional economies—either from the same region or from a newly developed and less saturated locale.

In this sense, the network is constantly changing, both because of the changes in the relationship of particular firms and executives to the underlying structure of regions and sectors and because of the changes in the relative importance of the regions and sectors themselves. These changes, like the enduring patterns discussed in chapter 7, trace and facilitate the flow of capital in the economy. They too symbolize and stabilize the hegemony of finance capital.

9 Hubs and Bridges: Unity and the Division of Labor in the Corporate Network

> Within the higher circles of the power elite, factions do exist; there are conflicts of policy; individual ambitions do clash. There are still enough divisions...to make for different methods of operation. But more powerful than these divisions are the internal discipline and the community of interests that bind the power elite together, even across the boundaries of nations at war.
>
> C. Wright Mills (1956: 283)

In chapter 8, we applied a directional analysis to the interlock network to help disentangle the relationships that create cohesive ties within regions and between regional groupings and the money market. In this chapter, we analyze the role of financial institutions in dampening conflict within the business world.

Specifically, we address three points. First, evidence presented in chapters 7 and 8 suggests that financial and nonfinancial corporations accumulate centrality in different ways. In the directional network, financial prominence is the result of bank representation on nonfinancial boards, while nonfinancial corporations gain centrality from sending officers to the boards of banks and insurance companies. In this chapter we wish to explore these differences in a more systematic way, comparing financial and nonfinancial centrality. We argue that the differences in interlock structure express different functions within the corporate world and that financial interlock arrangements enhance bank capacity to manage discretion over capital flows and, most particularly, to coordinate investment policy.

Second, we wish to investigate the differences in structural locations of banks and insurance companies. In chapter 3, we argued that the division of labor—commercial banks focus on short-term lending while insurance companies concentrate on long-term debt—thrusts banks into the position of primary determiners of lending commitments. This imposes upon banks the necessity of developing

203   **Hubs and Bridges: Unity and the
Division of Labor in the Corporate
Network**

a decision-making capacity and creates the main impetus for tight coordination between the two types of lending institutions. In this chapter, we explore the reflection of this symbiosis in the interlock network and discuss its significance for facilitating bank hegemony and reinforcing unity within the financial world.

Third, we have identified a system of regional groupings tied into a national network of capital flows and corporate coordination. In this chapter we explore more fully the role of interlocks in tying such groups together and integrating them into the national economy. This will provide a foundation for the detailed discussion in chapter 10 of the possible existence and development of competing financial groups.

To address these issues, we focus upon hubs, bridges, and sets (figure 9.1). A hub is a corporation at the center of a group of interlocked firms; a bridge connects two or more hubs; and a set is a small group of intensely interlocked companies, poorly integrated into the larger system. All three types may produce high centrality, although their interlock configurations are strikingly different.

We can extract different information about network structure if highly central firms are bridges, hubs, or members of sets. In chapter 7, for example, we analyzed the role of United California Bank in great detail, demonstrating that its network location in 1966 reflected its key position in a tightly connected set of California firms. From this we drew a number of important conclusions about the role of regional financial institutions, the role of interlocks in intercorporate affairs, and the genesis of multiple ties. The existence of sets in the interlock network demonstrates both the continued existence of stockholding empires (see chapter 6) and the ongoing importance of regional groupings.

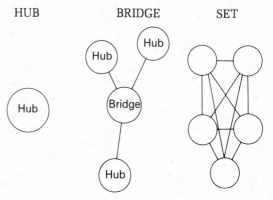

Figure 9.1. Hubs, bridges, and sets.

In this chapter, we focus primarily on hubs and bridges. As figure 9.1 indicates, a hub is the center of a group of interlocked companies that are not tied extensively to each other (as in a set). It thus dominates a sector of the network and is highly central. Hubs are generally tied together in the larger system, either through direct connections or through companies that perform a linking function. These links—bridges—are central because they are connected to a small number of highly central hubs (see Appendix 3; Mintz and Schwartz, 1981a).

Most very central firms act as both bridges and hubs. In the 1962 interlock matrix, for example, Metropolitan Life created links among five major hubs—Chase Manhattan, First National City, AT&T, Westinghouse, and General Electric—while acting as a hub in its own right for thirty-five less central companies. It is possible to discern different roles in the system by determining what proportion of a company's centrality derives from bridge relationships and what proportion derives from hub relationships. We can specify, for example, that, of Metropolitan Life's centrality score of .7316, it derived .1921 from its ties to five hubs and .5395 from the thirty-five smaller firms to which it was linked. We conclude that Metropolitan maintained a hub centrality of 72%.[1] In this context, a bridge obtains a large proportion of its centrality from bridging several highly central firms, while a hub obtains a large proportion of its centrality from ties to a great many less central companies. Hubs, then, interlock with many corporations, whereas bridges may be highly central while interlocking with significantly fewer companies.

Financial Hubs in the Interlock Network

Table 9.1 lists the major hubs (corporations with the highest amount of hub centrality) of the 1962 and 1966 full interlock networks. By and large, the lists are very similar to those for total centrality reported in chapter 7. In 1962, seventeen of the twenty most important hubs were among the twenty most central overall. In 1966, eighteen of the top twenty hubs were among the top twenty of the full system. Thirteen firms appeared as major hubs in both years. It is not surprising, therefore, that financial institutions—money market commercial banks most particularly—were the dominant firms in the network of hub centrality. Of the twenty-seven companies appearing as major hubs in either 1962 or 1966, twelve were banks, five were insurance companies, and one was an in-

Table 9.1
Twenty Most Important Hubs, 1962 and 1966: Full Network

Corporation	Type[a]	Hub Ranking		Degree of Hub Centrality		Hub Centrality as Percentage of Total Centrality	
		1962	1966	1962	1966	1962	1966
Morgan	Bank	1	2	.94	.79	94	92
Chemical Bank of New York	Bank	2	4	.78	.62	89	77
Chase Manhattan Bank	Bank	3	6	.73	.57	82	70
Equitable Life Assurance	Ins	4	1	.72	.84	81	84
First National City Bank	Bank	5	3	.72	.69	88	85
New York Life	Ins	6	15	.64	.35	77	50
Metropolitan Life	Ins	7	10	.54	.42	74	58
Mellon	Bank	8	8	.51	.50	81	78
Manufacturers Hanover	Bank	9	29	.50	.24	79	52
Southern Pacific Railroad	Trans	10	25	.46	.25	68	45
Bankers Trust	Bank	11	7	.45	.51	82	93
Harris Trust	Bank	12	19[b]	.40	.31	77	67
First National Bank of Chicago	Bank	13[b]	11	.38	.41	78	75
Pennsylvania Railroad	Trans	14	22	.37	.27	62	54
Irving Trust	Bank	15	42	.36	.15	69	45

Table 9.1 (cont.)

Corporation	Type[a]	Hub Ranking		Degree of Hub Centrality		Hub Centrality as Percentage of Total Centrality	
		1962	1966	1962	1966	1962	1966
International Harvester	Ind	16[b]	9	.34	.49	67	83
Insurance Company of North America	Ins	17	35	.32	.18	58	46
Westinghouse Electric	Ind	18	13	.30	.40	57	61
General Electric	Ind	19	26	.30	.25	55	51
Mutual of New York	Ins	20[b]	23	.30	.27	59	64
Lehman Brothers	Inv	55	5	.11	.59	55	83
United California Bank	Bank	245	12	.01	.41	7	66
General Motors	Ind	29	14	.22	.35	50	56
Pacific Mutual	Ins	48	16	.14	.32	50	53
Continental Illinois Bank	Bank	25	17[b]	.26	.32	60	70
American Telephone and Telegraph	Util	22	18	.27	.32	44	45
United States Steel	Ind	21	20	.28	.30	52	44

[a]For type abbreviations, see table 7.2.
[b]Not in top twenty for total centrality.

207   Hubs and Bridges: Unity and the
Division of Labor in the Corporate
Network

vestment bank. In 1962, the top nine hubs and thirteen of the top fifteen were financials; in 1966 the top eight hubs and twelve of the top thirteen were financials. Morgan, Chemical, Chase, and First National City were in the top six each year; only Manufacturers Hanover, among the New York money market banks, fell in rank. Equitable Life, New York Life, and Metropolitan Life, the main money market insurance companies, were included in both lists.[2]

Comparing the twenty most important hubs (table 9.1) with the most central organizations of the full network (table 7.3) indicates that financial institutions are much more likely to be hubs than comparably central nonfinancials. For example, in 1962, AT&T ranked eleventh in centrality (.61), while Manufacturers Hanover placed tenth (.63); among hubs, Manufacturers Hanover was ninth (.50), while AT&T ranked twenty-second (.27). AT&T derived a smaller proportion of its centrality from hub relationships (44% compared with 79%), reflecting its bridging role among eight financial institutions including Manufacturers Hanover, Chase, Morgan, Chemical, and First National City Bank. Manufacturers Hanover, on the other hand, had bridging relations with only three firms: Phelps Dodge, American Smelting, and AT&T. Phelps Dodge is an extreme example of high centrality due mainly to bridging: it was directly connected to thirteen firms of high centrality, eight of which were financial institutions. While its overall score was .52, twentieth on the list, its fifteen interlocks with less central corporations gave it a hub centrality score of only .15, ranking it forty-seventh among hubs. First National Bank of Chicago, on the other hand, while not among the most central corporations of the full network, was thirteenth among hubs, since only four of its ties were to other hubs. Phelps Dodge's hub portion of centrality was 28%, compared with 76% for First National Bank of Chicago.[3]

Table 9.2 compares the sources of centrality of the fifty most central financial and nonfinancial institutions of 1962 and 1966. These figures demonstrate that financials accumulate much higher proportions of hub centrality than their nonfinancial counterparts. In both years, top twenty financial firms achieved high rankings owing largely to their hub relationships: over 70% of their centrality derived from hub interlocks; top-ranked industrials barely reached a 50% level of hub centrality. Among firms ranked twenty-one to fifty, the same pattern was in evidence, although the proportions were lower: both banks and insurance companies in this group maintained about 60% hub centrality while industrials and other financials averaged under 40%.

208   **Hubs and Bridges: Unity and the
Division of Labor in the Corporate
Network**

Table 9.2
Hub Centrality as Percentage of Overall Centrality, 1962 and 1966: Full Network

Corporation Type	1962 Centrality Rank		1966 Centrality Rank	
	1–20	21–50	1–20	21–50
Nonfinancial firms	52 (7)[a]	38 (23)	56 (6)	35 (22)
Financial firms	79 (13)	54 (7)	72 (14)	50 (8)
Banks	82 (9)	66 (3)	75 (9)	62 (4)
Insurance companies	77 (3)	59 (2)	63 (4)	64 (1)
Other[b]	58 (1)	30 (2)	83 (1)	30 (3)

[a]Number of firms in parentheses.
[b]"Other financials" are diversified financial institutions except in 1966, when Lehman Brothers, an investment bank, was among the top twenty.

These findings dovetail nicely with the evidence presented in chapters 7 and 8 about the role of financial institutions in the American economy. Banks and insurance companies are the crucial hubs in the system, while highly central industrials derive a disproportionate amount of their centrality from a few ties to major financial institutions. These results indicate that the boards of directors of major banks and insurance companies are populated by individuals who sit on the boards of a great many firms, both large and small. Financials tend to connect to the widest spectrum of companies, reaching into many industries and sectors. Nonfinancial institutions, on the other hand, are more limited in their interlock patterns. They are more likely to tie to a few highly central financials.

This suggests that financial companies utilize interlocks as a method of outreach, information gathering, and system survey, while industrial firms depend upon interlocks for more limited goals. In terms of general information collection, then, financial institutions demonstrate the widest scan in the system. They exhibit a broad spectrum of ties to a wide range of firms. We argue that this expresses their responsibility for managing the allocation of investment capital—for distributing that part of loan capital that is not subject to structural constraint.

Whether viewed from an industrial or a financial perspective, interlocks are largely instruments of capital flow. Although they do facilitate the monitoring of loans, their structure suggests that their major function is aiding allocation.

209   Hubs and Bridges: Unity and the
Division of Labor in the Corporate
Network

Hubs and Bridges in the Directional Network

There are two additional patterns of interest in tables 9.1 and 9.2. First, insurance companies maintain slightly less hub centrality than commercial banks. Second, less central corporations of all types are not likely to be hubs. These trends help us address the other issues raised at the beginning of this chapter: the relationship between banks and insurance companies and the integration of regional groupings into the national network.

Since a directional analysis can disentangle the dense sets that characterize both regional groups and the multiple interlocks maintained between major banks and insurance companies, we use the directional network to explore these issues. Table 9.3 lists the percentage of hub centrality for the fifty most central firms in the directional networks of 1962 and 1966. We find the three patterns noted above: financial firms are more likely to be hubs; banks maintain more hub ties than insurance companies; and larger firms are most likely to be hubs.

The most striking new result in table 9.3 is the low proportion of hub centrality of insurance companies. Though their numbers are small—three in each year—the pattern is unmistakable: insurance companies have hub centrality profiles that more closely resemble industrial firms than financials. Tables 9.4 and 9.5, which list the twenty most important hubs and bridges of the 1966 directional network, underscore this result.[4] While eight commercial banks, including four money market institutions, qualify as major hubs, life insurance companies do not appear on the list. More striking is the inclusion of two insurance firms—Pacific Mutual and

Table 9.3.
Hub Centrality as Percentage of Overall Centrality, 1962 and 1966: Directional Network

Corporation Type	1962 Centrality Rank		1966 Centrality Rank	
	1–20	21–50	1–20	21–50
Nonfinancial firms	41 (10)[a]	24 (24)	52 (11)	35 (24)
Financial firms	77 (10)	52 (6)	75 (9)	54 (6)
Banks	87 (8)	38 (3)	86 (7)	55 (3)
Insurance companies	37 (2)	28 (1)	28 (2)	35 (1)
Other[b]	—	84 (2)	—	63 (2)

[a]Number of firms in parentheses.
[b]In 1962, "other financials" were diversified financials; in 1966 they were investment banks.

210   Hubs and Bridges: Unity and the
Division of Labor in the Corporate
Network

Table 9.4
Twenty Most Central Hubs, 1966: Directional Network

Corporation	Type[a]	Hub Ranking	Degree of Hub Centrality	Hub Centrality as Percentage of Total Centrality
Mellon	Bank	1	1.00	100
First National City Bank	Bank	2	.85	100
Chemical Bank of New York	Bank	3	.75	97
Morgan Guaranty Trust	Bank	4	.73	100
First National Bank of Chicago	Bank	5	.60	77
Broadway-Hale	Mer	6	.57	75
Continental Illinois Bank	Bank	7	.55	80
American Telephone and Telegraph	Util	8	.49	71
United California Bank	Bank	9	.48	
Sears[b]	Mer	10	.41	47
International Harvester	Ind	11	.41	61
TRW	Ind	12	.36	100
Lehman Brothers	Inv	13	.35	74
Pennsylvania Railroad	Trans	14	.30	64
Litton Industries[b]	Ind	15	.28	49
Bankers Trust	Bank	16	.27	73
Gillette	Ind	17	.27	52
National Distillers and Chemical[b]	Ind	18	.24	44
Amsted Industries	Ind	19	.24	100
Pacolet Industries	Ind	20	.24	48

[a]For type abbreviations, see table 7.2.
[b]Also appears in list of most central bridges.

Equitable Life—among the major bridges, the only financials to appear on this list.[5]

That insurance companies are hubs in the full network and bridges in the directional system suggests a paradox, since the directional system is part of the full network. This is explained, though, by the multiple ties between insurance companies and banks. In 1966 Equitable, for example, maintained six interlocks with Chase Manhattan Bank, four interlocks with Chemical Bank, and one interlock with First National Bank of Chicago, as well as a number of links to smaller banks. These major ties were created by exchanges of executives with Chase and Chemical as well as

211   Hubs and Bridges: Unity and the
          Division of Labor in the Corporate
          Network

Table 9.5.
Twenty Most Central Bridges, 1966: Directional Network

Corporation	Type[a]	Bridge Ranking	Degree of Bridge Centrality	Bridge Centrality as Percentage of Total Centrality
Sears[b]	Mer	1	.47	53
Pacific Mutual Life	Ins	2	.43	84
Inland Steel	Ind	3	.37	84
United States Steel	Ind	4	.36	90
Cyprus Mines	Ind	5	.35	70
Cummins Engine	Ind	6	.33	100
Southern California Edison	Util	7	.32	63
Lockheed	Ind	8	.30	75
National Distillers and Chemical[b]	Ind	9	.30	54
Swift	Ind	10	.29	84
Commonwealth Edison	Ind	11	.29	62
Litton Industries[b]	Ind	12	.29	51
Federated Department Stores	Mer	13	.29	67
Corning Glass Works	Ind	14	.29	69
Equitable Life Assurance	Ins	15	.29	62
Union Carbide	Ind	16	.29	88
Foremost-McKesson	Ind	17	.29	50
Proctor and Gamble	Ind	18	.29	62
Jones and Laughlin Steel	Ind	19	.29	50
Union Oil	Ind	20	.28	78

[a]For type abbreviations, see table 7.2.
[b]Also appears in list of most central hubs.

placement of an Equitable executive at First National Bank of Chicago. Other bank interlocks were the result of industrial executives' sitting on the board of Equitable and a bank simultaneously. Equitable's outside directors also sat on many industrial boards and created thirty interlocks for Equitable. In a directional analysis these ties are not counted, since they do not involve direct exchanges between companies. Thus, in the directional system, Equitable lost many indirect ties to less important companies, while the exchange of executives with major banks was left intact. In the directional network Equitable maintained only twenty of its original sixty-three interlocks, twelve of which were incoming. Most of its centrality (68%) derived from close connections to three banks, and

212   Hubs and Bridges: Unity and the
             Division of Labor in the Corporate
             Network

these links were sufficiently strong to make it highly central in the directional system.

Commercial banks, on the other hand, maintain a great many direct links to industrial corporations. In 1966, while Equitable sent representatives to the boards of only five nonfinancials, Chemical sent officers to the boards of twenty-one nonfinancials. This contrast clearly indicates that banks—not insurance companies—maintain a presence around the corporate world that allows for input from many different sectors. Insurance companies, owing to their institutional proximity to banks, share their directors and also share their information-gathering and capital-monitoring capability.

This pattern, in our opinion, is a structural trace of the division of labor between banks and insurance companies discussed in chapter 3. As short-term lenders, banks must evaluate and decide upon initial capital commitments. This necessitates current, ongoing interaction with all sectors of the economy and results in the direct relationships that produce interlock patterns. Banks are the primary hubs in the network because they are the primary decision makers.

We conclude that the division of labor between short-term and long-term lending has led to a set of institutional relationships between banks and insurance companies. The interdependence of the original arrangement is now characterized by an asymmetrical relationship in which banks are placed in a hegemonic position because of their decision-making role and because of the institutionalized dependence of insurance companies on bank information networks.

This arrangement, in turn, has profound consequences for interbank unity. Since insurers are involved in complicated interactions with more than one bank, they tie the banks together into loosely coordinated joint ventures. This loose unity extends beyond the important personal bonds that arise among bank executives who meet and interact on insurance company boards; it extends into the joint interest that major banks maintain in a shifting set of insurers. It reaches the level of direct symbiosis in attempting to find a common interest that will allow banks and their executives to guide the actions of the entire range of institutions that influence the health of insurance companies and banks.

Regional Groupings and National Integration

Tables 9.1 to 9.5 indicate that hub status is correlated with overall centrality in both the full and the directional networks. Al-

213   **Hubs and Bridges: Unity and the
          Division of Labor in the Corporate
          Network**

though this correlation is in part a consequence of the statistical dependence of the two calculations, it is also a result of the regionalization of the American economy. This can be seen when we note that three firms, all nonfinancials, appear as both major bridges and major hubs in the 1966 interlock network. These three companies—Sears, Litton, and National Distillers—were discussed in chapter 8 as examples of locally based national nonfinancials that created links between regional and national banks. This linking function explains their importance as bridges. They achieve their hub status through extensive interlocks inside their regions, partly as a cause and partly as a consequence of their national outreach. As we argued in earlier chapters, money market banks are interested in dynamic local firms whose leaders are well connected in the region and therefore usually sit on many boards. Local companies, especially banks, are interested in the information and expertise that these individuals acquire outside the area. In regional economies, therefore, a very different division of labor arises: industrial firms provide the linkage to the national system while dominant area banks are the backbone (and major hubs) of internal regional structures.

This pattern was evident in our analysis of the Chicago area and in the United California Bank example discussed in chapter 7. It can also be seen clearly in tables 9.6 to 9.8, which chart the 1962 interlocks of National City Bank, Hanna Mining, and Midland-Ross, the three most central firms in the Cleveland vicinity. National City, the dominant local bank, was the thirty-ninth most central firm in the 1962 list, but the Cleveland region was too small to figure prominently in the directional system. (In the 1962 directional analysis, National City Bank was thirty-fourth in centrality, Hanna 136th, and Midland-Ross 374th.) Nevertheless, it exhibits the exact pattern found in California and Chicago.

National City Bank (table 9.6) maintained forty-seven interlocks in 1962, seventeen of which were directional; thirty-eight ties, including all seventeen directional ties, were to twenty-three Cleveland firms. Of the remaining nine, four were to Pittsburgh companies that have maintained historical connections to Cleveland. The five interlocks to outside companies included one to Equitable Life and another to General Reinsurance, a diversified financial firm. National City Bank had only three interlocks with industrial corporations outside Cleveland, while it maintained some forty-two ties to local companies.

This is typical of regional banking institutions. Even Continental Illinois, despite its money market pretensions, maintained thirty-

Table 9.6
Interlocks of National City Corporation, 1962

Corporation	Regional Interlocks		Corporation	Other Interlocks	
	Total	Directional		Total	Directional
Cleveland Area			Equitable Life Assurance (NYC)	1	0
Midland-Ross	6	2	General Electric (NYC)ᵇ	1	0
Standard Oil (Ohio)	4	2	General Reinsurance (Greenwich, Conn.)	1	0
Cleveland Electric Illumination	3	1	McDermott (New Orleans)	1	0
Addressograph-Multigraph	2	2	Texaco (NYC)ᶜ	1	0
Clevite	2	1			
Reliance Electric	2	1	Total	5	0
Sherwin Williams	2	1			
Youngstown Sheet and Tube	2	1			
Warner and Swasey	1	1			
Carrier (Syracuse, N.Y.)	1	1			
Hanna Mining	1	1			
Marathon Oil	1	1			
TRW	1	1			
Anchor Hocking	1	1			
Armco Steel	1	0			
Bliss	1	0			
Consolidated Natural Gas (NYC)ᵃ	1	1			
Diamond Shamrock	1	0			
Ferro	1	0			
B. F. Goodrich (Akron, Ohio)	1	0			
Harris Intertype	1	0			
Republic Steel	1	0			
White Motor	1	0			
Total	38	17			

Table 9.6 (cont.)

Corporation	Regional Interlocks Total	Directional	Corporation	Other Interlocks Total	Directional
Pittsburgh area					
Consolidation Coal	1	0			
Jones and Laughlin Steel	1	0			
National Steel	1	0			
Westinghouse Electric	1	0			
Total	4	0			

a Service area: Pennsylvania, West Virginia, Ohio, and upstate New York.
b Main plant: Schenectady, New York.
c Historically located in Texas.

216   Hubs and Bridges: Unity and the
          Division of Labor in the Corporate
          Network

eight of forty-two nonfinancial interlocks and all twenty-five directional ties to companies in or near Chicago; Nortrust maintained all but one of its twenty-three nonfinancial interlocks (and all seven directional ties) to Chicago-area firms; and First National Bank of Boston maintained thirty-five of forty-seven (and seventeen of twenty-two directionals) to New England–area companies.

Hanna Mining (table 9.7) typifies a regional industrial gone national: of twenty-two interlocks, only eight (including six directional) were to firms in either the Cleveland or the Pittsburgh area, including one to National City Bank. The 14 outside ties included links to Bankers Trust and Mellon, as well as interlocks with companies in Philadelphia (Pennsylvania Railroad), Los Angeles (Southern California Edison), Saint Louis (Monsanto), and many in New York City. Hanna Mining was no longer an active participant in Cleveland regional affairs.

This is a typical pattern for mature national industrial firms that maintain only residual relations, usually financial, with their regions of origin. In 1962, General Motors maintained only one interlock (of thirty-six) in the Detroit area (to Detroit National Bank); its thirty-five other ties were geographically dispersed and included nine links to Mellon, Chase, First National Bank of Boston, Morgan, Western Bancorp, John Hancock Life, Metropolitan Life, and Mutual Life. Scott Paper maintained only five (of twenty-eight) links to its historical home, Philadelphia (including two to financials); its twenty-three other ties were spread around the country and included Chemical Bank, Continental Illinois, Morgan, Southeastern Bancorp, American Express, Metropolitan Life, and Southland Life.

Midland-Ross, in 1962, was a regional firm with some national outreach (table 9.8). It maintained sixteen of twenty-three interlocks (and nine of eleven directionals) to firms within the Cleveland-Pittsburgh area including six links to National City Bank. Among Midland-Ross's seven extraregional interlocks were links to three financial institutions: Lehman Brothers and Smith, Barney—both investment banks—and General Reinsurance, a diversified financial also tied to National City Bank. We see in this the potential for Midland-Ross to ascend from regional membership to connecting bridge. To do so, it would have had to continue to establish outside ties, especially to money market banks and insurance companies. It would then ultimately exit from the regional network and assume national status, as Hanna Mining has done.[6] The importance of these patterns can be best understood by reviewing the internal structure of the Chicago area. The regional

Table 9.7
Interlocks of Hanna Mining, 1962

Corporation	Regional Interlocks		Corporation	Other Interlocks	
	Total	Directional		Total	Directional
Cleveland area			Penn Central (Philadelphia)	1	1
National City Corporation	1	1	Texaco (NYC)	1	1
Midland-Ross	1	1	General Electric (NYC)[a]	2	1
Carborundum (Niagara Falls)	1	0	Southern California Edison (Los Angeles)	1	0
			Monsanto (Saint Louis)	1	0
Pittsburgh area			Chrysler (Detroit)	1	1
Mellon	1	0	Union Carbide (NYC)	1	0
National Steel	2	2	Republic Aviation (Farmingdale, N.Y.)	1	0
Wheeling Steel	1	1	Nabisco (NYC)[b]	1	0
Consolidation Coal	1	1	Bankers Trust (NYC)	1	1
			American Can (NYC)	1	0
			IBM (NYC)	1	0
			Ampex (Redwood, Calif.)	1	1
Total	8	6	Total	14	6

[a]Main plant: Schenectady, New York.
[b]Mainly located in the Midwest.

Table 9.8
Interlocks of Midland-Ross, 1962

Corporation	Regional Interlocks Total	Regional Interlocks Directional	Corporation	Other Interlocks Total	Other Interlocks Directional
Cleveland area			Lehman Brothers (NYC)	1	1
National City Corporation	6	2	Smith, Barney (NYC)	1	1
Sherwin Williams	1	1	Scott Paper (Philadelphia)	1	0
Standard Oil (Ohio)	1	1	General Reinsurance (Greenwich, Conn.)	1	0
Diamond Shamrock	1	1	Texaco(NYC)	1	0
Anchor Hocking	1	1	General Electric (NYC)	1	0
			Cerro (NYC)	1	0
Pittsburgh area					
Jones and Laughlin Steel	1	1	Total	7	2
Westinghouse Electric	1	1			
McDermott	1	0			
Consolidation Coal	1	0			
National Steel	1	0			
Total	16	9			

219   **Hubs and Bridges: Unity and the
Division of Labor in the Corporate
Network**

network includes three dominant banks—First National Bank of Chicago, Continental Illinois, and to a lesser extent Harris. These companies appear and reappear in our analyses as highly central in the national network and as Chicago-area hubs. Their centrality derives almost exclusively from their extensive links to local firms. They have few ties outside the region, and those are usually either nondirectional links to financials or interlocks created as a by-product of directional ties to local firms.[7]

Chicago-area industrials exhibit two patterns: intense local interlocking, and bridging ties between national and regional companies. In 1962, for example, Quaker Oats maintained fifteen of its seventeen interlocks with Chicago-area firms; International Harvester maintained thirty-nine of its forty-eight links within the region. Sears, on the other hand, maintained half of its thirty-two ties to outside firms, including interlocks with banks in New York (Manufacturers Hanover), California (Bank of America), and Texas (Republic National). Unlike Hanna Mining, however, Sears remained deeply enmeshed in the Chicago network, with multiple ties to First National Bank of Chicago, Continental Illinois, Inland Steel, and others. Sears was both a Chicago-area hub and a national bridge.

We conclude that regional groupings are tied together by a complex set of institutional and personal interdependencies. In each region, major local banks are intimately bound together with dominant local industrials by networks of capital flows, institutional dependencies, interlocking directorates, and long-term personal relationships. Smaller banks and nonfinancial institutions may contribute to the overall unity through partial participation in these interconnections, or they may become satellites of specific dominant firms or groupings.

These regional networks are linked into the national economy by major industrial firms, which undertake national expansion, money market borrowing, or both. The connections these firms establish with national banks and insurance companies create an implicit and explicit joint venture between regional banks and national banks. They also provide for the transmission of economic strategy in both directions and become an important incentive for further, more direct, cooperation. The direct involvement of life insurance companies in regional financing creates a second set of unifying bridges. These symbiotic ties between local areas and the national money market exercise a dampening effect on what might become competitive relations among regions and between regional and national banks.

220   Hubs and Bridges: Unity and the
       Division of Labor in the Corporate
       Network

Conclusion: The Institutional Skeleton of the Business Class

We are now in a position to describe the institutional structure that shapes the internal hierarchy of business and provides the foundation upon which bank hegemony is constructed. This portrait allows us to identify both the relationships that condition the activities of business leadership and the processes by which coordination and planning are facilitated.

Our exploration of the interlock network has expanded the description of the division of labor among banks that we developed in chapter 5. At the pinnacle of American financial and industrial structure are the money market banking institutions, located mainly in New York. The quasi-membership of First National Bank of Chicago, Continental Illinois, Mellon, and, more recently, Bank of America make this a select group of ten banks that, when united, are the only institutions capable of coordinating the broadest spectrum of American business. This hegemony is founded upon the control of capital flows and is both reflected and activated by the elaborate interpersonal network that connects the leadership of these financial corporations to the operating leadership of the dominant nonfinancial firms in the American economy. For the most part, these personal connections that tie business leadership together are traced (and further enhanced) by the web of interlocking directorates we have been exploring. The specific form of the interlock network is conditioned both by the importance of banks in determining the direction of capital flow and by the need for candid and expert information on the economic conditions in the diverse economic sectors affected by any important capital investment. The exchange of directors between banks and major industrial firms is therefore simultaneously an expression of and a condition for efficient planning and execution by bank decision makers. Ultimately the interlocks banks maintain with national industrial firms such as General Motors, United States Steel, and AT&T, as well as with major regional industrial companies, reflect this fundamental structural fact.

The role of the national banks is replicated, in part, by dominant regional banks in Chicago, Texas, Boston, California, and Philadelphia, and by subregional banks in Cleveland, Detroit, and other localities. Major local banks make decisions about the local allocation of capital and therefore decide to nurture certain sectors of the regional economy and abandon others. At the same time, the most successful industrial firms outgrow the region, either because their financing needs are greater than local capital supplies or be-

221   **Hubs and Bridges: Unity and the
          Division of Labor in the Corporate
          Network**

cause they begin to expand into other areas of the country and the world. When a regionally based company develops such a national presence, it develops connections to the national money market; and these ties provide both information about investment opportunities and access to large-scale lending consortia. They also transmit necessary information about local lending opportunities to the money market. Regionally based national firms thus form the bridges that tie the regional and national banks together, and their joint interest in these industrials produces a variety of unifying mechanisms that further consolidate the interests of the two sets of banks. Tendencies toward regional/national conflict are consequently muted and often suppressed.

The national insurance companies, notably Equitable Life, Mutual of New York, and Metropolitan Life, perform a dual role as independent capital suppliers and as long-term partners for major banks. Because banks specialize in short-term lending, they make the initial decision as to the direction of capital flows. These initial choices require broad decision-making capacity and usually constrain long-term lending decisions. Despite tendencies toward conflict, this creates a symbiosis that has prevailed in recent years and has produced long-term partnerships between insurance companies and banks, traced and enforced by multiple interlocks. Insurance companies, by and large, borrow the decision-making expertise of the banks through this exchange of personnel and through close working relationships.

This marriage of bank and insurance company capital produces a second-order relationship among the leaders of the national banks. Their cooperation, based on interlocks with insurance companies, as well as their ongoing involvement in numerous lending consortia, produce a joint interest among major banks. The money market institutions find themselves with very similar lending options and investment profiles. The bridging effect of insurance companies is therefore an important barrier to bank conflict.

We discern three different types of important nonfinancial corporations: national firms, regional firms, and regional/national bridges. National industrials that have, to a large extent, separated themselves from their historical regional bases are "relatively" autonomous. They may be free from the close interpersonal relationships that characterize regional groupings, and their connections to national financial institutions may not be as dense as those between banks and insurance companies. This distancing of national industrial corporations from both regional groupings and national cliques accounts both for the managerialists' pseudoinsight of au-

222   **Hubs and Bridges: Unity and the
Division of Labor in the Corporate
Network**

tonomy and for the sometimes pathological isolation of industrial leadership, a phenomenon forcefully described by Wright (1979) in his study of General Motors. This isolation should not, however, be confused with independence from all outside influence, especially from the hegemonic leadership of financial institutions.

The isolation of national industrial firms contrasts sharply with the integration of regional companies, which maintain personal connections to the business elite of their local areas. This integration provides a form of collective leadership that defeats isolation of the firm and bestows upon regional economies their unique dynamic. In these locales, it is possible for industrial firms to play economically dominant roles, despite the importance of regional banking institutions. Such domination is not a reflection of the absence of financial hegemony, but a socialized hegemony that allows for collective decision making about the flows of capital within the area.

At the same time, since most local economies cannot meet the financial needs of their largest and most important industrial firms, the region as a whole becomes subjected to the hegemony of national financial leadership. The tight-knit quality of regional groupings works to enhance their responsiveness to national financial decision making and thus enhances the importance of regional industrial leadership with national financial connections.

The bridging functions performed by companies such as Inland Steel appear to be short-lived. A successful firm that reaches outside its region may quickly abandon its local roots; its leadership may become less involved in the no-longer-relevant regional economy, and it may therefore lose its usefulness as a bridge.

This pattern of regional and national integration describes some three hundred to four hundred corporations that control over 50% of the financial and industrial assets of the country and dominate the economy as a whole. The remaining firms in our sample of over 1,100, as well as companies too small to be included in the population analyzed here, exist as satellites to dominant regional economies or dominant industrial firms. The analysis of the relationship between the auto industry and the auto supply industry (see chapters 1 and 2) offers a prototypical case of such interindustrial domination based on resource dependency relationships. Numerous other examples can be found and analyzed. They fit the broader system of hierarchical relationships: decisions about capital flow made in New York or Chicago will influence and condition the behavior of major industrial firms at the national and regional levels and will delimit the choices available to regional financial institutions. The secondary decisions made by these firms will, in turn, condition and constrain the activities of dependent smaller companies located in subregions.

Thus, the overall system is hooked together into a chain of hierarchical relationships loosely coupled and only problematically coordinated. The coordination, when it occurs, is maintained and conditioned by decisions about capital flows, which in turn condition other decisions about capital, which in turn condition still others. Ultimately those who determine major banking investments can rely, in many circumstances, on a careful analysis of the conditions created by initial investments to evaluate their consequences for the activities of a broad spectrum of corporations.

The institutional skeleton places enormous responsibility in the hands of financial leaders, imposing upon them the role of "organic" intellectuals, those who produce the guiding ideas that inform institutional action:

> For the organic intellectuals of the bourgeoisie, the specific criterion of definition is whether the intellectual activity is weighted toward the *administration of the affairs* of the class as whole, rather than narrow, personal, private interests. It is not a matter of whether these organic intellectuals consciously recognize that they are maintaining the domination of a class, but whether their mental activity in fact serves the crucial function of coordinating the many facets of systematic social hegemony. (Patterson, 1975: 274; see also Gramsci, 1971: 9)

10 Financial Groups and Intracapitalist Competition

> The ruling group . . . becomes a narrow clique which
> strives to perpetuate its selfish privileges by regulating
> or even suffocating the birth of opposing forces, even
> if these forces are homogeneous to the fundamental
> ruling interests.
>
> Gramsci, *The Ruling Prince*

The portrait of business structure hierarchy we are developing suggests that decisions on capital allocation produce a loosely coordinated system that in the long run serves the interests of major financial institutions. While our analyses of the interlock network have identified regional and subregional groupings, we have also found multiple connecting links between regional sections and the New York money market. And while we have stressed the critical role of national banks and insurance companies, we have argued that the competitive tendencies among them are subordinate to structural symbiosis.

This portrait of a relatively unfactionalized group of major financial institutions, capable of coordinating systemwide activities, contrasts sharply with traditional bank control theory, which posits the existence of a series of competing interest groups (Rochester, 1936; Sweezy, 1939; Perlo, 1957; Pelton, 1970). Baran and Sweezy (1966) rejected the concept but defined these groups as containing a "number of corporations under common control, the locus of power being normally an investment or commercial bank or a great family fortune" (p. 17). Such groups are expected to act in unison, maximizing group, rather than individual, profits and sacrificing individual need in favor of the broader interest of the group as a whole (Fitch and Oppenheimer, 1970a-c; Kotz, 1978; Niosi, 1978; Pelton, 1970; Perlo, 1957).

In this chapter, we address the issue of discrete interest groups.[1] Since the theory of bank hegemony emphasizes the structural interdependence of financial institutions, it does not predict the segmentation of corporations into competing interest groups. Rather than assuming the control of nonfinancial corporations by one (or a handful) of the most powerful banks and insurance companies, the model of financial hegemony argues that similarity in position over capital allocation generates a structural unity among financials and that they collectively play a coordinating role within the larger system. And, rather than the strategic control of a corporation by a particular financial, bank hegemony depends on the alteration of structural constraint made possible by financial unity to influence corporate policy. Thus, while bank control theory posits a system divided into discrete interest groups organized around competing financial institutions, bank hegemony assumes a loose community of interest among financials with overlapping ties to nonfinancial corporations.

Results reported in chapters 7–9 demonstrate that commercial banks interlock with the same set of nonfinancial institutions, indicating that there are multiple ties uniting major financials. At first glance, this would suggest that the interlock network is not characterized by discrete groups of corporations organized around particular banks. Under closer scrutiny, however, we see that this conclusion is premature. While specific nonfinancial corporations—those most involved in capital markets—link to a number of banks, other firms interlock with a much smaller set of companies. We noted that Exxon, for example, the largest oil company and second-largest industrial in the United States in 1962, ranked 273d in centrality in that year. This points to the small number of interlocks it maintained and to its limited role in the communication network formed by interlocking directorates. This raises the possibility, then, that the bridging roles played by capital-intensive nonfinancials, as well as by insurance companies, overlie a network characterized by interest-group formation; that we are viewing two networks, one defined by cross-cutting ties linking major banks while underneath remains a system divided into separate spheres of influence.

In this chapter we concentrate on this issue, although research on corporate clustering has not always done so. Early investigations addressed the question of bank control, but the rise of managerialism, and later resource dependency theory, carried with it the assumption of shifting alliances among basically autonomous firms. This created a corresponding shift in research focus: instead of

searching for clearly defined interest groups, investigations concentrated on areas of dense interaction with interlocking directorates as a useful measurement tool (Dooley, 1969; Sonquist and
Koenig, 1975; Allen, 1978; Pennings, 1980). The renewed interest
in bank control theory generated by Fitch and Oppenheimer (1970a-
c) led to a new wave of interest-group investigations (Bearden et
al., 1975; Mariolis, 1977a, 1984; Mintz and Schwartz, 1981a, 1983;
Mizruchi, 1982a,b; Bearden and Mintz, 1984).

In this chapter, we follow this tradition. We test for the existence
of coordinated cliques with internal cohesion and external conflict
as postulated by the theory of bank control. To do this, we avoid
measures that seek areas of dense interaction and, instead, use
interlocking directorates to identify discrete interest groups. If the
cross-cutting ties identified in earlier chapters overlie a system defined by financial interest groups, it would demonstrate the existence of competitive forces within the financial world that are not
mediated by trends toward structural unity as suggested by the
theory of bank hegemony. Financial prominence in the interlock
network would then be more consistent with a bank control interpretation.

Peak Analysis

Interest groups in the bank control tradition are characterized
by intragroup unity, on the one hand, and intergroup competition
on the other. Since major financial institutions typically dominate
these collectivities, a corporation cannot maintain ties to more than
one bank unless an alliance exists among the banks. Using these
assumptions, Mariolis (1977a, 1984) developed a method of analysis
that identifies discrete groups within an interlock system. Built on
the logic of centrality analysis (see chapters 7–9), peak analysis rests
on the following axioms:
1. A company is a peak if it is more central than all firms to
   which it is interlocked.
2. A company is in an interest group if every firm more central
   than it—to which it is interlocked—is in that group.
3. A firm that connects upward into two different groups is not
   a member of either group.[2]
Peaks are corporations that organize interest groups. The most central company in the network (Morgan Guaranty in 1962, for example) is a peak by definition, since it is more central than any
firm with which it interlocks. The second most central corporation

(Chase Manhattan in 1962) is a peak if and only if it does not interlock with a company more central than itself. In 1962, for example, Chase Manhattan did not maintain interlocks with Morgan, the only firm more central than itself. Since all its interlocks were with less central companies, Chase was a peak and defined an interest group.

A company is a member of an interest group defined by a peak if it interlocks with the peak and/or a company in the group defined by the peak that is more central than itself and if it does not tie to any other more central firm. Some corporations might interlock with more than one peak. For example, a firm might tie to both Morgan and Chase. Since theoretically, in the bank control paradigm, a company cannot be dominated by more than one bank, this firm would not belong to an interest group. From a measurement point of view, the firm would not be classified as a peak because it interlocks with companies more central than itself; it would not be a member of an interest group because it tied to two firms more central than itself that were in different groups.[3] Note that two corporations need not directly interlock to be members of the same interest group; they may tie to the group through a connection to the peak or to any of the group members. Hence, group members do not necessarily maintain interlocks with each other. Note also that, since corporations are not necessarily assigned to clusters, peak analysis will not automatically generate cliques. Since we are searching for competitive financial groupings, a measure that can tap the absence of such collectivities is crucial.[4]

Moreover, only one peak, the most central firm, is automatically generated in a given network. The maximum number of interest groups, on the other hand, is limited only by the number of firms in the system.[5] The number of potential clusters is equal to the number of peaks and can therefore vary greatly.

Finally, if cliques exist, they may be arranged hierarchically within the network. Those cliques with many members and those whose members are more central can be seen as more important. Hierarchy, therefore, is incorporated into the peak analysis on two levels: on the one hand, differential importance is attributed to the corporations within the cluster, the peak being the most important firm. On the other hand, one cluster may be more critical to the overall network than another.

Our portrait of the corporate world implies a dialectical relationship between tightly interlocked regional networks and the national money market, as well as a fragile unity among central financial firms. By searching for interest groups, we wish to explore whether these potential lines of cleavage are overcome by the unifying forces within the system. Hence we look for autonomous, competing cliques organized around financial institutions, which constrain the activities of member firms. Peak analysis offers the possibility of identifying such groupings by searching for discrete clusters that are more than areas of relative density in the interlock network.

Corporate Interest Groups

Tables 10.1 and 10.2 list the peaks and corresponding interest groups generated in the 1962 and 1966 interlock networks. Although peaks were identified, the system produced no important groupings. In 1962, five major peaks (all large banks) and four minor peaks were identified.[6] Only seven companies, however, were members of clusters; only three were associated with the major peaks. Although Morgan, in 1962 the most central peak, directly or indirectly tied to 987 less central companies, all of these firms

Table 10.1
Corporate Peaks of the 1962 Full Network

Peak	Type[a]	Centrality Rank	*Fortune* Rank	Number of Clique Members[b]	Number of Clique Candidates[c]
Morgan	Bank	1	5	0	987
Chase Manhattan Bank	Bank	2	2	2	987
Mellon	Bank	9	14	0	975
Manufacturers Hanover	Bank	10	4	1	977
Bankers Trust	Bank	14	9	0	966
Beneficial Finance	Div	996	—[d]	1	0
Associated Transportation	Trans	998	—[d]	1	0
Dillon Companies	Mer	1,000	—[d]	1	0
Heller International	Div	1,001	—[d]	1	0

[a]For type abbreviations, see table 7.2.
[b]Companies whose only ties to more central firms were to the peak or to other firms in the clique.
[c]Less central companies tied directly or indirectly to the peak and to at least one member of another clique.
[d]Not ranked by Fortune in 1962.

Table 10.2
Corporate Peaks of the 1966 Full Network

Peak	Type[a]	Centrality Rank	Fortune Rank	Number of Clique Members	Number of Clique Candidates
Equitable Life Assurance	Ins	1	1	2	972
Morgan	Bank	2	4	0	972
First National City Bank	Bank	5	3	0	972
Beneficial Finance	Div	978	—[b]	2	0
City Products	Ind	981	—[b]	5	0
Marine Bancorp	Bank	987	—[b]	1	0
Wheelabrator-Frye	Ind	989	—[b]	1	0
Seatrain Lines	Trans	991	—[b]	1	0
Associated Transport	Trans	993	49	1	0
Ashland Oil	Ind	995	116	1	0
Crown Central Petroleum	Ind	996	—[b]	1	0

[a]For type abbreviations, see table 7.2.
[b]Not ranked by Fortune in 1966.

also tied upward, directly or indirectly (through firms more central than themselves), to at least one other peak.

In 1966, three major peaks (two large banks and one insurance company) and eight minor peaks were identified, generating nine very small interest groups. Only fifteen companies were group members, and only two companies were associated with a major peak. Equitable, Morgan, and First National City Bank each tied directly or indirectly to 972 less central firms, but only Equitable maintained exclusive ties to any companies; it defined an interest group with two members.

Thus, we discern no exclusive sphere of influence for the central peaks in the network. The structural arrangements that produce cooperative consortia and other joint ventures also produce cross-cutting interlocks that link the banks to the same nonfinancials and thus indirectly to each other. To the extent that such interlocks represent viable communication linkages, they are symptomatic of limited competition and represent deterrents to its development.

It is important to note, however, that at least some of the meager clustering represents solid structural linkages. The two firms that appeared in the 1962 Chase Manhattan clique were Equitable Life and Chemical Bank. This grouping is historically significant: in the

early 1930s, Chase National Bank and Equitable Life Assurance
were linked through Rockefeller interests (Rochester, 1936: 55); and
a 1930 merger between Equitable Trust Company, a former subsidiary of Equitable Life, and the Chase National Bank produced
the largest banking establishment of the day (Collier and Horowitz,
1976: 159-61). Based on this evidence, Perlo (1957: 202-3) referred
to Equitable as one of the "Rockefeller insurance companies." Menshikov (1969: 267) offered a membership list of the Rockefeller
financial group that included three banks—Chase Manhattan,
Chemical, and the Bank of New York, and two life insurance companies—Equitable and Metropolitan. Pelton (1970: 21) placed Equitable, Chemical, and Chase in the "financial core of the Rockefeller circle." Knowles (1973: 5) also grouped the firms together in
his analysis of the Rockefeller interests. Though some of the evidence presented by these researchers may be questioned, a substantive relationship seems to have existed among these three major financial firms.

In the 1962 network, the Manufacturers Hanover Trust clique
contained one member: Reynolds Metal. Although the bank acted
as trustee for a $346 million loan, the actual bondholders—a group
of insurance companies—were not part of the clique. Menshikov
(1969: 215) classified Reynolds as a member of the Manufacturers
Hanover domain but offered no documentation for this coding. It
is therefore difficult to interpret this relationship.

The other three major peaks have no clique members, while the
remaining four cliques in the 1962 network were isolated dyads—
pairs of corporations that interlocked only with each other. Identifiable functional relationships existed in some of these cases. Beneficial Finance, for example, was paired to Western Auto Supply,
a wholly owned subsidiary. Associated Transport, a trucking company, was linked to Dana Corporation, a manufacturer of car, truck,
and bus parts. Dillon Company, an industrial firm located in Kansas,
was interlocked with Cessna Aircraft, also a Kansas concern. Walter
Heller International, the largest specialist in commercial construction financing, was paired to the Jim Walter Corporation, a manufacturer and financer of shell homes. The tiny clustering effect
thus reflects at least some structural relationships, although it is
definitely overshadowed by the absence of significant cliques.

Similar patterns were found in the 1966 interlock system, and
two results are of special interest. The Chase, Chemical, Equitable
triumvirate had endured with one modification—Chase was no
longer the peak; Equitable had assumed that role (see table 10.2).
Beneficial Finance and Western Auto Supply, paired in the 1962

network, were joined by Spiegel Company one year after its acquisition by Beneficial.[7]

The main conclusion we draw from these findings is that cliques do not appear to be a major characteristic of the corporate network. While discernible financial peaks emerge from the analysis, they do not maintain exclusive contact with a group of identifiable satellites; lesser network members cannot be placed in the domain of a single peak. In the 1962 network thirteen firms, approximately 1% of all corporations under investigation, were clique members. In 1966, fifteen companies, or less than 2% of the data set, belonged to clusters. Industrial firms tend to link to two or more peaks. This reflects the bridging function identified in chapter 9. It also suggests the unlikelihood that a single bank (or group of tightly connected financial firms) will unilaterally dominate the actions of industrial companies. Financial influence must be a coordinative, collective activity.[8]

This conclusion assumes that all interlocks reflect noncompetitive relations. While we believe that this is reasonable, there may be many circumstances in which an outside director is quite detached from the internal workings of a company. Viewing the interlock network as a general communication system, for example, deemphasizes the particular affiliations of a specific director. In this case, simultaneous directorships would not compromise competitive autonomy. As we have argued repeatedly, the exact content of a corporate interlock is difficult to discern without specific investigation, especially since the nature of the underlying relationships may change over time. However, certain types of interlocks are much less likely to represent structural relationships. Therefore they can be excluded from an analysis that seeks to understand the shape of structural control and influence.

There has been much discussion pointing to differential power within a board. Gordon (1945: 136–37), for example, has argued that certain "influential directors play a more important part in decision making and coordination than does the board of directors as a whole" (see also Pahl and Winkler, 1974). Following this logic, we seek to distinguish between important and less important directors. It seems likely, for example, that university presidents, museum directors, and other outsiders without full-time affiliations to major corporations are less influential and less active in interfirm coordination. It is possible that such outsiders could sit on two competitive boards without compromising autonomy.

To test the possibility that cliques are buried under a set of incidental interlocks, we ran a peak analysis after excluding all

interlocks created by individuals who were not principally employed by or affiliated with a corporation included in the study. As
table 10.3 indicates, a majority of excluded directors were businessmen. In 1962, 62.1% of all excluded interlockers (for whom
information was found) were principally connected to financial and
nonfinancial enterprises too small to be included among the *Fortune* listings; in 1966, 54.7% were affiliated with such companies.
An additional 11.5% in 1962 and 17% in 1966 were employed by
corporations in our population but did not serve on their boards of
directors. Lawyers accounted for 18.1% of the excluded individuals
in 1962 and 17.7% in 1966. Since these lawyers were virtually all
from corporate practices, the business world accounted for over
90% of the excluded directors in each year. Nonbusiness personnel,
7.4% of the total in 1962, were affiliated with academic institutions
(5.5%), foundations (1.4%), and government (0.5%).

In addition to excluding all interlocks created by individuals not
employed by firms in our population, we excluded secondary interlocks created by individuals affiliated to our sample. A representative of one company who sits on two other boards creates a
tie between the two host firms that may not reflect congenial relations. In analyzing this, we replicate the exclusion made in the
directional analyses of chapters 8 and 9, without the emphasis on
the direction of the main interlocks. Thus, we look only at those
interlocks in which an officer of one company sits on the board of
another. Since firms seldom offer competitors representation on
their boards, this network includes interlocks that should reflect
nonconflictual relationships.[9]

Table 10.3
Principal Affiliations of Excluded Directors, 1962 and 1966 (Percentage)

Affiliation	1962		1966	
Non-500 corporations, nonfinancial	44.2	(257)[a]	39.3	(215)
Non-500 corporations, financial	17.9	(104)	15.4	(84)
500 corporations, nondirector	11.5	(67)	17.0	(93)
Law	18.1	(105)	17.7	(97)
Nonbusiness	7.4	(43)	9.15	(52)
Other	0.9	(5)	1.1	(6)
Total	100.0	(581)	100.0	(547)

Note: In 1962, information was not available in 109 cases; in 1966, information
was not available in 182 cases.
[a]Number of cases in parentheses.

A peak analysis was performed on this "strong tie" network,[10] and fewer than 10% of the firms in our population were included in the resulting cliques (tables 10.4 and 10.5). In 1962, twenty-six peaks were identified. Eight of these were major peaks with direct or indirect ties to hundreds of firms in the system; one was a minor peak with ties to twenty-five firms; and seventeen were associated with isolated groups—fifteen dyads, one triad, and one quartet. The eight major peaks and the one minor peak were all commercial banks; the interest groups they defined were very small, from one to five companies. These results are consistent with findings for the full interlock network: the 1962 strong tie system is not characterized by the type of interest-group formation suggested by bank control theory. Financial institutions do not organize discrete groups of corporations; not only the most capital-intensive firms, but non-financial corporations in general interlock—directly or indirectly—with multiple banks and insurance companies, and exclusive spheres of influence do not underlie the more integrated communication system.

The largest clusters, those defined by the major and minor peaks, are nevertheless instructive to analyze. Most significantly, they reflect the larger structure of the network discussed in chapters 7–9. Note, for example, that the peaks are commercial banks rather than industrial firms or insurance companies; they are most likely to organize the scant degree of interest-group formation within the system. This is consistent with their position as the primary capital allocators of the economic sector. This also reflects the hub/bridge distinction developed in chapter 9. As in their role of hub, banks in the peak analysis are in the center of groups of corporations. Insurance companies do not occupy this position because commercial banks typically evaluate initial capital commitments whereas insurance companies utilize bank information sources in their capital-allocation decision making. And, since insurance companies depend on more than one bank in this capacity, they are forces for cohesion in the system, uniting various banks. Note that the major money market insurance companies—Equitable, Metropolitan, New York Life—are most active in this capacity. Other insurance companies are less likely to play this role, as is illustrated by the inclusion of two such firms—Aetna and Connecticut Mutual—in the First National City Bank clique and Connecticut General in the Bankers Trust grouping. Commercial banks are peaks and define interest groups because of their role in capital-flow decision making. Their separate spheres of influence point to competitive tendencies within the system, but the sparseness of member firms indicates that these tendencies are mediated by the bridging role of insurance companies as well as by an increasing set of structural interdependencies typified by interbank lending consortia. The very limited clustering in the interlock network, we submit, reflects this trend toward unity.

This same point is illustrated by the small number of major industrials in the most developed cliques. Like insurance companies, industrials involved in capital markets typically tie to more than one major financial institution. This serves a unifying function within the system, since multiple banks receive similar inputs. The results of the peak analyses extend this point. It is not only the most active corporate borrowers that integrate the system. The lack of well-defined interest groups demonstrates that nonfinancial corporations, in general, tie directly or indirectly to more than one of the largest banks in the system.

When we compare the three largest clusters in the 1962 strong-tie analysis, those associated with First National City Bank, First National Bank of Chicago, and Mellon, we see some interesting differences. First Chicago's clique contained five Chicago-area non-financials, suggesting some subdivision among the major Chicago banks; First National City's domain included two insurance companies and three industrials with no geographic coherence, while Mellon's clique was closest to a financial interest group. Within each clique, some of the relationships were substantively significant, demonstrating that peak analysis, as a method, clusters corporations with at least some visible ties. This is important even though a vast majority of intercorporate relationships are not identified by the analysis. The reasons for this will be discussed below.

The group defined by First National City Bank, containing Aetna Life, Anaconda, Connecticut Mutual Life, Mohasco, and United Aircraft (table 10.4), is only partly interpretable in terms of structural relations. While First National City has historically maintained extensive connections to insurance companies (Perlo, 1957: 329; United States Congress, 1968: 715), there is no specific evidence linking it to either Aetna or Connecticut Mutual. Nor could we discover evidence of enduring structural bonds with Mohasco, although First National City was the company's loan registrar. The Anaconda–First National City connection was, however, historically familiar, dating back to the 1930s (Rochester, 1936: 165) and continuing through the 1950s (Perlo, 1957: 175) and 1960s (Menshikov, 1969: 281; Kotz, 1978: 194). United Aircraft also maintained long-term ties to the bank (Leinsdorf and Etra, 1973: 102; Menshi-

Table 10.4
Corporate Clusters in the 1962 Strong-Tie Network

Peak	Type[a]	Centrality Rank	Fortune Rank	Number of Clique Members	Number of Clique Candidates	Clique Members
First National City Bank	Bank	1	3	5	771	Aetna Life Anaconda Connecticut Mutual Life Mohasco United Aircraft
Mellon National Bank	Bank	2	14	4	642	Alcoa Diamond Shamrock Pittston PPG
Morgan Guaranty Trust	Bank	3	5	2	799	Clorox Proctor and Gamble
Continental Illinois Bank	Bank	4	8	1	683	Link Belt
First National Bank of Chicago	Bank	5	10	5	678	Armour Chicago and Northwestern Hart, Schaffner and Marx MCA. Spiegel
Chase Manhattan Bank	Bank	6	2	1	738	Moore-McCormack
Bankers Trust	Bank	9	9	3	619	Connecticut General Life Emhart Lipton
Irving Trust	Bank	24	12	1	354	Sterling Drug

Table 10.4 (cont.)

Peak	Type[a]	Centrality Rank	Fortune Rank	Number of Clique Members	Number of Clique Candidates	Clique Members
Northwestern National	Bank	93	48	2	24	Control Data Northwest Bancorp
Beneficial Finance	Div[b]	866	—[b]	1	0	Western Auto
Riegel Paper	Ind	868	400	1	0	Riegel Textile
Blair	Inv	870	—[b]	3	0	Coastal States Producers Flavorland Industries Indian Head Mills
West Point–Pepperell	Ind	871	281	1	0	Liberty National Life
Kansas City Southern	Trans	876	—[b]	2	0	BMA Peabody Coal
Seagram	Ind	877	175	1	0	Rheingold
Fedders	Ind	881	—[b]	1	0	Colt Industries
Canteen	Mer	883	—[b]	1	0	Del E. Webb
Dillon Companies	Mer	885	—[b]	1	0	Cessna Aircraft
Heller International	Div[b]	886	—[b]	1	0	Jim Walter
Flying Tiger	Trans	889	—[b]	1	0	Signal Companies
United Merchants and Manufacturers	Ind	891	107	1	0	Fieldcrest Mills
Ohio Edison	Util	892	29	1	0	Tappan
North Carolina National Bank	Bank	895	—[b]	1	0	McClean Trucking
State Mutual of America	Ins	897	28	1	0	Norton
Guardian of America	Ins	899	35	1	0	Teachers Insurance
Dean Witter	Inv	901	—[b]	1	0	Varian Associates

[a]For type abbreviations, see table 7.2.
[b]Not ranked by Fortune.

kov 1969: 279; Perlo, 1957: 329), including an $85 million loan con-
sortium led by the financial (*Moody's Transportation Manual*, 1964:
1266).

The most significant aspect of the First National Bank of Chicago
cluster was its geographic coherence. Chapters 7 and 8 stressed the
importance of regional networks, and previous interlock investigations have uncovered regional groupings as well. Dooley (1969:
319) placed fourteen firms (including First National Bank of Chicago, Continental Illinois Bank, and Harris Trust) in the Chicago
cluster, while Allen (1978) placed nine companies (including First
National Bank of Chicago and Continental Illinois) in the same
group. These two analyses largely agreed on group membership
and differed from our listing.[11]

Perlo (1957: 333–34) also generated a group of Chicago corporations, using various classification criteria. He coded fifty-seven
firms as members. The Chicago cluster produced by the strong-tie
peak analysis used in this study did not contain other Chicago-area
banks, and only Armour, of the five nonfinancials, appears in Dooley's list. (An analysis of these discrepancies will be presented below.)

Solid underlying structural ties were found in two cases in the
Chicago cluster. First National Bank of Chicago owned 8.1% of Hart,
Schaffner and Marx and managed an employee benefit fund for the
company (United States Congress, 1968: 603); it also managed a
similar fund for Armour, although no stockholding relationship
could be discerned (United States Congress, 1968: 603). Although
First National was the transfer agent for Spiegel, Armour, and MCA,
this is not by itself an important relationship.[12] No functional ties
connected Chicago and Northwestern Transportation to other group
members.

The third-largest cluster was defined by Mellon National Bank,
the major financial institution in the Pennsylvania area, and included Aluminum Company of America (Alcoa), the largest aluminum producer in the world; PPG, one of the largest producers
of glass in the United States; Diamond Shamrock, a leading manufacturer of basic petrochemicals; and Pittston, a Virginia-based
coal company. All but Pittston have far-reaching historical ties to
the Mellon family. Alcoa was created by the Mellon family in the
late nineteenth century (Rochester, 1936: 65). In 1962, Mellon National Bank held 14% of the stock through nominees, and additional
shares were owned by individual family members (Larner, 1970:
73–74). As of the mid-1960s, Burch (1972: 41) estimated the total
stock interest at about 30%, and Patman (United States Congress,

1968: 762) cited 25.3% of the common and 15% preferred under Mellon control.

In 1966, 14.5% of Diamond Shamrock's stock was held by the bank (United States Congress, 1968: 761), and in 1971 the company announced a $50 million loan agreement headed by Mellon (*Moody's Industrial Manual*, 1971: 83).

Historically, there have been strong connections between PPG and the Mellons, but direct ownership ties could not be found. In fact, minority control of the company had for some years been with the Pitcairn family (Larner, 1970: 78–79), who in 1963 owned 29.8% of the outstanding stock (*Moody's Industrial Manual*, 1964: 1211). In 1936, Rochester (1936: 68) classified the firm as a member of the Mellon group, and Menshikov (1969: 302) suggested a Pitcairn-Mellon coalition. Patman (United States Congress, 1968: 761) found no stockownership links between the two firms but noted that Mellon managed five PPG employee benefit funds. Moreover, a recent chief executive of the bank was the son of a former PPG board chairperson (*New York Times*, September 29, 1974: F7). Although the exact significance of this type of interlock is never clear, the Mellon–PPG relationship appeared to be a strong, enduring one.

We could find no direct control relations between Mellon and Pittston, though its membership in the clique may be explained by its involvement in Pennsylvania-area coal, steel, and oil production. Coal and steel were the dominant industries in the area, and many of the most important local firms were directly tied to the Mellons. Koppers, a major producer of crude and refined coal products (*Moody's Handbook*, 1963: 307), was about 20% owned by Mellon interests (Burch, 1972: 54; United States Congress, 1968: 761); Consolidation Coal was considered by many to be within the Mellon domain (Perlo, 1957), and Jones and Laughlin Steel and Allegheny Ludlum Steel had long-term ties as well. Since Mellon National Bank was the leading financial institution in the area and heavily invested in these industries, its health was dependent upon their performance. Pittston's inclusion in the cluster therefore may have represented a functional relationship with well-integrated area corporations.

This interpretation raises a very important question, however. Why should Pittston be included while other, much more tightly connected firms were excluded from the Mellon clique? Posed on the general level, Why does a peak analysis identify some structural relationships while ignoring most others? The answer lies in the underlying dynamics that create the densely connected, highly integrated network of corporate ties we have been analyzing. Major companies—even those intimately connected to controlling banks—cannot satisfy all of their resource needs within an interest group. Loan capital, for example, is rarely provided by one financial institution (see chapter 3). Gulf Oil, 40% owned by the Mellon family, accumulated several hundred million dollars in debt in the early 1960s. These funds necessitated outside lenders, and in the 1970s a representative of New York banks chaired the investigation that ousted its leadership (Bearden, 1982).

Intraclique integrity cannot be expected in the context of such wide interdependencies. Major corporations are too large and too intertwined with the entire economy to isolate themselves in small groups. Even when closely aligned to a major bank, as in the case of Gulf Oil, outside companies and other financial institutions are an integral part of their environment. This interdependency undermines the intraclique coordination and interclique competition suggested by bank control theory. And this interdependency is reflected in the makeup of the Mellon cluster: not all "Mellon corporations" are included, but a sketchy outline of clique parameters appears.[13]

The 1966 strong-tie analysis produced many more cliques with sizable memberships (table 10.5), including a large (twenty-one-member) western group headed by United California Bank; a New York State–New England regional group (with eleven members) headed by Marine Midland Bank, and five money market cliques, including a Chase Manhattan cluster with nine members. In the absence of our previous finding, these results suggest the existence of coherent financial interest groups. But analyzed in conjunction with the results in tables 10.1, 10.2, and 10.4, table 10.5 reinforces our sense of the impermanence of corporate cliques. Though some group stability exists, the contrast between 1962 and 1966 demonstrates that corporate groupings are impermanent and therefore cannot reflect ongoing group-level coordination and control. Even if significant intragroup coordination could be demonstrated the groups include only 104 firms, a little over 10% of our population.[14]

And the corporations included in the 1966 domains were not drawn from among the largest firms. Only seven of the top one hundred industrials were included. Group members were disproportionately drawn from the smaller firms in our population and represented only a minor portion of corporate revenues.

From these results we conclude that financial interest groups, although marginally present in the network, were not the prevalent form of intercorporate organization in the 1960s. Membership was

Table 10.5
Corporate Clusters in the 1966 Strong-Tie Network

Peak	Type[a]	Centrality Rank	Fortune Rank	Number of Clique Members	Number of Clique Candidates	Clique Members
United California Bank	Bank	1	13	20	677	Alexander and Baldwin
						American President Lines
						Bancal Tri-state
						Broadway-Hale
						Cyprus Mines
						El Paso Natural Gas
						Hyster
						Lehman Brothers
						Litton Industries
						Lockheed
						Matson Navigation
						Metro-Goldwyn-Mayer
						Pacific Mutual
						Potlatch Forests
						Republic
						Southern California
						Edison
						Times-Mirror
						Trans World Airlines
						Twentieth Century-Fox
						Western Bancorp
Mellon National Bank	Bank	2	15	3	716	Diamond Shamrock
						Purolator
						Rockwell Manufacturing

Peak	Type[a]	Centrality Rank	Fortune Rank	Number of Clique Members	Number of Clique Candidates	Clique Members
First National City Bank	Bank	4	3	3	668	International Telephone and Telegraph Sybron Xerox
Continental Illinois Bank	Bank	5	8	3	689	Central Soya Link Belt Zenith
First National Bank of Chicago	Bank	7	10	5	740	Armour Brunswick International Minerals and Chemical MCA Time Incorporated
Morgan Guaranty Trust	Bank	9	4	2	680	Cities Service Texas Gulf Sulphur
Chemical Bank of New York	Bank	11	6	5	738	Armstrong Rubber Bordon Liggett and Myers National Sugar Refining Penn-Dixie
Chase Manhattan Bank	Bank	12	2	8	704	Borman's Commercial Solvents Combustion Engineering Essex International Grand Union Provident Life and Accident Shields and Company Moore-McCormack

Table 10.5 (cont.)

Peak	Type[a]	Centrality Rank	Fortune Rank	Number of Clique Members	Number of Clique Candidates	Clique Members
Bankers Trust	Bank	22	7	1	494	Grumman
Marine Midland Bank of New York	Bank	40	26	10	293	Amfac Avon Crum and Foster Houdaille Industries Loblaw Marine Midline Bank of Western New York Marine Midland Trust New York, New Haven and Hartford Pepsico Sun Chemical
Beneficial Finance	Div	866	—[b]	2	0	Spiegel Western Auto
Household Finance	Div	869	—[b]	1	0	City Products
Riegel Paper	Ind	871	442	1	0	Riegel Textile
National Bank of Commerce	Bank	873	—[b]	1	0	Marine Bancorp
Michigan National Bank	Bank	875	49	1	0	Wickes
General Tire	Ind	877	80	1	0	Frontier Airlines
Gulf and Western	Ind	879	247	1	0	Ward Food
Heller International	Div	881	—[b]	2	0	Jim Walter Barwick
American Export Isbrandtsen Lines	Trans	884	44	1	0	Wheelabrator-Frye

Table 10.5 (cont.)

Peak	Type[a]	Centrality Rank	Fortune Rank	Number of Clique Members	Number of Clique Candidates	Clique Members
Life and Casualty of Tennessee	Ins	886	46	1	0	Cook Industries
Dillon Companies	Mer	888	—[b]	1	0	Cessna Aircraft
Canteen	Mer	890	47	1	0	Del E. Webb
Continental Airlines	Trans	892	33	1	0	National General
Signal Companies	Ind	894	95	1	0	Flying Tiger
Warner Communication	Ind	896	—[b]	1	0	Fedders
Ohio Edison	Util	897	33	1	0	Tappan
Kansas City Southern	Trans	900	—[b]	1	0	Peabody Coal
United Merchants and Manufacturers	Ind	902	135	1	0	Fieldcrest Mills

[a]For type abbreviations, see table 7.2.
[b]Not ranked by Fortune.

minimal, group size was small, and the largest companies were not represented. Cliques only occasionally formed along functional lines; intragroup interaction patterns sporadically reflected meaningful relationships; and only some of the member firms were linked to the peak through ownership, long-term lending, or formal business relationships. The only striking regularity in these results is the existence of financial peaks.

We conclude that the trends toward financial unity outweigh the forces for competition. While we can discern the outlines of possible discrete groupings, the structures that impel unified action among financial institutions are currently dominant. These results are consistent with the theory of financial hegemony, which predicts the development of collective leadership (with all its contingencies) instead of interest-group competition as suggested by the theory of bank control.

This lack of interest-group formation appears to contrast sharply with previous interlock research. Dooley (1969), Sonquist and Koenig (1975), and Allen (1978) have used interlock patterns to identify and analyze financially centered regional groupings (see also Knowles, 1973; Kotz, 1978; Menshikov, 1969; Pelton, 1970). We argue that these studies, when scrutinized carefully, confirm the results reported here, since their groups are neither discrete nor coordinated. They are actually unsegregated areas of relative density in an otherwise integrated network.

Dooley's groups were not discrete: individual firms were included in a tight-knit clique if they tied to four or more members of the group. This produced a New York clique that included most of the firms in the other groups, so Dooley required six ties for admission into the New York cluster (pp. 319–20). The grouping procedure itself therefore reflected the numerous cross-cutting relationships among Dooley's cliques. Chase Manhattan, a central focus of the New York group, actually maintained four interlocks with Chicago and could have been considered a member of both the New York and the Chicago groups. Were Chase included in the Chicago grouping, several other New York firms with connections to both Chicago and Chase would have been included as well. Ultimately the entire New York cluster could be folded into the Chicago group.

Thus, at best, Dooley's procedure identified areas of relative density, not discrete groupings. Similarly, Sonquist and Koenig explicitly searched for areas of relative density and made no claims that their procedure identified discrete, exclusive, coordinated, or competing groups. Allen's use of factor analysis guarantees groupings based on relative density, regardless of the shape of the network. The actual results produce low factor loadings, a number of groups with shared members, and many instances of excluded firms with multiple interlocks into defined groups. Thus, here again we find no evidence for discrete clustering.

Other studies produce similar results. Bearden and Mintz (1984), using a 1976 data set of 252 corporations, found an identifiable group structure within the system. Their method, however, did not address the issues of domination or control. Bearden et al. (1975) and Mariolis (1977a, 1984) have searched for clusters using peak analysis. In Mariolis's studies, no clusters appeared. Bearden et al., using the same data set as the present study, found small, largely inconsequential groupings.

Mizruchi (1982a) compared the results of his peak analysis for 1969 with groupings obtained by Menshikov (1969), Kotz (1978), and Allen (1978). His conclusion nicely summarizes the weight of the evidence:

> After surveying the [existing] cliques and taking into account the large number of corporations not belonging to any particular group, it is difficult to avoid the conclusion that the concept of separate, specific interest groups is not very relevant for understanding the American corporate system. This does not mean that there are no specific centers of power in the economy, nor does it mean that there are no lasting historical relationships between particular corporations. What it does mean is that the idea that there are several different groups, regional or otherwise, in which competition forms the basis of their relations, may not be an accurate characterization of the system, if it ever was. (p. 161)

Conclusion

Our evidence emphasizes the lack of interest-group formation in the United States interlock network, and this finding argues against the type of corporate structure posited by one very important school of bank control theory (Rochester, 1936; Sweezy, 1939; Perlo, 1957; Menshikov, 1969; Pelton, 1970; Knowles, 1973). Although financial institutions are the organizing units of the system, the vast number of overlapping ties to the same set of nonfinancials suggests a level of unity not typically expected in bank control paradigms.

Nevertheless, many features of the network suggest that tendencies toward financial clustering remain. The unique position of commercial banks is the most important indicator of this potential. In each analysis reported above, including different years and different partitionings, we record large numbers of financial peaks. With few exceptions, these peaks are the most important banks in the United States, and most changes between 1962 and 1966 appear to reflect actual changes in the roles of the banks.

Banks dominate the network in complementary ways: they are the dominant hubs in a network made up of hubs and bridges, and they are the dominant peaks in a network made up of peaks and cross-cutting nonpeaks. It is important to scrutinize these results. Peaks are not necessarily hubs, and hubs are not necessarily peaks. A hub that has large numbers of ties to a great many companies may also be connected to another hub that is more central than itself. In this circumstance a hub would not be a peak (see Mintz and Schwartz, 1981b; Mariolis, Schwartz, and Mintz, 1979). Similarly, a firm may become a peak because it is tied to a number of firms less central than itself and is unconnected to the multitude of more central firms in other sectors of the system. If the less-central neighbors are hubs, this peak may not be a hub itself.

In a random system we would expect hubs and peaks to be different. The fact that major banks are both hubs and peaks, while other firms are neither, suggests two important facts about American business structure: first, money market banks and dominant regional banks maintain enormous outreach to a great many companies, a point we have made in many different contexts. Second, they maintain few connections to other major banks. Thus, the banks continue to have what might be called spheres of influence, although these spheres overlap rather than organize discrete clusters. The myriad of secondary connections does not, however, result in myriad direct connections among the banks themselves, as network theory would predict.

This separation among commercial banks cannot be explained by the Clayton Act prohibition against competitive interlocks, since the legislation precludes only interlocks among competing banks, and then only in the same region. This allows long-term relationships between national money market banks and powerful regional banks, among regional banks from different areas, or among regional and subregional banks with symbiotic investment profiles. Yet few such interlocks exist. Regional banks would appear as hubs, but not peaks, if such national regional interchanges were made. Ties of this sort would involve access to inside information and would be an effective deterrent to future competitive activities. With the current separation among banks, the suppression of competition emerges from a community of interest developed around joint ventures (largely consortium relationships), without effective long-term bonds. This, in our interpretation, points to a tendency toward the development of highly competitive relationships in the event of a breakdown in the structural ties that unify the system.

This interpretation is reinforced by the findings of other researchers. Mizruchi (1982a,b), in a comprehensive survey of changes in interlock networks from 1904 to 1974, performed peak analyses for each year in his data set. His results nicely match those reported here. Before 1935 there were no cliques, even of the small size uncovered in this investigation. This was a consequence, he suggests, of the domination the House of Morgan exercised over the corporate community as a whole. The rise of the Rockefellers to a competitive level in the 1930s, combined with the depersonalization and institutionalization of corporate leadership, resulted in the development of small groups in his 1935 sample. These clusters, for which extensive documentation is available, were both coherent in terms of structural relationship and consistent with theories of bank interest groups (Sweezy, 1939). They may explain the development of interest group theory during the 1930s. Since that time, although the basic groupings have remained the same (including a Chicago group, a Mellon group, and a shifting set of New York money market groups), they have never matured into large, competitive, and discrete interest groups. Nevertheless, the consistency of the groups, their development after the decline of the House of Morgan, and their match to the theory of financial interest groups all suggest that the tendency to form cliques remains a persistent and important one in American corporate structure.

This argument is reinforced by a major study by Fennema (1982), utilizing information on international bank consortia. Fennema demonstrates that, at the international level, particular American banks tend to group with particular foreign banks into discrete consortium cliques. Each of these groupings is stable over time, and they appear to compete with each other in the multinational lending market. This growth of cliques in world finance is in stark contrast to the cross-cutting ties that develop internally in the United States and appear to be expression of the competitive tendencies within the financial community. On the basis of these results, Fennema concludes that the possibility of conflict within the financial communities of individual countries remains alive and powerful.

It is suppressed, however, in the current situation by cross-cutting joint ventures and consortium relationships.

Finally, we see indications in the financial press of the tendency to develop interest groups. Perhaps the most notable example in recent years has been the rapid growth of California banks. Both BankAmerica and Western Bancorp are now major international banks with large assets for industrial and commercial lending. California financials, led by these two institutions, have declared themselves capable of meeting all capital needs for the region at least in principle, giving independence from the national financial community. This suggests the possibility of an internally coherent financial interest group capable of coordinating the activities of the many industrial companies within its realm.

This isolation has not developed, however. Instead, Bank-America, by entering international and national money markets, has become a leader in major national and international consortia. If it were to concentrate on a regional financial group, its capital commitments would prohibit entry into broader markets with expanded profit possibilities. Thus, BankAmerica was forced to choose between local hegemony and national and international prominence. The necessity to choose and the economic incentives for expansion are powerful forces for unity within the system that counteract competitive tendencies. Finally, by entering the money market, BankAmerica reinforced unity on a second level. By removing its capital commitments from California, it forced local firms to seek lenders from outside their region. This connected area nonfinancials to the national money market as well.

This example suggests that, while tendencies toward group competition are recurrent features of the system, forces for unity prevail in current circumstances. The results of the peak analysis reinforce this conclusion. While the presence of financial peaks points to the possibility of competing institutions, the cross-cutting ties among them and the corresponding absence of interest groups suggest unifying trends. These tendencies are consistent with the structural interdependence emphasized by the theory of financial hegemony.

11 Conclusion

> With the growth of corporations the manipulation of
> capital plays an increasingly important part in the eco-
> nomic process, and great banking and industrial
> monopolies develop which draw off an increasing share
> of the profits extracted from the working class.
>
> Anna Rochester (1936: 13)

The analysis of business relations presented in this book has led
us to conclude that structural constraint is the major mechanism
of intercorporate coordination in modern American capitalism and
that hegemonic relations, organized around the interests of financial institutions, are the main organizing principles of the business
world. At the same time, we would like to emphasize several things
about this hegemony. First, we stress that, while bank hegemony
is the defining characteristic of the system, financial power is limited; it is only in very broad strokes that coordination is established.
What emerges is a loosely coordinated system that financial institutions dominate in the long run, while considerable day-to-day
autonomy and flexibility exist for individual units.

Second, we stress that the primary source of this hegemony is
control over the direction of capital flows, not direct intervention
into corporate decision making or institutional stockholding. We
do note that bank's stockownership (dumping, in particular) provides a useful adjunct to their primary leverage, but hegemony
could be maintained in the absence of these mechanisms.

Third, we note that the unity among financial institutions upon
which bank hegemony is constructed is fragile. This is illustrated
by the occasional competitive bouts between national and regional
banks, between commercial banks and insurance companies, and
within loan consortia (see chapter 3). It is also suggested by the
presence of financial peaks in the interlock network (see chapter

10). At the present stage of American capitalism, however, these competitive tendencies seem to be outweighed by shared interests and common needs. The structural forces that produce financial hegemony appear, therefore, to create a pattern of temporary conflict followed by a return to equilibrium. Financial hegemony is not a static, tightly maintained process but a fluid one with changing alliances and periods of flux.

Fourth, we stress that interlocking directorates are not sources of hegemony, but a method for managing discretion. They could not be sources of hegemony because they give access to the apparatus of discretionary decision making and only indirectly offer the possibility of altering structural constraint. While hegemony offers the institutional leverage for system coordination, corporate interlocks provide the information necessary to implement that hegemony. Bank centrality in this context reflects the dominant position of financial institutions in capital-flow decision making.

Finally, we emphasize that the hierarchical structure of business relationships identified in the preceding chapters is the result of the importance of capital to even the largest and most powerful nonfinancial firms. The leverage that accrues with the capacity for coordinated decision making about capital flows—even the loose coordination of hegemony—is the most abiding and long-term external influence in corporate life. Therefore the influence of bankers is the most abiding and significant in the corporate world.

With these points stated, we turn to a discussion of the implications of bank hegemony for social policy formation. In chapter 2 we reviewed the debate over ownership and control of large corporations and outlined the political analyses that flow from differing viewpoints on corporate behavior. We recall that managerialism, resource dependency theory, and class cohesion theory view government as the key force for reconciling the contradictions of interest and conflicts of power within the world of big business. By allocating this role to government, Baran and Sweezy (1966), for example, argue that the location of social policy formation—insofar as it is shaped by decision making and not by the automatic forces of capital—resides in government. Our analysis introduces a very different logic into the process of social policy formation. The theory of financial hegemony implies that major decision making takes place in the boardrooms of financial institutions and that this decision making reverberates throughout the entire society, creating de facto policy without the mediation of public institutions.

Moreover, it is in this context that the differences between traditional bank control theory and bank hegemony become most important. As we stressed in chapters 2 and 4, the theory of bank control posits the strategic control of financials over nonfinancial firms. Bank hegemony, on the other hand, posits domination without strategic control. This distinction suggests that hegemony is, at the same time, less exact but more pervasive than control. While the direct suppression of competition offers an effective and predictable result, it is only under very special conditions that banks attain sufficient leverage over any particular firm to accomplish such tight coordination.

Bank control, therefore, depends on dyadic control relationships between a particular bank and a large set of otherwise unconnected companies. Hegemonic relations are broader and more far-reaching. Banks can affect firms or industries with which they do not deal directly. Nurturance of a particular sector—oil tanker construction, for example—changes the environment of the industry in general, thus affecting the conditions under which all shipbuilders operate. It also affects sectors related to shipbuilding, ranging from the fastener industry as a supplier to oil distributors as direct recipients of increased tanker capacity. Moreover, to the extent that capital invested in tankers is diverted from other needy sectors, the decision (discretionary, in this case) to develop this industry affects the operating environment of other potential investment outlets. Thus, the consequences of investment decisions reverberate through the system in untold numbers of ways.

The reaction of individual corporations or industries to such changes in the constraints under which they operate is much less predictable than the reaction to the dictates of outside strategic control. To the extent that there are numerous options in responding to changes in structural constraint—that is, if there is a discretionary component to subsequent decision making—then hegemony provides less predictable outcomes for financial firms than bank control. Control produces a tighter grip on policy formation, but the one-to-one relationship between a bank and a corporation required to activate that control is much harder to arrange. Hence hegemonic relations regulate a much larger segment of the business world, but in a looser fashion.

Hegemonic financial institutions cannot dictate policy either to the corporate sector or to government. Nevertheless, the direction of capital flows creates direct societal commitment to projects that affect the very texture of American life. Bank decisions that led to Third World lending in the 1970s, to encouraging leasing as a major new device for securing capital goods, to developing certain kinds of industries at the expense of others, and to financing private rather than public transportation were all part of ongoing business decision making. Once made, such decisions become more or less irrevocable societal commitments that no government entity could reverse.

The looseness of the process makes its influence more subtle than overt bank control, but this does not lessen the effects on social policy formation. Capital-flow decisions determine directions of development on the local, national, and even international levels that many students of political behavior impute to governments. The pervasiveness of financial hegemony reverberates not only through the economic sector but through American life in general.

In our view, then, the capacity of banks to provide coordination within the business community—even the loose coordination described in this book—coupled with their capacity to find a unified posture toward major flows of capital—even though experiencing significant conflict—creates a major form of social decision making that is not mediated by public institutions.

For the most part, discussions of the power of business have focused on its relation to government. In the classic power structure debate between elite theorists and pluralists, the dispute over the role of business has involved a dispute over the role of business in government. Much research has concentrated on the capacity of business to organize and mobilize as a force in the political domain. We conclude from our analysis of corporate structure that this is not the primary mechanism of business influence over social policy. Collective decision making within the business world directs capital flows that commit the resources of the country as a whole to the projects selected by financial institutions. This form of corporate coordination is, in our opinion, the primary decision-making apparatus in American society.

By extension, the capital-flow skeleton upon which business unity is constructed affects the more extensively studied area of business-government relations. Domhoff (1967, 1970, 1975, 1978, 1983), particularly, has carefully documented both the many connections between business and government and the repeated episodes of business unity that help to impose business interests on all levels of government.[1] Our analysis identifies the context in which business is able to achieve the underlying unity that allows business-sponsored policy-formation groups to achieve a unified stance and to produce the coordinated political action that Domhoff and others have documented.

Capital allocation decisions set the agendas even for collective political action. This is accomplished not through the strategic control of particular policy formation groups or philanthropic foundations, but by pursuing certain investment options at the expense of others and by developing certain industries and not others. Capital-flow decisions, therefore, affect policy-formation bodies and other groups charged with reconciling divergent business interests in the same way that they affect corporate policy: through hegemonic relationships. And it is from this that the possibility of a united stance toward public bodies is derived. Without this underlying structure, the many contradictions that divide business entities and create ongoing conflict among them would, as the pluralist argues, prevent the sort of united action necessary for business to impose its will on government as well as on the population the government is meant to serve.

In sum, then, the political life of America is intimately bound up with the structure of intercorporate affairs. The capacity for unity that flows from the hegemony of financial institutions allows for both a massive independent policymaking capacity within business and for a united business stance vis-à-vis the government.

In this book we have analyzed the role of financial institutions in intercorporate relationships, but we have not considered, in any detail at all, the role of the capitalist class—the group of individuals who lead major corporations—in this process. Class can be introduced into this analysis in two ways. As we pointed out in chapter 6, researchers studying inner-group cohesion have demonstrated that multiple directors are the main source of business leadership, and they argue that their involvement in diverse corporations allows them to generate and understand broader class interest (Useem, 1979, 1983). Moreover, bankers are more likely to occupy multiple directorships than their industrial counterparts (Allen, 1978; Bearden, 1982; Soref, 1980; Useem, 1980; Zeitlin, 1974). We can integrate this analysis of individuals with the theory of finance capital by noting that Hilferding (1910) called finance capital "capital controlled by banks and employed by industrialists" (quoted in Lenin, 1917a: 46). Hilferding (1910) thus viewed finance capital as the coalescence of bank and industrial capital. And rather than the domination of industrialists by bankers, he suggested the melding of the two into a single group of finance capitalists. As Zeitlin (1976) notes:

> Neither "financiers" extracting interest at the expense of industrial profits nor "bankers" controlling corporations, but finance capitalists on the boards of the largest banks *and* corporations preside over the banks' investments as creditors *and*

shareholders, organizing production, sales and financing, and appropriating the profits of their integrated activities. (p. 900; emphasis in the original)

By combining the conclusions of inner-group analysis with the theory of finance capital, we conclude that business leadership accrues to a special social type: a cohesive group of multiple directors tied together by shared background, friendship networks, and economic interests, who sit on bank boards as representatives of capital in general. We have argued throughout this book that banks are the primary mechanisms for collective decision making within the business sector. In the final analysis, however, we must ask whether the capitalist class expresses the interest of banks or, as Zeitlin (1974, 1976), Zeitlin, Newman, and Ratcliff (1976) and Ratcliff (1980a,b) suggest, banks are controlled by the class networks of those individuals who lead them.

Findings by Ratcliff (1979–80, 1980a,b) and Ratcliff, Gallagher, and Ratcliff (1979) suggest that decisions on capital allocation are affected by the needs of this inner group of finance capitalists. We find this evidence compelling. However, we note that it is only one component of decision making—the discretionary element—that is molded by the opinions of finance capitalists and conditioned by the class networks they create and inhabit. The structural constraints under which banks operate determine the options available to those decision makers. We argue, then, that banks occupy a position of structural importance in the economic sector; that their location places them in the center of capital allocation; and that allocation decisions are, in good part, constrained by the imperatives of the accumulation process. The interests of banks as organizations, therefore, in good part determine and constrain the interests of capital in general. They are, in this sense, vehicles for the class control of the economy. Finance capitalists—as a class—become agents of this structural compulsion, but they also must make real choices about which investment options to pursue. Their participation is in no way trivial. Without their input, capital would be allocated in different ways and in response to different pressures. Like everyone else, the capitalist class makes decisions but not under conditions of its own choosing.

Appendixes:
Data Collection and Analysis for the Mathematical Analysis of Corporate Networks (MACNET)

William Atwood
James Bearden
Peter Freitag
Carolyn Hendricks
Peter Mariolis
Beth Mintz
Mark Mizruchi
Donald Palmer
Michael Schwartz

1 Data Collection: Interlocking Directorates among Major American Corporations, 1962–66

The list of firms for this study was obtained principally from *Fortune* magazine (1963–74), which presents a yearly listing of the five hundred largest industrial corporations (ranked by sales) and the fifty largest firms in five other categories: commercial banks, life insurance companies, and utilities (all ranked by assets); transportation companies (ranked by operating revenues); and merchandising firms (ranked by sales).

In 1971 *Fortune* began listing the fifty largest diversified financial companies (ranked by assets). These are included in the data set, together with forty-seven firms listed in 1969 as "Big Companies That Don't Appear Anywhere Else."[1] The data set was further augmented by the fifty-seven leading investment banks for the decade 1960–69, obtained from Hillstrom and King (n.d.).[2]

The *Fortune* lists changed from year to year owing to the rapid growth of some firms, the relative decline of others, changes from one type to another, mergers of small companies that created one large firm, and acquisitions of established companies that destroyed their independent existence. To compile an accurate and complete listing of all large companies for the entire time period, we obtained a foundation list of 750 firms from the 1962 *Fortune* compilation. For each successive year, we compared the new *Fortune* list with the existing set of firms, recording changes in rank and type. Corporations listed by *Fortune* for the first time were added to the data set. Acquisitions of one firm by another were coded whenever *Fortune* recorded them.

Because of acquisitions, name changes, type changes, and mergers, there were considerable redundancies in the initial listing. These required coding decisions based upon further research into the history of the particular corporation. Some of the more common coding procedures were as follows:

Name changes. In several hundred instances, corporations changed their names during the period under study. For example, the 1962 list included Mergenthaler Linotype as the 217th largest industrial. The 1963 data did not list Mergenthaler Linotype, but a new company, Eltra, was listed at rank 228, and *Fortune* noted that Eltra was the new name for the company. In this case and others like it, all information for the corporation was transferred to the most recent identity, along with comments noting the name history. Previous identities were kept in the data set with cross-references to the main entry.

Acquisitions. A large number of acquisitions and mergers occurred between 1962 and 1974. For example, Red Owl Stores was a leading merchandising firm, ranked between thirty-eight and forty-five among retailers during the period 1962 to 1966. In 1967 it disappeared from the *Fortune* list, and a footnote indicated that it had been acquired by Gamble-Skogmo, the twenty-second-largest merchandiser in 1966. In this case and others like it, a corporation was coded as independent until the year it was acquired. From that point on it was treated as part of the parent corporation. In a few cases, usually involving insurance companies, acquisitions did not result in elimination from *Fortune*'s rankings. In these cases, the acquired firm maintained an independent existence and therefore was treated as such.

Concurrent acquisitions and name changes. Often, acquisitions and name changes occurred simultaneously. In order to determine which company was acquired and which did the acquiring, we used a special feature of the *Fortune* ranking system. Each year *Fortune* reported the rank the corporation was given in the previous year in addition to its current rank. This was used to determine the dominant corporation. In 1970, for example, Schering and Plough (two separate firms) were merged to form Schering-Plough (a single corporation), with an industrial rank of 266. The 1970 listing for Schering-Plough showed the previous year's rank as 406, while Plough was not ranked at all (though it had been in previous years). From this information, we concluded that Schering had acquired Plough.

These procedures uncovered only a portion of the redundancies in the data set. Many name changes and acquisitions were not noted by *Fortune*. Moreover, a great many corporations underwent name changes or participated in mergers before they were ranked by *Fortune* or after they had been dropped from its listings. We consulted the organizational biography of each corporation in the 1974 editions of *Moody's Manuals* (Industrial, Transportation, Public Utility, Bank and Finance, and the OTC Industrial Manual) to trace these changes.

Ultimately we obtained a list of 1,582 corporate names, including all names for every firm on our list. Since there were 401 single or multiple name changes,[3] there were 1,181 independent firms in our population.

The number of active companies varied for each year of our study. In 1962, the base year for our analysis, there were twenty-seven corporations that, though they would later be large enough to achieve *Fortune* 500 status, had not yet been incorporated.[4] The population for 1962 included 1,144 companies: all 750 firms that appeared in the 1962 *Fortune* listing, the seventeen largest investment banks, and 377 companies that were not listed in 1962 but would achieve *Fortune* 500 status between 1963 and 1974. The inclusion of these smaller corporations allowed us to analyze the position of growing companies before they rose to the highest levels of the corporate world.

To obtain directorate interlocks, the 1962 board membership of each corporation was obtained, primarily from *Standard and Poor's Register of Corporations, Directors and Executives, 1963*. For each individual, the following information was recorded: name, management position in the firm, if any, and, when available, an indication of primary affiliation.

There were eighty-six firms for which Standard and Poor's did not offer board members in 1962. The directorates of seventy-three of these companies were obtained from *Dun and Bradstreet's Million Dollar Directory* (1963), *Moody's Manuals* (1963), *Directory of Directors of New York* (1963), and the records of the Securities and Exchange Commission. The boards of thirteen corporations were not located in any of the sources consulted. Our analyses for 1962 are therefore based upon 1,131 firms.

Once the names were entered into the computer it was a relatively simple matter to sort them into alphabetical order. In each instance in which directors of different corporations had identical or similar names, it was necessary to determine whether these individuals were, in fact, the same person. For example, if F. P.

Heffelfinger of the Great Northern Railroad was found to be the same individual as the F. Peavey Heffelfinger of Northwest Bancorp, then the existence of an interlock between the two firms was demonstrated. Similarly, George Murname of Corning Glass Works and George Murname, Jr., of Inland Steel could conceivably be either the same person, father and son, or two unrelated directors. A rigorous checking procedure was undertaken to determine which of these potential name pairs actually referred to the same people. We consulted the following sources: *Standard and Poor's Directory of Directors, Moody's Manuals, Dun and Bradstreet's, Directory of Directors for the City of New York, Who's Who* (national and regional), and *Who's Who in Finance and Industry.* We considered listings of possible matches to be the same individual if (1) we found a source that listed him or her as a director of both companies or (2) we found identical birth dates for the two individuals. Using this procedure 11,252 interlocks were verified. Only 151 possible matches could not be conclusively validated or invalidated. These were coded as noninterlocks. Our data therefore has a margin of error of 1.5%, in the direction of underestimation.

2 Fundamentals of Centrality Analysis for Networks of Interlocking Directorates

Two sorts of interlock matrixes are analyzed in this book. The first includes all interlocks found in a particular year (either 1962 or 1966); the second includes only officer interlocks. A simple example will illustrate the difference between these two types of matrixes. In 1962 Charles H. Percy sat on the boards of Harris Trust, Bell and Howell, Burroughs, and Chase Manhattan Bank. His interlocks are presented in matrix form in table A.1, which includes twelve entries. The actual number of interlocks is half of that, since each tie is presented twice. This produces a very dense matrix, since Percy connects each firm to all the others. Figure A.1 is a graphic presentation of the matrix.

Noting that Percy was the chairman of the board of Bell and Howell allows for a reformulation of this graph. In some circum-

Table A.1
Combined Matrixes of Interlocks Formed by Charles H. Percy in 1962

	Harris Trust	Bell and Howell	Burroughs	Chase Manhattan Bank
Harris Trust	0	1	1	1
Bell and Howell	1	0	1	1
Burroughs	1	1	0	1
Chase Manhattan Bank	1	1	1	0

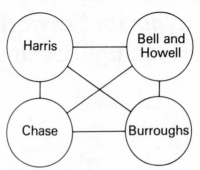

Figure A.1. Combined graph of all interlocks formed by Charles H. Percy in 1962 (each line represents an interlock).

Table A.2
Strong-Tie Matrix of Officer Interlocks Formed by Charles H. Percy in 1962

	Harris Trust	Bell and Howell	Burroughs	Chase Manhattan Bank
Harris Trust	0	1	0	0
Bell and Howell	1	0	1	1
Burroughs	0	1	0	0
Chase Manhattan Bank	0	1	0	0

stances, it is logical to assume that Percy's main role was to represent Bell and Howell to each of the other corporations. In this case, the ties he created among Harris Trust, Chase Manhattan, and Burroughs would be incidental to his primary role as agent for his home firm and, therefore, weaker than the direct, primary interlocks between Bell and Howell and the others.[1] These assumptions are incorporated into the matrix listed in table A.2, while figure A.2 is a graphic presentation of this primary or strong-tie network, representing only the three officer interlocks.

Consider figure A.1. Since each of the four corporations was connected to all the others, each was equally central in the system. Figure A.2, which excludes incidental interlocks, is very different. It is shaped like a wheel with Bell and Howell as the hub. Percy's position as chairman of Bell and Howell made it the most central corporation in the network created by his interlocks.

When the incidental interlocks are removed, it is easy to redraw figure A.2 and identify Bell and Howell as the central company of

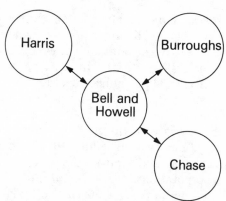

Figure A.2. Strong-tie graph of officer interlocks formed by Charles H. Percy in 1962 (each line represents an interlock, and the arrow indicates the direction of the interlock).

the network. It is impossible to do the same thing for the over 1,100 corporations in our population. We must therefore define centrality so it is measurable and may be expressed mathematically. Bonacich (1972) developed a measure of centrality for groups with overlapping membersip, and this was adapted to interlock networks by Mariolis (1975).[2]

The centrality of a corporation depends on three factors:
1. The number of firms with which it is interlocked.
2. The number of interlocks it maintains with each of the firms to which it is connected.
3. The centrality of the firms with which it is interlocked.

This can be expressed as

$$(1) \quad C_i \sim \sum_{j=1}^{n} r_{ij} * C_j \,,$$

where

r_{ij} = the intensity of the interlock between corporation i and corporation j with $r_{ii} = 0$,
C_j = the centrality of corporation j, and
n = number of corporations.

In matrix terms,

$$(2) \quad \lambda C = RC \,,$$

hence $(R - \lambda I)C = 0$.

Where λ is the largest eigenvalue of R, equation (1) can be expressed as

$$(3) \quad C_i = \frac{1}{\lambda} \sum_{i=1}^{n} r_{ij} C_j \,.$$

Bonacich (1972) shows that if $r_{ij} = r_{ji}$, this equation has a unique solution. If there are no discrete (totally unconnected) clusters, the first eigenvector will have all values greater than or equal to zero, and there will be negative or nonreal values in all other eigenvectors. If discrete clusters exist there will be as many positive vectors as clusters, each firm having a nonzero value in only one. Because the R matrix is sparse (less than 10% nonzero), the roots can be taken by computer.

Before centrality analysis, the most common method used in interlock investigations was to count the number of interlocks maintained by each firm and compare the varying frequencies over time and among corporations.[3] Mariolis (1975, 1978) found that centrality scores based on Bonacich's measure correlated .91 with the number of interlocks and therefore concluded that the two measures are somewhat interchangeable. However, Bonacich's measure is preferable for two reasons. First, because the centrality of each corporation is in part dependent on the centrality of the corporations with which it is linked, Bonacich's measure can identify strategically placed firms whose total interlock count is not great. This advantage is illustrated by the fact that among highly central firms—all of which have large numbers of interlocks—the correlation between number of ties and centrality is relatively low (often below .5).

Second, centrality analysis uses information on the intensity of interlocks, including adjustments for directionality (see below). Mizruchi and Bunting (1981) have demonstrated that this allows for a better fit with underlying control relationships for early twentieth century networks. Interlock intensity is incorporated into the basic centrality equation through varying the definition of r_{ij}. This flexibility makes the centrality measure a much more sensitive tool than the number of interlocks. Defining r_{ij} was, however, one of the more difficult tasks of this research.

The definition used by Mariolis was

$$(4) \quad r_{ij} = \frac{b_{ij}}{\sqrt{d_i d_j}},$$

where

b_{ij} = the number of interlocks between corporation i and corporation j (the number of individuals who were members of both boards),

d_i = the number of directors on the board of corporation i, and

d_j = the number of directors on the board of corporation j.

Clearly, with no interlocks,

$r_{ij} = 0$, since $b_{ij} = 0$,

and, if two corporations had identical boards,

$r_{ij} = 1$, since $b_{ij} = d_i = d_j$.

Defined in this way, r_{ij} can be interpreted as an intraclass correlation coefficient (see Mizuruchi et al., n.d.).

In searching for a definition of r_{ij} that discriminates between incidental and strong ties, we explored the nature of the centrality measure in a variety of situations. The simplest case is a triad in which A is tied to B and C, but B and C are not interlocked. In this case and all others using the Bonacich measure, the solution of the system of equations represented by $\lambda C = RC$ contains one arbitrary parameter. In our work, this parameter is chosen so that the most central corporation has a centrality of 1.0 and the remaining firms range between 0.0 and 1.0 in proportion to the centrality of the most central corporation.[4] With this method, when all ties are of equal strength, the value assigned to them affects the eigenvalue but not the centrality scorers (see Mizruchi et al., n.d.). Figure A.3 illustrates this principle and presents the solution for the simple triad. If all ties have an arbitrary strength of one unit, the largest eigenvalue is +1.41. A is the most central corporation, so $C_a = 1$. B and C both have centrality scores of .71. If, on the other hand, each of the corporations has ten board members, A and B have two directors in common, and A and C have two in common, the r_{ij} is the same for each tie:

$$r_{ab} = r_{ac} = \frac{2}{\sqrt{10 * 10}}.$$

The largest eigenvalue in this case is 0.28 instead of 1.41, but the centrality scores are identical to those found above.

By use of centrality analysis, we can draw a map of interlocks representing the structural arrangement among the corporations in a system. For example, centrality scores clarify the structure of the

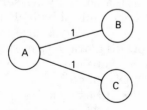
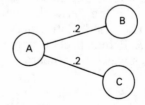

Figure A.3. Graph of simple triad of interlocks.

Solution:
$\lambda = +1.41 (= \sqrt{2}),0$
$C = 1.00$
$C = .71 (= 1/\sqrt{2})$
$C = .71 (= 1/\sqrt{2})$

Solution:
$\lambda = +.28 (= \sqrt{2/5}),0$
$C = 1.00$
$C = .71$
$C = .71$

diagram in figure A.4. When these interlocks are nondirectional and of equal intensity, the centrality scores for the ten companies in figure A.4 are (in order from one to ten): .45, .45, .45, 1.0, .82, .82, 1.0, .45, .45, .45. This information allows us to redraw interlock patterns into the polar diagram presented in figure A.5, with two corporations in dominant positions.

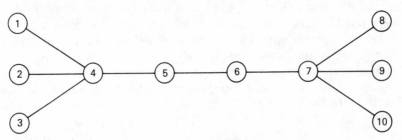

Figure A.4. Diagram of simple interlocks.

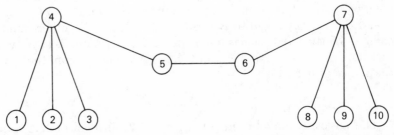

Figure A.5. Mapping of interlocks as determined by centrality scores.

These examples, however, are based on two simplifying assumptions: that all interlocks are of equal intensity and that primary and secondary interlocks are of equal significance. To illustrate how changing these assumptions affects the centrality measure, let us take the network created by two important individuals in 1962: Thomas S. Gates, president of Morgan Guaranty Trust, and Leroy A. Petersen, chairman of the board of Otis Elevator Company. Gates was on the board of the following companies:

		Number of Board Members
1	Morgan Guaranty Trust	22
2	Cities Service	18
3	Scott Paper	18
4	Smith Kline and French	16
5	Campbell Soup	12
6	Consolidated Edison	15

Petersen was on the board of these companies:

		Number of Board Members
6	Consolidated Edison	15
7	Otis Elevator	11
8	Irving Trust	20
9	Ruberoid	13
10	Metropolitan Life	24
11	Corn Products	15
12	Alco Products	14
13	Carrier	20

The map of these interlocks should be similar in structure to figure A.5, with clusters around Morgan and Otis connected only by the common link with Consolidated Edison, since it is the only board both men occupy. Taking into account all interlocks—officer and incidental—and defining r_{ij} as in the first equation above, centrality scores for the corporations in the network, from one to thirteen respectively, are .26, .28, .28, .29, .32, 1.0, .92, .74, .87, .69, .83, .85, and .74. The map of interlocks, ranked by the centrality scores, is presented in figure A.6.

Consolidated Edison, number 6 in the diagram, is the most central corporation. The result is intuitive when we note that it maintains interlocks with every other firm in the set (twelve in all), while no other company ties to more than seven others. For many analyses such logic is appropriate, and this result is meaningful and useful. If, however, we remember that this network was created by Gates and Petersen and that they were officers of Morgan and Otis, respectively, this result may seem distorted. Most of ConEd's interlocks were incidental. Otis Elevator, whose chief executive created nearly two-thirds of the links, is less central than ConEd. Even more disturbing is Morgan Guaranty's position; its officer created one-third of the interlocks, but it is the least central corporation in the entire network.

To take these concerns into account, we can eliminate the incidental interlocks from the network. Centrality scores for the network of officer ties, maintaining the definition of intensity and direction of interlocks used above, are as follows: .24, .07, .07, .09, .47, 1.0, .34, .42, .31, .39, .40, and .34, producing figure A.7. In this mapping, Otis Elevator is more central than all corporations to which it directly ties and is the most central firm in the whole network. ConEd, however, remains more central than all of the corporations in the Morgan grouping, although Morgan is now more central than its other interlock partners. This result suggests that eliminating

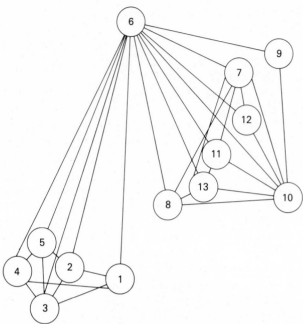

Figure A.6. Diagram of all interlocks created by Gates and Petersen.

Centrality

1	.26	Morgan Guaranty Trust	7	.92	Otis Elevator
2	.28	Cities Service	8	.74	Irving Trust
3	.28	Scott Paper	9	.87	Ruberoid
4	.29	Smith Kline and French	10	.69	Metropolitan Life
5	.32	Campbell Soup	11	.83	Corn Products
6	1.00	Consolidated Edison	12	.85	Alco Products
			13	.74	Carrier

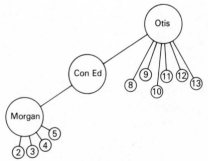

Figure A.7. Diagram of strong-tie officer interlocks created by Gates and Petersen.

incidental interlocks may provide a better portrait of underlying relationships.

It is apparent that this refinement does not eliminate all problems. The most disturbing fact is that the linking corporation in this network, ConEd, has much greater centrality than any of the members of the Morgan cluster. The reason for this becomes clearer if we examine our definition of r_{ij}, the measure of the intensity of relationship created by the interlocks. In our sample network, Petersen and Gates both sit on the board of ConEd. This creates one interlock between Otis and ConEd and one between Morgan and ConEd. By our first definition of r_{ij}, the intensity of these two interlocks is as follows:

$$r_{mc} = \frac{1}{\sqrt{22 * 15}} \qquad\qquad r_{oc} = \frac{1}{\sqrt{11 * 15}}$$

$$r_{mc} = .06 \qquad\qquad\qquad r_{oc} = .08 \quad.$$

The intensity of the interlock between Morgan and ConEd is only three-quarters the intensity of the interlock between Otis and ConEd. We have no reason to believe that such a variance in intensity between the two interlocks exists. Undoubtedly, the importance and strength of interlocks vary, but in this particular case the difference seems to be a consequence of the measurement. This can be seen by comparing the denominators of the two fractions above. The only difference is that Morgan's board has twice as many directors as Otis's. This difference means that ConEd's relationship with Otis is coded as much more intense than its relationship with Morgan. We disagree with this. We assume that the size of the board of the corporation at issue is the relevant unit to consider. This reflects the structure of intercorporate relations more accurately and is illustrated by incorporating this into the measure of intensity. If we define r_{ij} as $b_{ij}/\sqrt{d_j}$ and reconsider the ConEd–Morgan ConEd–Otis example, we see that

$$r_{mc} = \frac{1}{\sqrt{15}} \qquad\qquad r_{oc} = \frac{1}{\sqrt{15}}.$$

This finds the intensity of the ties between Otis and ConEd and Morgan and ConEd to be equal. Since we have no reason to think otherwise, we adopt $r_{ij} = b_{ij}/\sqrt{d_j}$ as our measure of intensity in full network analyses. We use the denominator $\sqrt{d_j}$ in all centrality analyses.

In addition, we add a further modification to the intensity measure in those instances in which asymmetry is introduced. The current definition is reflexive: the intensity of the interlock between Morgan and ConEd is assumed to be identical to the intensity of the interlock between ConEd and Morgan, even though it is a Morgan officer who has obtained a board position at ConEd, and not the other way around. We expect Gates to act mainly as a representative of Morgan interests to ConEd and only occasionally as a representative of ConEd to Morgan.

To include this difference, we have assigned 90% of the strength of an officer link to the sending company and 10% to the receiving company in all directional analyses. The modified r is defined as follows:

$$r_{ij} \text{ (sender)} = \frac{.9 * S_{ij}}{\sqrt{d_j}},$$

where S_{ij} = the number of officers of corporation i who sit on the board of corporation j;

$$r_{ij}(\text{receiver}) = \frac{.1 * T_{ij}}{\sqrt{d_j}},$$

where T_{ij} = the number of officers of corporation j who sit on the board of corporation i.

In general:

$$(5) \quad r_{ij} = \frac{b_{ij}}{\sqrt{d_j}},$$

where $b_{ij} = .9S_{ij} + .1T_{ij}$.

Using this definition of r_{ij}, the intensity of the tie between Morgan and ConEd in the example above was .232, and that between ConEd and Morgan was .026. The centrality scores for the thirteen companies in figure A.7 were calculated to be .30, .03, .03, .03, .03, .17, 1.0, .14, .14, .14, .14, .14, and .14, from one to thirteen respectively.[5] The associated map of interlocks is presented in figure A.8. Note that Otis is still the most central corporation, but Morgan has replaced ConEd as the second most central firm. ConEd, because of its ties to both Otis and Morgan, has more centrality than the corporations linking only to Morgan or Otis.

This is an agreeable result, considering our assumption that Gates and Petersen acted primarily as representatives of their companies. If, however, they created symmetrical relationships, the mappings

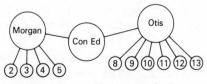

Figure A.8. Directional analysis of the interlocks created by Gates and Petersen.

in figures A.6 or A.7 would seem more appropriate. In chapters 6–10 we utilize symmetrical analyses of the full network (as illustrated in figure A.6) and directional analyses of the strong tie network (as illustrated in figure A.7) to get at different types of information. And in using each analysis, we test differing conceptions of the interlock network.[6]

3 Refinements in Centrality Analysis

Centrality analysis can be modified to meet the needs of particular research questions. In this book we use three refinements: the calculus of sources of centrality, hub and bridge analysis, and peak analysis. For additional discussion of such modifications, see Mizruchi et al. (n.d.).

The Calculus of Sources of Centrality

Since $C_i = (1/\lambda)\Sigma r_{ij}C_j$, it follows that the centrality of a particular firm can be said to be the sum of discrete quanta of centrality derived from the companies with which that firm is interlocked.

Using equation (3) (Appendix 2), we can express each quantum thus:

$$(6) \quad C_{ij} = \frac{r_{ij}}{\lambda}(C_j),$$

where

C_{ij} = the amount of centrality corporation i obtains because of its interlocks with corporation j.

Clearly,

$$(7) \quad C_i = \sum_{j=1}^{n} C_{ij}.$$

This equation allows us to calculate the most important relationships for a particular firm by assessing the largest C_{ij}. In this way, we can determine the proportion of centrality derived from particular types of relationships. For example, in chapter 6 we calculate the proportion of centrality derived from ties to large banks by summing the quanta of centrality from the banks and dividing by overall centrality.

The idea of partitioning centrality scores to understand the sources of a unit's centrality can be extended to consider changes in centrality over time. There are four ways for a firm's centrality to change: (1) establishment of new ties or breaking of old ties; (2) changes in the intensity (r_{ij}) of particular links; (3) changes in the centrality of the units with which a company is linked (C_j); and (4) changes in the eigenvalue as a result of increased or decreased interlocking in the system as a whole. We employ the following notation:

Characteristic	Year 1	Year 2	Change (Year 2−Year 1)
Centrality	C_{1i}	C_{2i}	$\Delta C_i = C_{2i} - C_{1i}$
Quanta of Centrality	C_{1ij}	C_{2ij}	$\Delta C_{ij} = C_{2ij} - C_{1ij}$
Intensity of relations	r_{1ij}	r_{2ij}	$\Delta r_{ij} = r_{2ij} - r_{1ij}$
Eigenvalue	λ_1	λ_2	$\Delta\lambda = \lambda_2 - \lambda_1$
Operant intensity (R_{ij})	r_{ij}/λ_1	r_{2ij}/λ_2	$\Delta R_{ij} = R_{2ij} - R_{1ij}$

Where
C_{1i} = the centrality of corporation i at time 1
C_{2i} = the centrality of corporation i at time 2, etc.
Changes in C_i between time 1 and time 2 can then be allocated as follows:

$$(8) \quad E(N)_i = \sum_{j=1}^{n} \Delta R_{ij} * C_{1j}$$

for all j such that $R_{1ij} = 0$ and $R_{2ij} > 0$ or $R_{1ij} > 0$ and $R_{2ij} = 0$, where

$E(N)_i$ = effects of changes in the number of corporations tied to corporation i.

$$(9) \quad E(R)_i = \sum_{j=1}^{n} \Delta R_{ij} * C_{1j}$$

for all j such that $R_{1ij} > 0$ and $R_{2ij} > 0$, where

$E(R)_{ij}$ = effects of changes in the intensity of relations between i and j.

$$(10) \quad E(C)_i = \sum_{j=1}^{n} \Delta C_j * R_{1ij} ,$$

where

$E(C)_{ij}$ = effects of changes in the centrality of j on the centrality of i.

(11) $E(N \times R)_{ij} = 0$,

where

$E(N \times R)_i$ = interaction effect between $E(N)_i$ and $E(R)_i$. This equals zero because we have controlled for the external effects of changes in the eigenvalue by dividing by λ in defining R_{ij} (see above).

Since an increase in R will cause an increase in C_j, which will in turn increase C_i, we can denote interaction effects as follows:

(12) $E(R \times C)_i = \sum\limits_{j=1}^{n} \Delta C_j * \Delta R_{ij}$, for all j such that $R_{1ij} > 0$ and $R_{2ij} > 0$

where

$E(R \times C)$ = interaction effect between $E(R)_i$ and $E(C)_i$.

(13) $E(N \times C)_i = \sum\limits_{j=1}^{n} \Delta C_j * \Delta R_{ij}$, for all j such that $R_{1ij} = 0$ and $R_{2ij} > 0$ or $R_{1ij} > 0$ and $R_{2ij} = 0$

where

$E(N \times C)$ = interaction effect between $E(N)_i$ and $E(C)_i$.

For the derivation of these effects, see Mizruchi et al. (n.d.).

For example: Let $r_{ij} = b_{ij}/d_j$,

where b_{ij} = number of interlocks between i and j

and d_j = number of directors of corporation j.

Consider a case in which a single tie between two firms is broken between time 1 (T1) and time 2 (T2). Then

$$r_{1ij} = \frac{1}{d_j},$$

$$r_{2ij} = 0,$$

$$\Delta r_{ij} = -r_{1ij},$$

$$\Delta R_{ij} = \frac{-r_{1ij}}{\lambda_1},$$

then

$$\Delta C_{ij} = 0 - R_{1j}C_{1j}$$

$$= -\frac{1}{\lambda_1 d_j} * C_{1j}.$$

Thus, we can say that corporation i lost $C_{1i}/\lambda_1 d_i$ in centrality owing to the broken interlock with j. It is important to note, however, that C_{ij} would not necessarily have remained the same even without the broken tie. As equations (9) to (13) reveal, changes in a number of system characteristics could produce changes in C_{ij} even if all r_{ij}'s remained constant.

This calculus of change in centrality is used in chapters 7 and 8.

Hubs and Bridges

The calculus of centrality allows us to analyze the components of a firm's centrality. A corporation can become central in one of two ideal ways: it can interlock with many relatively peripheral corporations, in which case we call it a hub; or it can interlock with a few relatively central corporations, in which case we call it a bridge. In chapter 9 we test our contention that financial corporations were central because they were hubs and that nonfinancial corporations were central because they were bridges.

For this study, we treated the hub/bridge distinction as a situational phenomenon. That is, within any group of connected firms, certain companies may be classified as hubs while others may be viewed as bridges or links between hubs. Morgan Guaranty, for example, the most central firm of 1962, could have derived its centrality from a multitude of ties to relatively unimportant companies or from its ties to several network leaders.

To distinguish between the two possibilities, we modified the measure of centrality. First we removed very central firms—potential hubs—from each company's list of total interlocks and recalculated its centrality score, thus producing a measure of network position unaffected by disproportionately strong direct connections. By removing the most central firms in a corporation's immediate environment, we could judge whether the unit was strategically important to the overall system or of interest in relation to the specific firms to which it linked.

We used a relative definition of very central: if a corporation that tied to the firm in which we were interested was 80% as central as that firm, it was considered a hub, and the centrality derived from this connection was interpreted as bridge centrality. The remaining centrality was interpreted as hub centrality. Thus

$$C_{Bi} = \frac{1}{\lambda} \sum_{j=1}^{n} r_{ij} C_j \text{ for all j such that } C_j \geq .8C_i$$

$$C_{Hi} = C_i - C_{Bi},$$

where

C_{Bi} = the bridge centrality of corporation i

C_{Hi} = the hub centrality of corporation i.

For example, in the full network of 1962, the second most central company, Chase Manhattan Bank, scored .9003, while the third, Equitable Life, had a score of .8957. Because it was directly tied to Chase Manhattan, Equitable contributed substantially to Chase's centrality. Using our situational definition of hub centrality, Equitable would be considered a hub in Chase's environment if its centrality score was 80% or more of the score of Chase. Eighty percent of Chase's centrality (.90) was .72. Thus, all firms directly linked to Chase with a score of .72 or more were considered hubs. Equitable's centrality of .8957 (rounded to .90) qualified for this classification. Similarly, the fourth most central organization in the 1962 full network, Chemical Bank (.88 centrality), interlocked with Chase and was considered a hub in Chase's environment as well. Metropolitan Life, with a centrality score of .73, was tied to both Chase and Morgan (1.0 centrality). It was considered a hub in Chase's network, but since its score was less than 80% of Morgan's it was not a hub in Morgan's environment. Southern Pacific (centrality .68) also maintained interlocks with Chase and Morgan, but its centrality was less than the cutoff point of 80% for both firms, and it therefore was not considered a hub for either company.

The hub centrality for Chase was thus calculated by subtracting from its total (.90) the amount of centrality derived from its ties to Equitable, Chemical, and Metropolitan. This figure was useful in assessing the degree to which Chase tied to relatively unimportant firms in the system (see chapter 9). Bridge centrality—the sum of the centrality derived from Chase's ties to Equitable, Chemical, and Metropolitan—allowed us to assess the degree to which Chase mediated relationships among other important companies. In chapter 9, hub centrality is the major tool in analyzing particular aspects of business structure.

Peak Analysis

Centrality analysis lends itself to a unique clique-detection (or clustering) technique, peak analysis (Mariolis, 1977a, 1984). Most of the commonly used clique-identification techniques group units together based on criteria of "structural equivalence" (Lorrain and White, 1971). That is, two units are said to be structurally equivalent if they have similar relations with other elements in the system. Factor analytic and block modeling approaches are explicitly based on these criteria (Breiger, Boorman, and Arabie, 1975). Graph theoretical and multidimensional scaling approaches, while not explicitly based on structural equivalence groups, usually produce almost identical results (Allen, 1982; Burt, 1979).

Peak analysis is based on the assumption of hierarchically based groupings. It was specifically designed to examine the thesis that the economy was organized in a series of interest groups, each dominated by a particular financial institution (Mariolis, 1977a,

1978). Our analysis follows this precedent.[1] The measure is designed to identify highly central but unrelated corporations that have a particular group of firms in their spheres of influence. With this in mind, our definitions are as follows:

1. A firm is a peak and defines a cluster if it is more central than any corporation (unit) with which it interlocks.
2. A firm is a member of the cluster defined by peak p if every more central unit with which it is linked is also in that cluster.

Stated mathematically:

$E_i \neq 0$ iff for all j, $r_{ij} \neq 0 \Rightarrow C_i > C_j$.

Corporation j is a member of E_i iff for all K, $r_{jk} \neq 0$ and $C_k > C_j \Rightarrow$ k is a member of E_i,

where

E_i = the cluster associated with unit i,

r_{ij} = measure of association (see above),

C_i = centrality of unit i.

In previous applications of peak analysis (Bearden et al., 1975; Mariolis, 1977a; Mintz, 1978; Mizruchi, 1982a), when all ties were counted, one huge cluster generally emerged. However, when we define ties created by officer-directors as strong ties and all other ties as weak, we can remove the weak ties from the system and generate a different picture. Bearden et al. (1975), for example, found five separate cliques in the strong-tie network of 1962. Mizruchi found from five to nine cliques in four different years between 1935 and 1975.

Results of the peak analysis are reported in chapter 10.

Notes

Introduction

1. A notable exception is Patterson (1975). Lukes (1974) develops a similar conceptualization of power without calling it hegemony. Sonquist and Koenig (1975), Koenig, Gogel, and and Sonquist (1979), Koenig and Gogel (1981), Domhoff (1978), and Bonacich and Domhoff (1977) analyze the concept of class hegemony, and excellent empirical work describing structural hegemony is found in Seybold (1978) and Fields (1982). For Gramsci on structural hegemony, see especially "The State and Civil Society" (In Gramsci, 1971: 210–76). See also Williams (1977).

2. We wish to specifically acknowledge the importance of other researchers in reporting and analyzing the significance of interlock patterns. We hope that the citations in chapters 6–10 offer sufficient documentation of the creativity and intellectual resourcefulness exhibited by scholars in this field.

3. See, for example, *Business Week* (April 26, 1969: 44); *New York Times* (Feb. 21, 1969: 63); *Dun's* (March, 1970: 69). See chapter 1 for an account of this fascinating and instructive episode.

4. See, for example, *Business Week* (Feb. 8, 1969: 34; March 29, 1969: 35–37; Feb. 28, 1970: 36–37; May 23, 1970: 34–35; July 13, 1970: 26–27; Oct. 17, 1970: 54; Dec. 19, 1970: 42), *Fortune* (June 15, 1968; Aug. 1, 1969: 136–41; May, 1970: 275).

5. See, for example, *Fortune* (Jan., 1959: 79–82; July, 1959: 112–17; March, 1961: 142–47), *Business Week* (Aug. 13, 1960: 30–31; Oct. 15, 1960: 68; Feb. 17, 1962: 112 *Forbes* (July 1, 1961: 11–14; Dec. 15, 1961. See also chapter 2 below.

6. Note, however, that the partisan quality of legal cases may limit their usefulness as historical evidence.

Chapter 1

1. This account of the Leasco tender for Chemical Bank is based on Glasberg (1981, 1982). See also Austin (1973).

2. A meeting actually took place between Steinberg and Renchard, but apparently no effort was made to convince Steinberg to desist (Glasberg, 1981).

3. This account of Henry Ford II's relationship to Ford Motor Company is based on Weymouth (1978); New York Times (April 15, 1977: D1; July 14, 1978: A1; July 15, 1978: 1, 23; March 4, 1980: D1); Fortune (Aug. 14, 1978: 13; June 16, 1980: 82–86); and Business Week (May 2, 1977: 31; June 25, 1979: 35; March 31, 1980: 39). See also Brough (1977).

4. Some publicized examples are Edwin Land of Polaroid, William Paley of CBS, Fairleigh Dickinson, Jr., of Becton-Dickinson, Robert A. Uhlein, Jr., of Schlitz, Harold Geneen of International Telephone and Telegraph, Nathan Cummings of Consolidated Foods, and Raymond C. Firestone of Firestone.

5. Kotz (1978) makes the same distinction, using the terms "control" and "managing." Pahl and Winkler (1974) also offer a similar analysis.

6. See, for example, Louis Yeager's (29% of stock) intervention in Ward Foods (Business Week, Feb. 14, 1977: 37); the Pew family (28% of stock) chief executive ousters at Sun Oil (Business Week, June 2, 1980: 70–74); and William S. Paley's (6% of stock, former chief executive) repeated interventions and ousters at CBS (Business Week 26, 1980: 128–32; New York Times, April 24, 1977: F17; May 15, 1980: A1; May 23, 1980: D1).

7. Such "coups d'etat" are not at all unusual, though they rarely explode into confrontations. At Firestone, barely two years after the retirement of Raymond C. Firestone, the Firestone family (with 25% of the stock) had lost control of policy. The one remaining family member on the board of directors lamented: "the others are frustrated, standing on the sidelines, and unity is difficult to get from them" (Business Week, Feb. 11, 1980: 62–63).

Top management of Litton Industries extracted a commitment (which was not broken) from Teledyne chairman Henry E. Singleton that he would not attempt to translate Teledyne's 28% holding in Litton into a device for control; and that if he sold the stock Litton itself would have the right of first refusal. (Business Week, Sept. 17, 1974: 112–13). At GAF in 1970, the Milstein family, which owned an apparently controlling share of the stock, was dissatisfied with what it called "gross mismanagement" by and "excessive compensation" to chief executive Jesse Werner. They sought his ouster, but they failed to win either a board vote or a proxy fight and were forced to accept his continued incumbency (New York Times, July 31, 1977: 3–5).

8. The notion of hegemony was first developed by Gramsci (1957, 1971, 1973, 1979a,b). Our usage of it in an institutional rather than ideological context owes much of its development to Patterson (1975), who applied it to the institutionalization of popular culture. Sonquist and Koenig (1975), Koenig, Gogel and Sonquist (1979), Gogel (1977), Domhoff (1978), Bonacich and Domhoff (1977), and Koenig and Gogel (1981) apply this term to class relations, while Zeitlin, Ewen and Ratcliff (1974), and Zeitlin, Neuman and Ratcliff (1976); discuss these sorts of relationships without utilizing the term "hegemony." These ideas are further developed by Ratcliff (1979–80, 1980a,b) and Ratcliff, Gallagher, and Ratcliff (1979) with

regard to bank domination of the Saint Louis economy. The arguments contained in these analyses have greatly influenced the conceptualization presented here.

9. Aldrich (1979: 269–73) offers a similar description of asymmetrical interdependence. However, he is not concerned with the possibility of utilizing such asymmetries to create overt control relationships. See also Pfeffer and Salancik (1978).

10. See *Business Week* (Jan. 31, 1977: 60–66; Feb. 7, 1977: 8; Dec. 26, 1977: 33); *New York Times* (Feb. 17, 1977: 57; March 31, 1977: D1; July 9, 1973: F1; Jan. 31, 1980: D1).

11. There is no evidence that such control was ever exercised in this instance, though it is a frequent occurrence in modern business, as we demonstrate in chapters 2–4. A particularly good illustration of this process occurred in 1978, when name-brand manufacturers used the threat of refusing to supply financially troubled Allied Supermarkets to gain eleven of twelve seats on its creditor committee. This gave them direct control, which they utilized to their own advantage: one change they initiated was to discontinue house brands in favor of exclusive use of their own national brands (*Business Week*, Nov. 20, 1978: 48; May 26, 1980: 93–96).

Chapter 2

1. It is interesting to note that Hilferding (1910) and Lenin (1917a) anticipated both managerial logic and the Marxian counterargument: "It is characteristic of capitalism in general that the ownership of capital is separated from the application of capital to production" (Lenin, 1917a: 69).

2. Nichols (1969: 55) has distinguished between "sectional managerialists," who argue that management will be self-interested, and the "nonsectionalists," who view the corporate manager as socially responsible. The former include Baldwin (1964), Burnham (1941), Earley (1957), Marris (1964), and Rose (1967). The latter include Berle (1957), Child (1969a), Drucker (1943), and Kaysen (1957). For a discussion of these issues, see also Child (1969b: 40–43).

3. Differences do remain among managerialists about the extent to which the drive for profit guides the behavior of the modern corporation. Most agree, however, that profit maximizing is much less important than in previous stages of economic development and that profit-seeking behavior is more a part of managerial discretion and less reflective of a structural constraint (for an exception to this logic, see Marris, 1964).

4. For example, for many years the Rockefeller family controlled the bulk of the oil industry in America. Even after they were forced to divide Standard Oil into six independent corporations, they maintained stockholding control over all six (Kolko, 1962). Thus they prevented the sort of "destructive" competition that would have helped their customers (and perhaps their employees) while reducing the overall profitability of the industry. This form of outside ownership suppresses the competitive tendencies brought about by the profit-maximizing dynamic. Analogously, standard Marxist accounts of the early twentieth century—the era of "finance capital"—argue that the dependence of major firms on loan capital created control relationships between major banks and nonfinancial firms. In exchange for capital infusions, industrial corporations were forced to honor the policies and interests of the banks they dealt with. This domination was often used by the banks to impose a cooperative demeanor on otherwise competitive enterprises, thus benefiting the industry as a whole while injuring those firms that would have survived severe competition. (See Brandeis, 1914; Rochester, 1936.)

5. TNEC (1940), Villarejo (1961), Chevalier (1969, 1970), Burch (1972), Zeitlin (1974, 1976), Kotz (1978), Scott (1979).

6. Rochester (1936), Perlo (1957), Lintner (1966), Menshikov (1969), Pelton (1970), Knowles (1973), Fitch and Oppenheimer (1970a-c), Fitch (1972), Gogel (1977), Kotz (1978), Glasberg (1981, 1982).

7. Feshbach and Shipnuck (1972), Aldrich and Pfeffer (1976), Pfeffer and Novak (1976), Gogel (1977), Aldrich (1979), Pfeffer and Salancik (1978), Whitt (1979–80, 1981, 1982), Useem (1982).

8. Zeitlin (1974), Zeitlin and Norich (1979), James and Soref (1981), Useem (1980), Herman (1981).

9. In 1979, when threatened with bankruptcy, Chrysler announced a rebate plan for new-car customers. This was the first instance of price competition during the fifteen-year Chrysler financial crisis, and even at this point—the most desperate circumstances in the history of the firm—the use of rebates rather than actual price reductions indicates the temporary nature of this move. Moreover, the long-term strategy of Chrysler, and the auto industry as a whole, was increased prices that would offset decreased sales. Such a strategy assumed not only the absence of price competition, but also the successful involvement of foreign manufacturers in price escalation (*Business Week*, March 24, 1980: 78–80; *Fortune*, June 16, 1980: 82–86).

10. Galbraith (1952) developed a similar argument, using the concept of "countervailing power" to describe the circumstance in which a tendency toward competition is suppressed by the inevitable counteraction of another large societal entity capable of frustrating these competitive tendencies. In Galbraith's rendering, however, consumers, unions, and other large formations participate in the cooperation that flows from mutual deterrence. See Whitt (1982) for a discussion of this. For Baran and Sweezy, the outcome of mutual deterrence is, by and large, class unity within business.

11. See also O'Connor (1968, 1972), Miliband (1969), and Sweezy (1972). As Baran and Sweezy (1966: 66–67) note, their analysis departs from the traditional Marxist characterization of the role of government, developed most forcefully in Lenin's *State and Revolution* and in Marx's *The Civil War in France*. For Lenin, the state represents an instrument of struggle for capitalists against workers and other ordinary citizens, not an instrument of intraclass conflict resolution. While the state could potentially operate in both roles simultaneously, as O'Connor (1973) suggests, the attribution of this role to the state contradicts, at least in part, Lenin's vision of a highly integrated and tightly unified capitalist class. This view, presented in his essay *Imperialism* and further developed in *The State and Revolution*, suggests that the capitalist class exists as a class independent of the state apparatus. The state therefore becomes "the executive committee of the ruling class"; It executes policies determined by the ruling class and is not itself a policymaker. Baran and Sweezy use the phrase "executive committee of the ruling class" in its more modern sense, as both a policymaking and a policy-enforcing body.

Thus, for Lenin, the operation of the state was mainly a matter of determining the best method for imposing ruling-class policy on the general population. For Baran and Sweezy, the state must calculate and discover the best policies for the ruling class and then impose them upon some corporate capitalists as well as on the general population. Needless to say, this interpretation is infinitely more complicated than the original Leninist conception, and it implies the creation of mechanisms that are not necessary to the Leninist view of government. Most particularly, it necessitates means for discovering the interests and strengths of various internal fractions within the business class, and it presumes a set of procedures for determining overall class interest.

12. This idea has been incorporated into almost all sides of the recent structuralist/instrumentalist debate. See Miliband (1969), Poulantzas (1973), Offe (1973), O'Connor (1973), Esping-Anderson et al. (1976), and Gold, Lo and Wright (1975). The contrary viewpoint is most forcefully argued in Holloway and Picciotto (1977).

13. See Pfeffer and Salancik (1978: chapter 3) for an especially lucid rendering of this logic.

14. Bank control theory derives from Hilferding's (1910) theory of financial capital, which has been interpreted in two ways: as a theory of bank domination of nonfinancial firms and as a coalescence of bank and industrial capital resulting in a mutual, rather than dominance, relationship between the two. Following Fennema's lead (1982: 18), we refer to the former as a bank control theory and the latter as the theory of finance capital. See also Niosi (1978) and Soref (1980). Major recent expressions of bank control theory can be found in Fitch and Oppenheimer (1970a–c), Menshikov (1969), and Kotz (1978). See also Knowles (1973) and Pelton (1970). For earlier work, see Rochester (1936) and Perlo (1957). See Didonato et al. (n.d.) for a review of early bank control theory.

15. For documentation of the continuing dependence of major corporations on outside finance, see Lintner (1966), Gogel (1977), Zeitlin (1974), and Stearns (1982). See also chapter 4 below.

16. See chapter 4 for a more detailed discussion of bank control theory.

17. The best expression of this logic can be found in Fitch and Oppenheimer (1970a–c). Kotz (1978) argues that the main mechanism for bank control is institutional stockholding rather than loans. Menshikov (1969) is less precise in describing the mechanism involved in bank control, as are Knowles (1973) and Pelton (1970).

18. This account of capital surplus in the mid-1970s is based on the following sources: Business Week (Oct. 12, 1976: 91; March 28, 1977: 106; Sept. 19, 1977: 55; Nov. 18, 1977: 176–84; Jan. 16, 1978: 78–80; Jan. 30, 1978: 62; March 13, 1978: 62–68; April 10, 1978: 74; Sept. 18, 1978: 97–126; Oct. 30, 1978: 162–65; Dec. 10, 1979: 99–100) Forbes (May 1, 1977: 23–24; March 20, 1978: 79; May 1, 1978: 114) New York Times (Feb. 13, 1975: F19; Feb. 6, 1977: F9).

19. For a detailed discussion of the connection between surplus capital and the merger wave of the period, see Business Week (Nov. 14, 1977: 179; March 30, 1981: 46–47), New York Times (March 16, 1981: D1; April 12, 1981: F3). For information about the development of the commercial paper market see chapter 5 below.

20. This discussion of the late 1970s capital shortage is based on the following sources: Business Week (June 30, 1980: 56–135; June 1, 1981: 55–100; Aug. 18, 1980: 84–88; Sept. 22, 1980: 103–4; April 6, 1981: 58–69). Specific industries were particularly hard hit, including automakers (New York Times, April 21, 1981: D3; Yago and Schwartz, 1981), mining (Business Week, Sept. 24, 1979: 104–12; March 30, 1981: 46–47; New York Times, Sept. 22, 1980: 103; March 16, 1981: D1; April 12, 1981: F3; June 1, 1981: 35), airlines (Business Week, May 15, 1981: 144–49; Fortune, Oct. 20, 1980: 50–56), computers (Business Week, March 23, 1981: 82–84), semiconductors (New York Times, May 19, 1981: D1), and even investment banking (Business Week, May 18, 1981: 108–14).

21. This chronology of the Braniff crisis is drawn from Business Week (Nov. 5, 1979: 104–12; Dec. 17, 1979: 40; March 17, 1980: 153–59; June 30, 1980: 45; July 28, 1980: 43; Aug. 11, 1980: 26–27; Dec. 29, 1980: 44), New York Times (June 10,

1980: D1, D4; Oct. 3, 1980: D1, D4; Oct. 7, 1980: D5; Jan. 28, 1981: D3; April 16, 1981: D5).

22. Despite the rescue attempt, Braniff declared bankruptcy the following year (*Dun's Business Monthly*, June, 1982: 29)

23. This argument is fully developed in chapter 3. For an illuminating analysis of this asymmetry, see Lenin (1917a: chapter 3), especially pp. 31–37.

Chapter 3

1. This discussion of commercial paper is based on material from *Business Week* (March 13, 1976: 91; June 30, 1977: 109; Oct. 30, 1978: 62–64; Dec. 10, 1979: 99; March 30, 1981: 11; April 13, 1981: 82–86), *Forbes* (May 1, 1978: 114), and *New York Times* (Feb. 6, 1977: 9).

2. This discussion of pension funds is based on material from Schotland (1977), Kotz (1978: 69–71), *Fortune* (July 31, 1978: 750); *Business Week* (Oct. 16, 1978: 76; Aug. 13, 1979: 57; Sept. 17, 1979: 13, 33), and *New York Times* (March 4, 1980: D1). See chapter 4 for a detailed discussion of institutional investing.

3. A major exception to this rule occurred during the New York City financial crisis, when otherwise unsellable bonds were bought by city workers' pension funds. Ironically this action was initiated by New York City's lenders, the money market banks. See McCue (1977), *New York Times* (Jan. 12, 1972: 1; Dec. 3, 1974: 1; July 31, 1974: 1; June 5, 1975: 31), *Fortune* (March, 1975: 106; Dec., 1975: 104), and *Wall Street Journal* (May 4, 1975: 14; June 4, 1976: 11; April 23, 1977: 24; Nov. 18, 1976: 18; Sept. 8, 1975: 33; Nov. 14, 1975).

4. See Rifkin and Barber (1978) for an excellent discussion of the abuses of pension management, including investment of union pensions in nonunion or antiunion companies (see also *Business Week*, Sept. 17, 1979: 33).

5. This discussion of trust-department investment is based on material from Schotland (1977), Kotz (1978: 69–71), *Newsday* (Aug. 7, 1977: 56), *Business Week* (July 25, 1980: 53; Dec. 29, 1980: 138), *Forbes* (April 17, 1978: 113), and *New York Times* (April 2, 1975: 55; Feb. 15, 1977: 40; Oct. 11, 1979: D1; March 7, 1980: 76; Oct. 7, 1980: D2).

6. This account of the Security National crisis is taken from *New York Times* (Feb. 28, 1975: 43, 53; Jan. 15, 1975: 27, 34). See also Heller and Willatt (1977) for descriptions of major bank crises and scandals in the 1970s.

7. Shares in Security National had sold at $40. as recently as 1970.

8. See below for a fuller description of these events.

9. "While Bunting [the old chief executive officer] wanted First Pennsylvania to compete with money market institutions, Butler [the new chief executive officer] is repositioning the company as a 'regional' bank, focusing on lending to businesses in its area. He is also emphasizing international lending, but mostly· to local companies doing business overseas or to help entice foreign companies to locate facilities in or near Philadelphia" (*Business Week*, Feb. 4, 1980: 28).

10. These figures are taken from an unpublished study by Steven Cohen of Columbia University. We thank him for permission to report these data.

11. Material for this discussion is derived mainly from Glasberg (1982). See also Austin (1973), *Business Week* (July 19, 1976: 60–62), and *New York Times* (Dec. 17, 1976: D2).

12. This discussion is based on the reports in the *New York Times* (March 2, 1975: E1; July 1, 1975 4) and *Business Week* (April 4, 1972: 114–116).

13. For an excellent discussion of international bank consortia, see Fennema (1982).

14. Assertions by managerialists and some Marxists that the automobile industry was self-financing (Sweezy, 1972; Baran and Sweezy, 1966; Galbraith, 1967) are incorrect. Highway building and other supports were publicly financed using funds borrowed from the money market (Yago, 1983; Caro, 1974). The manufacturers themselves relied on enormous infusions of borrowed money as well. Alfred Sloan (1965), the head of General Motors, wrote: "to meet the planned expansion we had to go to the capital markets ... for a total of $846.5 million" (p. 207).

15. See, for example, Ratcliff (1980a,b).

16. The accepted standard in the 1970s set $90 million as the limit for regional lending consortia; larger loans were referred to the money market. Late in the decade, California banks constructed consortia as large as $500 million, while in Texas 80% of the loan moneys for national firms came from outside lenders (*Business Week*, April 17, 1978: 66–72; May 30, 1977: 79–80; Nov. 7, 1977: 64–68; *New York Times*, May 25, 1980: F1).

17. In 1979 Citicorp, once again a trend setter, acquired a potentially controlling interest in a small Chicago-area bank with the apparent goal of using it as a device for overcoming unfamiliarity with potential customers (*Business Week*, April 7, 1980: 29–30; Nov. 7, 1977: 64–68; Oct. 23, 1978: 116–17; May 11, 1981: 119–20).

18. Lieberson (1961) suggests that a similar relationship exists between large regional banks and smaller banks within the Chicago region. Ratcliff (1980) presents evidence of another sort of division—between commercial lending and house mortgages in Saint Louis.

19. This account of the First Pennsylvania rescue is based on material from *Fortune* (June 2, 1980: 48–50), *Business Week* (Feb. 4, 1980: 28–29; Jan. 19, 1981: 27–48), and the *New York Times* (April 27, 1980: D1; April 28, 1980: D1; May 29, 1980: D5; June 1, 1980: F2; Jan. 6, 1981: D1).

Chapter 4

1. "For example, if a bank had made large loans to a corporation which was experiencing financial difficulty, it might be in the bank's best interest to pressure another corporation under its control to increase purchases of the first corporation's product" (Kotz, 1978: 136).

2. See also Pelton (1970), Knowles (1973), and Menshikov (1969). Lenin (1917a: 118–55) did not posit the development of financial groups, arguing instead that cycles of tight-knit unity among finance capitalists alternated with periods of competition and disunity.

3. See especially Fitch and Oppenheimer (1970a-c), Fitch (1972), Gogel (1977), and Kotz (1978, 1980).

4. A systematic analysis of bank intervention would require a separate research effort with substantial resources. A representative sample of major corporations could be selected and studied over a period as long as a decade. The business press, government documents, financial and business reports, and interviews could supply the detailed information necessary to offer precise estimates of the frequency, nature, and consequences of bank intervention.

5. For coverage of the International Harvester crisis see *New York Times* (Feb. 23, 1981: D4; March 10, 1981: D1; March 31, 1981: D1); and *Business Week* (April 27, 1981: 44; June 22, 1981: 66–72).

6. In the UMM bankruptcy, lenders received 100% of debt owed; in Korvette only 50% was recovered. See table 4.1 for sources.

7. Chapter 11 refers to the section of the federal bankruptcy law under which the bankruptcy is filed.

8. This was the case of Food Fair Stores, a Philadelphia-based supermarket chain.

9. Those familiar with the New York City fiscal crisis of the 1970s will note the similarity between the Emergency Financial Control Board, which oversaw the city's affairs, and the creditors' committees mandated by chapter 11 bankruptcy law. It seems likely that the financial community, familiar with bankruptcy law and comfortable with its operation, utilized this model in their relationship with New York City (McCue, 1977).

10. This account of the Daylin bankruptcy is based on *Wall Street Journal* (Oct. 15, 1976: 32), *Business Week* (Nov. 15, 1976: 43), and *New York Times* (June 11, 1978: F1).

11. This account of the Penn Central bankruptcy is based on *Wall Street Journal* (Oct. 15, 1976: 32), *Business Week* (Nov. 15, 1976: 43), and *New York Times* (June 11, 1978: F1).

12. This account of the Rohr crisis is taken from *Business Week* (Feb. 28, 1977: 86–87), and *New York Times* (July 30, 1980: D1).

13. This account of the Cook Industries crisis is taken from *New York Times* (Sept. 28, 1976: 60; June 6, 1977: 46), and *Business Week* (June 13, 1977: 42; June 20, 1977: 30; June 30, 1978: 22–23).

14. A similar event occurred at Farah, where banks forced William F. Farah, founder and dominant stockholder, out of management and off the board of directors. By raising sufficient cash to repay the loans, Farah restored his control of the company (*Business Week*, April 11, 1977: 40; Dec. 5, 1977: 44; April 10, 1978: 44; Oct. 9, 1978: 56; *New York Times*, June 15, 1977: D14).

15. Herman (1981:128) notes that the power of loan covenants is difficult to assess, although "the fact is inescapable that some power and influence must flow from the fixing of guideposts under loan agreements, the right to veto actions ... and the need to waive violations of the agreement." In sum, however, he argues that this power and influence is typically not realized, that "banker encroachments on managerial prerogatives are not great," and that "bankers fear adverse publicity associated with intervention and are often trapped in the boat with existing management, which frequently is able to preserve power well into insolvency." As we make clear below, we believe this conclusion is overdrawn.

16. Farah later regained control by raising money and repaying the debt. See note 14 above.

17. See Mintz and Schwartz (1982) for a detailed discussion of this episode.

18. Ironically, the initial popularity of pension funds was interpreted by many as a move toward "people's capitalism," since pension investments gave workers equity in corporate America. As it became clearer that these owners were indeed separated from control of the invested companies, this idea lost its appeal. See Perlo (1958).

19. In 1935, congressional hearings identified eighty-one firms in which investment companies held 10% or less of their voting stock, sixty-eight firms in which between 10% and 50% was held, and thirty-eight cases in which over 50% was held (Soldofsky, 1971: 155).

20. For discussions that preceded Patman, see Goldsmith (1954), Harbrecht (1959), and Wrightsman (1964). For later sources, see Greenough and King (1976), Herman (1981), and Rifkin and Barber (1978).

21. Not all researchers accept this notion of fiduciary responsibility. Rifkin and Barber (1978: 93–95) argue that pension funds are propping up American industry; that as the rate of return on stock purchases continues to decline, fewer individuals are investing in the market; and that the "smart money" got out, while pension funds absorbed the difference.

22. Note that this same problem applies to the Wall Street rule. At times, potential losses created by the sale of large blocks of stock make this an impractical method of withdrawing from a disagreement with management. As Herman and Safanda (1973: 112) suggest: "Realistically speaking, adherence to the Wall Street rule, in this case, would have been an impossibility, since the bank held close to 10% of the outstanding stock. . . . The marketability of this amount of stock was further limited because the bank's holdings were equal to approximately 30% of the preceding year's trading in the issue. The bank, in this instance, was locked in by the large size of its holdings, as well as by a close customer relationship that added to the difficulty in deciding to sell in any volume."

23. Herman (1975: 137) notes that in the early 1970s Chase reported a pension fund account loss of more than $1 billion. He also presents data from a study of performance rates of thirty funds owned by the Bell System. In this case, in 1967–68, the banks underperformed the market; in 1969–70 they came close to it, and they outperformed it in 1971–72 (Herman, 1975: 137).

24. See also Rifkin and Barber (1978) and Schotland (1977: 200).

25. Herman and Safanda (1973) provide a multitude of examples of banks' sacrificing the profits of their trust department customers in order to advance other interests. See pages 93, 94, 96, 97, 98n.15, 99n.16, 108, 109, and 112–13.

Chapter 5

1. This chronology of farm co-op expansion is taken from Business Week (Feb. 7, 1977: 54–64).

2. This discussion of the shipbuilding industry is based on material from Business Week (Feb. 10, 1975: 36; May 1, 1978: 80–81; Oct. 6, 1980: 38–40); New York Times (Aug. 29, 1976: 3–1; Sept. 15, 1977: D1, D11; July 9, 1978: 3.1; Feb. 12, 1981: D1); and Wall Street Journal (June 25, 1975: 36).

3. See Zeitlin and Norich (1979), James and Soref (1981), and Herman (1981), for recent evidence on this matter. Useem (1980) provides a lucid review of the debate and concludes that profit maximization remains the major force in corporate affairs.

4. The threat of bank crisis as described here is not an abstract analytic construction. "Silent runs" such as those described by Zeitlin (1976) have been the major cause of bank crises in the late 1970s (see chapter 3). This discipline is, of course, inexact and often inefficient.

5. Business Week (Nov. 5, 1979: 105; June 30, 1980: 45).

6. In arguing against the theory of banker control, Sweezy (1972: 189) suggests that giant multinational firms are closer to financial than production units and play the role in modern capitalism that Lenin (1917a) imputed to banks.

7. Forbes once referred to the period in the late 1960s when conglomerates were most under attack as the "conglomerate shakeout" because so many firms were reduced back to more coherent enterprises (June 26, 1978). By the late 1970s, the process of slimming down conglomerates became known as "enterprise restructuring" (New York Times, Jan. 11, 1981: F1). For examples see Bordon, Esmark, GAF, City Investing, Gulf and Western, Rapid-American, and Genesco.

8. Information on Ling's instructive career can be found in Brown (1972); *Fortune* (June, 1973: 134–40, 220–30; Jan., 1976: 32); and *New York Times* (Feb. 8, 1975: 33).

9. *New York Times* (May 1, 1980: D1, D15; May 30, 1980: 30). For an account of this episode, see Abolafia (1981).

10. This chronology of overseas banking in the 1970s is taken from the following sources, unless otherwise noted: *Business Week* (Aug. 7, 1977: 62; Nov. 7, 1977: 64–70; April 7, 1980: 29–30; Sept. 22, 1980: 34; June 23, 1980: 120–21; Oct. 6, 1980: 38–40); *Fortune* (Sept. 22, 1980: 125); *New York Times* (Aug. 29, 1976: 3.1; March 6, 1977: F-5; Sept. 15, 1977: D1; June 5, 1980: D4; May 31, 1978: D11; April 14, 1980: A1; April 21, 1980: D1; May 5, 1980: D1; Sept. 9, 1980: D1; Sept. 22, 1980: D1; Sept. 23, 1980: D1; Nov. 19, 1980: D1; April 4, 1981: D5); *Forbes* (May 15, 1978: 96); Egan (1980); Brooks (1981).

11. For example, Argentina (*Business Week*, Dec. 1, 1980: 99) and Turkey (*Business Week*, Dec. 15, 1980: 81).

12. Both the banks and the Polish government were set back by the militance of Polish workers, and their joint efforts to achieve increased foreign exchange were—at least temporarily—frustrated. This is not an isolated case. In Argentina, for example, bank-mandated policies of fiscal austerity were defeated when degenerating economic conditions threatened to trigger mass unrest (*New York Times*, April 2, 1981: D5).

Chapter 6

1. Allen (1974, 1978), Bearden (1982), Bearden et al. (1975), Berkowitz et al. (1979), Bunting (1976, 1977), Burt (1979, 1980a,b), Burt, Christman, and Kilburn (1980), Fennema (1982), Galaskiewicz and Wasserman (1981), Gogel (1977), Gogel and Koenig (1981), Koenig (1979), Koenig, Gogel, and Sonquist (1979), Koenig and Gogel (1981), Kotz (1978), Levine (1972), Mariolis (1975, 1978), Mintz (1978), Mintz and Schwartz (1981a,b, 1983), Mizruchi (1982a, 1983), Mokken and Stokman (1974, 1979), Norich (1980), Ornstein (1980, 1982), Palmer (1980, 1983a,b), Pennings (1980), Sonquist and Koenig (1975), Stokman, Zeigler, and Scott (1984), and United States Senate (1978).

2. For reviews of the interlock literature, see Bearden et al. (1975), Fennema and Schijf (1979), Glasberg and Schwartz (1983), DiDonato et al. (1984), and Soref (1979). See Ornstein (1982) and Palmer (1980, 1983a,b), for evidence that questions traditional interpretations.

3. See Brandeis (1914), Rochester (1936), Sweezy (1939), United States Federal Trade Commission (1951), Perlo (1957), and United States Congress, (1913, 1965, 1968).

4. Many capitalist families operate either through diversified investment portfolios managed by family offices (Collier and Horowitz, 1976; Dunn, 1979–80) and/or through a single corporation the family owns and controls (e.g., the Firestone family in Firestone Tire). In these instances control relationships with other firms, even when traced by board membership, appear as institutional ties with the family office or the main corporate holding.

5. See *Business Week* (Feb. 11, 1980: 78-79); *New York Times* (April 7, 1980: D4).

6. See *Business Week* (Nov. 22, 1976: 133–39; March 27, 1978: 54); *New York Times* (Feb. 1, 1981: F1).

7. Glasberg (1981, 1982); *Business Week* (Dec. 31. 1979: 40; Oct. 6, 1980: 106; March 16, 1981: 144–50); *New York Times* (March 27, 1980: D6).

8. See *Business Week* (Oct. 25, 1976: 80–83); *Fortune* (April 21, 1980: 62–72); *Forbes* (June 26, 1978: 33–34).

9. *Moody's Industrial Manual* (1967); *Business Week* (May 17, 1976); Burch (1972). In 1977, Kaiser Industries was dissolved, and the network began to disintegrate (*Business Week* (May 2, 1977: 38; July 11, 1977: 26–27).

10. That interlocks do not trace control with regularity is also consistent with Hirsch's (1982) findings that corporate directors do not view interlocks as mechanisms of power.

11. Pfeffer and Salancik (1978), Pfeffer (1972), Aldrich (1979), Aldrich and Pfeffer (1976), Burt (1979), Burt, Christman, and Kilburn (1980), and Pennings (1980).

12. The implicit conflict of interest illustrated by Smith's dual roles is a matter of considerable concern and debate in the business community, especially in the case of commercial and investment bank representation on industrial boards. Mace (1971) has numerous references to this issue. Brown and Smith discuss it (1957: 1146), as do Bacon and Brown (1977: 93). See also *Business Week* (June 25, 1979: 70–78) and chapter 7 below.

13. Domhoff (1970, 1975, 1978) suggests that nongovernment policy planning groups—the Council on Foreign Relations, the Committee for Economic Development, and the Business Council, for example—serve to mediate among the different interests within the capitalist class. See also Burch (1980–81, 1981).

14. See also Stigler (1968). More complete analyses of interlocks as relations among individuals can be found in Koenig, Gogel, and Sonquist (1979), Palmer (1980), Bearden (1982), and Useem (1983).

15. Glasberg (1981) illustrates another device by which outsiders can effectively oppose corporate policy. Bank outsiders on the Leasco board acquired information about Leasco's strategy for taking over Chemical Bank; this information was transmitted to Chemical and was used in developing countermoves.

16. The findings of Koenig, Gogel, and Sonquist (1979) were consistent with Palmer's. Glasberg (1982) and Bearden (1982) provide further evidence in support of these results. See also Ornstein (1982).

17. Bearden et al. (1975), Berkowitz (1982); Berkowitz et al. (1979), Bunting (1976, 1977), Burt (1979, 1980a,b, 1982), Burt, Christman, and Kilburn (1980), Fennema (1982), Galaskiewicz and Rauschenbach (1979), Glasberg (1981), Gogel and Koenig (1981), Koenig and Gogel (1981), Kotz (1978), Levine (1972), Mariolis (1975, 1978), Mintz and Schwartz (1981a,b, 1983), Mizruchi (1982a, 1983), Mokken and Stokman (1979), Norich (1980), Ornstein (1980), Palmer (1983a,b), Roy (1983a,b).

18. *New York Times* (Jan. 3, 1977: 33; Jan. 4, 1977: 37); *Business Week* (April 11, 1977: 29; April 3, 1978: 71–74).

Chapter 7

1. For a complete description of this data set, see Appendix 1. See also Bearden et al. (1975).

2. For reviews of interlock literature see Fennema and Schijf, (1979), Soref (1979), and DiDonato et al. (n.d.).

3. For recent data sets see Allen (1974), Bearden and Mintz (1984), Bunting and Barbour (1971), Dooley (1969), Mariolis (1975), and Mizruchi (1982a). For the European case, see Stokman, Zeigler, and Scott (1984), and for analyses of the transnational network, see Fennema (1982) and Fennema and Schijf (1984).

4. These figures refer to the total number of interlocks maintained rather than the number of corporations to which a company connects. For example,

in 1962 Chase Manhattan Bank tied to fifty-four different companies while maintaining multiple ties to several of those firms. It shared two directors with AT&T, three directors with American Express, three with Equitable Life, four with Metropolitan Life, and so on for a total of sixty-six interlocks. In 1962, banks shared directors with an average of 18.5 corporations while industrials connected to an average of 7.7 firms. We report total number of interlocks unless otherwise specified.

5. See also Mizruchi (1982a), Mizruchi and Bunting (1981), and Pennings (1980).

6. For a detailed analysis of this pattern, see Bearden (1982).

7. Lewis H. Young, editor-in-chief of *Business Week*, wrote: "management is primarily concerned with personal compensation, career growth, job security, appreciation of stock prices to make options valuable, or all or some of these" (Young, 1978: 54). This point is amply illustrated and acknowledged by business practice. International Harvester created a "novel" compensation package for chief executive officer Archie McCardell: "so that his interests will parallel those of outside investors in the company's stock" (*Fortune*, May 19, 1980: 93). Such efforts are not always successful. At Genesco, chief executive officers of acquired firms were given profit-sharing incentives to keep them at the helm after acquisition. Many of these executives built up short-term profits, collected bonuses, and left their firms behind (*Business Week*, June 22, 1980: 80). Similarily, mergers are often occasions for divergent executive/stockholder interests: "the management of a target company who fights tooth and nail is more anxious to protect its own interest [autonomy] than that of its stockholders" (*Forbes*, May 1, 1977: 104). The literature on intercorporate relations addresses this point as well. Berle and Means (1932), for example, wrote: "the separation of ownership and control produces a condition where the interests of owners and of ultimate managers may, and often do, diverge" (p. 7). The literature, however, has concentrated on the profit-seeking behavior of the corporation given the possibility of differences in interest. See chapter 2 above.

8. See Pfeffer and Salancik (1978) for the best evidence on mergers and joint ventures.

9. For a detailed discussion of centrality analysis, see Appendixes 2 and 3. See also Mariolis, Schwartz, and Mintz (1979), Mariolis (1975, 1977b, 1978), Bearden, et al. (1975), Mintz (1978), Mizruchi and Bunting (1981), and Mizruchi (1982a).

10. This report of second-order interlocks is an overestimate. Kodak, for example, directly interlocked with B. F. Goodrich and the Great Atlantic and Pacific Tea Company, each of which, in turn, tied to the Ford Motor Company. This is coded as indirect ties to two companies. Similarly, Eastman Dillon is interlocked with Food Fair and Lowenstein and Sons, which both maintain ties to Botany Industries. In this instance, Eastman Dillon is credited with two second-order interlocks.

11. On a range of 0 to 1.0, Eastman scores .03 in centrality, Kodak .14. For a discussion of the meanings of the scores themselves, see Appendix 3.

12. The most obvious nominees would be First National Bank of Chicago (twenty-sixth in centrality), Continental Illinois (thirty-fourth), First National Bank of Boston (seventy-eighth), and First Pennsylvania Corporation (sixty-eighth).

13. The same analysis applies to other high-asset West Coast banks (Wells Fargo and Security Pacific). Today, Bank of America is much more important, though it remains less prominent in commercial circles than its asset rating (currently number two) would suggest. In 1979 *Business Week* still classified it as a regional bank.

14. Ratcliff and his colleagues have analyzed the relation between network centrality and decision-making preeminence among Saint Louis area banks. They found that centrality is more important than the size of the institution in determining lending policy, institutional importance, and the civic prominence of executives (Ratcliff, 1980a,b; Ratcliff, Gallagher, and Ratcliff, 1979).

15. When Zender left Distillers in 1963 his successor, William P. Marsh, was also invited onto the Chemical Bank board. This indicates the importance placed on access to Distillers executives by Chemical's leadership.

16. In 1975, the only year for which we can obtain figures, 28% of all capital investment was in nuclear power plants.

17. Allen (1974, 1978), Bearden et al. (1975), Bunting (1976–77), Bunting and Barbour (1971), Burt, Christman, and Kilburn (1980), Dooley (1969), Galaskiewicz and Wasserman (1981), Levine (1972, 1977b), Mariolis (1975, 1977a,b, 1978), Mintz (1978), Mintz and Schwartz (1981a,b), Mizruchi (1982a), Mizruchi and Bunting (1981), Pennings (1980), and Sonquist and Koenig (1975). See Ornstein (1980) for the Canadian network and Stokman, Zeigler, and Scott (1984) for the European case.

18. Mariolis and Jones (1982), using the same data set used in this book correlated numbers of interlocks and non-directional and directional centrality for 1962, 1964, and 1966. They found correlations above .9 for all three measures, a stunning result considering the high turnover rates of director interlocks.

19. While most interlock analysts expect long-term trends along with some change, no extant theory predicts major alterations in the network over a four-year period. Mizruchi (1982a), Bunting and Barbour (1971), Allen (1978), and Dooley (1969) have all undertaken analyses of long-term trends, and their results are consistent with the analysis presented here. Mizruchi, in the most comprehensive of these studies, found that the network centrality of railroads and investment banks in the early part of the century dissipated as the economic importance of these institutions declined. (See Kotz, 1978, for an excellent discussion of the changing role of investment banks.) At the same time, commercial banks and insurance companies generally maintained and even increased their importance.

20. Information on interlocking directorates of 1969 was generously supplied by Peter Mariolis. The data sets under investigation are not strictly comparable. The Mariolis network included the interlocks of the 797 largest corporations in the United States that year, excluding investment banks. For a detailed analysis of the 1969 data, see Mariolis (1975, 1977a) and Levine (1977b). Note also that the definition of interlock intensity in the present investigation is different from the one used by Mariolis. See Appendix 2.

21. See Appendix 3 for the derivation of these percentages.

22. See Zeitlin (1974) for a persuasive expression of this view.

23. In 1969, Citibank initiated the structural transformation of money market banks into what has become known as "one bank holding companies" (see chapter 4). Though Walter Wriston is often credited with developing the bank holding company, it had actually been pioneered by Western Bancorp and Marine Midland.

24. UCB maintained multiple ties with the following nonfinancials: Cyprus Mines (four), Rockwell International (two), Litton (two), Lockheed (two), Southern California Edison (three), Times-Mirror (two), TWA (two), and Union Oil (two). It has also had seven interlocks with Pacific Mutual Life.

25. See Appendix 2 for an explication of the ways multiple ties increase the centrality of the companies connected by them.

26. The 1933 Banking and Security Act technically barred such ties, although the act has been only sporadically enforced.

Chapter 8

1. Although we have pointed out that interlocks reflect both structural and personal relationships, this analysis considers directional ties to be structural.

2. All directional ties are primary, by definition. A primary tie is a directional tie when asymmetry is assumed.

3. Palmer (1980, 1983a) found that almost all interlocks that actually reflect ongoing structural relations between two firms are primary—that is, they are created by the election of an officer of one firm to the board of another. Mizruchi and Bunting (1981) have demonstrated that, for the early twentieth century, centrality analysis of directional interlocks provides the best portrait of the intercorporate hierarchy, and Bearden et al. (1975) presented results indicating that directional analyses uncover corporate groupings that are invisible when the full network is analyzed. Finally, Pennings (1980) found that directional links from major banks to major industrial firms are the strongest (and often the only) correlate of corporate efficiency. For a detailed discussion of this distinction see Appendix 2. For analyses of the differences between directional (or primary) interlocks and nondirectional (secondary or incidental) interlocks, see Bearden et al. (1975), Mizruchi (1982a) Mizruchi and Bunting (1981), Palmer (1980, 1983a,b); and Pennings (1980). Pfeffer and Salancik (1979) and Burt, Christman, and Kilburn (1980) assume this distinction but do not incorporate it into their analysis.

4. See chapter 6 for a detailed discussion of this logic.

5. The 1962 network yields similar results. We chose 1966 for this discussion because it includes California regional firms that were not prominent in 1962.

6. The three insurance companies among the twenty most central corporations of the 1966 directional network are similar to industrials, not banks. The bulk of their centrality derived from links to banks. This finding will be discussed at length in chapter 9.

7. We should keep in mind that this chart maps only the most important links. Were we to trace all links, each region would include many more firms, and the entire network would be too dense to interpret.

8. Despite Hunter's (1953) pioneering effort, community studies have often ignored or underestimated the importance of these tight business networks (Dahl, 1961). The work of Ratcliff and his collaborators on Saint Louis is a notable exception. Many of the ideas and arguments presented here derive from their work (Ratcliff, 1979–80, 1980a,b; Ratcliff, Gallagher, and Ratcliff, 1979). See also Domhoff (1978) and Ewen (1978) for important contributions to this literature.

9. There are, however, reasons for bankers, especially money market bankers, to refuse industrial board memberships. First, regional friendship networks are denser and more enduring and often contain economic substance. Therefore reciprocal ties are more frequent and more necessary on the local level. Second, the top executives of money market banks cannot usually advance their own careers by joining the boards of much smaller nonfinancial firms. Third, whereas outsiders on bank boards participate in decisions of overarching importance to themselves and their home companies, bankers on industrial boards usually participate in decisions subsidiary to those they undertake at their principal affiliation.

10. See Useem (1982, 1983) for a stunning analysis of the foundations and implications of classwide rationality in the United States and Britain.

Chapter 9

1. To calculate hub centrality we must determine which firms in a company's environment are hubs. That is, when do we treat an interlock as a hub

tie? In the present investigation, a firm j is considered an important influence in the environment of corporation i if the centrality of j is at least 80% of the centrality of i. Thus, any company whose centrality is 80% or more of the overall centrality of the corporation under investigation is considered a hub; centrality derived from interlocks with this hub is counted as bridge centrality. Varying the definition (to as low as 60% or as high as 90%) does not alter the results substantially. See Appendix 3. See also Mintz (1978), Mariolis, Schwartz, and Mintz (1979), and Mizruchi et al. (n.d.).

An example will illustrate this procedure. Chase Manhattan was the second most central firm in the full network of 1962, maintaining a centrality of .9003. Equitable Life, the third most central company, had a score of .8957 and interlocked to Chase. Since 80% of Chase's centrality (.9003) is .7202, Equitable (.8957) qualifies as a hub in Chase's environment. New York Life (.8264) and Metropolitan Life (.7316) were both tied to Chase and were treated as hubs, while Southern Pacific (.6843) was not because its centrality was less than 80% of Chase's. This analysis of Chase indicates that it derived bridge centrality from its ties to the three insurance companies (totaling .1720) and its remaining (.7283) centrality from its role as a hub to fifty-one other companies. Thus Chase had .7283, or 81%, hub centrality and .1720, or 19%, bridge centrality.

2. Centrality analysis is highly sensitive to multiple interlocks (see Appendix 2), especially tightly connected sets such as the Kaiser group (see chapter 6) or temporary perturbations (e.g., United California Bank, chapter 7). These arrangements are very rare. In 1962, there were only forty-eight dyads with more than three links, and above a certain point, multiple ties are indistinguishable; five ties do not represent greater proximity than three. Our analysis therefore treats all links covered by three or more interlocks as three interlocks; our directional analyses utilize the comparable maximum of 1.5. See Mintz (1978), and Mizruchi et al. (n.d.) for a fuller discussion of this issue.

3. Although the hub centrality list largely replicates overall centrality, the differences are instructive. The three firms that in 1962 were among the most central companies, but that were not important hubs, were AT&T, United States Steel, and Phelps Dodge, all industrials. Of the three companies that were not among the top twenty in total centrality but appeared as important hubs, two (First National Bank of Chicago and Mutual of New York) were financials. In 1966, two companies (Western Bancorp and Southern Pacific) appeared among the most central but not among the important hubs; both were replaced by banks (Harris and Continental Illinois).

In 1962, six companies ranked higher as hubs than in the overall network; four were banks and one was an insurance company; five companies ranked lower as hubs—only one was a financial firm. Of eight nonfinancials, four ranked lower as hubs than in overall centrality. Only one of fifteen financials was less important as a hub. The 1966 figures are less dramatic but are consistent with these (see Mintz, 1978).

4. Results for 1962 are similar, but difficulties of exposition preclude reporting them here. See Mintz (1978) for further evidence.

5. In 1962, nine banks and one insurance company (New York Life) appeared among the hubs, while one bank (Nortrust) and two insurance companies were major bridges.

6. National firms tend to be headquartered in New York, and the national characteristics of these technically New York companies allow them to transcend geographic considerations. J. P. Stevens for example, headquartered in New York, is incorporated in Delaware, maintains sales offices in Allentown, Atlanta,

Boston, Buffalo, Cleveland, Charlotte, Chicago, Cincinnati, Dallas, Detroit, Los Angeles, New York, Philadelphia, Pittsburgh, Saint Louis, and San Francisco, and operates over seventy-five plants, most of which are located in North and South Carolina (*Moody's Industrial Manual*, 1971: 1335). Hence, the assignment of Stevens to a New York group by virtue of general office location is analytically deceptive. Historically, it belongs in the southeastern region, but by 1962 it maintained only three ties to that area (Duke Power, Daniel Construction, and Georgia-Pacific).

7. Smaller regional banks are not hubs, but bridges. Nortrust Corporation, for example, the thirty-seventh most central company in the 1962 directional network, maintained nineteen local Chicago-area interlocks and four national links; its seven directional ties were local. This configuration created a bridging pattern within the region, and all of Nortrust's 1962 centrality was bridge centrality.

Chapter 10

1. An earlier version of parts of this chapter is found in Mintz and Schwartz (1983).

2. See Appendix 2 for a fuller, more mathematical exposition of peak analysis. This technique has been successfully applied by Mariolis (1977b, 1978, 1984), Bearden et al. (1975), Mintz (1978), Mintz and Schwartz (1983), and Mizruchi (1982b).

3. We will use the terms cluster, clique, and interest group interchangeably.

4. All other clique-detection methods utilized in interlock research do not allow for a null finding. See Dooley (1969), Allen (1978), and Sonquist and Koenig (1975).

5. That the total number of peaks is limited by the degree of system interlocking can be illustrated by the following example. Assume ten corporations arranged by centrality, with company 1 the most central and company 10 the least central. Firm 1, by definition, is a peak. If corporation 2 is not directly linked to 1, it too is a peak. Similarly, if 3 is linked to neither 1 nor 2, it is a peak. Assume that firm 4 directly interlocks with 2—4 is a member of 2's clique. Corporation 5 does not tie to firms 1–4 and hence is a peak. If 6–10 interlock with any organization more central than themselves, they are not peaks. In this case, then, out of the ten firms, four peaks are present. Using the same corporation numbers, assume a system of greater density. Firm 1 is still a peak. In this case, however, assume that 2 ties to 1—it is not a peak. If 3 interlocks with 2, it is a member of 1's clique. Similarly, assume that 4 ties with 3, that 5 ties with 4, that 6 ties with 5, and so on. There is only one peak in the network. Nevertheless, the larger the system, the greater the number of potential peaks.

6. The minor peaks, in this case, are isolated pairs of companies connected only to each other and not to the broader network. These will be discussed below.

7. The largest group in the 1966 network was an isolated grouping (interlocked only with each other) headed by City Products that included Household Finance, Walter Heller International, the Jim Walter Corporation, the Fidelity Corporation, and E. T. Barwick. The exact relationships that create this group are partly apparent, but some are difficult to discern.

Household Finance, the most important specialist in small loans in the United States, owned City Products (*Moody's Bank and Finance Manual*, 1967). Group members seemed to share financial interests: Walter Heller was a consumer loan concern that had recently expanded into international finance; Jim Walter derived an important portion of total revenues from the consumer loans, and Fidelity Corporation (a diversified financial organization), was actively engaged in a variety of lending functions and capital supply (Moody's Bank and Finance Manual, 1967). Since these firms were not grouped together in the 1962 network, it is interesting to note certain changes in their business profiles. Heller entered the field of consumer finance late in 1962; Jim Walter formalized its financial operations in 1965 with the acquisition of Brentwood Financial Corporation (Moody's Bank and Finance Manual, 1967); and Household Finance's purchase of City Products was consummated sometime between 1962 and 1965. E. T. Barwick, the sixth member of the clique, apparently had little in common with other grouped firms.

Five new isolated dyads appeared in the 1966 network: Marine Bancorp and its subsidiary National Bank of Commerce; Wheelabrator-Frye and its major stockholder American Export Industries; Ashland Oil and Refining and National Industries, both Kentucky oil companies; Crown Central Petroleum and Columbia Pictures, apparently unrelated; and Pueblo International and Seatrain Lines, also unrelated.

Of the nine clusters in the 1966 network, then, potential relationships among clique members can be traced in seven cases. Some intergroup ties were clearer than others, some probably stronger than others. Relationships based on ownership, mutuality of need, location, and supplier-consumer links were either verified or directly suggested.

8. For a similar argument using a different method, see Mintz and Schwartz (1981a). Similar results were also found by Mariolis (1977b, 1978, 1984) and Mizruchi (1982b).

9. In excluding incidental interlocks and those created by individuals from outside the population under investigation, we are excluding a great many relevant ties. However, since we wish to provide the best chance of uncovering cliques, it is wise to err in this direction.

10. Sweezy (1939) referred to these ties as primary interlocks. See also Bearden et al. (1975).

11. Allen's Chicago firms included Borg-Warner, Commonwealth Edison, Continental Illinois, First National Bank of Chicago, Illinois Central Industries, Inland Steel, International Harvester, Sears, and Standard Oil of Indiana. Dooley's group included Armour, Commonwealth Edison, Continental Illinois, First National Bank of Chicago, Harris Trust, Illinois Central, Inland Steel, International Harvester, Montgomery Ward, People's Gas, Pure Oil, Sears, Standard Oil, and Swift. A much better fit is found between Allen and Dooley, with eight shared firms. It should be stressed that, in 1962, First National Bank of Chicago maintained primary interlocks with seven of the corporations included in Allen's and Dooley's groups. Note also that three different methods of clique detection were used to generate the three different membership lists under consideration, that data years varied, and that neither Dooley nor Allen used a procedure that allowed a null result.

12. MCA is not a Chicago organization. With principal offices in New York and important business dealings in California, its connection to the Midwest is not at all clear.

13. The remaining results of the 1962 strong-tie analysis replicate those already discussed. Bankers Trust generated a clique that contained Connecticut General Life, Emhart, and Lipton. While the bank owned 6.4% of Connecticut General, there is no evidence linking the two financial companies' loan activities. There were no direct ownership ties between Lipton and Bankers Trust; Lipton was, in fact, a wholly owned subsidiary of the Dutch firm Unilever (Moody's Industrial

Manual, 1971), which maintained no apparent links to Bankers Trust. The bank was the transfer agent for Emhart, but ownership links did not parallel this tie. Lipton and Emhart did not relate on a functional level, and no evidence appeared linking either company to Connecticut General Life.

Blair and Company, an investment bank located in New York, was the peak of a four-corporation group with little structural coherence. Neither regional homogeneity, overlapping industries, nor ownership ties linked the included firms. The Morgan group included Proctor and Gamble and its wholly owned subsidiary Clorox. Proctor and Gamble used Morgan as a debt trustee. Western National Bank of Minnesota defined a domain that included its parent company, Northwest Bancorp, and Control Data, for which it served as registrar.

Kansas City Southern, a Missouri railroad, was the nonfinancial peak of a group that included BMA, a diversified investment house, and Peabody Coal, one of the largest coal mining firms in the country. Clique membership seemed to be organized around geographic proximity, since each firm was headquartered in Missouri.

14. As in the 1962 strong-tie analysis some substantive relations were uncovered by the peak analysis and, like the 1962 system, corporations were organized around different criteria in different contexts. Unification by geographic location was illustrated in the case of the United California Bank group, which included only three corporations (Lehman Brothers, Metro-Goldwyn-Mayer, and Trans World Airlines) not located in the Far West. Functional relationships were in evidence within the group as well. Ownership lines were reflected in at least two cases: Alexander and Baldwin owned Matson Navigation, and Western Bancorp owned the United California Bank. Competitors were found: Matson Navigation was in direct competition with American President Lines, as determined by standard industrial classification numbers. Litton and Lockheed overlapped as well. Potential customer-supplier lines existed, as illustrated by El Paso Natural Gas and Southern California Edison, or Times-Mirror (newspaper publisher) and Potlatch Forests (paper producer). A commercial bank–insurance company link was also present.

Other clusters demonstrated the same pattern of functional interconnections. Three of the five members of the First National Bank of Chicago group were located in Illinois (Armour, Brunswick, and International Minerals and Chemical); direct product competition occurred between Armour and International Minerals and Chemical, and the First National Bank of Chicago managed two employee benefit funds for International Minerals (United States Congress, 1968: 605). Similarly, Continental Illinois defined a cluster of midwestern firms in which it managed an employee benefit fund for one company and served as registrar for a second.

Chemical Bank managed employee benefit funds for four of its five clique members and acted as transfer agent for three. First National City Bank held 5% of the stock of Xerox (United States Congress, 1968: 713), served as registrar for International Telephone and Telegraph (*Moody's Handbook of Common Stock*, 1967: 504), and managed employee benefit funds for two of its members (United States Congress, 1968: 713). In addition, Sybron and Xerox shared product lines. The Chase Manhattan clique was not randomly assembled either. Intercorporate ties reflected stockownership: Chase held 5.1% of the common stock and 9.1% of the preferred stock of Commercial Solvents as well as 8.5% of Moore-McCormack (United States Congress, 1968: 702). Potential lines of competition existed: Borman's versus Grand Union. Possible financial alliances occurred: Chase, Provident Life and Accident, and the investment bank of Shields and Company were mutually grouped. In addition, Chase served as transfer agent for four members and registrar for one (*Moody's Handbook of Common Stock*, 1967) and managed employee benefit funds for two firms (United States Congress, 1968: 702, 704). Similar relationships existed within the Marine Midland clique as well.

Chapter 11

1. See also Baltzell (1964), Burch (1980–81), Dye (1976), Dye and Pickering (1974), Eakins (1966), Freitag (1975, 1981, 1983), Mills (1956), Mintz (1975), Salzman and Domhoff (1979–80), Shoup and Minter (1977), Sklar (1980), and Useem (1979–80). For European examples, see Mokken and Stokman (1979).

Appendix 1

1. The *Fortune* magazine "Directory of the 500 Largest Industrial Corporations," the other *Fortune* listings, and most other sources of corporate data present information on the year preceding publication. Hence when we speak, for example, of the 1962 list of corporations and directors we are referring to information from the 1963 volumes of *Fortune* magazine and *Standard and Poor's Register* respectively.

Because of difficulty in obtaining accurate financial information, privately held corporations otherwise large enough to be included are not listed by *Fortune*. Burch (1972: 14, 180) has identified 33 such firms that were large enough to be included in the 1965 listing. Four of these were included in other *Fortune* lists, leaving twenty-nine large firms that merit inclusion. A preliminary analysis from a variety of sources suggests that the actual number of large firms that are not included may be as high as one hundred for the entire period under investigation.

2. The leading investment banks were defined as those managing or comanaging $500 million or more during the decade 1960–69 ("leading underwriting managers," p. 308) and those whose share of the actual underwriting exceeded $500 million ("leading underwriting participants," p. 28).

3. The Kinney Service Corporation, for example, changed its name to Kinney National Services, Incorporated, in 1966, to Kinney Services, Incorporated, in 1971, and then to Warner Communications in 1972.

4. Despite these additions, later years show a smaller population size, since 115 firms that existed in 1962 subsequently merged with other companies.

Appendix 2

1. For a full discussion of this distinction, see Palmer (1980). See also Palmer (1983a, b). For an empirical test of the importance of this distinction, see Mizruchi and Bunting (1981) and Mizruchi (1982a).

2. The method has since been successfully applied by Bearden et al. (1975), Mariolis (1975, 1978), Mizruchi (1982a), Mizruchi and Bunting (1981), Mintz and Schwartz (1981a, b, 1983), and Roy (1983b).

3. See, for example, Rochester (1936), United States Federal Trade Commission (1951), and Dooley (1969).

4. Roy (1983b), in applying centrality analysis to sectoral interlocks, set the centrality of the most central industry equal to λ, thus facilitating comparisons of connectivity over time.

5. Because the matrix produced by this method is asymmetrical (r_{ij} is not equal to r_{ji}), more than one eigenvalue can produce an all-positive eigenvector, or alternative sets of centrality scores. In this book we analyze only the first eigenvector.

6. One further difficulty we found with this measure is its great sensitivity to skewed distributions of correlation scores. For example, the four Kaiser Companies shared at least six officers each, and Hunt Foods and Industries sent five of its officers to McCall. This sort of overlap is extremely unusual in modern corporations—only 0.66% of all ties in 1962 involved more than three interlocks. The inclusion of uncorrected extreme figures obliterates the balance in centrality scores, because the Bonacich measure requires a continuous distribution of scores to yield interpretable results.

Therefore, when the number of ties between two corporations was discontinuously high, the distribution curve of the entries in the matirix is skewed and the calculation of C becomes too sensitive to those corporations. We have corrected for this problem in the analysis of our data by not counting more than three ties between any two corporations. Kaiser Aluminum and Chemical and Kaiser Cement and Gypsum had eight officer interlocks, but in our 1962 analysis we used only three. Thus in all procedures involving centrality measurement in the full network, $b_{ij} \leq 3$. By the same logic, for directional analysis, we set $b_{ij} \leq 1.5$.

Appendix 3

1. For an extensive discussion of this topic, as well as an empirical comparison between peak analysis and factor analysis, see Mizruchi, 1982b.

References

Abolafia, Mitchel
    1981   Taming the market: Bases of control in commodity futures markets. Ph.D. dissertation, SUNY at Stony Brook.

Aldrich, Howard
    1979   *Organizations and environments.* Englewood Cliffs, N.J.: Prentice-Hall.

Aldrich, Howard, and Jeffrey Pfeffer
    1976   Environments of organizations. *Annual Review of Sociology* 2:79–105.

Allen, Michael
    1974   Interorganizational elite cooptation. *American Sociological Review* 39:393–406.

    1978   Economic interest groups and the corporate elite structure. *Social Science Quarterly* 58:597–615.

    1982   The identification of interlock groups in large corporate networks: Convergent validation using divergent techniques. *Social Networks* 4:349–66.

Austin, Peter
    1973   Annuals of finance: The go-go years, III. *New Yorker* (August 13) 34:534.

Bacon, Jeremy, and James Brown
    1977   *The board of directors: Perspectives and practices in nine countries.* New York: Conference Board.

Baldwin, William
1964   The motives of managers, environmental restraints and the theory of managerial enterprise. *Quarterly Journal of Economics* 78:238–56.

Baltzell, E. Digby
1964   *The Protestant establishment.* New York: Random House.

Baran, Paul, and Paul Sweezy
1966   *Monopoly capital.* New York: Monthly Review Press.

Bauer, Raymond, Ithiel de Sola Poole, and Lewis A. Dexter
1963   *American business and public policy: The politics of foreign trade.* New York: Atherton Press.

Baum, David, and Ned Stiles
1965   *The silent partners: Institutional investors and corporate control.* Syracuse: Syracuse University Press.

Bearden, James
1982   The board of directors in large U.S. companies. Ph.D. dissertation, SUNY at Stony Brook.

Bearden, James, William Atwood, Peter Freitag, Carol Hendricks, Beth Mintz, and Michael Schwartz
1975   The nature and extent of bank centrality in corporate networks. Paper presented at the meetings of the American Sociological Association, San Francisco.

Bearden, James, and Beth Mintz
1984   Regionality and integration in the United States interlock network. In *Corporations and corporate power,* ed. Frans Stokman, Rolf Zeigler, and John Scott. Oxford: Polity Press.

Bell, Daniel
1961   The breakup of family capitalism. In *The end of ideology.* New York: Collier.

1973   *The coming of post-industrial society.* New York: Basic Books.

Berkowitz, S. D.
1982   *An introduction to structural analysis: The network approach to social research.* Toronto: Butterworth.

Berkowitz, S. D., Peter Carrington, Yehuda Kotowitz, and Leonard Wavarman
1979   The determination of enterprise groupings through combined ownership and directorship ties. *Social Networks* 1:415–35.

Berle, Adolph
1957   *Economic power and the free society.* New York: Fund for the Republic.

1959   *Power without property.* New York: Harcourt Brace.

Berle, Adolph, and Gardiner Means
1932   *The modern corporation and private property.* New York: Harcourt, Brace and World.

Bonacich, Phillip
1972   Techniques for analyzing overlapping memberships. In *Sociological methodology 1972*, ed. Herbert L. Costner. San Francisco: Jossey-Bass.

Bonacich, Phillip, and G. William Domhoff
1977   Overlapping memberships among eight clubs and policy groups of the American ruling class: A methodological and empirical contribution to the class hegemony paradigm of power structure. Paper delivered at the meetings of the American Sociological Association, Chicago.

Brandeis, Louis
1914   *Other people's money.* New York: Frederick A. Stokes Company.

Breiger, Ronald, Scott Boorman, and Phipps Arabie
1975   An algorithm for clustering relational data with applications to social network analysis and comparison with multi-dimensional scaling. *Journal of Mathematical Psychology* 12:328–83.

Brooks, John
1981   The money machine. *New Yorker* 58:41–61.

Brough, James
1977   *The Ford dynasty.* New York: Doubleday.

Brown, Courtney C., and E. Everett Smith, eds.
1957   *The director looks at his job.* New York: Columbia University Press.

Brown, Stanley
1972   *Ling: The rise, fall and return of a Texas titan.* New York: Atheneum.

Bunting, David
1976   Corporate interlocking. *Journal of Corporate Action* 1:6–15.
1977   Corporate interlocking. *Journal of Corporate Action* 2:27–37, 3:4–11, 4:39–47.
1983   Origins of the American corporate network. *Social Science History* 7:129–42.

Bunting, David, and Jeffrey Barbour
1971   Interlocking directorates in large American corporations, 1896–1964. *Business History Review* 45:317–35.

Burch, Philip, Jr.
1972   *The managerial revolution reassessed.* Lexington: D. C. Heath.

1980–81 *Elites in American history*, vols. 1–3. New York: Holmes and Meier.

1981   The business roundtable: Its make-up and external ties. *Research in Political Economy* 4:101–27.

Burnham, James
1941   *The managerial revolution.* New York: John Day Company.

Burns, Tom
1974   On the rationale of the corporate system. In *The corporate society*, ed. Robin Marris. New York: John Wiley.

Burt, Ronald
1979   A structural theory of interlocking corporate directorates. *Social Networks* 1:415–35.

1980a   Cooptive corporate actor networks: A reconsideration of interlocking directorates involving American manufacturing. *Administrative Science Quarterly* 25:557–82.

1980b   On the functional form of corporate cooptation: Empirical findings linking the intensity of market constraint with the frequency of directorate ties. *Social Science* 9:146–77.

Burt, Ronald, Kenneth Christman, and Harold Kilburn, Jr.
1980   Testing a structural theory of corporate cooptations: Interorganizational directorates as a strategy for avoiding market constraints on profits. *American Sociological Review* 45:821–41.

Caro, Robert
1974   *The power broker: Robert Moses and the fall of New York.* New York: Alfred Knopf.

Chemical New York Corporation
1975   *Annual report.* New York: Chemical New York Corporation.

Chevalier, J. M.
1969   The problem of control in large American corporations. *Anti-Trust Bulletin* 14:163–80.

1970   *La structure financière de l'industrie américaine.* Paris: Editions Cujas.

Child, John
1969a   *British management thought: A critical analysis.* London: Allen and Unwin.

1969b   *The business enterprise in modern industrial society.* London: Collier-Macmillan.

Cohen, Robert
1980   Structural change in international banking and its implications for the U.S. economy. In *Special study on economic change*, ed. Joint Economic Committee of the United States Congress, 96th Congress, 2d session, Washington, D. C.: Government Printing Office. 9:501–15.

Collier, Peter, and David Horowitz
1976   *The Rockefellers: An American dynasty.* New York: Holt, Rinehart and Winston.

Consolidated Edison
1975   *Annual report.* New York: Consolidated Edison.

Dahl, Robert
1961   *Who governs? Democracy and power in an American city.* New Haven: Yale University Press.

Daughen, Joseph, and Peter Binzen
1971   *The wreck of the Penn Central.* Boston: Little, Brown.

De Vroey, Michel
1975   The owner's interventions in decision making in large corporations: A new approach. *European Economic Review* 6:1–15.

DiDonato, Donna, Davita Glasberg, Beth Mintz, and Michael Schwartz
n.d.   The social history of interlock research: Theoretical orientations, empirical results, and social consequences, 1913–1970. In *Perspectives in organizational sociology,* ed. Sam Bachrach, vol. 3. Greenwich, Conn.: JAI. Forthcoming.

Directory of directors for the city of New York
1963–74 New York: Directory of Directors Company.

Domhoff, G. William
1967   *Who rules America?* Englewood Cliffs, N.J.: Prentice-Hall.
1970   *The higher circles.* New York: Random House.
1975   Social clubs, policy-planning groups and corporations: A network study of ruling-class cohesiveness. *Insurgent Sociologist* 5:173–84.
1978   *Who really rules?* New Brunswick, N.J.: Transaction.
1979   *The powers that be.* New York: Random House.
1983   *Who rules America now?* Englewood Cliffs, N. J.: Prentice-Hall.

Dooley, Peter
1969   The interlocking directorate. *American Economic Review* 59:314–23.

Drucker, Peter
1943   *The future of industrial man.* London: Heinemann.
1976   *The unseen revolution: How pension fund socialism came to America.* New York: Harper and Row.

Dun and Bradstreet's million dollar directory
1963–74 New York: Dun and Bradstreet.

Dunn, Marvin
1979–80 The family office as a coordinating mechanism within the ruling class. *Insurgent Sociologist* 93:8–23.

Dye, Thomas
1976   *Who's running America? Institutional leadership in the United States.* Englewood Cliffs, N. J.: Prentice-Hall.

Dye, Thomas, and John Pickering
1974   Governmental and corporate elites: Convergence and specialization. *Journal of Politics* 36:900–925.

Eakins, David
1966   The development of corporate liberal policy research in the United States, 1885–1965. Ph.D. dissertation, University of Wisconsin.

Early, James
1957   Economics, organizational theory, and decision-making. *American Economic Review* 47:33–35.

Egan, Jack
1980   The money men: New York's top bankers. *New York Magazine* 1 (Dec.):31–38.

Esping-Anderson, Gosta, Roger Friedland, and Erik O. Wright
1976   Modes of class struggle and the capitalist state. *Kapitalistate* 4–5:186–220.

Evans, Peter
1979   *Dependent development: The alliance of multinational, state, and local capital in Brazil.* Princeton: Princeton University Press.

Ewen, Lynda
1978   *Corporate power and urban crisis in Detroit.* Princeton: Princeton University Press.

Exxon Corporation
1975   *Annual report.* New York: Exxon Corporation.

Fennema, Meindert
1982   *International networks of banks and industry.* Boston: Martinus Nijhoff.

Fennema, Meindert, and B. Schijf
1979   Analyzing interlocking directorates: Theory and method. *Social Networks* 1:297–332.

1984   The transnational network. In *Corporations and corporate power*, ed. Frans Stokman, Rolf Zeigler, and John Scott. Oxford: Polity Press.

Feshbach, Dan, and Les Shipnuck
1972   Regional government: A national perspective. *Pacific Research and World Empire Telegram* 4:19–22.

Fields, Karen
1982   Political contingencies of witchcraft in colonial Central America: Culture and the state in Marxist theory. *Canadian Journal of African Studies* 16:567–93.

Fitch, Robert
1972   Sweezy and corporate fetishism. *Socialist Revolution* 12:93–127.

Fitch, Robert, and Mary Oppenheimer
1970a–c Who rules the corporations? *Socialist Revolution* 4:73–108, 5:61–114, 6:33–94.

Frank, Andrie Gunder
1966   *Capitalism and underdevelopment in Latin America*. New York: Monthly Review Press.

Freitag, Peter
1975   The cabinet and big business: A study of interlocks. *Social Problems* 23:137–52.

1981   Class struggle and the rise of government regulation. Ph.D. dissertation, SUNY at Stony Brook.

1983   The myth of corporate capture: Regulatory commissions in the United States. *Social Problems* 30:480–91.

Galaskiewicz, Joseph, and Barbara Rauschenbach
1979   Patterns of interinstitutional exchanges: An examination of linkages between cultural and business organizations. Paper presented at the meetings of the American Sociological Association, Boston.

Galaskiewicz, Joseph, and Stanley Wasserman
1981   Change in a regional corporate network. *American Sociological Review* 46:475–84.

Galbraith, John
1952   *American capitalism, the concept of countervailing power*. Boston: Houghton Mifflin.

1967   *The new industrial state*. New York: New American Library.

Glasberg, Davita
1981   Corporate power and control: The case of Leasco Corporation versus Chemical Bank. *Social Problems* 29:104–16.

1982   Corporations in crisis: The significance of interlocking directorates. Ph.D. dissertation, SUNY at Stony Brook.

Glasberg, Davita, and Michael Schwartz
1983   Ownership and control of corporations. *Annual Review of Sociology* 9:311–32.

Gogel, Robert
  1977   Interlocking directorships and the American corporate net-
          work. Ph.D. dissertation, University of California, Santa Bar-
          bara.

Gogel, Robert, and Thomas Koenig
  1981   Commercial banks, interlocking directorates and economic
          power: An analysis of the primary metals industry. *Social Prob-
          lems* 29:117–28.

Gold, David, Clarence Lo, and Erik O. Wright
  1975   Recent developments in Marxist theories of the state. *Monthly
          Review* 27:29–43.

Goldsmith, Raymond
  1954   *The share of financial intermediaries in national wealth and
          national assets, 1900–1949.* New York: National Bureau of Eco-
          nomic Research.

Gordon, Robert
  1945   *Business leadership in the large corporation.* Washington, D. C.:
          Brookings Institution.

Gramsci, Antonio
  1957   *The modern prince and other writings.* Trans. Louis Marks. New
          York: International Publishers (6th printing, 1975).

  1971   *Selections from the prison notebooks.* New York: International
          Publishers.

  1973   *Letters from prison.* Selected, translated and introduced by Lynne
          Lawner. London: Jonathon Cape.

  1979a   *Gramsci and Italy's passive revolution.* Ed. John A. Davis. New
          York: Barnes and Noble.

  1979b   *Gramsci and Marxist theory.* Ed. Chantel Mouffe. Boston: Rout-
          ledge and Kegan Paul.

Greenough, William, and Francis King
  1976   *Pension funds and public policy.* New York: Columbia Univer-
          sity Press.

Grossman, Karl
  1980   *Cover up: What you are not supposed to know about nuclear
          power.* New York: Permanent Press.

Group of Thirty
  1982   *How bankers see the world financial market* (pamphlet). New
          York: Group of Thirty.

Hancock, R.
  1980   The social life of the modern corporation: Changing resources
          and forms. *Journal of Applied Behavioral Science* 16:279–98.

Harbrecht, Paul
   1959   *Pension funds and economic power.* New York: Twentieth Century Fund.

Heller, Robert, and Norris Willatt
   1977   *Can you trust your bank?* New York: Charles Scribner's Sons.

Herman, Edward
   1973   Do bankers control corporations? *Monthly Review* 25:12–29.
   1975   *Conflicts of interests: Commercial bank trust departments.* New York: Twentieth Century Fund.
   1979   Kotz on banker control. *Monthly Review* 31:46–57.
   1980   Reply to David Kotz. *Monthly Review* 32:61–64.
   1981   *Corporate control, corporate power.* New York: Cambridge University Press.

Herman, Edward, and Carl Safanda
   1973   Proxy voting by commercial bank trust departments. *Banking Law Journal* 90:91–115.

Hilferding, R.
   1910   *Finance capital.* Paris: Minoit. 1981 translation, London: Routledge and Kegan Paul.

Hillstrom, Roger, and Robert King
   n.d.   *1960–1969: A decade of corporate and international finance.* New York: IDD.

Hirsch, Paul
   1982   Network data versus personal accounts: The normative culture of interlocking directorates. Paper presented at the meetings of the American Sociological Association, San Francisco.

Holloway, John, and Sol Picciotto
   1977   Capital, crisis and the state. *Capital and Class* 7:76–101.

Hunter, Floyd
   1953   *Community power structure: A study of decision makers.* Chapel Hill: University of North Carolina Press.

Hutchinson, Harry
   1977   *Money, banking and the United States economy.* New York: Appleton-Century-Crofts.

James, David, and Michael Soref
   1981   Managerial theory: Unmaking of the corporate president. *American Sociological Review* 46:1–18.

Katona, George
   1957   *Business looks at banks.* Ann Arbor: University of Michigan Press.

Kaysen, Carl
    1957   The social significance of the modern corporation. *American Economic Review* 47:311–19.

Knowles, James C.
    1973   *The Rockefeller financial group.* Module 343:1–59. New York: Warner Modular Publications.

Koenig, Thomas
    1979   Interlocking directorates among the largest American corporations and their significance for corporate political activity. Ph.D. dissertation, University of California, Santa Barbara.

Koenig, Thomas, and Robert Gogel
    1981   Interlocking directorates as a social network. *American Journal of Economics and Sociology* 40:37–50.

Koenig, Thomas, Robert Gogel, and John Sonquist
    1979   Models of the significance of interlocking corporate directorates. *American Journal of Economics and Sociology* 38:173–83.

Kolko, Gabriel
    1962   *Wealth and power in America.* New York: Praeger.

Kotz, David
    1978   *Bank control of large corporations in the United States.* Berkeley: University of California Press.
    1979   The significance of bank control over large corporations. *Journal of Economic Issues* 13:407–26.
    1980   Reply to Edward Herman. *Monthly Review* 32:57–60.

Larner, Robert J.
    1970   *Management control and the large corporation.* New York: Dunellen Publishing Company.

Leinsdorf, David, and Donald Etra.
    1973   *Citibank.* New York: Grossman.

Lenin, V. I.
    1917a   *Imperialism: The highest stage of capitalism.* 1968 edition. New York: International Publishers.
    1917b   *The state and revolution.* 1973 edition. Peking: Foreign Languages Press.

Levine, Joel
    1972   The sphere of influence. *American Sociological Review* 37:14–27.
    1977a   The network of corporate interlocks in the United States. Paper presented at the meetings of the American Sociological Association, Chicago.
    1977b   The theory of bank control: Comment on Mariolis' test of the theory. *Social Science Quarterly* 58:506–10.

Lieberson, Stanley
1961   The division of labor in banking. *American Journal of Sociology* 66:491–96.

Lintner, John
1966   The financing of corporations. In *The corporation in modern society*, ed. E. S. Mason. Cambridge: Harvard University Press.

Lorrain, François, and Harrison White
1971   Structural equivalence of individuals in social networks. *Journal of Mathematical Sociology* 1:49–80.

Lukes, Steven
1974   *Power: A radical view.* London: Macmillan.

McConnell, Grant
1962   *Steel and the presidency.* New York: Norton.

McCue, Dennis
1977   An economy in conflict with democracy: A case study of the financial crisis in New York City. Honors thesis, SUNY at Stony Brook.

Mace, Myles
1971   *Directors: Myth and reality.* Boston: Harvard University Press.

Magdoff, Harry
1978   *Imperialism: From the colonial age to the present.* New York: Monthly Review Press.

Mariolis, Peter
1975   Interlocking directorates and the control of corporations. *Social Science Quarterly* 56:425–39.

1977a   Interlocking directorates and finance control: A peak analysis. Paper presented at the meetings of the American Sociological Association, Chicago.

1977b   Type of corporation, size of firms and interlocking directorates: A reply to Levine. *Social Science Quarterly* 58:511–13.

1978   Bank and financial control among large U.S. corporations. Ph.D. dissertation, SUNY at Stony Brook.

1984   Interlocking directorates and financial groups: A peak analysis. *Sociological Spectrum.* In press.

Mariolis, Peter, and Maria Jones
1982   Centrality in corporate interlock networks: Reliability and stability. *Administrative Science Quarterly* 24:571–84.

Mariolis, Peter, Michael Schwartz, and Beth Mintz
1979   Centrality analysis: A methodology for social networks. Paper presented at the meetings of the American Sociological Association, Boston.

Marris, Robin
1964   *The economic theory of managerial capitalism.* London: Macmillan.

Marx, Karl
1894   *Das Kapital.* Hamburg: Verlag von Otto Meissher. 1967 translation. New York: International Publishers.
1940   *The civil war in France.* New York: International Publishers.

Menshikov, Sergei
1969   *Millionaires and managers.* Moscow: Progress Publishers.

Meussen, W., and L. Cuyvers
1984   The interaction between interlocking directorates and economic behavior of companies: An exploratory comparison of the U.S., Belgium and the Netherlands. In *Corporations and corporate power,* ed. Frans Stokman, Rolf Zeigler, and John Scott. Oxford: Polity Press.

Miliband, Ralph
1969   *The state in capitalist society.* New York: Basic Books.

Mills, C. Wright
1956   *The power elite.* New York: Oxford University Press.

Mintz, Beth
1975   The president's cabinet, 1897–1972: A contribution to the power structure debate. *Insurgent Sociologist* 5:131–48.
1978   Who controls the corporation? A study of interlocking directorates. Ph.D. dissertation, SUNY at Stony Brook.

Mintz, Beth, Peter Freitag, Carol Hendricks, and Michael Schwartz
1976   Problems of proof in elite research. *Social Problems* 23:314–24.

Mintz, Beth, and Michael Schwartz
1981a   Interlocking directorates and interest group formation. *American Sociological Review* 46:851–69.
1981b   The structure of intercorporate unity in American business. *Social Problems* 29:87–103.
1982   Capital flows and the creation of social policy. Paper delivered at the meetings of the International Sociological Association, Mexico City.
1983   Financial interest groups and interlocking directorates. *Social Science History* 7:183–204.

Mizruchi, Mark
1982a   *The American corporate network: 1904–1974.* Beverly Hills: Sage.
1982b   Interest groups in the American corporate elite, 1900–1975. Paper presented at the meetings of the American Sociological Association, San Francisco.
1983   The structure of relations among large American corporations. *Social Science History* 7:165–82.

Mizruchi, Mark, and David Bunting
  1981   Influence in corporate networks: An examination of four measures. *Administrative Science Quarterly* 26:475–89.

Mizruchi, Mark, Peter Mariolis, Beth Mintz, and Michael Schwartz
  n.d.   *Centrality analysis of network data.* Forthcoming.

Mokken, Robert, and Frans Stokman
  1974   Interlocking directorates between large corporations, banks and other financial companies and institutions in the Netherlands in 1969. Paper presented at the meetings of the European Consortium for Political Research, Strasbourg.

  1978   Traces of power IV: The 1972 intercorporate network in the Netherlands. Paper presented at the meetings of the European Consortium for Political Research, Grenoble.

  1979   Corporate government networks in the Netherlands. *Social Networks* 1:333–58.

Moody's handbook of common stock
  1963–74 New York: Moody's Investors Service.

Moody's manuals
  1963–74 New York: Moody's Investors Service.

Morganthau, Hans
  1922   *All in a lifetime.* Garden City, N.Y.: Doubleday.

Myers, Gustave
  1936   *History of the great American fortunes.* New York: Modern Library.

Ney, Richard
  1970   *The Wall Street jungle.* New York: Grove Press.

Nichols, Theo
  1969   *Ownership, control and ideology.* London: George Allen and Unwin Ltd.

Niosi, Jorge
  1978   *The economy of Canada.* Montreal: Black Rose Books.

Norich, Samuel
  1980   Interlocking directorates, the control of large corporations and patterns of accumulation in the capitalist class. In *Classes, class conflict, and the state,* ed. M. Zeitlin. Cambridge: Winthrop Publishers.

O'Connor, James
  1968   Finance capital or corporate capital? *Monthly Review* 20:30–35.

  1972   Question: Who rules the corporation? Answer: The ruling class. *Socialist Revolution* 7:117–50.

  1973   *The fiscal crisis of the state.* New York: St. Martin's Press.

Offe, Claus
    1973   The abolition of market control and the problem of legitimacy. *Kapitalistate* 1:109–16.

Ornstein, Michael
    1980   Assessing the meaning of corporate interlocks: Canadian evidence. *Social Science Research* 9:287–306.

    1982   Interlocking directorates in Canada: Evidence from replacement patterns. *Social Networks* 4:3–25.

Pahl, Raymond E., and John Winkler
    1974   The economic elite. In *Elites and power in British society,* ed. P. Stanworth and A. Giddens. Cambridge: Cambridge University Press.

Palmer, Donald
    1980   Broken ties: Some political and interorganizational determinants of interlocking directorates among large American corporations. Paper presented at the meetings of the American Sociological Association, New York.

    1983a   Broken ties: Interlocking directorates and intercorporate coordination. *Administrative Science Quarterly* 28:40–55.

    1983b   On the significance of interlocking directorates. *Social Science History* 7:217–31.

Pam, Max
    1913   Interlocking directorates: The problem and its solution. *Harvard Law Review* 26:467–92

Patman Committee
    1968   *Commercial banks and their trust activities: Emerging influence on the American economy.* Washington, D.C.: U.S. Government Printing Office.

Patterson, Tim
    1975   Notes on the historical application of Marxist cultural theory. *Science and Society* 39:257–91.

Pelton, Richard
    1970   *Who really rules America?* Somerville, Mass.: New England Free Press.

Pennings, Johannes
    1980   *Interlocking directorates.* San Francisco: Jossey-Bass.

Perlo, Victor
    1957   *The empire of high finance.* New York: International Publishers.

    1958   People's capitalism and stock ownership. *American Economic Review* 48:333–47.

Pfeffer, Jeffrey
1972   Size and composition of corporate boards of directors: The organization and its environment. *Administrative Science Quarterly* 17:218–28.

Pfeffer, Jeffrey, and P. Novak
1976   Joint ventures and interorganizational interdependence. *Administrative Science Quarterly* 21:398–418.

Pfeffer, Jeffrey, and Gerald Salancik
1978   *The external control of organizations: A resource dependence perspective.* New York: Harper and Row.

Poulantzas, Nicos
1973   *Political power and social classes.* London: New Left Review.

Ratcliff, Richard
1979–80 Capitalist class structure and the decline of older industrial cities. *Insurgent Sociologist* 9:60–74.

1980a   Banks and corporate lending: An analysis of the impact of the internal structure of the capitalist class. *American Sociological Review* 45:553–70.

1980b   Banks and the command of capital flows: An analysis of capitalist class structure and mortgage disinvestment in a metropolitan area. In *Classes, class conflict and the state*, ed. M. Zeitlin. Cambridge, Mass.: Winthrop Publishers.

Ratcliff, Richard, Mary Elizabeth Gallagher, and Kathryn Strother Ratcliff
1979   The civic involvement of bankers: An analysis of the influence of economic power and social prominence in the command of civic policy positions. *Social Problems* 26:298–313.

Reed, Edward, Richard Cotter, Edward Gill, and Richard Smith
1976   *Commerical banking.* Englewood Cliffs, N.J.: Prentice-Hall.

Rifkin, Jeremy, and Randy Barber
1978   *The North will rise again: Pensions, politics and power in the 1980s.* Boston: Beacon Press.

Rochester, Anna
1936   *Rulers of America.* New York: International Publishers.

Rose, Arnold
1967   *The power structure.* New York: Oxford University Press.

Roy, William
1983a   Interlocking directorates and the corporate revolution. *Social Science History* 7:143–64.

1983b   The interlocking directorate structure of the United States. *American Sociological Review* 48:248–57.

Salzman, Harold, and G. William Domhoff
    1979–80 The corporate community and government: Do they interlock?
        Insurgent Sociologist 9:121–35.
    1983   Nonprofit organizations and the corporate community. *Social
        Science History* 7:205–16.

Schotland, Roy
    1977   Testimony on pension simplification and investment rules at
        joint hearing before the subcommittee on private pension plans
        and Employee Fringe Benefits of the Committee on Finance
        and the Select Committee on Small Business. United States
        Senate, May 10–July 17, 189–246.

Schwartz, Michael
    1976   *Radical protest and social structure: The Southern Farmers' Al-
        liance and the one crop cotton tenancy system.* New York: Ac-
        ademic.
    1977   An estimate of the size of the Southern Farmers' Alliance, 1884–
        1890. *Agricultural History* 51:756–68.

Scott, John
    1978   The intercorporate configuration: Substructure and superstruc-
        ture. Paper presented at the meetings of the European Con-
        sortium for Political Research, Grenoble.
    1979   *Corporations, classes and capitalism.* London: Hutchinson Uni-
        versity Library.

Seybold, Peter
    1978   The development of American political sociology. Ph.D. dis-
        sertation, SUNY at Stony Brook.

Shoup, Laurence, and William Minter
    1977   *The imperial brain trust.* New York: Monthly Review Press

Simon, Herbert
    1966   Theories of decision making in economics and behavioral sci-
        ence. In *Surveys of economic theory*, vol. 3, ed. E. A. Robinson.
        New York: American Economic Association.

Sklar, Holly
    1980   *Trilateralism.* Boston: South End Press.

Sloan, Alfred
    1965   *My years with General Motors.* Garden City, N.Y.: Doubleday.

Soldofsky, Robert
    1971   *Institutional holdings of common stock, 1900–2000.* Michigan
        Business Studies, vol. 18. Ann Arbor: University of Michigan.

Sonquist, John, and Thomas Koenig
    1975   Interlocking directorates in the top U.S. corporations: A graph
        theory approach. *Insurgent Sociologist.* 5:196–230.

Soref, Michael
  1976   Social class and a division of labor within the corporate elite: A note on class, interlocking and executive committee membership of directors of U.S. industrial firms. *Sociological Quarterly* 17:360–68.

  1979   Research on interlocking directorates: An introduction and a bibliography of North American sources. *Connections* 2:84–86.

  1980   The finance capitalists. In *Classes, class conflict and the state,* ed. M. Zeitlin. Cambridge, Mass.: Winthrop Publishers.

Stallings, Barbara
  1982   International lending and the relative autonomy of the state: Twentieth century Peru. Paper delivered to World Congress of Sociology, Mexico City.

Standard and Poor's register of corporations, directors and executives
  1963–74 New York: Standard and Poor's Corporation.

Standard and Poor's stock market encyclopedia
  1963–74 New York: Standard and Poor's Corporation.

Stearns, Linda
  1982   Corporate dependency and the structure of the capital market. Ph.D. dissertation, SUNY at Stony Brook.

Stigler, George
  1968   *The organization of industry.* Homewood, Ill.: Irwin.

Stokman, Frans, Rolf Zeigler, and John Scott, eds.
  1984   *Corporations and corporate power.* Oxford: Polity Press.

Sweezy, Paul
  1939   Interest groups in the American economy. In *The structure of the American economy,* ed. National Resources Committee. Washington, D.C.: U.S. Government Printing Office.

  1972   The resurgence of finance-capital: Fact or fancy? *Socialist Revolution* 8:157–90.

Sweezy, Paul, and Harry Magdoff
  1975   Banks: Skating on thin ice. *Monthly Review* 26:1–21.

Temporary National Economic Committee (TNEC)
  1940   *The distribution of ownership in 200 largest nonfinancial corporations.* Monograph 29. Washington, D.C.: U.S. Government Printing Office.

Tinnen, David
  1973   *Just about everyone vs. Howard Hughes.* Garden City, N.Y.: Doubleday.

United States Congress, House of Representatives, Committee on Banking and Currency, Subcommittee on Domestic Finance

1913   *Investigation of concentration of control of money and credit.* Washington, D.C.: U.S. Government Printing Office.

1968   *Commercial banks and their trust activities: Emerging influence on the American economy.* 90th Congress, 2d session. Washington, D.C.: U.S. Government Printing Office.

United States Congress, House of Representatives, Committee on the Judiciary, Antitrust Subcommittee

1965   *Interlocks in corporate management.* Washington, D.C.: U.S. Government Printing Office.

United States Federal Trade Commission

1951   *Report on interlocking directorates.* Washington, D.C.: U.S. Government Printing Office.

United States Securities and Exchange Commission

1938–42 *Investment trusts and investment companies.* Vols. 1–4. Washington, D.C.: U.S. Government Printing Office.

United States Senate, Committee on Banking and Currency

1955   *Stock market study.* Washington D.C.: U.S. Government Printing Office.

United States Senate, Committee on Governmental Affairs, Subcommittee on Reports, Accounting and Management

1978   *Interlocking directorates among the major U.S. corporations.* Washington D.C.: Government Printing Office.

United States Senate, Committee on Government Operations

1973   *Disclosure of corporate ownership.* Washington, D.C.: U.S. Government Printing Office.

1976   *Institutional investor's common stock.* Washington, D.C.: U.S. Government Printing Office.

Useem, Michael

1978   The inner group of the American capitalist class. *Social Problems* 25:225–40.

1979   The social organization of the American business class. *American Sociological Review* 44:553–71.

1979–80 Which business leaders help govern? *Insurgent Sociologist* 9:107–20.

1980   Corporations and the corporate elite. *Annual Review of Sociology.* 6:41–78.

1982   Classwide rationality in the politics of managers and directors of large corporations in the United States and Great Britain. *Administrative Science Quarterly* 27:199–226.

1983   The inner circle: Large corporations and business politics in the U.S. and U.K. New York: Oxford University Press.

Villarejo, Don
1961   Stock ownership and the control of corporations. Somerville, Mass.: New England Free Press.

Weymouth, Lally
1978   The saga of Henry Ford II. New York Times Magazine, March 5, 12–17, 59–78.

Whitt, J. Allen
1975   Means of movements: The politics of modern transportation systems. Ph.D. dissertation, University of California, Santa Barbara.
1979–80 Can capitalists organize themselves? Insurgent Sociologist 9:51–59.
1981   Is oil different? A comparison of the social backgrounds and organizational affiliations of oil and non-oil directors. Social Problems 29:142–15.
1982   Means of motion. Princeton: Princeton University Press.

Who's Who in America
1963–74 Chicago: Marquis Who's Who.

Williams, Raymond
1977   Marxism and literature. Oxford: Oxford University Press.

Wright, J. Patrick
1979   On a clear day you can see General Motors. New York: Avon.

Wrightsman, Dwayne
1964   An analysis of the extent of corporate ownership and control by private pension funds. Ph.D. dissertation, Michigan State University.

Yago, Glen
1980   Corporate power and urban transportation: A comparison of public transit's decline in the United States and Germany. In Classes, class conflict and the state, ed. M. Zeitlin. Cambridge, Mass.: Winthrop Publishers.
1983   The decline of public transportation in Germany and the United States. New York: Cambridge University Press.

Yago, Glen, and Michael Schwartz
1981   Welfare for corporations: What's good for Chrysler is bad for us. Nation 233:200–203.

Young, Lewis
1978   The claimants for influence within the corporation. In Running the American corporation, ed. American Assembly. Englewood Cliffs, N.J.: Prentice-Hall.

Zeitlin, Maurice
   1974   Corporate ownership and control: The large corporation and
           the capitalist class. *American Journal of Sociology* 79:1073–1119.
   1976   On class theory of the large corporation: Response to Allen.
           American Journal of Sociology 81:894–903.

Zeitlin, Maurice, Linda Ewen, and Richard Ratcliff
   1974   The "inner group": Interlocking directorates and the internal
           differentiation of the capitalist class in Chile. Paper presented
           at the meetings of the American Sociological Association, Mon-
           treal.

Zeitlin, Maurice, W. Laurence Newman, and Richard Ratcliff
   1976   Class segments: Agrarian property and political leadership in
           the capitalist class of Chile. *American Sociological Review*
           41:1006–29.

Zeitlin, Maurice, and Samuel Norich
   1979   Management control, exploitation and profit maximization in
           the large corporation. *Research in Political Economy* 2:33–62.

Index

This index includes subjects, personal names, cited authors, and corporate names. Corporate names are indicated by small capitals.